CHENG CHUNG BOOK CO., LTD.

CHENG CHUNG
BOOK CO., LTD.

CHENG CHUNG
BOOK CO., LTD.

CHENG CHUNG BOOK CO., LTD.

新版 實用
視聽華語

PRACTICAL AUDIO-VISUAL
CHINESE
2ND EDITION | 3

主 編 者◆國立臺灣師範大學
編輯委員◆范慧貞・劉秀芝(咪咪)・蕭美美
策 劃 者◆教育部

# 再版編輯要旨

　　本書原版《實用視聽華語》1、2、3冊，自1999年9月出版以來深受海內外好評，並廣被採用至今。

　　本書七年來使用期間，曾收到國內外華語教學界、各大學華語教學中心或華語文教師及學生對本書建設性的批評與建議。

　　適逢2003年美國大學委員會宣布AP(Advance Placement)華語測驗計畫──針對已在美國實行的第二語言教學考試，作了一次改革性的創舉，此項壯舉，影響了今後華語文教材編寫、師資培訓、教學方法及測驗等內容之改進，並在第二語言教學上建立了要實現的五大目標，即──Five C's：1.溝通(Communication)，2.文化(Cultures)，3.多元(Connection)，4.辨思(Comparisons)，5.實用(Communities)。

　　本書原為臺灣師範大學編輯委員會負責編寫，教育部出版發行，目前著手改編之理由：一是採納各方使用者之意見，修改不合時宜之內容。二是響應國際華語文教學趨勢，配合第二語言教學之五大目標進行修正。

　　本次再版修訂之內容及過程如下：

　　本教材在改編之前邀請教育部對外華語小組、原教材編輯者、華語文專家學者，商定改編計畫。對原書之課文內容、話題調整、詞彙用法及練習方式等相關各項問題，廣徵各方意見，並達成協議，進行大幅度變動與修改。

　　原版《實用視聽華語》1、2、3共三冊，再版後將原第1冊改為1、2兩冊；原第2冊改為3、4兩冊；原第3冊保持一冊，改為第5冊。新版《實用視聽華語》共分1、2、3、4、5五冊。每套教材包括課本、教師手冊、學生作業簿等三冊，每課均附有語音輔助教具。

　　新版《實用視聽華語》第1冊共十二課，重點在於教授學生的基本發音、語法及常用詞彙，以達到使用華語基本實用語言溝通的目的。本冊課文調整後之生字共314個，生詞449條，語法句型50則。

　　《實用視聽華語》第2冊共十三課，延續第1冊實際生活用語，並達到使用流利華語，表達生動自然的語用技巧。生字共303個，生詞481條，語法句型39則。

《實用視聽華語》第3冊共十四課，內容著重在校園活動和日常生活話題。生字共600個，生詞1195條，語法句型137則。每課加附不同形式之手寫短文。

　　《實用視聽華語》第4冊共十四課，延續介紹中華文化，包括社會、歷史、地理、人情世故。生字共625個，生詞1250條，語法配合情境介紹句型119則。每課加附手寫短文。

　　《實用視聽華語》第5冊共二十課，課文介紹中華文化之特質及風俗習慣；以短劇、敘述文及議論文等體裁為主，內容則以民俗文化、傳統戲劇、文字、醫藥、科技、環保、消費、休閒等配合時代潮流，以提高學生對目前各類話題討論的能力。本冊生詞667條，連結結構之句型91則。每課除課文外，另附有閱讀與探討、佳文欣賞及成語故事。

　　本書所有的生字與生詞及第1、2冊課文，拼音係採用1.國語注音；2.通用拼音；3.漢語拼音並列，以收廣為使用之效。

　　每冊教材所包括的內容大致如下：1.課文、對話；2.生字、生詞及用法；3.語法要點及句型練習；4.課室活動；5.短文；6.註釋。

　　本書第1、2冊由王淑美、盧翠英兩位老師負責改編工作；第3、4冊由范慧貞、劉咪咪兩位老師負責改編工作；第5冊由張仲敏、陳瑩連兩位老師負責改編工作；英文由任友梅小姐工作群翻譯。並由林姿君小姐、陳雅雪老師、林容年老師及三位助理完成打字及整理全稿工作。插圖則由張欣怡小姐補充設定完成。

　　本書在完成修改稿後，曾邀請華語文專家學者進行審查，經過修訂後定稿。審查委員如下：陳純音教授、曾金金教授、陳俊光教授、陳浩然教授。

　　本書改版作業歷時半年有餘，在臺灣師大國語中心教材組陳立芬老師等工作人員之全力配合下得以完成，感謝所有盡心戮力參與編輯的作者及審核的委員，使這部修訂版《實用視聽華語》得以出版。各位教學者使用時，請不吝指教並匡正。

主編 葉德明
2007年3月

# 新版 實用視聽華語
## PRACTICAL AUDIO-VISUAL CHINESE 2ND EDITION
## 3 CONTENTS

再版編輯要旨

| | | |
|---|---|---|
| 第一課 LESSON 1 | 新室友 | 1 |
| 第二課 LESSON 2 | 吃什麼好 | 31 |
| 第三課 LESSON 3 | 我想去臺灣 | 61 |
| 第四課 LESSON 4 | 談談地理吧 | 91 |
| 第五課 LESSON 5 | 氣候跟出產 | 123 |
| 第六課 LESSON 6 | 考不完的試 | 149 |
| 第七課 LESSON 7 | 念大學容易嗎 | 177 |
| 第八課 LESSON 8 | 你也打工嗎 | 207 |

| | | |
|---|---|---|
| 第九課 LESSON 9 | 誰最漂亮 | 237 |
| 第十課 LESSON 10 | 你選誰 | 261 |
| 第十一課 LESSON 11 | 臺灣故事 | 289 |
| 第十二課 LESSON 12 | 看球賽 | 317 |
| 第十三課 LESSON 13 | 過節了 | 345 |
| 第十四課 LESSON 14 | 放假到哪裡去 | 375 |
| INDEX I | 詞類略語表 | 403 |
| INDEX I | 文法練習索引 | 404 |
| INDEX II | 生詞索引 | 411 |

# 第一課　新室友

■臺灣的大學女生宿舍（張欣怡　攝）

（大學學生宿舍電梯門口，高偉立在等電梯。林建國跟爸爸、媽媽拿著行李走過去。）

建國：我的房間在五樓。（電梯門開了，四人走進去）

偉立：嗨！你們好。

媽媽：你會說中文啊？

偉立：我學過一點兒。我是中文系二年級的學生。

建國：我是新生。我叫林建國。你呢？

偉立：我是William。我的中文名字是高偉立。

建國：這是我爸媽。

偉立：林先生，林太太[1]，幸會，幸會[2]。

爸媽：你好！（出了電梯）

偉立：我也住五樓。你住幾號房？

建國：五〇六。

偉立：真的嗎？我也住五〇六。Great！噢，對了[3]。太棒了。

媽媽：是啊！真沒想到建國的室友會說中文。（進了房間）

建國：這是我的床吧？（把東西放下，上下左右看一看）**嗯，看起來還不錯，就是**舊了一點。

媽媽：舊一點**沒關係**，你自己弄乾淨**就好了**。（對偉立）以後要麻煩你照顧他了。這是他第一次離開家。

建國：媽！我不是小孩子了。

媽媽：好，好，我知道。可是他是二年級，知道的**總是**多一點。

爸爸：我們做父母的**總是**不放心，擔心孩子不會照顧自己。

偉立：我父母本來也一樣，後來我開始送報、幫忙做家事，因為我做得還不錯，他們慢慢兒地就放心了。

媽媽：難怪有人說西方小孩比東方小孩獨立。

建國：那是因為你們從來不讓我們獨立。

媽媽：我們覺得把書念好最重要[4]，總是鼓勵你們多念書，所以沒叫你們做家事，也不希望你們去打工。好了[5]，**還是先把箱子裡的東西拿出來吧**！（打開箱子）

建國：你看，我說得沒錯吧！你又要幫我做了。

媽媽：對不起，我又忘了。好，好，你就自己**來吧**！

建國：你放心，沒問題。我們去吃飯吧！我餓了！

爸爸（對偉立）：要不要一起去？

偉立：謝謝，我吃過了。

媽媽：那[6]就走吧！別忘了鑰匙，還有夾克，外邊涼。

※　　※　　※　　※　　※　　※

（在宿舍裡，偉立正在看報）

偉立：回來**啦**[7]？你爸媽呢？

建國：回去了。

偉立：**看起來**你爸媽好像很關心你。

建國：是啊！可是我媽太嘮叨，有時候我真受不了。

偉立：那[6]你一定很高興可以住校了？可是大概**過不了**幾天，你就會想他們了。你們在家都說中文嗎？

建國：我十歲的時候，全家就從臺灣移民到這裡來了。我爸媽怕我們把中文忘了，所以在家的時候，一定要我們說中文。你呢？你為什麼要學中文？

偉立：我幾年前在國家地理雜誌裡看到一篇文章，介紹臺南的孔廟，看了以後，就開始**對**孔子跟中華文化**有興趣**了。

建國：你的中文說得不錯，口音不太重。你們中文課都學些什麼？有沒有意思？

偉立：說話跟寫字。我覺得很有意思，可是寫字比較難。

建國：我也不太會寫。那⁶我也去選你們的課，好不好？

偉立：好啊！

■大學女生宿舍門口（范慧貞提供）

第一課　新室友

■臺南孔廟（行政院新聞局　葉銘源攝）

■臺南孔廟入口（行政院新聞局　葉銘源攝）

■臺南孔廟大廳（行政院新聞局提供）

## 生詞及例句

**1** 室ㄕˋ友ㄧㄡˇ (shìhyǒu) (shìyǒu)　　N：roommate, housemate

我跟小李以前是室友，現在不住在一起了。

**2** 電ㄉㄧㄢˋ梯ㄊㄧ (diàntī)　　N：elevator, lift（M：部）

梯ㄊㄧ子ㄗ˙ (tī·zih) (tī·zi)　　N：ladder

樓ㄌㄡˊ梯ㄊㄧ (lóutī)　　N：stairs

東西太重了，別走樓梯，坐電梯吧！

**3** 行ㄒㄧㄥˊ李ㄌㄧˇ (síng·lǐ) (xíng·lǐ)　　N：luggage

我上次去日本帶了兩件行李，一個箱子，一個袋子，裝的東西不多。

第一課　新室友

**4 系ㄒㄧˋ (sì) (xì)**　N/M：department (in colleges)

張：你在大學念哪一系？
王：我念中文系。

**5 新ㄒㄧㄣ 生ㄕㄥ (sīnshēng) (xīnshēng)**

N：freshman, first-year student, new student

小高是中文系今年的新生，不是舊生。

**6 幸ㄒㄧㄥˋ 會ㄏㄨㄟˋ (sìnghuèi) (xìnghuì)**　IE：It is a pleasure to meet you!

張：我來介紹一下，這是李先生，這是高先生。
高：李先生，你好。
李：幸會，幸會。

**7 棒ㄅㄤˋ (bàng)**　SV：to be good, fine, excellent

那個學生的歌，唱得真棒！我聽了還想再聽。

**8 沒ㄇㄟˊ 關ㄍㄨㄢ 係ㄒㄧˋ (méi//guān·sì) (méi//guān·xi)**

IE/VO：It's not important, It doesn't matter, It's nothing, It's all right/not related, no relationship to X

(1) 張：對不起，我來晚了。
　　李：沒關係，我沒等多久。
(2) 你不打電話給老師也沒什麼關係，他已經知道你不去了。

**關ㄍㄨㄢ 係ㄒㄧˋ (guān·sì) (guān·xi)**　N：relationship

(1) 最近我們國家跟那個國家的關係不太好，你最好不要去旅行。
(2) 我跟我室友的男朋友都姓陳，可是我們沒有什麼關係。

**9 照ㄓㄠˋ 顧ㄍㄨˋ (jhàogù) (zhàogù)**

V/N：to look after; to take care of/care, attention

(1) 再見了，好好地照顧自己。
(2) 謝謝老師這三年的照顧。

7

## 實用視聽華語 3

**10** 總是 (zǒngshìh) (zǒngshì)　A：always, invariably

人總是會生病的，身體好也得小心。

**11** 擔心 (dān//sīn) (dān//xīn)　VO/SV：to worry/ worried, concerned

(1) 妹妹好晚才回來，媽媽擔了半天的心。
(2) 老李母親病得很重，他擔心得不得了。

**12** 難怪 (nán'guài)　A：no wonder

張：小張在美國住了十年。
王：難怪英文說得那麼好。

**13** 西方 (sīfāng) (xīfāng)　N：the West, Occident

會說中文的西方人多不多？

東方 (dōngfāng)　N：the East, Orient

東方學生上課的時候不太喜歡問問題嗎？

**14** 獨立 (dúlì)　V/SV：independent, to be independent

(1) 美國是一七七六年獨立的。
(2) 小王很獨立，什麼事都自己做。

**15** 從來不 (cóngláibù)　A：never (habitual)

張：你們喝不喝酒？
王：我從來不喝酒，謝謝你。
李：我從來沒喝過酒，可是今天想喝一點。

**16** 鼓勵 (gǔlì)　V/N：to encourage, urge/encouragement

(1) 老師常常鼓勵我們上課的時候要多問問題，不要只聽老師說。
(2) 孩子都需要父母的鼓勵，要是孩子做錯事，父母告訴他們下次應該怎麼做，比打他們有用多了。

## 第一課　新室友

**17 打開 (dǎ//kāi)** RC：to open up

這個窗戶壞了，我打不開。

**18 來 (lái)** V：to do (something implied in the context)

(1) 你要吃什麼，自己來，不必客氣。
(2) 張：我替你拿行李。
　　李：謝謝，我來，我自己來。

**19 夾克 (jiákè)** N：jacket

運動的時候穿的外套，臺灣人叫夾克。

**20 關心 (guānsīn) (guānxīn)** V/N：to be concerned about/concern

(1) 謝先生太忙，沒有時間關心孩子的健康。
(2) 我的病已經好了，謝謝你的關心。

**21 嘮叨 (láo·dāo)**

SV/V：to be a nag, to be repetitive in speech/to nag at

(1) 孩子常常覺得自己的父母很嘮叨。
(2) 不是你媽媽喜歡嘮叨你，你自己想想，她說了這麼多次，你聽了沒有？

**22 受不了 (shòu·bùliǎo)**

RC：cannot stand, cannot bear, unable to endure

天氣這麼熱，誰都受不了啊！

**23 會 (huèi) (huì)** AV：will, shall

今天晚上會不會下雨？

**24 全家 (cyuánjiā) (quánjiā)** N：the entire family

我們全家都出去了，所以沒有人接你的電話。

9

全(cyuán) (quán)　SV/A：entire, whole

(1) 去年全年的國家地理雜誌，本來我都有，現在小王拿走了一本，就不全了。
(2) 我的錢全都給你了，我現在一毛錢也沒有了。

全國 (cyuán'guó) (quán'guó)　N：the whole nation

全校 (cyuánsiào) (quánxiào)　N：the whole school

全世界 (cyuán shìhjiè) (quán shìjiè)　N：the whole world

完全 (wáncyuán) (wánquán)

A：completely, wholly, totally, fully, entirely

我沒學過法文，你說的法國話，我完全不懂。

## 25 移民 (yímín)　V/N：to migrate/an immigrant

(1) 王先生打算明年移民到美國去。
(2) 紐約這幾年有很多臺灣去的新移民。

## 26 地理 (dìlǐ)　N：geography

地圖 (dìtú)　N：map（M：張）

## 27 雜誌 (zájhìh) (zázhì)　N：magazine（M：本）

## 28 篇 (piān)　M：[used for papers, literary articles, essays, etc.]

## 29 文章 (wúnjhāng) (wénzhāng)

N：essay, literary article（M：篇）

李老師那篇文章寫得真棒，你看了沒有？

## 30 孔廟 (Kǒng Miào)　N：Confucius temple

廟 (miào)　N：temple（M：座）

10

臺北也有孔廟。每年九月二十八日孔子生日的時候，都要在孔廟慶祝。

### 31 中華文化 (Jhōnghuá wúnhuà) (Zhōnghuá wénhuà)

N：Chinese culture

中華(Jhōnhuá) (Zhōnghuá)　AT：Chinese

文化(wúnhuà) (wénhuà)　N：Culture

孩子要聽父母的話，是中華文化很重要的一部分。

### 32 興趣 (sìngcyù) (xìngqù)　N：interest

這幾年，小王最大的興趣是學中文。

有興趣 (yǒu sìngcyù) (yǒu xìngqù)

SV：to be interested, have an interest in

我最有興趣的功課是地理。

對(X)有興趣 [duèi(X)yǒu//sìngcyù] [duì(X)yǒu//xìngqù]

PT：to have an interest in (X), to be interested in (X)

我對寫毛筆字很有興趣。

有趣 (yǒucyù) (yǒuqù)　SV：interesting, fascinating, amusing

王老師的話真有趣，大家聽了都笑了。

### 33 口音 (kǒuyīn)　N：accent (for a spoken language)

小英男朋友的紐約(Niǔyuē, New York)口音不太好懂。

### 34 選 (syuǎn) (xuǎn)　V：to select, to choose

這兩張畫，你選一張掛上吧！

## 嘆詞跟語助詞　Interjections and Particles

1. 嗨 (hài)　　I：Hi! [greeting]

   嗨！你好！

2. 噢 (òu)　　I：Oh! [sudden realization]

   噢，我想起來了！

3. 嗯 (·m)　　P：mmm! [contentment]

   嗯！你說得一點都不錯！

4. 啦 (·la)

   P：[combined sounds of "le" and "a", denoting exclamation or interrogation]

   吃飽啦？

## 專有名詞　Proper Names

1. 林建國 (Lín Jiànguó)　　Lin, Jianguo
2. 高偉立 (Gāo Wěilì)　　Gao, Weili
3. 臺灣 (Táiwān)　　Taiwan
4. 國家地理雜誌 (Guójiā Dìlǐ Zájhìh) (Guójiā Dìlǐ Zázhì)
   National Geographic Magazine
5. 臺南 (Táinán)　　Tainan
6. 孔子 (Kǒngzǐh) (Kǒngzǐ)　　Confucius (551-479 B.C.)

## 注釋

1. 高偉立說："林先生，林太太……。"　In Chinese society, it is impolite to address friends' (peers') parents as ×先生 or ×太太. They should be called 伯父 (bófù) and 伯母 (bómǔ). 伯父 is one's father's elder brother. 伯母 is the wife of one's father's elder brother. Evolving from a long tradition, this custom helps to promote a feeling of cordial familiarity

and makes one feel like part of an extended family. Now people in Taiwan often use other more informal terms——X伯伯, X媽媽. (伯伯 means the same as 伯父)

2. "幸會,幸會。" is used when one is first introduced to somebody, but it is seldom used among the younger generation. Instead they usually say, "很高興認識你。" or "你好。".

3. Here, 對了 does not mean "correct." It is similar to saying: "By the way……" or "Oh, yes,……" as an introduction to a statement which the speaker suddenly thinks of or remembers.

4. "我們覺得把書念好最重要。" is a commonly held notion in Chinese society. In traditional China, people of learning, 士 (shì), occupied the highest class of the society. Only they could be officials who served the emperor after they had passed the government exams. Chinese people still believe that effective study will lead to a successful future, bringing honor to oneself and one's family. Therefore study is of primary importance.

5. "好了,還是先把箱子裡的……。" This 好了 is used to suggest to others that they close the issue. It is similar to saying: "Okay, okay. Let's……".

6. "那就走吧!" "那你一定很高興…。" "那我也去選你們的課。" If 那 or 那麼 is at the beginning of a sentence, serving as a way to connect the sentence to what was said earlier, it means "then" "in that case", or "So".

7. 回來啦? is a common form of greeting and functions in much the same way as "Hi, how are you doing?" or "Hi, what's up?" The most common Chinese greeting is "吃過飯了沒有?" or "吃飽了沒有?" Depending on the situation, simple and obvious facts are mentioned and used as greetings to start a conversation, such as:"出去啊?", "回家啦?", "上街啊?", "上哪兒去啊?" etc. The speaker does not necessarily expect an extended answer. Usually a simple "是啊!" is considered satisfactory.

## 文法練習

一

(I) (topic) V起來……

　　V as if, (looks as if, sounds as if, etc.)

◎看起來還不錯,……
　It looks as if it's not too bad……

用法說明：說話者對主題(topic)所做的評斷、估計或推測。「起來」的後面常是SV，或描寫、修飾性的短句，主題可省略。

Explanation: The pattern is used to show the speaker's estimation or assessment of the topic. Following 起來 is often an adjective or a descriptive, modifying clause. The subject can be omitted.

### 練習　把下面各句改成「V 起來」的句子。

1. 你穿這件衣服非常漂亮。
   You look very beautiful wearing this outfit.
   →這件衣服，你穿起來非常漂亮。
   　You look very beautiful wearing this outfit.

2. 我媽媽嘮叨的時候，我真受不了。
   _____

3. 那件事說容易，做大概不容易。
   _____

4. 算一算王老師的年紀，已經六十歲了。
   _____

5. 這個盒子太大，恐怕不方便帶。
   _____

6. 照顧那麼多病人，一定很麻煩。
   _____

---

(II) (topic)看起來……，就是……。

It looks......, one thing however......

◎看起來還不錯，就是舊了一點。
　It looks pretty good; however, it's a little old.

第一課　新室友

用法說明：前句是說話者對主題表面、正面的評斷，後句則是說話者對主題唯一不滿意之處。

Explanation: The first part of the sentence is the speaker's appraisal of the outward appearance of the subject. The latter part the sentence states a point which makes the speaker less than completely satisfied with the subject.

▼ 練習　用「看起來……，就是……。」及所給提示回答下面問題。

1. 你覺得這個房子怎麼樣？（乾淨、不夠大）
   What do you think about this house? (clean, not big enough)
   → 看起來很乾淨，就是不夠大。
   　It appears to be very clean, but it's not big enough.

2. 那個盤子非常漂亮，你為什麼不買？（太貴了）
   ＿＿＿＿＿＿＿＿＿＿＿＿＿＿＿＿＿＿＿＿＿＿＿

3. 你不喜歡我新買的汽車嗎？（很好、只有兩個門不方便）
   ＿＿＿＿＿＿＿＿＿＿＿＿＿＿＿＿＿＿＿＿＿＿＿

4. 你剛剛吃的那個蛋糕好像很好吃，真的好吃嗎？（太甜了）
   ＿＿＿＿＿＿＿＿＿＿＿＿＿＿＿＿＿＿＿＿＿＿＿

5. 我買的這個桌子好不好？（不錯、矮了點）
   ＿＿＿＿＿＿＿＿＿＿＿＿＿＿＿＿＿＿＿＿＿＿＿

二　……沒關係，……就好了。

It doesn't matter ......., ...... then it'll be fine.

◎舊一點沒關係，你自己弄乾淨就好了。
　It doesn't matter that it's a little old. You clean it yourself, and then it'll be fine.

用法說明：前句情況雖然不好，但問題不大，後句的辦法或情形就可以解決。有讓步的意思。

Explanation: Although the situation stated at the beginning of the sentence is a problem, it is

15

not a big one. The latter portion of the sentence shows how the problem can be resolved. This pattern implies that one is making concession.

### ▼ 練習　請回答問題。（學生不會時，老師可給括弧中的提示）

1. 書架壞了，怎麼辦？（再買一個）
   The bookcase is broken. What should we do? (buy another)
   →壞了沒關係，再買一個就好了。
   It doesn't matter if it's broken. Just buy another (and the problem will be resolved).

2. 今天沒買到肉，吃什麼？（有青菜）
   _____

3. 這兩個字，他寫錯了，沒關係吧？（改一改）
   _____

4. 小王的生日舞會，我不去，行不行？（送份禮物）
   _____

5. 你穿這件衣服，你男朋友不喜歡怎麼辦？（我自己喜歡）
   _____

### 三　總是 always/invariably

◎他是二年級，知道的總是多一點。
　He is a sophomore; he will invariably know a little more (than you).

◎我們做父母的總是不放心，……。
　We parents never stop worrying, ……

用法說明：「總是」的用法有兩種：(1)跟「常常」的意思差不多，但事情發生的頻率更高。正、反兩面的情形都可用。(2)表示一定存在的事實。如果「總是」後面有助動詞，「是」可省略。句尾常有「的」，表示肯定。

Explanation: There are two uses for 總是：(1) It is similar to 常常 (often), but the rate of occurrence is higher ("very, very often" "always"). It can be used in both positive and negative implications. (2) It indicates the invariability of a fact. If 總是 is followed by an auxiliary verb, then 是 can be omitted. 的 is often placed at the end of the sentence to express certainty.

## ▼ 練習

### （一）請把「常常」換成「總是」，然後加一個句子說明頻率較高的原因。

1. 我常常在那家飯館吃飯。
   I often eat at that restaurant.
   → 我總是在那家飯館吃飯，因為飯館就在學校旁邊。
   　I always eat at that restaurant because it's right next to the school.

2. 這個字，我常常寫錯。（很難寫）
   _____

3. 我室友常常很晚起來。（天天都睡得很晚）
   _____

4. 我常常打電話給媽媽。（不喜歡寫信）
   _____

5. 老師說的話，小李常常聽不懂。（中文不好）
   _____

### （二）請用「總是」完成下面對話。

1. 張：我覺得我的孩子長得好慢，他什麼時候才會長大啊？
   　　I think that my son is growing really slowly. When will he grow up?
   李：別急，孩子總是會長大的。
   　　Don't worry, children all grow up eventually.

2. 張：你為什麼一定要住在學校附近呢？郊區的房子便宜多了！
   李：住在學校附近_____，上課下課不必坐車，走路就到了。

3. 張：你怎麼帶這麼多錢出門？
   李：我怕不夠，多帶些錢_____。

4. 張：我已經學了五百個中國字了，還不能看中文報嗎？
   李：當然不行，想看中文報＿＿＿＿＿＿。

5. 張：我從來沒生過病，沒想到今天也感冒了。
   李：人＿＿＿＿＿＿，身體好也得小心。

## 四　還是……吧！ (after considering the options) it's best to

◎還是先把箱子裡的東西拿出來吧！
I think we should unpack the trunk first. (Though not explicitly stated, the option here is whether to continue debating or unpack the trunk first.)

用法說明：「還是……」是表示說話者比較主題之各種情況後，做出的結論，「吧」表示建議。

Explanation: 還是 indicates that the speaker has a conclusion after considering different situations. 吧 shows that the statement is a proposal or suggestion.

### (I) 還是……

**練習　用「還是……」完成下面各句。**

1. 夏天太熱，冬天太冷，還是秋天最舒服。
   Summer is too hot and winter is too cold. Fall is still the most comfortable.

2. 用刀叉吃中國菜不方便，還是＿＿＿＿＿＿。（筷子）

3. 你這個辦法太好了，別人都想不出來，還是＿＿＿＿＿＿。（聰明）

4. 我病了，只有老王來看我，還是＿＿＿＿＿＿。（關心我）

5. 那個房子一百多萬，我們都買不起。小陳買了，還是＿＿＿＿＿＿。（有錢）

## (II) 還是……吧！

**練習** 用「還是……吧」及所給提示回答下面各問題，需要的話並說明做此選擇之理由。

1. 你打算開車去，坐飛機去？（開車太累、坐飛機）
   Do you plan to go by car or by plane?
   →開車去太累，還是坐飛機去吧！
   　It's too tiring to drive. I think it's better to fly.

2. 我們去游泳，怎麼樣？（天氣這麼冷、跳舞）
   _____

3. 這個橘子太酸了！（吃蘋果）
   _____

4. 我想看電影，可是沒錢！（在家看電視）
   _____

5. 吃飯的時間到了，我這封信還沒寫完，怎麼辦？（菜冷了就不好吃了、先吃飯）
   _____

## 五　來　to do

◎好，好，你就自己來吧！
　Okay, okay, then just do it yourself.

用法說明：「來」可以表示「做」某件事，但這「某件事」必需是雙方都知道所指為何的某事。

Explanation: 來 can be used to mean "to do" some action, and the action referred to by 來 must be understood by both the speaker and the listener.

▼ 練習　　請用「來」完成下面對話。

1. 姐姐：媽媽不在家，我又要做飯，又要洗碗，真麻煩！
   Elder sister: Mom isn't home. I have to cook, and I have to wash the dishes, too. What a pain!
   妹妹：你做飯吧！洗碗，我來。
   Younger sister: You cook. I'll do the dishwashing.

2. 張：這麼重的箱子，你一個人搬得動嗎？
   李：當然搬不動，＿＿＿＿＿＿。

3. 張：謝謝你給我們準備了這麼多好吃的東西。
   李：沒什麼，別客氣！想吃什麼，＿＿＿＿＿＿。

4. 小兒子：每次都是哥哥開車，今天讓我開，好不好？
   爸爸：不行，你剛學會，那條路又不好走，還是＿＿＿＿＿＿。

5. 太太：有人來了，我去開門。
   先生：＿＿＿＿＿＿，你看電視吧！

---

六

(I) (S) V 不了幾 M(N)，(S) 就……

before a few M (N) occurs, (S) will ......

◎……大概過不了幾天，你就會想他們了。
………before long, you'll probably be missing them.

用法說明：本句是由RC「V不了」跟「不／沒V＋幾＋M＋N」兩個句型合成的。意思是前句情況不會維持很久或動作次數不會太多，就會發生後句的情況。

Explanation: This sentence pattern is a combination of the RC pattern "V 不了" and the pattern "不／沒 V＋幾＋M＋N". It means that the situation presented in the first clause will not be completed before the situation in the second clause occurs.

▼ 練習　　請用本句型改寫下面各句。

1. 李小姐常常只走三、五分鐘就累了。
   Miss Lee often gets tired after just three or five minutes of walking.

第一課　新室友

→ 李小姐走不了幾分鐘，就累了。
　Miss Lee can't even walk for a few minutes without getting tired.

2. 王小姐總是只吃一兩口東西，就不吃了。
_____

3. 也許只能穿幾次，這件衣服就不能穿了。
_____

4. 我弟弟每天念書，只念兩三頁，就想出去玩。
_____

5. 林先生很忙，每次來，說兩三句話，就要走。
_____


## (II) (S) 沒 V 幾 M(N),(S) 就……了

**用法說明：**如果是已經發生的實際情況，就得用這個句型。
Explanation: If the sentence is describing an actual situation that has already occurred, then this pattern must be used.

▼ **練習**　請把下面各句改成「沒 V 幾 M (N),(S) 就……了」，並說明兩句的分別。

1. 李小姐走不了幾分鐘，就累了。
　Miss Lee can't even walk for a few minutes without getting tired.
→ 李小姐沒走幾分鐘，就累了。
　Miss Lee hadn't even walked for a few minutes before she got tired.

2. 王小姐吃不了幾口，就不吃了。
_____

3. 也許穿不了幾次，這件衣服就不能穿了。
_____

21

4. 我弟弟每天念書,念不了幾頁,就想出去玩。
   _____

5. 林先生很忙,每次來,說不了幾句話,就要走。
   _____

## 七　S對……有興趣　S is interested

◎ 我幾年前在國家地理雜誌裡看到一篇文章……,看了以後,就開始對孔子跟中華文化有興趣了。
I once saw an article in National geographic Magazine………… . After I saw it I started to be interested in Confucius and Chinese culture.

用法說明:在中文裡,當事者有興趣的對象、事物應在「有興趣」之前。「對」是「對於」的意思。
Explanation: In Chinese, the thing that the subject is interested in should be placed before 有興趣. 對 means "concerning, toward, in".

▼ 練習　請改寫下面各句。

1. 跳舞,我非常有興趣。
   Dancing? I am very interested in this.
   → 我對跳舞非常有興趣。
     I am very interested in dancing.

2. 照像,我有很大的興趣。
   _____

3. 打網球,我爸爸越來越有興趣了。
   _____

4. 什麼運動,林小姐都沒有興趣。
   _____

5. 做家事，我女朋友一點興趣都沒有。

___

## 八　歎詞跟語助詞的用法
### The use of Interjections & Modal Particles
### (I) 歎詞　Interjections

歎詞通常位於句首，每個歎詞包含一定的意義，與後面句子的意思有關聯。但歎詞沒有確切的詞彙意義，語調高低長短不同時，意思也不同。

Interjections are usually placed at the beginning of sentences and do not always have concrete, translatable definitions. However, they always express a specific tone related to the sentence that follows. As the pitch and length of the interjection varies, so does its implication.

### （一）噢 Oh

◎噢，對了！
Oh! Right! or Oh! Yes! (I remember!)

**用法說明：**表示醒悟、領會，語調低而短。
Explanation: This indicates realization or understanding. The tone is low and short.

▼ **練習**　在句首加上「噢」，並注意說時之語調。

1. 我懂了。
   I understand.
   → 噢，我懂了。
   　Oh! I understand.

2. 你就是張先生的弟弟。

___

3. 我想起來了。

___

4. 你不喜歡吃肉。
___

## （二）嗯 Mmm

◎嗯，看起來還不錯，……
Mmm, it looks pretty good,…………

**用法說明**：語調低降，表示滿意、讚許。
Explanation: The pitch is low and falling, indicating satisfaction or approval.

▼ **練習**　在句首加上「嗯」，注意說時之語調。

1. 這件衣服真好看。
   This article of clothing is really nice.
   → 嗯，這件衣服真好看。
   　 Mmm, this article of clothing is really nice.

2. 還是你說得對。
___

3. 你媽做的菜好吃多了。
___

4. 這樣做就對了。
___

## (II) 語助詞　(modal) particles

語助詞一般位於句末，讀作輕聲，所表示的語氣由其語調和語言環境來決定。現僅介紹與課文相同之用法。

Particles are usually placed at the end of sentences and read in neutral tone. Its implications are determined by the tone of voice and context. Though particles can have many uses, here, only explanations for their use in the text are given.

## 第一課　新室友

### （一）啦

◎回來啦?!
　You're back?!

用法說明：「啦」是「了」跟「啊」的合音，用於打招呼，語調較低。「了」表示完成、改變或即將發生，「啊」在此表示疑問，或不確定的意思。

Explanation: 啦 is the combined sound of 了 and 啊, and it is used as a greeting and spoken with a slightly low tone. 了 indicates completion, change, or the imminence of an action, while 啊 indicates doubt or uncertainty.

**練習**　根據所給情況及提示，用「啦」打招呼。

## A. 完成　showing completion

1. 看見朋友從飯館出來。（吃）
   You see some friends come out from a restaurant. (eat)
   →吃飽啦?! 或：吃過啦?!
   　You're finished eating? or: You've eaten?

2. 下午五點多，看見朋友從公司出來。（下班）
   _____

3. 早上看見家裡的客人從房間出來。（起來）
   _____

## B. 改變　showing change

1. 朋友病了一個禮拜以後，第一次來上課。
   This is the first time your friend comes to class after a week of illness.
   →你好啦?!
   　You're well now?

2. 看見朋友開著一輛新車來上班。（買新車）
   _____

3. 一進門看見弟弟的朋友要回家。（不坐）

## C. 即將發生（常跟「要」連用）

showing the imminence of an action or situation

1. 看見朋友把他家裡的桌子、椅子搬上車。
   You see your friend moving the table and chairs from his house to his car.
   →你們要搬家啦?!
   　You're moving?

2. 看見同學拿著行李要上車。（走）

3. 下班以後在車站看見朋友在等車。（回家）

## 課室活動　　Classroom Activities

一、Divide the students into pairs. As the course has just begun, it is assumed they do not know one another. Give them a couple of minutes to get acquainted by asking one another questions in Chinese. Then ask each student to take turns introducing his/her partner to the class. If time is limited, just select a few students.

　　Some suggested getting-acquainted questions include:

1. 你姓什麼？叫什麼？
2. 你家在哪裡？
3. 你現在住在哪裡？宿舍嗎？
4. 你父母做什麼工作？
5. 你是哪一系的學生？
6. 沒有課的時候，你喜歡做什麼？
7. 你為什麼要學中文？

## 二、討論問題 (Discussion)
1. 你也覺得西方小孩比東方小孩獨立嗎？你的想法怎麼樣？
2. 要是你是父母，你覺得怎麼做會讓孩子比較獨立？
3. 說說你第一次離開家，長時間住在外面的感覺。

## 短文　　　　　高偉立的日記[1]

八月三十一日　星期日　雨

太棒了！我的室友是台灣人，他們全家是八年前從台灣移民來的。我跟他們都說中文，這好像是我第一次說那麼多中文。

林建國瘦瘦的，不怎麼高，很像他爸爸。他看起來人很好，我們大概過不了多久，就可以是好朋友了。他住校，他媽媽好像比他還緊張，總是想幫他做這個、做那個。他爸爸很少說話，可是對我很客氣。記得去年爸媽送我來的時候，也告訴我要好好地照顧自己，可是不像林建國的父母那樣——什麼都不放心。

林建國也要選中文系的課，他一定學得比較快、比較好，我得更用功才行，以後有什麼不懂的地方，就可以問他了。

## Vocabulary:

1. 日記 (rìhjì) (rìjì): diary

### 高偉立的日記[1]

　　　　　　　　　　　　　　八月三十一日　星期日　雨

　　太棒了！我的室友是台灣人，他們全家是八年前從台灣移民來的。我跟他們都說中文，這好像是我第一次說這麼多中文。

　　林建國瘦瘦的，不怎麼高，很像他爸爸。他看起來人很好，我們大概過不了多久，就可以是好朋友了。他住校，他媽媽好像比他還緊張，總是想幫他做這個、做那個。他爸爸很少說話，可是對我很客氣。記得去年爸媽送我來的時候，也告訴我要好好地照顧自己，可是不像林建國的父母那樣——什麼都不放心。

　　林建國也要選中文系的課，他一定學得比較快、比較好，我得更用功才行。以後有什麼不懂的地方，就可以問他了。

# 第二課　吃什麼好

■華人常吃的菜跟湯：紅燒肉　　蛋花湯
　　　　　　　　　　酸辣湯　　青豆蝦仁
　　　　　　　　　　宮保雞丁　芥蘭牛肉
　　　　　　　　　　　　　　　糖醋排骨

（在飯館）

服務生：請進。幾位？

偉立：兩個。（對建國）生意真好，快客滿了。

服務生：請跟我來。（到一個沒人的桌子前面）請坐。這是菜單，你們先看看。

偉立：我們吃特餐吧！比較快，也比較便宜。

建國：什麼好吃？

偉立：我最喜歡他們的七號紅燒豬肉。十四號青豆蝦仁[1]也不錯。要是你喜歡吃辣的，可以試試十三號宮保雞丁。

建國：說得我更餓了。我就要宮保雞丁吧！

偉立：我還是吃紅燒豬肉。

服務生：兩位想點什麼？決定了嗎？

偉立：我們吃特餐，一個七號，一個十三號。

服務生：喝什麼湯呢？我們有酸辣湯跟蛋花湯。

偉立：我要酸辣湯，你呢？

建國：我也要酸辣湯。

偉立：可不可以快一點兒？我餓得不得了！

服務生：可以。謝謝，馬上就來。

（服務生把他們點的東西送來）

偉立：請你給我們筷子，好不好？

服務生：沒問題。（服務生走開）

服務生（把筷子拿來）：請慢用[2]。

（偉立要建國看旁邊那一桌）

偉立：**欸**！你看她們吃的是什麼？

建國：我也不知道，有青花菜，胡蘿蔔，還有肉。她們說的好像是中文，你敢不敢問她們？

偉立：怎麼不敢？怕什麼？！（轉頭對那一桌的女孩兒）對不起，你們是中國人吧？

美真：我們是臺灣來的。

偉立：請問你們吃的是什麼菜？

美真：我吃的是芥蘭牛肉[3]。她吃的是糖醋排骨。

偉立：糖醋是什麼？

台麗：就是菜裡面放了糖跟醋，吃起來酸酸甜甜的。

建國：我媽很喜歡，我們家常吃。你們是什麼時候來的？

美真：上個月才來的。我叫謝美真。

台麗：我叫陳台麗，也是上個月來的。我們都是來留學的。

建國：我叫林建國，他是我室友高偉立。

偉立：很高興認識你們！怎麼樣？這裡的菜味道好不好？

美真：還可以，可是跟我們平常吃的不一樣。也許這裡的人喜歡這樣的口味。**對**我們**來說**，每個菜吃起來都差不多。

台麗：**就是嘛**！而且你看，你們這裡是先喝湯，我們在臺灣是先吃飯。

美真：對啊！這就叫「中菜西吃」[4]。不過總是比學校餐廳好。學校餐廳的大鍋菜，吃**來**吃**去**就那幾樣。真膩！

偉立：所以我們有時候得出來換換口味。
台麗：想我們在臺灣的時候，要吃**什麼**就**有什麼**。**連**半夜**都**找得到地方吃。臺灣小吃、美國速食、法國大餐，什麼都有。
美真：要是你去臺灣住幾個月，你一定會胖**得**上不了飛機[5]。麥當勞、炸雞、水餃、北京烤鴨、廣東點心，（叫服務生算帳）**只要**你想得出來，**就**吃得到。
偉立：真的啊？
建國：上次我姑姑[6]來，也這麼說。有機會我也要回去看看。

（服務生送來甜點跟帳單）

美真：（拿起帳單）對不起，我們還有課，先走了。這個給你們吃吧。我們沒有飯後吃甜點的習慣。再見。
建國：謝啦。**欸**，能不能把你們的手機號碼留給我？大家都是臺灣來的**嘛**！
美真：沒問題！

## 第二課　吃什麼好

| 飯湯免費請自助，最低消費每人一道菜 ||||||||||
|---|---|---|---|---|---|---|---|---|---|
| 桌號： ||||||||請先付款||
| 價目 | 品　　名 | 數量 | 價目 | 品　　名 | 數量 | 價目 | 品　　名 | 數量 |
| 60元 | 招牌快餐 | | | 洋蔥牛肉 | | | 鹽酥青蚵 | |
| 60元 | 焢肉快餐 | | | 青嫩牛肉 | | | 紅燒鱈魚 | |
| 60元 | 豬腳快餐 | 100元 | 蔥爆牛肉 | | 140元 | 糖醋鱈魚 | |
| 70元 | 魚排快餐 | | 京醬肉絲 | | | 紅燒牛腩 | |
| 70元 | 肉排快餐 | | | 蒜泥白肉 | | | 青椒雞丁 | |
| 80元 | 雞腿快餐 | | | 培根高麗菜 | | | 糖醋雞丁 | |
| 80元 | 牛腩快餐 | | | 鐵板豆腐 | | | 蝦仁豆腐 | |
| 50元 | 炒青菜 | ✓ | | 蛤仔魚瓜 | | | 清炒蝦仁 | |
| | 炸豆腐 | | 120元 | 筍絲大腸 | | | 宮保蝦仁 | |
| | | | | 焢肉筍絲 | | 150元 | 糖醋蝦仁 | |
| 60元 | 豆干肉絲 | | | 炒三鮮 | | | 蔥燒鮮蚵 | |
| | 蘿蔔煎蛋 | | | 炒花枝 | | | 薑絲大場 | |
| | 蔥花煎蛋 | | | 炒蛤仔 | | | 脆皮大腸 | |
| | 麻婆豆腐 | | | 糖醋里肌 | | | 紅燒獅子頭 | |
| | 肉醬豆腐 | | 120元 | 梅干扣肉 | | | 豆瓣魚 | |
| 70元 | 開陽白菜 | | | 杏菜銀魚 | | 200元 | 鹽酥虱目魚 | |
| | 蕃茄炒蛋 | | | 白切雞 | | | 鐵板蝦仁豆腐 | |
| | 紅燒肉 | | | 糖醋花枝 | | | 清蒸鱈魚 | |
| | 桂竹筍肉絲 | | 130元 | 宮保花枝 | | 時價 | 豆酥鱈魚 | |
| | 雪菜肉絲 | | | 宮保魷魚 | | | 清蒸鯧魚 | |
| | 芙蓉煎蛋 | | | 紅燒魚 | ✓ | | 豆酥鯧魚 | |
| 70元 | 滷豬腳 | | | 五更腸旺 | | | 鹽酥鯧魚 | |
| | 回鍋肉 | ✓ | | 蔥油雞 | | 時菜 | | |
| | 苦瓜肉絲 | | 140元 | 宮保雞丁 | | | | |
| | 魚香茄子 | | | 蝦仁角瓜 | | 總計 | | |
| | 肉醬茄子 | | | 炒青蚵 | | | | |

■ 菜單（劉秀芝提供）

實用視聽華語 3
Practical Audio-Visual Chinese

## 生詞及例句

**1 服務生／服務員 (fúwùshēng/fúwùyuán)**

N：attendant, service person, waiter

這家咖啡店的服務生，男的比女的多。

**服務 (fúwù)** N/V：service/to serve, give service to

(1) 如果你覺得這家旅館的服務太差，下次就不要再去住了。
(2) 你們要不要喝茶？我年紀最小，我替大家服務。

**2 客滿 (kèmǎn)** IE：full house, sold out, no vacancy

那家旅館常常客滿，去晚了就沒有房間了。

**客人 (kèrén)** N：visitor, guest

**滿 (mǎn)** SV/RE：to be full

(1) 瓶子裡水已經滿了，不能再裝了。
(2) 這條路在火車站旁邊，所以什麼時候都停滿了車。

**3 菜單 (càidān)** N：menu

這個菜單上的菜，我差不多都吃過。

**名單 (míngdān)** N：roster of names, name list

**通知單 (tōngzhīdān)** N：notification, notice slip

**單子 (dān·zih) (dān·zi)** N：a list

**4 特餐 (tècān)** N：a special dish of a restaurant, a special dish of the day

**套餐 (tàocān)** N：combo; combo meal

要是你點套餐，飯、菜、湯都有了，比單點 (single order) 便宜。

## 第二課　吃什麼好

**5 紅燒 (hóngshāo)**　V/AT：to braise or stew in soy sauce

(1) 這條魚要是紅燒，加鹽 (yán, salt) 跟醬油 (jiàngyóu, soy-bean sauce) 就行了。
(2) 這盤紅燒牛肉，你大概放了太多鹽，好鹹！

**燒 (shāo)**　V：to cook; to burn; to stew after frying

(1) 趙太太一定在六點以前把飯菜燒好，等先生下班回來吃飯。
(2) 小孩子不可以玩火，不小心燒了房子怎麼辦？

**6 豬肉 (jhūròu) (zhūròu)**　N：pork

**豬 (jhū) (zhū)**　N：pig, hog, swine

**7 青豆 (cīngdòu) (qīngdòu)**　N：green peas

**8 蝦仁 (siārén) (xiārén)**　N：shelled shrimp

**蝦 (siā) (xiā)**　N：shrimp

**9 辣 (là)**　SV：to be hot, spicy

這個湯又酸又辣，叫酸辣湯。

**10 青花菜 (cīnghuācài) (qīnghuācài)**　N：broccoli（M：棵 kē）

**11 胡蘿蔔（紅蘿蔔）(húluó·bo) (hóngluó·bo)**

N：carrot（M：根 gēn）

**蘿蔔 (luó·bo)**　N：radish, turnip

**12 敢 (gǎn)**　AV：to dare

外面太黑了，李小姐不敢一個人出去。

**13 糖醋 (tángcù)**　V/AT：cooked with sweet-and-sour sauce

(1) 要是你喜歡酸酸甜甜的味道，這些肉，我們就糖醋吧！
(2) 糖醋魚是我家常吃的菜。

醋 (cù)　　N：vinegar

**14** 排骨 (páigǔ)　　N：spareribs; a chop; a rib

排骨飯、排骨麵都可以說是臺灣的速食。

**15** 留學 (lióusyué) (liúxué)　　V：to study abroad

我姐姐打算畢業以後，到英國去留學。

留學生 (lióusyuéshēng) (liúxuéshēng)
N：student studying abroad

留 (lióu)　　V：to remain, to stay; to keep, reserve; to detain

(1) 哥哥還沒回來，我們給他留些飯菜吧！
(2) 我留張先生吃飯，可是他一定要走。

留起來 (lióu//cǐ·lái) (liú//qǐ·lái)
RC：to save, to put away for later use

這些紙別扔了，留起來下次用吧！

**16** 口味 (kǒuwèi)　　N：taste, flavor（M：種）

我們兩個人的口味不一樣，你喜歡吃甜的，我愛吃鹹的。

**17** 而且 (érciě) (érqiě)　　CONJ：moreover, in addition, furthermore

我要準備明天的功課，而且我很累，不想出去。

**18** 不過 (búguò)　　CONJ/A：but, however/only, merely

(1) 烤肉的味道不錯，不過我更喜歡炸雞。
(2) 王小弟不過是個孩子，你不必跟他生氣。

**19** 餐廳 (cāntīng)　　N：dining hall; restaurant （M：家）

這家餐廳的菜又便宜又好吃。

第二課　吃什麼好

**20 大鍋菜 (dàguōcài)**

N：food prepared in a big pot, institutional food (made in mass quantities)

大鍋菜裡有肉、有菜，可是因為鍋太大，東西太多，味道沒有自己家裡做的好吃。

**鍋 (guō)**

N/M：cooking pot (container used for cooking food)/Measure for cooked food

我上次去看我男朋友，想做一鍋湯給他吃，可是找不到大一點兒的鍋。

**平底鍋 (píngdǐguō)**　N：a pan; a griddle

**21 膩 (nì)**　SV/RE：to be bored with, tired of

(1) 天天吃一樣的東西，一定會覺得很膩。
(2) 這個歌越聽越好聽，聽了這麼多次，我還沒聽膩。

**22 連……都 (lián .... dōu)**　PT：even

老林什麼都忘了，連自己的名字都忘了。

**23 半夜 (bànyè)**　N：midnight, in the middle of the night

我弟弟昨天晚上玩到半夜兩點才回家。

**24 小吃 (siǎochīh) (xiǎochī)**

N：food served at a night market stall, a street stall, a small diner, etc., which can be eaten as a meal, a snack, or a side dish

**25 速食 (sùshíh) (sùshí)**　N："fast food"

**速食麵 (sùshíhmiàn) (sùshímiàn)**　N：instant noodles

**26 大餐 (dàcān)**　N：an abundant meal on special occasions

今天是老李的生日，他請我們吃大餐，有魚、有肉、有蝦、還有甜點，吃了三個小時還沒吃完。

39

實用視聽華語 3

27 水餃 (shuěijiǎo) (shuǐjiǎo)　N：boiled Chinese dumplings

餃子 (jiǎo·zih) (jiǎo·zi)

N：Chinese dumpling made of various fillings stuffed in a dough wrapper

28 烤鴨 (kǎoyā)　N：roast duck

鴨子 (yā·zih) (yā·zi)　N：duck（M：隻）

29 算帳（賬）(suàn//jhàng) (suàn//zhàng)

VO：to settle accounts, figure out a bill

(1) 你吃飽了吧？可以叫小姐來算帳了吧？
(2) 我們今天一共吃了多少錢，那個小姐算了半天的帳了，還沒算出來。

帳單 (jhàngdān) (zhàngdān)

N：a bill (at a restaurant, shop, etc.)（M：張）

30 姑姑 (gū·gu)　N：aunt, father's sister

31 機會 (jīhuèi) (jīhuì)　N：chance, opportunity

有機會我想到法國去旅行。

32 甜點 (tiándiǎn)　N：dessert

33 習慣 (síguàn) (xíguàn)　V/N：to get used to, to be accustomed to/habit

(1) 我習慣看著報吃早飯。
(2) 我知道晚睡是壞習慣，可是很難改。

34 手機/大哥大/行動電話

(shǒujī/dàgēdà/xíngdòng diànhuà)

N：cell phone; cellular phone; mobile phone

我打手機給小王，他沒開機，我沒辦法，只能留言給他。沒想到才說了兩句話，我的手機就沒電了。

40

第二課　吃什麼好

## 歎詞跟語助詞　Interjections and Particles

1. 欸（ㄟˋ,ㄟˊ,ㄟˇ）(èi, éi, ěi)　I：[to attract attention or express surprise]

   (1) 欸，把那封信拿給我。
   (2) 欸？小王怎麼還沒來？
   (3) 欸？你怎麼可以站在床上？

2. 嘛 (·ma)　P：[used at end of a sentence implying that what precedes it is obvious]

   張：王先生的中文怎麼那麼棒？
   李：他是中國人嘛！

## 專有名詞跟菜名　Proper Names & dish Names

### 專有名詞　Proper Names

1. 謝美真 (Xiè Měijhēn) (Xiè Měizhēn)　Xie, Meizhen
2. 陳台麗 (Chén Táilì)　Chen, Taili
3. 麥當勞 (Màidāngláo)　McDonald's
4. 北京 (Běijīng)　Beijing
5. 廣東 (Guǎngdōng)　Canton

### 菜名　Dish Names

1. 紅燒豬肉 (hóngshāo jhūròu) (hóngshāo zhūròu)
   pork braised in soy sauce
2. 青豆蝦仁 (cīngdòu siārén) (qīngdòu xiārén)
   green peas and shelled shrimp
3. 宮保雞丁 (gōngbǎo jīdīng)　Kongbao chicken
4. 酸辣湯 (suānlà tāng)　hot and sour soup
5. 蛋花湯 (dànhuā tāng)　egg drop soup

6. 芥ㄐㄧㄝˋ蘭ㄌㄢˊ牛ㄋㄧㄡˊ肉ㄖㄡˋ (jièlán niúròu) (jièlán nióuròu)    beef and kale
7. 糖ㄊㄤˊ醋ㄘㄨˋ排ㄆㄞˊ骨ㄍㄨˇ (tángcù páigǔ)    sweet and sour spareribs

## 注釋

1. "……七號紅燒豬肉。十四號青豆蝦仁……" Usually there are no numbers for dishes on restaurant menus in Taiwan.

2. 請慢用 is said by a person (perhaps a host or waiter) who has just served a dish. It literally means "Take your time to eat it" and is equivalent to the Western expression, "Enjoy your meal."

3. 芥蘭牛肉  芥蘭 is Chinese kale. It is hard to find this vegetable in the United States, so most Chinese restaurants there use broccoli as a substitute. However they still name the dish "kale." That is why in the text 建國 said there were broccoli, carrots and meat in the girl's plate.

4. 中菜西吃 means to eat Chinese food in a Western fashion. It can be done in several different ways. Some examples are having the soup course first, changing some of the ingredients and eating a dish without rice. Chinese use chopsticks to take food from communal dishes placed in the center of the table to their individual rice bowls. The meat or vegetable is placed on top of the rice, the entire bowl is raised to the mouth, and then the food is transferred into the mouth using chopsticks. Some people have adopted the Western custom of using plates rather than bowls and of using serving utensils for communal dishes. Sometimes the dishes are also passed around rather than left in the center of the table for the entire meal.

5. "你一定會胖得上不了飛機" means "You will certainly become too fat to get on the plane." This exaggeration is meant as a joke. In general, Chinese are not very sensitive to being fat. While being skinny is in fashion among many younger people, the older generation still think being a little fat is good. It is symbol of being able to afford a good life.

6. 姑姑 is one's father's sister. If she is married, she may be called 姑媽. Mother's sister is called 阿姨 (āyí) or 姨媽 (yímā). The name given the wife of one's father's younger brother is 嬸嬸 (shěn·shen), while the wife of one's mother's brother is known as 舅媽 (jiùmā).

## 文法練習

### 一　V/SV 得 N/PN ……N/PN V/SV 得……
### V/SV to the point that N/PN ......

◎說得我更餓了。
As you say that, I feel even hungrier.

◎你一定會胖得上不了飛機。
You'll certainly become too fat to get on the plane.

用法說明：「得」前面的動詞或 SV 常是原因，「得」後面的補語表示結果和程度。即某動作或狀態使當事者出現某種情態。而且該結果和程度多半是誇張的或不好的。當事者可在句首，亦可在「得」之後。當事者在「得」之後時，有被動的感覺。

Explanation: The verb or SV preceding 得 is often a cause or reason, while the information after 得 is a resulting outcome or level of completion. This outcome or level of completion is often exaggerated for emphasis or effect, and usually has a negative tone. The subject being spoken about can be placed at the beginning of the sentence or after 得. When it is placed after 得, the sentence has a passive tone.

### 練習

#### (I) V 得……

（一）請用「V 得 N/PN……」改寫下面各句。

1. 王先生吃了很多，所以走不動了。
   Mr. Wang ate a lot, so he can't walk.
   → 王先生吃了很多，吃得他走不動了。
   Mr. Wang ate so much that he can't walk.

2. 我打了四個小時的球，累極了。
   _____

3. 老王喝了太多酒，不會走路了。
   _____

4. 我們談了很久，就忘了吃午飯了。
   _____

5. 書上的字太小，老高看了以後就頭疼了。
   _____

(二) 請把下面各句改成「N/PN＋V得……」句子，如果當事者相同，第二個主語應該省略。

1. 王先生吃了很多，吃得他走不動了。
   Mr. Wang ate so much that he can't walk.
   → 王先生吃了很多，吃得走不動了。
   　Mr. Wang ate so much that he can't walk.

2. 我打了四個小時的球，打得我累極了。
   _____

3. 老王喝了太多酒，喝得他不會走路了。
   _____

4. 我們談了很久，談得我們忘了吃午飯了。
   _____

5. 書上的字太小，看得老高頭疼了。
   _____

## (II) SV得……

(一) 請用「SV 得 N/PN……」完成下面各句。

1. 我走了一天的路，累得我一坐下就睡著了。
   I walked for a full day, and was so tired that I fell asleep as soon as I sat down.

2. 小林越來越胖，胖得他＿＿＿＿＿＿＿＿＿＿＿＿＿＿＿＿＿。

3. 昨天晚上太冷，冷得我媽媽＿＿＿＿＿＿＿＿＿＿＿＿＿＿＿。

4. 火車快開了，小張還沒來，急得他女朋友＿＿＿＿＿＿＿＿＿。

5. 這個橘子真酸，酸得我＿＿＿＿＿＿＿＿＿＿＿＿＿＿＿＿＿。

(二) 請用「N/PN＋SV得……」及提示回答下面各題。

1. 聽說你弟弟很高興，他有多高興？
   I heard that your little brother is very happy. How happy is he?
   → 他高興得跳起來了。
   　He's so happy that he jumped for joy.

2. 你有多餓？（可以吃下一頭牛）
   ＿＿＿＿＿＿＿＿＿＿＿＿＿＿＿＿＿＿＿＿＿＿＿＿＿＿＿

3. 你爸爸非常忙嗎？（沒有時間吃飯）
   ＿＿＿＿＿＿＿＿＿＿＿＿＿＿＿＿＿＿＿＿＿＿＿＿＿＿＿

4. 李先生真的很氣嗎？（說不出話來）
   ＿＿＿＿＿＿＿＿＿＿＿＿＿＿＿＿＿＿＿＿＿＿＿＿＿＿＿

5. 你為什麼不喜歡很香的花呢？（受不了）
   ＿＿＿＿＿＿＿＿＿＿＿＿＿＿＿＿＿＿＿＿＿＿＿＿＿＿＿

## 二　對 NP 來說…… As far as NP is concerned

◎對我們來說，每個菜吃起來都差不多。
　For us, every dish tastes about the same.

**用法說明：**「對」後面的當事者，本句型是站在當事者立場，表示意見或看法。
Explanation: Following 對 is a person or group. This sentence pattern speaks from this person or group's point of view, expressing their opinions or thoughts.

▼ 練習　　請用「對……來說……」回答問題。

1. 日本人說中國字不難寫，你們美國人呢？

Japanese say that Chinese characters aren't difficult to write. What about you Americans?

→ 對我們美國人來說，中國字很難寫。
　　So far as Americans are concerned, Chinese characters are very difficult to write.

2. 你覺得宮保雞丁好吃嗎？
　　_____

3. 一年級的新生每星期上二十個小時的課，多不多？
　　_____

4. 學校的學生太少，好不好？
　　_____

5. 一件衣服一千塊，貴不貴？
　　_____

### 三　就是嘛！　That's right! Indeed!

◎ 美真：……對我們來說，每個菜吃起來都差不多。
　　台麗：就是嘛！
　　Meizhen: For us, every dish tastes about the same.
　　Taili: Indeed!

### (I) 嘛

用法說明：「嘛」是語助詞 (P)，放在句子後面，語調低，對顯而易見的事情表示肯定的語氣，有「本來就是這樣，本來就應該這樣」的意思。因為「嘛」前的句子是敘述一顯而易見的事，沒有「嘛」就沒有「你應該知道」的含義。

Explanation: 嘛 is a particle. It is placed at the end of a sentence and pronounced with a low pitch, indicating definite affirmation of a preceding statement. The connotation is that "this is invariable and is fitting and appropriate". The statement preceding 嘛 describes an obvious matter, and 嘛 implies that "one ought to know this."

## 練習

### (一) 用「嘛」完成下面對話。

1. 李：我弟弟什麼都不會，什麼都不懂。
   Lee: My brother can't do anything, and he doesn't understand anything.
   張：他還是個孩子嘛！
   Chang: C'mon, he's still a child!

2. 李：小錢的中文說得真好。
   張：_____！

3. 李：這一課，我有很多地方都不懂，怎麼辦？
   張：_____！

4. 李：王小姐為什麼還沒來？
   張：_____！

5. 李：你為什麼不坐電梯？
   張：_____！

### (二) 把下面句中的「嘛」去掉，並比較兩句的不同。（可用英文）

1. 累了就休息嘛！
   If you're tired, just take a rest then! (Implies: It's obvious! You ought to know that!)
   → 累了就休息。
   If you're tired, then take a rest. (No implication of: "It's obvious! You ought to know that!")

2. 你覺得冷就多穿點衣服嘛！
   _____

3. 老丁這麼嘮叨，誰受得了嘛！
   _____

4. 用筷子吃飯是中國人的習慣嘛！
   _____

5. 我們是好朋友，我幫你是應該的嘛！
   _____

## (II) 就是嘛！ Indeed!

用法說明：表示完全同意對方的觀點、說法或意見。意思是「事情就是你說的那樣」。

Explanation: This indicates that you totally agree with another's point of view, opinion, or statement. It means "the situation is exactly as you stated".

▼ 練習　用「就是嘛」完成下面對話。

1. 張：不準備，考試當然考不好啊！
   Chang: If you don't prepare, of course you'll do poorly on the test!
   王：就是嘛！
   Wang: I couldn't agree more.

2. 張：身體不健康，有錢有什麼用？
   王：_____！

3. 張：現在是冬天，可是熱得跟夏天一樣！
   王：_____！

4. 張：住得近比住得遠方便，他為什麼要搬家？
   王：_____！

5. 張：這家餐廳的菜這麼難吃，怎麼會客滿？
   王：_____！

## 四　V來V去

◎學校餐廳的大鍋菜，吃來吃去就那幾樣。
After repeatedly eating the school cafeteria's mass-produced food, one still just finds those same few dishes.

用法說明：強調不斷重覆某一動作，由於動詞不同，而有兩種不同意思：(A) 不停地往返來回不同的地方。(B) 某個動作被重覆多次以後，說詞者或當事者得到某種看法或感想。「V來V去」後不可再加賓語 (O)。

Explanation: This pattern shows that an action is continually repeated. Depending on what verb is used, there are two poddible meanings: (A) Continual movement between two different locations. (B) Repetition of an action upon many different objects which leads the speaker or person involved to develop a conclusion. An object cannot be placed after "Ｖ來Ｖ去".

## 練習　請改寫下面各句。

A. Different locations

1. 林太太急得在屋子裡從這邊走到那邊，從那邊走到這邊。
   Mrs. Lin was so anxious she walked from here to there and there to here in the house.
   → 林太太急得在屋子裡走來走去。
      Mrs. Lin was so anxious she paced back and forth in the house.

2. 小孩子不應該在街上從這裡跑到那裡，從那裡跑到這裡。
   _____

3. 王小姐的工作就是每天從這個城市飛到那個城市，從那個城市飛到這個城市。
   _____

4. 我哥哥把這張桌子從這裡搬到那裡，又從那裡搬到這裡，怎麼放都覺得不好。
   _____

5. 這些書，你每天從家裡帶到學校，又從學校帶回家，不麻煩嗎？
   _____

B. Repeated action upon different objects

1. 我聽過很多歌，還是覺得這首歌最好聽。
   I've listened to many songs, but still thinks that this song is the best.
   → 我聽來聽去還是覺得這首歌最好聽。
      I've repeatedly listened to many songs, but still thinks that this song is the best.

2. 小趙要買生日禮物給女朋友，想了半天，才決定買一本書。
   _____

3. 說了那麼多，大家都覺得是你的錯。
   _____

4. 穿了這麼多家公司的鞋，還是這家的最舒服。
___

5. 老陳太高，那條褲子他比了半天，都覺得不夠長。
___

### 五

#### (I) ……QW……就……QW……

◎在臺灣要吃什麼就有什麼。
In Taiwan, whatever you'd want to eat is readily available.

用法說明：疑問代詞 (QW) 表示任指，前後兩個疑問代詞指的是同一事物。意思是「隨便，都可以，只要合乎『就』前面的希望、要求或需求，沒有特別的限制」。如果 QW 是「誰」，第二個「誰」也可以放在「就」的前面。

Explanation: Both QWs in this pattern represent the same desired object. This pattern shows that anything which fits the conditions described before 就 is easily available, without any special restrictions. If the QW is 誰, the second 誰 can also be placed in front of 就.

▼ 練習　　請用「……QW……就……QW……」回答下面問題。

1. 張：對不起，我來晚了，我應該坐哪兒？
   Chang: Sorry, I'm late. Where should I sit?
   李：你想坐哪兒，就坐哪兒。
   Lee: Sit wherever you want.

2. 張：我們明天去紐約，誰去買票？
   李：___

3. 張：你的錢不夠啊？你想借多少錢？
   李：___

4. 張：我不知道怎麼幫他，怎麼辦？
   李：___

5. 張：我什麼時候去你家比較好？
   李：_____

## (II) QW＋SV 就 V＋QW ＆ 怎麼 SV 就怎麼 V

用法說明：用法與 (I) 一樣，但意思是：只要合乎「就」前面的條件即可。「多少」、「幾」，不適用本句型。而「誰」和「什麼時候」則應在 V 前面。

Explanation: The usage here is similar to (I) above. However, this pattern means that whatever fits the conditions described before 就 is acceptable. 多少 and 幾 should not be used with this pattern. And 誰 or 什麼時候 must be placed before, not after, the verb.

▼ 練習　用「QW＋SV 就 V＋QW」或「怎麼 SV 就怎麼 V」回答下面問題。

1. 張：這幾個錶，你要買哪個？
   Chang: Which watch do you want to buy?
   李：哪個便宜，我就買哪個。
   Lee: Whichever one is cheaper, that's the one I'll buy.

2. 張：我們現在去哪裡吃飯？
   李：_____

3. 張：事情還沒做完，我們兩個，誰可以先離開？
   李：_____

4. 張：我把小李的車弄丟了，你覺得我什麼時候可以告訴他？
   李：_____

5. 張：我家玩的東西很多，你想玩什麼？
   李：_____

6. 張：我們怎麼去紐約？
   李：_____

## 六　連……都／也……　　even ......

◎連半夜都找得到地方吃。
Even in the middle of the night you can find a place to eat.

用法說明：說話者認為「連」後面的情況是不平常的，有強調的意思。N、SV、V、VO、S-V，或短句都可放在連的後面。

Explanation: The speaker thinks that the situation mentioned after 連 is unusual or worthy of note and thus uses this pattern for emphasis. N, SV, V, VO, S-V of a simple sentence all can be placed after 連.

**練習**　　用「連……都／也……」改寫下面各句。

### (一) 連 N/NP 都／也……

1. 我太忙，沒時間吃飯。
   I'm too busy. I don't have time to eat.
   → 我太忙，連飯都沒時間吃。
   I'm too busy. I don't even have time to eat.
   or → 我太忙，連吃飯的時間都沒有。
   I'm too busy. I don't even have the time to eat.

2. 這件事太容易了，小孩子也會做。
   _____

3. 高先生真有錢，他買得起飛機。
   _____

### (二) 連 VO 都／也……

1. 我太忙，沒時間吃飯。
   I'm too busy. I don't have time to eat.
   → 我太忙，連吃飯都沒時間。
   I'm too busy. I don't even have time to eat.

2. 你今天怎麼了？看電影也沒興趣了嗎？
   _____

3. 王小明什麼都不會，打電話也不會。

## （三）連 S-V 都／也……

1. 這件衣服太小，我最小的弟弟也穿不下。
   This article of clothing is too small. My youngest brother can't get it on either.
   → 這件衣服太小，連我最小的弟弟穿都穿不下。
   This piece of clothing is too small; even my youngest brother can't get it on.

2. 那個菜很辣，墨西哥 (Mòsīgē) (Mòxīgē, Mexico) 人都受不了。

3. 這個字眞難寫，老師也寫不好。

## （四）連 clause（短句）都／也……

1. 老師請客，你不去，不太好吧？
   The teacher invited us. It would be a bad idea for you not to show up, don't you think?
   → 連老師請客你也不去，不太好吧？
   Even with the teacher inviting us you're not going to show up. That's not too good, don't you think?

2. 你眞奇怪！為什麼不許我說話？

3. 媽媽太緊張了，爸爸做事，她也不放心。

## （五）連 V 都／也　不／沒 V……

1. 我女朋友接到我的信，沒看就扔了。
   My girlfriend received my letter and threw it away without reading it.
   → 我女朋友接到我的信，連看都沒看就扔了。
   My girlfriend received my letter and threw it away without even reading it.

2. 我去借錢，他什麼都沒想就說不行。

3. 我弟弟病了，今天不想玩了。
_____

4. 我吃得太飽了，站不起來了。
_____

### (六) 連SV都／也 不／沒SV

1. 這個東西一點都不甜，怎麼能叫糖呢？
   This thing isn't sweet at all. How can it be called candy?
   → 這個東西連甜都不甜，怎麼能叫糖呢？
      This thing isn't even sweet. How can it be called candy?

2. 這杯茶不熱了，真難喝。
_____

3. 老趙說錯了話，大家都看著他，可是他的臉一點也沒紅。
_____

### 七 只要……，就…… As long as...... (then) ......

◎只要你想得出來，就吃得到。
Whatever you can think of to eat is available.

用法說明：「只要」後面是假設的唯一條件，如果合於此條件就有「就」後面的結果。只能用於一般或未來的情況，已經發生的則不適用。因為只有一個條件，感覺上不太難做到。

Explanation: Following 只要 is a single hypothetical stipulation. As long as this stipulation is met, then the situation after 就 will result, since the condition is relatively simple and easy to satisfy. This pattern can only be used to describe habitual or future situations. It cannot be used for an action which has already occurred.

▼ 練習　　用「只要……，就……。」回答下面問題。

1. 你願意搬到那兒去住嗎？
   Are you willing to move there?
   → 只要去學校方便，我就願意。
      As long as it's convenient to go to school from there, I'm willing.

2. 我們明年都可以畢業嗎？
   _____

3. 你的車，今天晚上可以借我嗎？
   _____

4. 我們什麼時候去野餐？
   _____

5. 我越來越胖，怎麼辦？
   _____

## 八　歎詞「欸」的用法　　The use of "欸" Interjection

◎欸，你看，她們吃的是什麼？
Hey, look! What is it that they are eating?

用法說明：語調高降（第四聲）表示招呼並提醒別人注意，或答應別人的叫喚。語調高揚（第二聲）表示驚訝，或忽然想起。語調曲折（第三聲）表示不太同意。用於較熟的朋友之間。

Explanation: When the tone starts high and descends (fourth tone), this indicates a greeting that is meant to get another's attention or answer another's call. When the tone starts fairly high and ascends (second tone), this indicates that one is surprised or has suddenly thought of something. When the tone drops and then rises (third tone), this indicates that one disagrees. This interjection is very informal and is used in more casual settings.

▼ 練習

（一）根據所給的情況及提示，用「欸」(èi) 招呼並提醒對方注意。

1. 看見同學沒拿書就走了。
   You see a classmate leaving without taking his/her book.
   → 欸，你忘了拿書了！
   　 Hey! You forgot to take your book!

2. 上課的時間到了，可是室友還在看報。
   _____

3. 弟弟的女朋友進來,可是弟弟在寫功課,沒看見。

## (二) 用「欸」(èi) 答應別人的叫喚。

1. 建國!建國!你快來!
   Jian Guo! Jian Guo! Come here quickly!
   → 欸!來了!
   　 Ok, I'm coming!

2. 張小姐!

## (三) 用「欸」(éi) 表示驚訝。

1. 已經十點了,看見哥哥還沒去上班。
   It's already ten o'clock, and you see that your brother hasn't gone to work yet.
   → 欸,你怎麼還在家?
   　 Huh? Why are you still home?

2. 覺得朋友今天來得比平常早。

3. 服務生送來一個你沒點的菜。

## (四) 用「欸」(éi) 表示忽然想起。

1. 聽到別人說要寄信,想起寫好的信也還沒寄。
   You hear someone say they are going to mail a letter and (suddenly) remember that you still haven't mailed a letter that you finished writing (either).
   → 欸,我的信也還沒寄。
   　 Oh! I still haven't mailed my letter yet either!

2. 要去開車的時候,找不到鑰匙。

3. 打工的時候忙得不得了,餓了才想起來忘了吃午飯。

（五）用「欸」(ěi) 表示不太同意。

1. 你聽見弟弟對他同學說話不太客氣，你覺得這樣不對。
   You hear your little brother impolitely talking to his classmate. You feel that it is not proper to talk in this way.
   → 欸，對同學說話怎麼這麼不客氣！？
   　Hey, how come you are so impolite to your classmate?

2. 你看見室友把髒東西扔到窗戶外面去。
   _____

3. 你看見好朋友的小孩吃飯的時候玩筷子。
   _____

| 課室活動 | Classroom Activities |
|---|---|

## 一、角色扮演 (Role Playing)

Ask for three volunteers. Two of them act as friends going to a Chinese restaurant. The third acts as their waiter. The two friends first place their order. After being served, one of them is appalled to find a hair（一根頭髮 yìgēn tóufǎ）in a dish. What would they do in this situation? Have the students speak and act out their reactions. Give them two minutes to prepare. A fourth role may be added-that of the owner of the restaurant, the 老闆 (lǎobǎn) or the manager（經理）.

## 二、討論問題 (Discussion)

1. 你最喜歡吃什麼？為什麼？
2. 華人吃的東西，你覺得最好吃/難吃的是什麼？
3. 用圖片 (picture) 或實物 (object) 介紹你們國家最特別的一種吃的東西。
4. 貴國人吃飯的習慣，有什麼跟臺灣人一樣或不一樣的地方？

蚊子 (wénzi, mosquito)
咬 (yǎo, to bite)

牠 (tā, it)

## 短文　　　　建國給父母的信

爸：
媽：

　　你們好！上課已經一個多禮拜了，我在這裏一切都好，請放心。姐姐怎麼樣？我還沒給她打電話。你們一定沒想到我會用中文寫信吧？這學期我選了中文系的課，應該多練習寫字。

　　昨天我跟高偉立去市區一家廣東飯館吃飯，那裏的菜都是高偉立喜歡的口味，吃起來不怎麼樣，還是媽媽做的好吃。不過高偉立常去，他特別喜歡那裏的紅燒豬肉。如果他吃過媽媽做的宮保雞丁，就一定不會再想去那家飯館了。

　　我們在吃飯的時候，認識了兩個剛來的女留學生。她們在我們學校念研究所。聽她們說在台灣要吃什麼，就有什麼，說得高偉立對台灣更有興趣了。

　　我的信寫得不錯吧？希望爸爸看了會高興得給我多寄點錢來。先謝謝了！我要去上課了，有空再給你們寫信。

　　　敬祝
健康、快樂！

　　　　　　　　　　　　　　　兒　建國　敬上
　　　　　　　　　　　　　　　　　九月十日

## Vocabulary:

1. 敬 (jing): means to respect. 敬上 means to respectfully offer to a superior. When one writes a letter to his/her elders, one should place 敬上 after his/her signature.

### 建國給父母的信

爸：
媽：

　　你們好！上課已經一個多禮拜了，我在這裏一切都好，請放心。姐姐怎麼樣？我還沒給她打電話。你們一定沒想到我會用中文寫信吧？這學期我選了中文系的課，應該多練習寫字。

　　昨天我跟高偉立去市區一家廣東飯館吃飯，那裏的菜都是高偉立喜歡的口味，吃起來不怎麼樣，還是媽媽做的好吃。不過高偉立常去，他特別喜歡那裏的紅燒豬肉。如果他吃過媽媽做的宮保雞丁，就一定不會再想去那家飯館了。

　　我們在吃飯的時候，認識了兩個剛來的女留學生。她們在我們學校念研究所。聽她們說在台灣要吃什麼就有什麼，說得高偉立對台灣更有興趣了。

　　我的信寫得不錯吧？希望爸爸看了會高興得給我多寄點錢來。先謝謝了！我要去上課了，有空再給你們寫信。
　　敬祝
健康、快樂！

兒建國敬上[1]<br>九月十日

# 第三課　我想去臺灣

■學生註冊情形（吳俊銘攝）

（高偉立敲辦公室的門）

教授：請進。

偉立：張老師，您好！我來請教幾個問題，昨天已經跟您約好了。

教授：好的[1]，請坐。有什麼問題？有什麼需要我幫忙的？

偉立：謝謝。我覺得這兒沒有說中文的環境，我想得去臺灣或中國大陸**才**能把中文學好。**不知道**我們跟那邊的學校有沒有交換計畫？

教授：有。你打算什麼時候去？

偉立：**要是**可能**的話**，明年就去。

教授：很好。我們跟臺灣的大學、大陸的大學都有交換計畫。有一年的，也有兩三個月的暑期班。這些資料，我們系的網站上都有，你可以上網去看看，要申請**的話**，就自己下載申請表。

偉立：好。容不容易申請？申請的人多不多？

教授：這**要看**你的成績了。你先填申請表，再寫一份兒學習計畫。

偉立：然後呢？

教授：你還得申請成績單，再請老師寫一封推薦信。把這些東西一起交給系辦公室。記得要在二月一號以前交來！

偉立：我大概需要準備多少錢？機票貴不貴？

教授：每個地方不一樣。**等**你決定去哪兒以後，我**再**告訴你。機票**嘛**，當然是越早訂越便宜。

第三課　我想去臺灣

# 國立台灣師範大學國語教學中心

入學申請表
## MTC APPLICATION FORM

*Please TYPE or PRINT in clear Chinese or English. Documents that are not clear will not be considered
*請正反兩面皆以中文或英文書寫整齊(打字更好)否則不予考慮。

*1- 英文姓名 ENGLISH NAME
- Last: Ray
- First: Sarah
- Middle: Emily

*2- 中文姓名 CHINESE NAME: 

*3- 國籍 NATIONALITY: Canadian

*4- 出生日期 DATE OF BIRTH: 12 Month 24 Day 1981 Year

5- 性別 SEX: ☐Male ☒Female

6- 現任職務 PRESENT OCCUPATION: Student

7- 永久地址 HOME ADDRESS AND PHONE
- No. and Street: 25 Femia St.
- City: Godrich
- State (or Province): Ontario
- Country, Postal (Zip) Code: Canada, B3S 1V1
- E-mail: sarahray@hotmail.com
- Phone: 1(412)439-2121　Fax: 1(412)439-2122

*8- 通訊地址 MAILING ADDRESS (Complete only if different from home address)
Send mail to home address after ___/___/___ (month/day/year)
- No. and Street:
- City:
- State (or Province):
- Country, Postal (Zip) Code:
- E-mail:
- Phone:　　Fax:

本欄請勿填寫（辦公室用）FOR OFFICE USE ONLY

| 收件 | 年 月 日 | 護照 | 簽證 | 來台 年 月 日 |
|---|---|---|---|---|
| 電話 | | | 入學編號 | |
| ☐ | | | ☐ ✓ | |
| ☐ | | | ☐ ✗ | |
| ☐ | | | | |

■ 學生入學申請表（范慧貞提供）

偉立：有沒有我可以申請的獎學金？
教授：當然有。
偉立：要是申請不到，我能不能**一邊**學中文，**一邊**教英文[2]？
教授：臺灣有一些補習班[3]請外國人教英文，不過你是學生，還是學中文比較重要。要是真的還有困難，我們再想辦法補助。
偉立：那麼學分怎麼算呢？
教授：**要看**你在那邊念了什麼書，念了多少時間以後才能決定。
偉立：聽說有的學校跟我們沒有交換計畫，可是也不錯，能不能給我介紹幾個？學費都很貴嗎？
教授：不一定。所有的資料我這兒都有，你需要**的話**，隨時歡迎你來拿。都聽明白了吧？
偉立：明白了。謝謝您。

　　　　※　　※　　※　　※　　※　　※

(教室外面)
偉立：嗨！美真，你好。很高興又碰見你了。
美真：你好，高偉立[4]。你去哪裡啊[5]？
偉立：圖書館，你呢？
美真：我剛下課，想到美容院去剪頭髮[6]。
偉立：我想問你幾個問題，你有時間嗎？

美真：沒關係。我還有半個鐘頭。
偉立：明年我想到臺灣去學中文。**不知道**臺灣的物價怎麼樣？生活容易不容易？
美真：這兩年物價比較高。不過你會說英文，在臺灣找工作不難，生活應該沒有問題。
偉立：住呢？房子好不好找？房租貴不貴？
美真：學校附近有很多分租給學生的房間，也可以幾個學生合租一個公寓，大家合起來付房租。有些外國學生住在臺灣人家裡，**要是**房東願意**的話**，房租可以少算一點，**有時候**房東還會讓你在他們家吃飯。市區的房租比郊區的貴，當然也**得看**是什麼樣的房子。
偉立：那交通方便嗎？需不需要自己有車？
美真：在臺灣坐公車最方便，沒有車不是問題。而且計程車也不貴，叫車很容易。哎喲[7]！我得走了，要不然就來不及了，我們下次再談吧！
偉立：好啊！你快走吧！謝謝你啦！
美真：哪裡[8]，別客氣。

■ 房屋招租廣告（范慧貞提供）

第三課　我想去臺灣

## 生詞及例句

**1 敲 (ciāo) (qiāo)**　V：to knock; to beat; to tap; to pound

吃飯的時候，媽媽不讓我用筷子敲碗。

**2 辦公室 (bàngōngshìh) (bàngōngshì)**　N：office（M：間）

　　教室 (jiàoshìh) (jiàoshì)　N：classroom

　　休息室 (siōusíshìh) (xiūxíshì)　N：lounge, lobby, foyer

**3 教授 (jiàoshòu)**　N：professor（M：位）

張教授已經在我們大學教了二十年的書了。

**4 約 (yuē)**　V/N：to make an appointment/appointment, engagement

(1) 我打電話約他今天晚上去看電影。
(2) 我今晚已經有約了，明天再跟你去吃飯，好不好？

　　約會 (yuēhuèi) (yuēhuì)　V/N：to have a date/date

(1) 你今天穿得這麼漂亮，跟誰約會啊？
(2) 像你這麼好的女孩子，禮拜六怎麼可能沒約會？

**5 請教 (cǐngjiào) (qǐngjiào)**　V：to ask advice, to consult with

(1) 高先生，有一件事我不太清楚，想跟您請教請教。
(2) 要是你有不懂的問題，應該去請教老師。

**6 環境 (huánjìng)**　N：environment, surroundings, financial conditions (of a family)

(1) 小李家附近的環境真不好，又髒又亂。
(2) 小王家環境很好，所以他從來不必打工。

67

## 實用視聽華語 3

**7** 交換 (jiāohuàn)　V：to exchange, swap

明天舞會完了以後，大家要交換禮物。

交 (jiāo)　V：to hand in, give to, pass on to

請你替我把這張名單交給謝老師。

交朋友 (jiāo//péngyǒu)　VO：to make a friend

偉立最近交了幾個臺灣朋友，所以常常有機會說中文。

**8** 計畫 (jìhuà)　V/N：to plan, to map out/plan, project, program

(1) 我計畫明年夏天到臺灣去學兩個月中文。
(2) 我的計畫是找到工作以後再買車。

**9** 暑期班 (shǔcíbān) (shǔqíbān)　N：summer school, summer session

去年夏天小張在那所學校念了兩個月的暑期班。

**10** 資料 (zīhliào) (zīliào)　N：materials; data, information

你寫這篇文章需要的資料，圖書館都有。

**11** 網站 (wǎngjhàn) (wǎngzhàn)　N：website

Yahoo、Google 都是最受歡迎的網站。

上網 (shàng//wǎng)　VO：to log on to the Internet, to use the Internet

網路 (wǎnglù)　N：internet

現在網路上什麼都有，要查資料，上網就行了。

網址 (wǎngjhǐh) (wǎngzhǐ)　N：internet address

你打錯了網址，難怪進不了那個網站。

### 網誌／部落格 (wǎngjhìh) (wǎngzhì/bùluògé)

N：weblog/blog

現在很多人都喜歡在網誌上寫文章，我也開了個部落格，把我的日記都放在裡面。

### 12 申請表 (shēncǐngbiǎo) (shēnqǐngbiǎo)

N：application form（M：張）

申請 (shēncǐng) (shēnqǐng)　V：to apply for

很多人都想申請那個電腦公司的工作。

表 (biǎo)　N：table, form, list（M：張）

### 13 下載 (siàzài) (xiàzài)　V：to download

我的電腦真慢，下載一張照片，用了這麼多時間。

### 14 填 (tián)　V：to fill in; to stuff

我的申請表只填了姓名、地址，忘了填電話號碼。

### 15 成績 (chéngjī)　N：grade (at school), academic record, achievement

(1) 小王這學期特別用功，所以成績很好。
(2) 恭喜你找到工作了！只要你好好地做，要不了幾個月，就會有好成績。

成績單 (chéngjīdān)　N：report card, transcript（M：張）

(1) 你看我的成績單，就知道我上學期有多用功。
(2) 小張進公司半年以後，就交出了一張漂亮的成績單，幫公司多做了好幾百萬的生意。

### 16 學習 (syuésí) (xuéxí)　V：to study; to learn

住校是一個學習獨立的好機會。

## 17 推薦信 (tuēijiànsìn) (tuījiànxìn)　　N：letter of recommendation

現在找工作，大概都需要有推薦信。

### 推薦 (tuēijiàn) (tuījiàn)　　V：to recommend

因為成績好，小高一畢業，老師就推薦他去一家銀行工作了。

## 18 訂 (dìng)

V：to conclude, draw up (a treaty, an agreement, etc.); to order, subscribe to; book, make reservations (in a hotel, restaurant, theater, etc.)

我們下個星期去旅行，旅館房間已經訂好了。

## 19 獎學金 (jiǎngsyuéjīn) (jiǎngxuéjīn)　　N：scholarship, fellowship

小陳申請到了我們大學中文研究所的獎學金，每個月五百塊錢。

### 金子 (jīnzih) (jīn·zi)　　N：gold（M：塊）

## 20 補習班 (bǔsíbān) (bǔxíbān)

N：tutorial school (a private institution that offers tutoring in various subjects), cram school（M：家）

我媽覺得我的成績不夠好，所以我下了課，還要去補習班上課。

### 補習 (bǔsí) (bǔxí)　　V：to receive tutoring

我妹妹想去美國，可是英文不好，所以得先補習。

### 補助 (bǔzhù)　　V/N：to subsidize/a subsidy, allowance

(1) 你買車的錢不夠，公司可以補助你一點。
(2) 家裡環境不好的學生，可以跟學校申請補助。

### 補課 (bǔ//kè)　　VO：to have/to give a make-up lesson

張老師說他今天不舒服，不能來上課，下禮拜一給你們補課。

## 第三課　我想去臺灣

**21** 請 (cǐng) (qǐng)　V：to hire someone to do something

我們公司事情越來越多，得再請一個人幫忙了。

**22** 困難 (kùnnán)　N/SV：difficulty/to be difficult, hard

(1) 你要是有什麼困難，找他幫忙一定沒問題。
(2) 老謝病了，好像連說話都很困難。

**23** 學分 (syuéfēn) (xuéfēn)　N：academic credits

我們每個禮拜上三小時的中文課，可以算三個學分。

**24** 學費 (syuéfèi) (xuéfèi)　N：school tuition fees

這個大學的學費很貴，沒有錢的人念不起。

水費 (shuěifèi) (shuǐfèi)　N：water bill

電費 (diànfèi)　N：electricity bill

電話費 (diànhuàfèi)　N：telephone bill

旅費 (lyǔfèi) (lǚfèi)　N：travel costs

**25** 所有的 (suǒyǒu·de)　AT：all

小王不是只有地理考得好，他所有的功課都很棒。

**26** 明白 (míng·bái)　V/SV：to understand, realize, know/to be clear

(1) 你要是還不明白，可以請老師再說一次。
(2) 老錢的信寫得這麼明白，他不想借錢給你，你怎麼看不懂呢？

**27** 碰見 / 碰到 (pèng//jiàn /pèng//dào)

RC：to meet unexpectedly, to run into, to chance upon

(1) 昨天我在街上碰見一個好久不見的老朋友。
(2) 明天星期六沒課，我恐怕碰不見小王。

碰 (pèng)　　V：to touch, bump

老李很怕別人把他的東西弄髒，所以他的東西都不讓別人碰。

碰上 (pèng//·shàng)　　RC：to run up against, to come across

老張沒有工作，又生病了，要是你碰上這樣的事，你怎麼辦？

28 美容院 (měiróngyuàn)　　N：beauty parlor（M：家）

美容 (měiróng)　　V：to have plastic surgery; beauty treatment for the face

林小姐覺得自己的鼻子不夠高，就決定去美容，請醫生把她的鼻子做高一點。

理髮廳 (lǐfǎtīng)　　N：barber shop（M：家）

29 剪頭髮 (jiǎn//tóu·fǎ)　　VO：to give/get a haircut

剪 (jiǎn)　　V：to cut (with scissors), to clip, to trim

老林覺得那條褲子太長，就剪短了一點。

剪刀 (jiǎndāo)　　N：scissors, clippers（M：把）

頭髮 (tóu·fǎ)　　N：hair (on the human head)（M：根 gēn / 頭）

我哥哥覺得理髮廳剪的頭髮，樣子不好看，所以我姐姐上美容院做頭髮的時候，他也跟著去剪頭髮。

30 物價 (wùjià)　　N：price of goods

日本的物價高，我什麼都買不起。

房價 (fángjià)　　N：housing prices

菜價 (càijià)　　N：vegetable prices; food prices

這裡的菜價很便宜，可是房價越來越高。住比吃貴多了。

價錢 (jiàqián)　　N：price; cost

這本書的價錢不貴，只要五塊錢。

### 31 生活 (shēnghuó)　　N/V：life/to live

(1) 這幾年你哥哥在外國的生活怎麼樣？吃、住、念書都習慣了嗎？
(2) 這裡的物價這麼高，怎麼生活？

### 活 (huó)　　SV/V：to be alive, living/to live

(1) 這條魚剛離開水，還是活的。
(2) 人活著就得吃飯，所以我得工作。

### 生活費 (shēnghuófèi)　　N：living expenses, cost of living

你父親每個月給你多少生活費？吃、住都夠用嗎？

### 32 付 (fù)　　V：to pay

今天我請你吃飯，當然應該我付錢。

### 33 房租 (fángzū)　　N：rent

這個房子很舊，所以房租比較便宜。

### 租 (zū)　　V：to rent

我沒車，打算租輛車去東部旅行。

### 分租 (fēnzū)　　V：to sublet, to rent separately

這個房間我們不用，分租給別人吧！

### 合租 (hézū)　　V：to jointly rent, rent together, share rental

我們四個人在學校附近合租了一個大房子。

### 合起來 (hé//cǐlái) (hé//qǐ·lái)　　RC：to join, combine; together

老張搬家，我們五個同學合起來買了一個衣櫃送給他。

### 出租 (chūzū)　　V：to be for rent; offer for rent; rent to others

租出去 (zū//chūcyù) (zū//chū·qù)　RC：to rent out

張：請問，你有房間出租嗎？
李：對不起，已經租出去了。

### 34 公寓 (gōngyù)

N：apartment building, multi-story multi-family dwelling（M：棟dòng / 間）

### 35 房東 (fángdōng)　N：landlord

二房東 (èrfángdōng)　N：subleasor

張小姐把她租的公寓分租一個房間給我，所以她是我的二房東。

房客 (fángkè)　N：tenant

### 36 交通 (jiāotōng)　N：transportation; traffic

這裡公共汽車很多，交通很方便。

通 (tōng)

V/SV/RE：to go, move or flow unobstructed; to communicate/open, passable/unobstructed

(1) 我很久沒跟李文德通信了，他好嗎？
(2) 我鼻子不通，大概感冒了。
(3) 這個電話壞了，我打了很多次，都打不通。

### 37 計程車 (jìchéngchē)　N：taxi（M：輛 / 部）

叫車 (jiào//chē)　VO：to get a cab, to call a cab, to hail a cab

小張喝了太多酒，不敢開車回家，手機又沒電了，不能打電話叫計程車，站在路邊，等了半天，才叫到一輛計程車。

### 38 來不及 (lái·bùjí)

RC：to have insufficient time, to be too late (to do something)

飛機三點起飛，現在才一點，還來得及。

## 第三課　我想去臺灣

▼ **歎詞**　　Interjections

1. 哎ㄞ·喲ㄧㄠ (āi·yāo)　I: [indicating surprise or discontent]

   哎喲，我的頭好疼啊！

▼ **專有名詞**　Proper Names

1. 中ㄓㄨㄥ國ㄍㄨㄛˊ大ㄉㄚˋ陸ㄌㄨˋ（大ㄉㄚˋ陸ㄌㄨˋ）(Jhōngguó Dàlù) (Zhōngguó Dàlù)
   Mainland China

▼ **注釋**

1. 好的　means "Yes." This 的 is a particle, indicating certainty and making the tone of 好的 polite and gentle. 是的 functions the same way.

2. "……教英文"　English teaching positions are governed by R.O.C.'S Foreign Labor Laws. Students desiring more information on teaching English in Taiwan should contact the nearest local representative agency.

3. 補習班　means "tutorial school". There are many different kinds of 補習班 in Taiwan, most of which are privately run. People go to 補習班 for special tutoring in a vast array of subjects. Although the most popular courses are review courses to prepare for various examinations (college entrance exams, TOEFL, civil service exams, etc.), there are also programs for such things as learning languages, driving, cooking, playing musical instruments, etc.

4. "你好，高偉立。"　The Chinese student called William by his full Chinese name, not only the first name. Chinese students at school address one another using their full names, as does the teacher. In other circumstances such as at work, however, it is not polite to address peers using their full names unless they are friends. The first name is used alone only by family and close friends. Younger people should not address older people by their first name nor their full name, but instead should address them by their surname plus a title or by the name of their relationship.

5. "你去哪裡啊？"　is a greeting. See Note 5 of Lesson 1. It is the same as asking "上哪兒去啊？". It is not necessary to describe one's destination in detail. An appropriate reply might be "出去。", "上街。", or "去買東西。" etc.

6. "到美容院去剪頭髮。"　means to go to the beauty parlor to have one's hair cut. It is not necessary to make an appointment to have one's hair done in Taiwan. In the United States, however, sometimes one has to make an appointment before going to a barbershop or a beauty parlor. This is why in the text 美眞 says she has a half hour.

7. 哎喲 is used when something unexpected or unpleasant happens. This interjection is spoken mostly by women.
8. Here, 哪裡 does not mean "where?" It is used when one receives praise or gratitude from other people. It is similar to saying: "It's really nothing."

## 文法練習

### 一 才 only if

◎我想去臺灣或中國大陸才能把中文學好。
I think that only by going to Taiwan or Mainland China can one be proficient in Chinese.

用法說明：前句是後句的必要條件，如果不具備前句的條件，絕不可能達成後句的情況。第二課的「只要……，就……」是假設性的狀況，而「才」不但可以用在一般及未來的情況，已發生的也適用，語氣也強許多。

Explanation: The first clause of the sentence describes requirements for the second clause. If the requirements are not met, it is impossible to achieve the situation described in the second clause. This pattern is different from "只要……，就……" (see Ch. 2). 才 describes the relative difficulty of a situation and means "only if this requirement is met can one ……," "只要……，就……" on the other hand describes the relative ease of a situation and means "all must do is meet this requirement."

### 練習

(一) 請用「才」回答下面問題。

1. 你明天要去游泳嗎？
   Do you want to go swimming tomorrow?
   → 天氣好，我才去。
     I'll only go if the weather is nice.

2. 你姐姐願意租這個房子嗎？

3. 你的照像機可以借我用一天嗎？
   _____

4. 你說你不喜歡他，你昨天為什麼要跟他出去呢？
   _____

5. 老趙的病怎麼好得那麼快？
   _____

6. 大學生都可以喝酒嗎？
   _____

7. 你每天晚上都看電視嗎？
   _____

8. 你常在學校後面的那個飯館吃飯嗎？
   _____

## （二）請把下面各句改成「才」的句子，並比較兩句的不同。

1. 只要你會說英文，就可以做這個工作。
   As long as you can speak English, you can do this job
   → 你會說英文，才可以做這個工作。
   　You can only do this job if you can speak English.

2. 只要你去，我就去。
   _____

3. 只要明天不下雨，我就參加。
   _____

4. 只要你對別人好，別人就會對你好。
   _____

5. 只要你好好念書，就能畢業。
   _____

## （三）請改正下面各句，並說明原因。

1. 只要我問老李，他就告訴我了。(sic.)
   → 只要我問老李，他就會告訴我。

All I have to do is ask him, and he will tell me.
→ 我問老李,他才告訴我的。
He told me only after I asked him.

2. 只要你給錢,趙先生就賣給你了。
_____

3. 只要你寫完功課,我就讓你看電視了。
_____

## 二 不知道…… I wonder ......

◎不知道我們跟那邊的學校有沒有交換計畫?
I wonder if we have an exchange program with schools there?

◎不知道臺灣的物價怎麼樣?
I wonder how prices are in Taiwan?

**用法說明**:「不知道」表示疑問,前面的主語 (S)「我」省略了。有時是婉轉提出問題,希望對方回答。

Explanation: The subject, 我 normally placed before 不知道 has been omitted. This pattern indicates doubt and is sometimes a subtle way to propose a question in the hope that the other will answer.

### ▼ 練習

**(一) 請按提示用「不知道」發問,再請另一學生回答。**

1. 跟一個同學談王老師的病,想知道他現在怎麼樣了。
   Discuss Teacher Wang's illness with a classmate. You'd like to know how he is now.
   → 不知道他的病好了沒有?
   答:聽說好多了。
   A: I wonder if Teacher Wang has recovered from his illness?
   B: I heard he's feeling much better.

2. 跟一個剛認識的朋友談到一部電影，想約他一起去看。
   _____

3. 跟老師談到一本有名的書，希望老師借給你看。
   _____

4. 跟朋友談到現在租的房子不好，想搬家，希望朋友幫忙找。
   _____

5. 跟同學談學校的交換計畫，想知道高偉立參加不參加。
   _____

## （二）請按提示用「不知道」表示疑問，並不期待對方回答。

1. 明天要去旅行，今天天氣不好，怕明天會跟今天一樣。
   You're going on a trip tomorrow. Today's weather is not very good, and you're afraid it will be the same tomorrow.
   → 不知道明天的天氣怎麼樣？
   　　I wonder what the weather will be like tomorrow.

2. 要去看一個同學，怕他不在家。
   _____

3. 買了一個禮物要送給女朋友，希望她喜歡。
   _____

4. 覺得餓了，希望媽媽已經把飯做好了。
   _____

5. 快要考試了，怕考試太難，自己考不好。
   _____

## 三　（要是）……的話　if……

◎要是可能的話，明年就去。
　If it is possible, then I will go next year.

◎要申請的話，就自己下載申請表。
　If you want to apply, you can download the application form yourself.

◎你需要的話，隨時歡迎你來拿。
　If you need it, you are welcome to come over and get it anytime.

◎要是房東願意的話，房租可以少算一點。
　If the landlord is willing, then the rent can be made a little cheaper.

用法說明：這個句型跟「要是……」完全一樣。「要是」與「的話」可以並用，也可以省略其一。
Explanation: This sentence pattern is exactly the same as 要是. Both 要是 and 的話 can either be used together or alone.

**練習**　請用「（要是）……的話」把兩個句子合成一個。

1. 你吃膩了，我們換換口味吧！
   You had enough of this type of food. Let's try another type of dish.
   → 要是你吃膩了的話，我們就換換口味吧！
   　If you had enough of this type of food, then let's try another type of dish.

2. 你關心我。你就不應該離開我。
   _____

3. 你喜歡吃這種口味。你可以點宮保雞丁。
   _____

4. 王太太有空。我們今天就請她照顧這個孩子。
   _____

5. 小陳還是不明白。他最好去請教張老師。
   _____

## 四　要/得看……　depends on ......

◎這要看你的成績了。
　This depends on your academic performance.

◎要看你在那邊念了什麼書，……
　That depends on what books you study there, ……

◎當然也得看是什麼樣的房子。
　Of course it also depends on what kind of room it is.

用法說明：所談的事情由「看」後面的情況決定。「看」後面的短句可能包括：a. 疑問詞(QW)、b. 選擇式(A/not A)、c. 兩個相對的單音節、d. 如果語言環境清楚，前三種亦都可省略。

Explanation: The matter being discussed depends upon the situation stated after 看. 看 can be followed by a clause with: a. a question word, b. a choice type question, c. a two opposite single-syllable stative verb. d. If the context is obvious, then nothing needs to follow 看.

### ▼ 練習　請用「要/得看……」回答下面各問題。

1. 你明天一定要去嗎？
   Will you definitely go tomorrow?
   → a. 不一定，要看天氣怎麼樣。
   　　 No, not necessarily. It depends on what the weather is like.
   → b. 要看天氣好不好。
   　　 It depends on whether the weather is good.
   → c. 要看天氣好壞。
   　　 It depends on whether the weather is good (or bad).
   → d. 要看天氣。
   　　 It depends on the weather.

2. 小林想走路去，還是坐車去？
   _____

3. 你要不要買那個照像機？
   _____

81

4. 這本書多久可以看完？
___

5. 你什麼點心都喜歡吃嗎？
___

## 五　等……再……　after ...... then ......

◎ 等你決定去哪兒以後，我再告訴你。
I will tell you (more information) after you have decided where to go.

用法說明：當事者等某（些）情況發生，或某（些）動作完成以後，再做其他的事。
Explanation: The party involved will wait for a certain situation or action to occur before performing the action stated at the end of the sentence.

### ▼ 練習

（一）請用「等……，再……」回答下面各問題。

1. 我們現在可以走了嗎？
   Can we go now?
   → 等吃完飯、洗好碗再走吧！
   　Let's go after we finish eating and washing the dishes.

2. 你搬家已經好幾天了，哪一天買床啊？
   ___

3. 這個消息，我什麼時候可以告訴他？
   ___

4. 下個星期要考試，這個週末你還回家嗎？
   ___

5. 天這麼黑，我們怎麼去找他呢？
   ___

## （二）請改正下面各句，必要時可請學生說明原因。

1. 先雨停了以後，我再回家。(sic.)
   → 等雨停了以後，我再回家。
     I will go home after the rain has stopped.

2. 你先大了，再搬到外頭住。
   _____

3. 現在太貴，先便宜了再買吧！
   _____

4. 爸爸先回來，我們再吃飯。
   _____

5. 先病好了，再出去玩。
   _____

## 六　嘛

◎ 機票嘛，當然是越早訂越便宜。
Plane tickets …… Of course, the earlier you reserve them, the cheaper they are.

用法說明：「嘛」亦可寫作「麼」，語調低而緩，在句中表示停頓，大部分是說話者為了考慮下面的話該怎麼說，有時是為了喚起聽者的注意。

Explanation: 嘛 could also be written as 麼. The tone is low and extended, marking a pause in the middle of the sentence. It is usually used when the speaker wants to think about his/her following statement. Sometimes it is used to summon the listener's attention.

▼ 練習　　請完成下面對話。

1. 張：游泳、跳舞，你都喜歡嗎？
   Chang: Do you like both swimming and dancing?
   李：游泳，我很喜歡；跳舞嘛，我一點興趣都沒有。
   Lee: Swimming, I like very much. Dancing, I am not interested in at all.

2. 張：一天三餐，你都吃得這麼多嗎？
   李：早飯、晚飯，我吃得比較多，<u>午飯嘛，　　　　　　　</u>。

3. 張：這次考試難不難？
   李：大家都說很難，<u>我嘛，　　　　　　</u>。

4. 張：你要不要參加下星期的舞會？
   李：我還沒決定。參加嘛，怕沒時間準備考試；<u>不參加嘛，　　　　　　　　</u>。

5. 張：這學期學的功課都很容易。
   李：這學期很容易，<u>下學期嘛，　　　　　　　</u>。

## 七　一邊……，一邊……

### simultaneously V1 and V2; V1 and V2 at the same time

◎我能不能一邊學中文，一邊教英文？
Can I study Chinese and teach English at the same time?

**用法說明**：同時做兩件事情。這兩件事必須是實際的動作，而不是情況或狀態。
Explanation: Two actions are performed at the same time. The two items must be actions, not situations or circumstances.

### ▼ 練習

（一）請用「一邊……，一邊……」改寫下面各句。

1. 我明年要念大學，也要工作。
   Next year I will go to college, and I will also work.
   → 我明年要一邊念大學，一邊工作。
   Next year I will both go to college and work at the same time.

2. 大家一起唱歌、跳舞，非常熱鬧。
   _____

3. 我哥哥總是在吃早飯的時候看報紙。
   _____

4. 老丁熱得受不了了，走進門的時候就開始脫衣服了。
   _____

第三課　我想去臺灣

5. 很多人開車的時候，也跟旁邊的人談話。
   _____

(二) 請改正下面各句，並說明原因。

1. 小錢一邊生病，還一邊工作。
   Little Qian is both sick and still working (sic.) [生病 is not an action and thus not be used with this pattern.]
   → 小錢生病了還工作。
   　Little Qian is sick, and yet he's still working.

2. 張先生總是一邊坐飛機，一邊看書。
   _____

3. 我喜歡一邊睡覺，一邊聽歌。
   _____

4. 昨天晚上我妹妹一個人在家，一邊怕，一邊哭。
   _____

5. 我一邊想，一邊生氣。
   _____

## 八　……，有時候 N 還……　sometimes ...... even ......

◎……房租可以少算一點，有時候房東還會讓你在他們家吃飯。
　…… the rent can be made a little cheaper, and sometimes you will even be invited to have a meal at the landlord's house.

**用法說明**：這個「還」有「程度更進一步」的意思。
Explanation: This 還 means that the intensity or degree is one level stronger.

▼ 練習　　請完成下面各句。

1. 他一生氣就哭，有時候還丟東西打人。
   As soon as he gets angry he cries, and sometimes he even throws things at people.

2. 我哥哥常玩到很晚才回家，有時候還_____。

3. 他每個月的錢都不夠用，<u>有時候還_____</u>。

4. 我爸爸年紀很大，可是每天慢跑，<u>有時候還_____</u>。

5. 這個學生很少做功課，<u>有時候還_____</u>。

## 九　歎詞「哎喲」的用法　The use of Interjection "哎喲"

◎哎喲！我得走了，要不然就來不及了，……
Oh no! I have to go; otherwise I won't make it, ……

用法說明：「哎喲」，語調低降，放在句首，表示驚訝、驚喜、驚懼、焦急的叫聲，有時也是疼痛時的呻吟。為女性比較常用之歎詞。有時有誇張的語氣。

Explanation: The tone of 哎喲 starts low and descends. Placed at the beginning of a sentence, it shows amazement, pleasant surprise or sudden fright. It can also be a cry of despair or pain. This interjection is often used by females. Sometimes it is a tone of exaggeration.

**練習**　請根據下面情況用「哎喲」表示驚訝、驚喜、驚懼、焦急跟疼痛。

1. 你的頭疼得不得了。
   You have an unbearable headache.
   →哎喲，我的頭好疼啊！
   　Ow! My head really hurts!

2. 你坐在窗戶前面看書，有人丟球，把你的窗戶打破了。
   _____

3. 走在街上，有人從後面搶走了你的錢包。
   _____

4. 跟朋友約好三點見，三點二十五分了他還沒來，你還有別的事情，三點半一定得走。
   _____

5. 有人敲門，開門一看，是多年不見的老朋友。
   _____

## 課室活動　　Classroom Activities

### 一、角色扮演 (Role Playing)

1. Select two of the students or ask for volunteers. One is looking for a place to rent, while the other is the landlord. The renter goes to see a place and engages the landlord in conversation. They can talk about 房租, 水費, 電費, 電話費, and rules of the house. Give them two minutes to prepare.

2. Ask for another two volunteers. One is the landlord（房東）, the other is a poor tenant （房客） who has not paid rent for two months. It is the day the tenant should pay the rent, so the landlord comes. Their conversation is about how to solve the problem of the unpaid rent. Give them two minutes to prepare. Some helpful supplementary words are: 借 (jiè, to loan), 利息 (lìxí, interest), 求 (qiú, to ask; to beg).

### 二、討論問題 (Discussion)

1. 留學生在新環境會碰到哪些問題或困難？
2. 談談你在外國租房子的經驗 (experience)。
3. 說說你學中文的苦跟樂。
4. 你參加過交換計畫嗎？你對交換計畫有興趣嗎？為什麼？

## 短文　　　　　　　廣告₁

**學中文的同學們：**

　　想把中文學得更好嗎？有興趣參加我們的交換計畫到台灣去嗎？想不想在一個完全用中文的環境裡學習中文呢？

　　我們這裡有最好的中文老師，上課方法又新又有趣。我們用的書又有意思又有用。上過我們的課，要不了幾個月，就可以用中文跟朋友討論₂問題了。

　　你可以跟台灣學生同住大學宿舍，也可以租房子，住在台灣人家裡，自己看看台灣人的生活習慣。宿舍有餐廳，學校附近有不少小飯館，可以試試很多口味的菜。學校就在市區，交通方便，去哪裡都很容易。

　　每年分兩個學期，每班最多十人，每週上課十小時。暑期班兩個月，每週上課二十小時，學期當中學校會帶學生出去旅行兩次。

　　要是想知道得更清楚，請來信或電話，我們就寄資料給你。

　　　　　　　　　　　　　　　××大學₃中文系
　　　　　　　　　　　　　　　地址：…………
　　　　　　　　　　　　　　　電話：…………
　　　　　　　　　　　　　　　網址：http//www.xxx.edu.xx

## Vocabulary:

1. 廣告 (guǎnggào): advertisement
2. 討論 (tǎolùn): to discuss
3. ××大學："a certain" university. X is used to represent the name of an exisiting person, place, time or thing, whose exact identity or date cannot either be remembered or be revealed, such as "Mr. X in X city..." It Should be pronounced as "某ㄇㄡˇ mǒu".

# 第四課　談談地理吧

■臺灣風景：中部橫貫公路上的九曲洞（師大國語中心提供）

（郵局門口，李平拿著包裹走出來）

偉立：嗨！李平[1]，有包裹啊[2]？

李平：嗯，我女朋友寄來的。我兩天前才收到她的簡訊，說要寄東西給我，沒想到這麼快就到了。那天我不在家，郵差留了張通知給我，說有我的掛號包裹。我今天下了課就過來拿了。

偉立：難怪這麼高興，原來是接到了女朋友寄來的東西。
（李平笑笑）**哇！好漂亮的郵票！臺灣的嗎？**

李平（指著郵票）：這是我們故宮博物院[3]裡的東西。

偉立：故宮博物院？

李平：是臺灣最大的博物館。裡面的東西又多又好。外國人到了臺灣，都一定會去參觀。

偉立：這個博物館在哪兒？

李平：在臺北郊區。臺北在臺灣北部，是我們最大的城市。欸，臺灣在哪裡，你知道吧？

偉立：當然知道！別以為我什麼都不懂，好不好？臺灣是一個島，在亞洲，在中國大陸東南方。

李平：對！臺灣離大陸一百多公里，坐飛機到日本只要三個小時。

偉立：噢，對了，臺灣有多大[4]？

李平：差不多跟荷蘭一樣大。

偉立：那很小嘛！

李平：是很小。**除了**海邊有一些平原**以外**，中部**都**是山。臺

第四課　談談地理吧

■臺北故宮博物院（吳俊銘攝影）

灣全島人口**加起來**有兩千多萬，大部分都住在西部。
偉立：為什麼都住在西部？東部不好嗎？
李平：東部很好啊！只是平原比較小，颱風、地震比較多。
　　　而且從大陸過來的人[5]，都是先到西部。
偉立：嗯，這跟我們正相反。我們東部、西部有山，當中有
　　　平原。從歐洲來的移民，都是先到東部。
李平：臺灣東部發展比較慢，是因為中部山太多，交通不方
　　　便。你們中部是平原，為什麼很晚才往西發展呢？
偉立：因為從中西部越往西走越高，有高山，有高原，還有
　　　沙漠，都不適合人住。後來政府鼓勵年輕人到西部去，
　　　西部才發展**起來**。

■臺北一○一大樓：二○○七年世界最高的大樓（范慧貞攝）

李平：臺灣是在中部橫貫公路⁶開好以後，去東部的人才多起來的。

偉立：開這條路一定很辛苦吧？

李平：**雖然**很辛苦，**可是**值得。有了這條路，**不但**東部開始發展，大家**也**有機會欣賞到太魯閣峽谷的風景。去過

的人，沒有一個不說好的。

偉立：太魯閣？不知道跟美國的大峽谷比起來怎麼樣？

李平：不一樣的美，你去看了就知道了。

偉立：除了這條路以外，從西部到東部沒有河嗎？

李平：我們的河都是從山區往東或往西流到海裡，而且都不

■臺灣風景：花蓮長春祠（行政院新聞局提供）

長，對交通沒有什麼幫助。
偉立：山區的河大概都這樣。我們平原上有一條從北往南流的大河，對我們的農業有很大的幫助。
李平：對了，你喜歡游泳，那你到臺灣去的時候，一定要去墾丁。墾丁在臺灣最南邊，是臺灣第一個國家公園[7]。那裡的海灘又漂亮又乾淨，連冬天都可以游泳。
偉立：去這些地方交通方便嗎？
李平：臺灣的交通方便極了，除了公路、鐵路跟飛機以外，另外還有高速公路跟高速鐵路。你什麼時候去？要是我不在臺灣，我可以請家人帶你去。
偉立：那太好了！

■臺灣風景：墾丁國家公園（師大國語中心提供）

第四課　談談地理吧

## 生詞及例句

**1** 包裹 (bāoguǒ)　　N：parcel, package

**2** 收到 (shōu//dào)　　RC：to receive, to get, obtain

我收到學校的通知單，才知道我拿到獎學金了。

收起來 (shōu//qǐ·lái)　　RC：to put away

天氣涼了，夏天的衣服可以收起來了，明年再拿出來穿。

收 (shōu)　　V：to collect, gather, receive

我的房東每個月十號來收房租。

**3** 簡訊 (jiǎnsyùn) (jiǎnxùn)

N：text message from a cell phone（M：通／封）

我同學剛剛發 (to send) 了一通簡訊給我，祝我生日快樂，我也馬上給他回了一封，謝謝他。

**4** 掛號 (guà//hào)　　VO：to register

(1) 我媽給我寄了個包裹，裡面有吃的，也有穿的。因為是掛號，應該不會丟，可是怎麼還沒到？
(2) 在臺灣，去看病的時候，要先掛號，拿到號碼，再到醫生的房間外面等。

**5** 原來 (yuánlái)

A：originally, formerly, at first; (indicating discovery of the truth) it turns out that ......

(1) 老王原來住在北京，現在搬到上海去了。
(2) 原來李先生是中國人，難怪他的中文這麼好。

**6** 郵票 (yóupiào)　　N：postage stamp（M：張／套）

97

這封信,我要寄到德國,五毛錢的郵票,夠不夠?

**7** 指 (jhǐh) (zhǐ)　　V：to point at, to point to, to point out

請你指給我們看,哪輛車是你的?

**8** 博物館 (bówùguǎn)　　N：museum

**9** 參觀 (cān'guān)　　V：to visit (a place, exhibition, etc.)

我們能不能參觀你們怎麼上課?

**10** 以為 (yǐwéi)　　V：to think, assume (incorrectly)

我以為小林是坐飛機去的,原來他自己開車去了。

**11** 島 (dǎo)　　N：island

日本是一個島國,北邊有很多小島。

**12** 除了……以外 (chú·le …… yǐwài)　　PT：besides, except for

(1) 除了你以外,人人都知道明天要考試。
(2) 除了中文以外,我還會說法文。

除(÷) (chú)　　V：to divide

除法 (chúfǎ)　　N：division (in mathematics)

我妹妹才念小學一年級,只學過加法,還沒學除法。

**13** 平原 (píngyuán)　　N：plains, flat lands

美國中西部是一個大平原。

高原 (gāoyuán)　　N：plateau

中國西南部的高原上,二〇〇六年就可以通火車了。

第四課　談談地理吧

### 14 人口 (rénkǒu)　　N：population

世界上的人口越來越多了，過不了幾年，恐怕就到七十億了。

### 口 (kǒu)　　N/M：mouth/M for family members, wells; mouthful

(1) 不乾淨的東西不要吃，小心「病從口入 (bìng cóng kǒu rù, illness finds its way in by the mouth)」。
(2) 小王家一共有五口人，兩個大人，三個小孩。

### 15 颱風 (táifōng) (táifēng)　　N：typhoon

臺灣每年夏天跟秋天都有颱風。

### 16 地震 (dìjhèn) (dìzhèn)　　N：earthquake

我媽不願在這裡買房子，因為地震太多。

### 17 相反 (siāngfǎn) (xiāngfǎn)

SV/N：to be the opposite, to be contrary/the opposite

(1) 我喜歡大家一起玩，小張跟我相反，他喜歡一個人去玩。
(2) 「冷」的相反是「熱」。

### 18 發展 (fājhǎn) (fāzhǎn)　　V/N：to develop, expand/development, expansion

(1) 這裡交通方便，所以發展得很快。
(2) 你不用功念書，以後能有什麼發展？

### 19 沙漠 (shāmò)　　N：desert（M：片）

沙漠裡，綠洲(an oasis)才有水。

### 沙 (shā)　　N：sand

### 20 適合 (shìhé) (shìhé)　　V/SV：to be suited to, suitable for ...... (X)

(1) 你這件衣服太緊，不適合運動的時候穿。
(2) 我這雙鞋不太高，上班的時候穿比較適合。

合ㄏㄜˊ適ㄕˋ (héshìh) (héshì)　　SV：to be suitable, appropriate

我想這個工作對你不合適，因為你不喜歡早起。

合ㄏㄜˊ (hé)　　V：to suit, agree with

這個公寓太小，我們家人多，不合我們的需要。

21 政ㄓㄥˋ府ㄈㄨˇ (jhèngfǔ) (zhèngfǔ)　　N：government

22 年ㄋㄧㄢˊ輕ㄑㄧㄥ人ㄖㄣˊ (niáncīngrén) (niánqīngrén)

　　N：young person, young people

年紀大的人常常不懂年輕人做的事。

年ㄋㄧㄢˊ輕ㄑㄧㄥ (niáncīng) (niánqīng)　　SV：to be young

我年輕的時候很喜歡跳舞，現在老了，跳不動了。

輕ㄑㄧㄥ (cīng) (qīng)　　SV：to be light (in weight)

箱子裡沒什麼東西，很輕。

23 開ㄎㄞ路ㄌㄨˋ (kāi//lù)　　VO：to open up a new road

要是這裡開一條路，對大家都方便。

24 辛ㄒㄧㄣ苦ㄎㄨˇ (sīnkǔ) (xīnkǔ)

　　SV：to be difficult, hard, painful, exhausting; to experience difficulty, hardship, pain, exhaustion

陳老師每天教五個小時的書，非常辛苦。

苦ㄎㄨˇ (kǔ)　　SV/N：to be toilsome, hard; sad; bitter/toil, hardship

(1) 這次醫生給我的藥，真苦。
(2) 老高這幾年都沒有工作，生活很苦。
(3) 先生離開我了，我一個人又要工作，又要照顧孩子，沒有人知道我心裡的苦。

第四課　談談地理吧

吃ㄔ苦ㄎㄨ (chī//kǔ)
VO：to bear (or endure) hardships; to suffer hardships; to have a rough time

(1) 我哥哥在外國留學的頭一年，碰到很多困難，吃了很多苦。
(2) 俗話 (súhuà, proverb, saying) 說：「吃得苦中苦，方為人上人」，現在辛苦一點沒關係，以後就好了。

25 雖ㄙㄨㄟ然ㄖㄢ (suīrán)　A：though, although

雖然坐電梯很快，可是走樓梯對身體比較好。

26 值ㄓ得ㄉㄜ (jhíh·dé) (zhí·dé)

SV/A：to be worth while, worth (doing something)

(1) 做這件事用了很多時間，可是學到不少東西，非常值得。
(2) 那部電影很不錯，可以學到很多東西，值得看。

值ㄓ (jhíh) (zhí)　V：to be worth (time, money, effort)

這棟公寓我買的時候只要十萬，現在值三十萬了。

值ㄓ錢ㄑㄧㄢ (jhíh//cián) (zhí//qián)　SV/VO：to be valuable, costly

(1) 沒關係，小偷偷走的都是不值錢的東西。
(2) 五百塊太貴了，這個照像機不值那麼多錢！

27 不ㄅㄨ但ㄉㄢ (búdàn)　A：not only

(1) 趙太太喜歡旅行，她不但去過歐洲，也去過亞洲。
(2) 這件衣服不但大，而且長，你穿不適合。

但ㄉㄢ是ㄕ (dànshìh) (dànshì)　CONJ：but, still, however

雖然他的成績不錯，但是不一定申請得到獎學金。

28 欣ㄒㄧㄣ賞ㄕㄤ (sīnshǎng) (xīnshǎng)　V：to appreciate, to admire

(1) 我很不欣賞小陳，因為他太隨便。
(2) 我沒學過中國字，所以不懂怎麼欣賞毛筆字。

101

## 29 峽谷 (siágǔ) (xiágǔ)　　N：canyon, gorge

## 30 流 (liú)　V：to flow

這條河是從山區流過來的。

### 河流 (héliú)　N：river

地圖上的河流都是藍色的。

## 31 幫助 (bānghù) (bāngzhù)　　V/N：to help, assist, aid/assistance, aid

(1) 有錢的人應該幫助沒錢的人。
(2) 運動對健康有很大的幫助。

## 32 農業 (nóngyè)　N：agriculture, farming

這個地方有很多高山，不能發展農業。

### 農人 (nóngrén)　N：farmer

老王是個農人，一直住在鄉下，沒去過大城市。

### 農民 (nóngmín)　N：peasant, peasantry

颱風過了以後，要是生活有困難，農民都可以跟政府申請補助。

## 33 國家公園 (guójiā gōngyuán)　N：national park

## 34 海灘 (hǎitān)　N：seashore, beach

夏天的時候，很多人去海邊玩，海灘上躺滿了人。

### 沙灘 (shātān)　N：beach

小孩喜歡在沙灘上用沙跟水做房子、火車……什麼的。

## 35 高速公路 (gāosù gōnglù)　N：expressway, freeway（M：條）

第四課　談談地理吧

公路 (gōnglù)　N：highway（M：條）

臺灣有些公路，經過海邊或山裡，風景真不錯。

馬路 (mǎlù)　N：road, street, avenue（M：條）

在市區過馬路的時候，一定要小心兩邊來的車。

36 鐵路 (tiělù)　N：railway, railroad（M：條）

經過臺北市區的鐵路搬到地下以後，交通就不像以前那麼亂了。

高速鐵路 (gāosù tiělù)　N：high-speed railway

(1) 從臺北到高雄 (Gāoxióng, Kaohsiung)，開車走高速公路，最快要四個小時，坐高鐵，九十分鐘就到了。
(2) 臺灣從南到北有高速公路跟高速鐵路，從東到西還有快速道路 (express way)，交通非常方便。

鐵 (tiě)　N：iron（M：塊）

37 另外 (lìngwài)　DEM/A：another, the other/in addition, additionally

(1) 我有兩位中文老師，一位姓王，另外一位姓張。
(2) 我給李老師打了電話，另外還給他寫了一封信。

## ▼ 歎詞跟語助詞　Interjections and Particles

1. 嗯 (·en)　I：[used to indicate agreement]

   嗯，你說得很對。

2. 哇 (·wa)　I/P：[used to indicate surprise, approval./ 啊 is replaced by "哇" if the final word in a sentence ends with "u", "ao", or "ou".]

   (1) 哇！你們家的房子好大啊！
   (2) 您今天真早哇！

## 專有名詞　Proper Names

1. 李平 (Lǐ Píng)　Li, Ping
2. 故宮博物院 (Gùgōng Bówùyuàn)　National Palace Museum
3. 亞洲 (Yǎzhōu) (Yǎ Zhōu)　Asia
4. 荷蘭 (Hélán)　Netherland
5. 中部橫貫公路 (Jhōngbù Héngguàn Gōnglù) (Zhōngbù Héngguàn Gōnglù)　the Central Trans-island Highway
6. 太魯閣峽谷 (Tàilǔgé Siágǔ) (Tàilǔgé Xiágǔ)　Taroko Gorge
7. 大峽谷 (Dà Siágǔ) (Dà Xiágǔ)　Grand Canyon
8. 墾丁 (Kěndīng)　Kenting

## 注釋

1. 李平 is a person's name. 李 is the surname and 平 is the first name. First names normally consist of two syllables. but sometimes people have single syllable names. One syllable first names are known as 單名. One can tell parents' expectations for their children from the names they give them. For example, the parents of 林建國 probably hope that he will one day contribute to the development of the country.

2. "有包裹啊？" is a greeting. See Note 5 of Lesson 1.

3. 故宮博物院, the National Palace Museum, stands on a scenic hillside setting in the northern suburbs of Taipei. The museum collection is the result of a successive Chinese imperial collection which was started by a Sung Dynasty emperor over a thousand years ago. This collection was passed down and added to from one generation to the next and from one dynasty to the next. In 1925, one year after the last emperor moved out of the Imperial Palace, the National Palace Museum was established, making the greatest collection of Chinese art in the world accessible to the public. During the 1930s and 40s the collection was transferred to various locations in mainland China to protect it from damage during the Sino-Japanese War and the Chinese Civil War. The collection was brought to Taiwan in 1949, and it was opened to the public at its present site in 1965. The Museum's collection now stands at close to 700,000 pieces.

4. "臺灣有多大？" The area of Taiwan, not including the small islands that surround it, is 35,824 square kilometers. The area of Holland is 41,526 square kilometers.

5. "而且從大陸過來的人……" Before 鄭成功 (Zhèng Chénggōng) and his troops drove the Dutch off of Taiwan island in December 1661, the Dutch had controlled Taiwan for thirty-eight years. Emperor 康熙 (Kāngxī) of the Ching Dynasty proclaimed in 1684 that Taiwan was a territory of China. People from the southeastern coast of China started to move to Taiwan in large groups about three hundred years ago. They settled on plains along the west coast. In addition to descendants of the people who came from mainland China, Taiwan is also home to descendants of aborigine tribes which were already on the island before the new settlers arrived. Today there are altogether 13 aboriginal tribes on Taiwan, numbering approximately 390,000 persons, which accounts for less than two percent of the total population.

6. 中部橫貫公路, the Central Trans-Island Highway, consists of a main road with two branches. The main road is from 東勢 (Dōngshì), on the west side, to 太魯閣 (Tàilǔgé), on the east side. Construction started in July 1956 and was completed in April 1960. The total length of the highway is 194.2 km. Along the road there are many high mountains, precipices, cliffs and virgin forests. The Central Trans-Island Highway was very difficult to construct. Frequent typhoons and earthquakes caused temporary setbacks. (The Northern Trans-Island Highway was completed in 1966. while the Southern Trans-Island Highway was finished in 1972.) The area along the Central Trans-Island Highway comprises the main part of 太魯閣國家公園, Taroko National Park, established in November 1986 as the fourth national park on Taiwan. The park, known for its high mountains and marble gorges, is a natural museum of geology.

7. 墾丁國家公園 Kenting National Park, the first national park established on Taiwan, is on the southern most tip of Taiwan. Established in September 1982, it ranges from the Pacific Ocean to the Taiwan Strait, from the Pashih Channel to the north side of Mount Nanjen (南仁山). With a total area of 32,631 hectares (80,632 acres), it is the only national park in the tropical region of Taiwan. Within the park are hills, flatlands, lakes, grasslands, forests, beaches, coral reefs and many other landforms.

## 文法練習

### 一　好 SV 的 N！　What a SV N!

◎好漂亮的郵票！
What a pretty stamp!

用法說明：「好」在這個句型中是副詞 (A)，有「非常、這麼」的意思。是感歎的語氣。也可以用「DEM-M-N 好 SV」的型式，如「這張郵票好漂亮」，但僅有敘述的意味。

Explanation: 好 is an adverb in this sentence pattern, meaning "very", "what a ......", or "such a ......". It has an exclamatory tone. 好 can also be used as an adverb in the pattern "DEM-M-N 好 SV". as in 這張郵票好漂亮, but in this pattern it is merely descriptive and carries no exclamatory tone.

**練習**　根據所給情況，用「好 SV 的 N！」表示感歎。

1. 看到一個五歲的孩子在用電腦畫畫兒。
   You see a five-year old child drawing pictures on a computer.
   →好聰明的孩子！
   　What a smart child!

2. 朋友說他的照像機是五百塊買的。
   _____

3. 朋友告訴你他上次去的那個地方夏天有五個月。
   _____

4. 走進弟弟的房間，看見報紙在地上，書在床上，衣服在桌子上。
   _____

5. 同學的媽媽只有三十六歲，看起來像他姐姐。
   _____

## 二

**(I) 除了……以外／之外，都……**

Except for/other than ...... all the others ......

◎除了海邊有一些平原以外，中部都是山。
Except for some plains along the coast, the central part (of Taiwan) is all mountains.

**(II) 除了……以外／之外，還……**

other than/besides ...... there is ......

◎臺灣的交通方便極了，除了公路、鐵路跟飛機以外，另外還有高速公路跟高速鐵路。
Taiwan's transportation is extremely convenient: besides public roads, railways, and airways, there are also freeways and high-speed railways.

用法說明：「除了」表示「不算在裡面」。後面可用名詞、動詞、SV 或短句。(I)(II) 用法不完全相同：(I) 不算特殊的，說明相同的，所以第二個短句常用「都」或「全」。(II) 不算已經知道的，說明其他的，所以第二短句中，常有「還」或「也」等字。這個句型可以只說「……以外」，也可以只說「除了……」。主語可以放在第一個短句前，也可以放第二個短句前。

Explanation: 除了 expresses exclusiveness. Following 除了 is a noun, a verb, a stative verb, or an entire clause. The usage in patterns (I) and (II), however, is not entirely identical: (I) The first clause indicates an exception to the norm, and either 都 or 全 is placed in the second clause. (II) The first clause shows part of a sequence, and 還 or 也 is used in the second clause to complete the sequence. In this pattern, "除了……" and "……以外" can each be used together or alone. The subject can be placed at the beginning of either the first clause or the second clause.

### 練習

**（一）請用「除了……以外，都……」回答下面各題。**

1. 張：老王那麼會做生意，別的事情一定也做得很好吧？

Chang: Old Wang can manage business affairs so well; he is also capable of doing other things, isn't he?

李：你看錯了，除了做生意以外，別的事情他都不會。

Lee: You are wrong about him. Other than manage business affairs, he can't do anything else.

2. 張：小林家每個人都像他那麼高嗎？
   李：_____

3. 張：這家餐廳都客滿了，是因為今天是週末嗎？
   李：_____

4. 張：李子很好吃啊！你怎麼不吃？你不喜歡吃水果嗎？
   李：_____

5. 張：我什麼時候可以給你打電話？你上午有課嗎？
   李：有，_____.

**(二) 請用「除了……以外，還……」提出問題。**

1. 張：我昨天去超市買了一個大西瓜。
   Chang: I bought a watermelon at the supermarket yesterday.
   李：我知道你喜歡吃水果，除了西瓜以外，你還買了什麼？
   Lee: I know you like to eat fruits. Besides watermelon, what else did you buy？

2. 張：下禮拜五我二十歲生日，要請全班同學吃蛋糕。
   李：_____

3. 張：我打算暑假去歐洲旅行，我會去英國和法國。
   李：_____

4. 病人：我大概感冒了，有一點頭疼。

   醫生：_____

5. 張：我做錯事的時候，我媽會罵(mà, to scold)我。
   李：_____

## 三　加起來　put together/added together

◎臺灣全島的人口加起來有兩千多萬。
The total population of the island of Taiwan adds up to more than 20 million.

用法說明：「加起來」意思是「加在一起」，跟第一課的「看起來」、第二課的「吃起來」用法不同。

Explanation: 加起來 means "put together" or "added together". This usage is not the same as 看起來 (Ch.1) or 吃起來 (Ch.2).

### 練習　請用「加起來……」回答下面問題。

1. 你們兩個人的錢買這本書，夠不夠？
   Do you (plural) have enough money to buy this book?
   → 我們兩個人的錢加起來才夠。
   　We only have enough if we put our money together.
   → 我們兩個人的錢加起來還不夠。
   　We don't have enough even when we put our money together.

2. 這個學期一共有幾天假？
   _____

3. 你常旅行，去過多少國家了？
   _____

4. 這個學期中文系有多少學生？
   _____

5. 聽說全世界最重的人有四百多公斤，我們五個人才兩百多公斤。
   _____

## 四　V/SV起來　start to V/become SV

◎……政府鼓勵年輕人到西部去，西部才發展起來。
The government encouraged young people to go the West; only then did the West begin to develop.

◎……中部橫貫公路開好了後，去東部的人才多起來的。
Only after the Central Trans-Island Highway opened did the number of people who went to the East start to increase.

用法說明：這個「起來」表示一個動作或一種狀態「開始」並持續下去，所描述的多為非常態的情況。這種用法「起來」常放在句尾，後面沒有修飾性的 SV 或短語，且多以 RC 的 actual type 肯定型式出現，偶爾也可以 potential type 表示。如有賓語，應該插在「起來」中間，成為「V 起 O 來」。

Explanation: This 起來 indicates that an action or situation starts and continues. Usually, what is being described is an abnormal situation. This use of 起來 is often found at the end of a sentence and is not followed by a SV or clause. It is usually used as a positive form resultative compound in actual type form; occasionally it is used in potential type form. If there is an object, this object should be inserted between 起 and 來, so it becomes "V 起 O 來".

## ▼ 練習

### (一) 請用「V 起來」改寫下面各句。

1. 那個故事說到一半，她就開始哭了。
   She started crying halfway into the story.
   → 那個故事說到一半，她就哭起來了。
   She came to tears halfway into the story.

2. 這個孩子疼得開始叫了。
   _____

3. 我覺得他的話很有趣就笑了。
   _____

4. 還沒說兩句話，張先生就開始打李先生了。
   _____

5. 老師還沒叫他念書，他就開始念了。
_____

## （二）請用「SV 起來」改寫下面各句。

1. 老師一說要考試，我們就開始緊張了。
   As soon as the teacher said we would have a test, we started to feel anxious.
   → 老師一說要考試，我們就緊張起來了。
   As soon as the teacher said we would have a test, we became anxious.

2. 他病了好久，可是現在慢慢地好了。
   _____

3. 還沒到六月，天氣已經開始熱了。
   _____

4. 這條街上的店一多，就會越來越熱鬧了。
   _____

5. 大部分的人到了四十歲就開始胖了。
   _____

## （三）請用「V 起 O 來」回答問題。

1. 今天早上的天氣很好。現在是下午。下雨了。這時候你會說什麼？
   The weather was good this morning. It is in the afternoon. It's raining. What will you say in this situation?
   答：今天早上天氣很好，怎麼下午下起雨來了？
   Answer: The weather was nice this morning. Why is it raining in the afternoon?!

2. 現在是下午三點，你看見媽媽開始做晚飯了。你會跟媽媽說什麼？
   答：現在才三點，_____？

3. 你室友從來不喝酒，可是你現在看見他在喝酒，你會跟他說什麼？
   答：你從前不喝酒的，_____？

4. 你朋友告訴你他現在在學中文，可是你記得他以前說中文很難聽、很奇怪。這時候你會說什麼？
   答：你從前說中文很難聽，_____？

5. 你弟弟非常不喜歡做家事,可是你今天看見他在洗全家人的衣服。這個事情你可以怎麼說?
   答:我從來沒看過我弟弟做家事,_____?!

### 五 雖然……,可是…… Although .......,

◎雖然很辛苦,可是值得。
Although it's very hard work, it's worth it.

**用法說明:**本句型表示讓步,承認「雖然」後的短句是事實,但「可是」後的短句並不因此而不成立。「雖然」可省略,一般不省略「可是」,但如後半句中有「還是」,例如:「雖然他常送我禮物,(可是)我還是不喜歡他。」,此「可是」可以省略。請注意,只有「可是」,沒有「雖然」的句子,僅表示語氣轉折,與「雖然……可是……」的句子,語境並不相同。

**Explanation:** This sentence pattern shows that one concedes or admits that the phrase following 雖然 is true, but the phrase following 可是 is unaffected by this fact. 雖然 can be omitted, but 可是 usually cannot be omitted. If 還是 is placed in the second clause, then 可是 can be omitted, e.g. "雖然他常送我禮物,(可是)我還是不喜歡他"。Be aware that sentences with only 可是, and no 雖然, indicate a change in tone. Their context is different from sentences with the "雖然……可是……" pattern.

▼ 練習    請用「雖然……,可是……」完成下面對話。

1. 張:你為什麼要學中文?我聽說中國字非常難寫。
   Chang: Why do you want to study Chinese? I heard that Chinese characters are difficult to write.
   李:寫中國字雖然麻煩,可是很有意思。
   Lee: Although writing Chinese characters is tedious, it's very interesting.

2. 張:小王昨天就感冒了,沒想到今天還來上課。
   李:_____。

3. 張:這件衣服價錢不便宜,你真的要買嗎?
   李:_____。

4. 張:你怎麼不認識他?你們不都是去年從紐約大學畢業的嗎?

第四課　談談地理吧

　　李：＿＿＿＿＿＿＿＿＿＿＿＿＿＿＿＿＿＿＿＿＿＿＿＿＿＿＿＿＿＿。

5. 張：你那麼有錢，給他一點，有什麼關係嘛！
　　李：＿＿＿＿＿＿＿＿＿＿＿＿＿＿＿＿＿＿＿＿＿＿＿＿＿＿＿＿＿＿。

## 六　不但……，也／而且（也）／並且（也）……
### not only …… but also

◎不但東部開始發展，大家也有機會欣賞到太魯閣峽谷的風景。
Not only did the East begin to develop, but every body also got an opportunity to see the beautiful Taroko Gorge scenery.

用法說明：「不但……也……」表示不只是「不但」後面的情況，還有「也」後面的情況，有更進一步的意思。如果前後兩短句的主語相同，主語在「不但」前面。如果兩主語不同，主語在「不但」的後面，及「也」的前面（如前面例句）。此句型與「除了……以外，還……」語境不同。「除了」的句型表示除去已知，加以補充。（請參考本課文法二）

Explanation: "不但……也……" means "not only …… but also ……" indicating "furthermore." If the subject of the two clauses is the same, it should be placed before 不但. If the subjects are different, one should be placed after 不但, and the other should be placed before 也. Its context is different from the one of "除了……以外……，還……" — the situation after 還 is merely additional to the situation after "除了……以外……".

▼練習　請用「不但……，也……」回答下面各句，再改成「除了…以外，還…」的句子，並加以比較。

1. 張：你剛剛去超市，只買了西瓜嗎？
   Chang: You went to the suppermarket just now, you only bought watermelons?
   李：我不但買了西瓜，也買了蘋果。
   Lee: I not only bought watermelons; I also bought apples.
   李：除了西瓜以外，我還買了蘋果。
   Lee: Besides watermelons, I also bought apples.

2. 張：你的二十歲生日，只要請全班同學吃蛋糕嗎？
   李：＿＿＿＿＿＿＿＿＿＿＿＿＿＿＿＿＿＿＿＿＿＿＿＿
   李：＿＿＿＿＿＿＿＿＿＿＿＿＿＿＿＿＿＿＿＿＿＿＿＿

3. 張：你暑假去歐洲旅行，只要去英國跟法國嗎？
   李：_____
   李：_____

4. 醫生：你覺得不舒服，只有一點頭疼嗎？
   病人：_____
   病人：_____

5. 張：你爸爸生氣的時候，會亂扔東西嗎？
   李：_____
   李：_____

6. 張：大家都說小李媽媽好像他姐姐，是因為他媽媽看起來很年輕嗎？
   李：_____
   李：_____

7. 張：你說這個地方不適合人住，是因為常有颱風嗎？
   李：_____
   李：_____

8. 張：這次旅行，只有小王要參加嗎？
   李：_____
   李：_____

9. 張：你想搬家，是因為你現在租的房子房租太貴嗎？
   李：_____
   李：_____

## 七　沒有一 M (N) 不 / 沒……的

### every, everyone (not a single N is not)

◎去過的人，沒有一個不說好的。

Everyone who has been there says it is good. (literally: "Of the people who have been there, there is not a single one who doesn't say it is good.")

用法說明：兩個否定就變肯定，強調沒有一個例外，語氣比直接肯定更強，句子較富變化。句末的「的」表示肯定。

Explanation: Two negatives form a positive. Emphasizing that there are no exceptions, this pattern carries a stronger tone than the simple positive form and adds variation to the sentence. The 的 at the end of the sentence expresses certainty.

### 練習　請用「沒有一 M (N) 不／沒……的」改寫下面各句。

1. 那些人，每一個我都認識。
   I know every one of those people.
   → 那些人，沒有一個我不認識的。
   I know every one of those people (literally: Of those people, there isn't one that I don't know).

2. 我剛剛說的話都是真的。
   _____

3. 這個人真聰明，什麼事情都會做。
   _____

4. 我妹妹住校以後，天天都想家。
   _____

5. 張老師寫的書，我都看過了。
   _____

## 八　N1/NP1 跟 N2/NP2 比起來……
### comparing N1 with N2

◎ 不知道跟美國的大峽谷比起來怎麼樣？
   I wonder how it compares to the Grand Canyon in America?

用法說明：把 N1 跟 N2 或 NP1 跟 NP2 比較一下，做一評斷，評斷的句子要有描寫程度的副詞，如：多了、一點或比較等。語言環境清楚時，N1/NP1 可以省略。

Explanation: When you compare N1 with N2 or NP1 with NP2 and reach a judgment, the sentence with the comparison needs to have an adverb of degree, such as 多了，

一點，or 比較。When N1/NP1 is clear from context, it may be omitted.

### 練習　請用「N1 / NP1 跟 N2 / NP2 比起來」回答下面問題。

1. 我覺得我媽真嘮叨！
   I think my mom is really a nag！
   → 你媽跟我媽比起來，我媽嘮叨多了。
   Comparing your mom and my mom, my mom is much more of a nag.

2. 中國的四川 (Sìchuān, Swechwan) 菜跟墨西哥 (Mòxīgē, Mexico) 菜都很辣吧？

3. 政府的獎學金跟學校的獎學金，哪一種容易申請？

4. 巴西 (Bāxī, Brazil) 人口多，還是印度 (Yìndù, India) 人口多？

5. 在餐廳打工很辛苦，在超級市場呢？

## 九　歎詞跟語助詞的用法
## The use of Interjections & Modal Particles

### （一）嗯

◎嗯，我女朋友寄來的。
Uh huh, it is from my girlfriend.

用法說明：「嗯」為歎詞，語調低降，用於回應，表示肯定對方的說法。「嗯」的後面大多有補充說明，也可免掉。

Explanation: 嗯 is an exclamation which has a low and descending tone. It is used to affirm something the other party has said. 嗯 is usually followed by a supplementary explanation, but this explanation may be omitted.

### 練習　用「嗯」完成下面對話。

1. 張：你下了課就回家嗎？
   Chang: Are you going home right after class?
   李：嗯，下了課就走。
   Lee: Uh huh, I'm going right after class.

2. 張：一邊念書，一邊工作很辛苦吧？
   李：_____。

3. 張：你打算明天去參觀博物館嗎？
   李：_____。

4. 張：這部電影真值得看。
   李：_____。

5. 張：高速公路對城市的發展很有幫助。
   李：_____。

### （二）哇

◎哇！好漂亮的郵票！
Wow! What a beautiful stamp!

用法說明：「哇」用在句首做歎詞時，語調降，當面高聲表示稱讚、羨慕、驚喜或訝異。這種用法年輕人用得較多。如放在句尾做語助詞，是 u, ou, ao 跟「啊」的合音。

Explanation: When 哇 is used as an interjection at the beginning of a sentence with a high and falling tone, it indicates praise, admiration, pleasant surprise, or astonishment. This usage is more common amongst young people. If 哇 is used as a particle at the end of a sentence, it is the combined sound of "u", "ou", "ao" and "啊 (a)".

### 練習

（一）根據所給情況，用「哇」表示稱讚、羨慕、驚喜或訝異。

1. 一開門看見女朋友穿了一件漂亮的新衣服。
   As soon as you open the door, you see your girlfriend wearing a beautiful new

outfit.
→ 哇！你今天好漂亮！
　Wow! You look gorgeous today!

2. 吃了朋友買的葡萄，味道好極了。
___

3. 朋友告訴你他爸爸送他一輛汽車。
___

4. 走進廚房，看見媽媽做了很多好菜。
___

5. 看到室友半個鐘頭就把一個月的髒衣服洗好了。
___

(二) 請念下面各句，並注意句尾「啊」的變音。

1. 你早啊！
   Good morning.
   → 你早哇！
   　Good morning!

2. 那個人好高啊！
___

3. 走啊！你還等什麼？
___

4. 她為什麼哭啊？
___

5. 好啊，就這麼辦。
___

| 課室活動 | Classroom Activities |

一

1. Play the game 接詞, "connecting words." It is better to have the students sit in a circle. The instructor starts the game by saying a two or three syllable word. The teacher then asks a student to form a new word which begins with the last syllable (or one of the syllables if the last is too difficult) of the previous word, e.g., 同學→學生→生氣→汽水→水果→(Homophones are permitted.)

2. As a penalty, those who fail to keep the "merry-go-round" moving has to give a short summary of his/her hometown to the class. The summary should include the following information: 在哪裡？有多大？有多少人口？什麼最有名？風景怎麼樣？

二、討論問題 (Discussion)

1. 你對臺灣知道多少？請你說說看。
2. 你介紹你們國家的時候，一定會說到的是什麼？為什麼？
3. 你們國家有沒有人口問題？有什麼樣的人口問題？

## 短文　　簡介台灣（一）

台灣是一個長長的小島，南北長三百九十四公里，東西最寬的地方有一百四十二公里，跟荷蘭差不多一樣大。台灣在中國大陸東南方，離大陸有一百三十多公里。東邊是太平洋，西邊是台灣海峽。

除了台灣這個島以外，附近還有七十七個小島。島上平地非常少，大部分是山。最高的山是玉山，有三千九百五十二公尺高。台灣在火山帶上，所以地震特別多。又因為山多，所以河流不但短，而且都流得很急。最長的河是濁水溪，只有一百八十六公里。

台灣雖然小，可是可以看到很多種地形，而且都有不一樣的美，所以大家都說台灣的風景好極了。

一共有兩千多萬人住在這個又小山又多的島上，所以人口問題是政府最關心的事。

## Vocabulary:

1. 簡介 (jiǎn jiè) (jiǎnjiè): brief introduction
2. 寬 (kuān): wide
3. 荷蘭 (Hélán): the Netherlands
4. 太平洋 (TàipíngYáng): Pacific Ocean
5. 海峽 (hǎisiá) (hǎixiá): strait
6. 玉山 (Yùshān): Mt. Jade
7. 火山帶 (huǒshān dài): volcanic range
8. 濁水溪 (Jhuóshuěi sī) (Zhuóshuǐ Xī): Zhuoshui River
9. 地形 (dìsing) (dìxíng): topography

### 簡介¹ 台灣（一）

台灣是一個長長的小島，南北長三百九十四公里，東西最寬²的地方有一百四十四公里，跟荷蘭³差不多一樣大。台灣在中國大陸東南方，離大陸有一百三十多公里。東邊是太平洋⁴，西邊是台灣海峽⁵。除了台灣這個島以外，附近還有七十七個小島。

島上平地非常少，大部分是山。最高的山是玉山⁶，有三千九百五十二公尺高。台灣在火山帶⁷上，所以地震特別多。又因為山多，所以河流不但短，而且都流得很急。最長的河是濁水溪⁸，只有一百八十六公里。

台灣雖然小，可是可以看到很多種地形⁹，而且都有不一樣的美，所以大家都說台灣的風景好極了。一共有兩千多萬人住在這個又小山又多的島上，所以人口問題是政府最關心的事。

# 第五課　氣候跟出產

■稻米（范慧貞提供）

（公共汽車站）

偉立：奇怪！今天**怎麼回事**？等了這麼久，都沒有車來！

台麗：是啊！平常都很準時的。（咳嗽）

偉立：你病啦？我剛剛就覺得你的聲音不太對。

台麗：已經一個多星期了，我**以為**只是小感冒，**沒想到**咳了這麼久，今天好像還有一點發燒。

偉立：看醫生了沒有？

台麗：我吃了一些家裡帶來的藥，可是沒什麼用。我想我應該跟醫生約個時間去看病了。天氣這麼冷，我的身體還不能適應。

偉立：臺灣現在還很暖和嗎？

台麗：臺灣熱的時間很長，這時候大概還有三十度。

偉立：啊？差那麼多！難怪你會生病。那冬天也不冷嗎？

台麗：冬天差不多是十五度。**再冷也**不會到零下[1]。因為臺灣北部常下雨，而且我們房子裡大部分不裝暖氣，所以覺得比較冷。**一般來說**，南部晴天的時候多，比北部暖和[2]。聽說臺灣的天氣跟你們的南部差不多。

偉立：那麼，一年四季都很舒服吧？

台麗：也不一定，夏天又濕又熱，**並不**舒服。春天秋天的氣溫變化很大[3]，很容易感冒。

偉立：我們春秋天早晚的氣溫也差很多。冬天很冷，常常下雪，尤其是颳**起**風**來**，真是冷得受不了。

台麗：那我怎麼辦？

偉立：別怕，車裡、房子裡都有暖氣，不要在外面太久，就沒問題了。冬天穿的衣服、鞋子你都準備好了嗎？

台麗：帶了件雪衣，別的我想到時候再買。不知道下**起**雪**來**是什麼樣子？

偉立：下雪的時候到處都是白的，很漂亮。不過雪融化了以後，路上又髒又滑，這時候你就會覺得還是夏天好了。夏天只有中午比較熱，晚上就涼快了。

（台麗又咳嗽）

偉立（拿出一個蘋果）：啊，我有一個蘋果，給你吧，病人。我們有句話說：「一天吃一個蘋果，就不必看醫生了。[4]」

台麗：謝謝。你們的蘋果**是**很好吃，可是我現在最想的就是鳳梨。臺灣的鳳梨又香又甜，顏色也很漂亮。

偉立：李平也這麼說。他還說他家那兒有一條河，附近出產的米跟西瓜是全臺灣最好吃的[5]。

台麗：對，對，對，真的很不錯。除了鳳梨、西瓜以外，還有香蕉、葡萄…好多好多水果。

偉立：我們南部也出產很多水果，**像**葡萄柚、柳橙、香蕉、葡萄、李子**什麼的**。

台麗：你們中西部大平原出產的小麥、玉米是有名的，我們每年都進口不少。

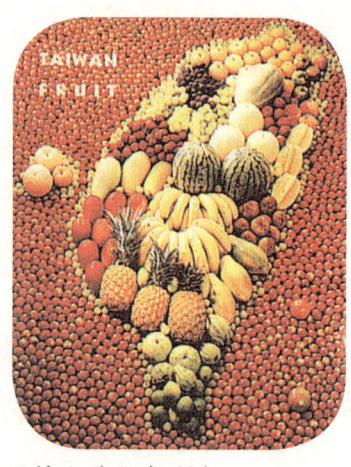

實用視聽華語 3
Practical Audio-Visual Chinese

■臺灣的水果（臺灣省青果運銷合作社提供）

■做糖用的甘蔗（范慧貞提供）

偉立：你們喜歡喝茶，臺灣也產茶嗎？

台麗：北部山區出產的茶很多、也很好。算起來我們的天然資源並不多，尤其是礦產，像煤、石油差不多都沒有，所以政府跟農民都在研究怎麼樣可以有更多更好的農產品，現在不但夠自己吃，還可以出口了。

偉立：我知道，在你心裡，臺灣什麼都好。

台麗：那當然。你知道我還想什麼嗎？海鮮。臺灣的魚蝦又便宜又新鮮，種類又多。看！你害我更想家了。

（公共汽車來了）

偉立：真對不起。我的車來了，我得走了。再見。

台麗：再見。

## 生詞及例句

**1 氣候 (qìhòu)**　　N：climate

這裡的氣候不錯，冬天不冷，夏天也不熱。

**2 出產 (chūchǎn)**　　N/V：natural product, product/to produce

(1) 我們的出產不夠，所以得跟外國買。
(2) 你們那裡出產什麼水果？

**產 (chǎn)**　　V：to produce, yield

臺灣山區產茶嗎？

**3 準時 (jhǔnshíh) (zhǔnshí)**　　A/SV：to be punctual, on time

(1) 今天你來晚了，請你明天準時來。
(2) 王先生跟人約會總是很準時。

**4 咳嗽 (késòu)**　　V/N：to cough/a cough

**咳 (ké)**　　V：to cough

(1) 我上個星期開始咳嗽，咳了好幾天了。
(2) 小張的咳嗽還沒好。

**5 發燒 (fā//shāo)**　　VO：to have fever

(1) 天氣這麼熱，你穿了外套還說冷，你是不是發燒了？
(2) 王老師的孩子發了三天的高燒，都是四十一、二度，家人都很著急。

**6 適應 (shìhyìng) (shìyìng)**　　V：to adapt to

我剛搬家，對新環境還不太能適應。

## 第五課　氣候跟出產

**7 暖和 (nuǎn·huo)**　　SV：to be warm

外面好冷，一進門就覺得暖和多了。

**8 度 (dù)**　　M：degrees [unit of measure for angles, temperature]

臺北最熱的時候，有三十八度多。

**9 零下 (língsià) (língxià)**　　N：below zero

這幾天冷得不得了，夜裡都是零下兩三度。

**10 裝暖氣 (jhuāng//nuǎncì) (zhuāng//nuǎnqì)**

VO：to equip with heating

小陳的房間裡沒裝暖氣，所以比較冷。

**裝 (jhuāng) (zhuāng)**　　V：to install; to load, pack, fill

你為什麼不把電話裝在客廳裡？

**暖氣 (nuǎncì) (nuǎnqì)**　　N：heating; warm air

**冷氣 (lěngcì) (lěngqì)**　　N：air conditioning; cold air

**11 一般來說 / 一般說來 / 一般而論**

(yìbān lái shuō/yìbān shuō lái/yìbān ér lùn)

IE：generally speaking

一般來說，臺灣人喝茶的比喝咖啡的多。

**一般 (yìbān)**　　AT：common, general

在臺灣，一般六樓的公寓都有電梯。

**12 晴天 (cíngtiān) (qíngtiān)**　　N：clear day, sunny day

**晴 (cíng) (qíng)**　　SV：sunny

129

這幾天一直下雨,等天晴了,再搬家吧!

**13.** 濕/溼 (shīh) (shī)　　SV：to be damp, moist, humid, wet

冬天下雨,又冷又濕,很不舒服。

濕度 (shīhdù) (shīdù)　　N：humidity

臺灣夏天因為濕度高,覺得特別不舒服。

濕熱 (shīhrè) (shīrè)　　SV：to be hot and humid

濕熱的地方,吃的東西特別容易壞。

**14** 並 (bìng)　　A：used before a negative for emphasis (see 文法練習第五)

(1) 學中文並沒有你想的那麼難。
(2) 張:你為什麼到你爸爸公司去上班?
　　李:我並不願意去,可是我爸爸一定要我去。

並且/而且 (bìngcǐe / ércǐe) (bìngqiě / érqiě)

CONJ：and, besides, moreover, furthermore

小李的成績原來就很棒,而且申請獎學金的人不怎麼多,所以他一申請,就拿到了。

**15** 氣溫 (cìwūn) (qìwēn)　　N：air temperature

這幾天的氣溫很高,熱得不得了。

體溫 (tǐwēn)　　N：body temperature

要是你的體溫三十八度,你就生病了。

溫度 (wēndù)　　N：temperature

烤雞的時候,溫度不能太低。

**16** 變化 (biànhuà)　　N：change, transformation

130

第五課　氣候跟出產

臺北市這幾年的變化很大，很多地方我都不認得了。

變ㄅㄧㄢˋ (biàn)　V：to change, become different, to transform

我妹妹小時候很難看，現在大了，變漂亮了。

17 尤ㄧㄡˊ其ㄑㄧˊ是ˋ (yóucíshìh) (yóuqíshì)　A：especially, above all

我什麼水果都喜歡吃，尤其是西瓜。

18 颳ㄍㄨㄞ風ㄈㄥ (guāi//fōng) (guā//fēng)　VO：for wind to blow

現在外面颳著風、下著雨，你還要出去嗎？

19 雪ㄒㄩㄝˇ衣ㄧ (syuěyī) (xuěyī)　N：snow suit

雪ㄒㄩㄝˇ鞋ㄒㄧㄝˊ (syuěsié) (xuěxié)　N：snow shoes

20 到ㄉㄠˋ處ㄔㄨˋ (dàochù)　N：everywhere

今天放假，街上到處都是人，你開車要慢一點。

21 融ㄖㄨㄥˊ化ㄏㄨㄚˋ (rónghuà)　V：to melt, to thaw

是下雪的時候冷，還是雪融化的時候冷？

22 滑ㄏㄨㄚˊ (huá)　SV/V：to be slippery, smooth/to slip, skate, slide, glide

(1) 剛下過雨，路上很滑，你走慢一點吧！
(2) 地上有水，他走路不小心，就滑倒 (huádǎo, to slip and fall) 了。

23 鳳ㄈㄥˋ梨ㄌㄧˊ (fènglí)　N：pineapple

24 香ㄒㄧㄤ蕉ㄐㄧㄠ (siāngjiāo) (xiāngjiāo)

N：banana（M：根 gēn / 串 chuàn / chuàn）

25 葡ㄆㄨˊ萄ㄊㄠˊ柚ㄧㄡˋ (pútáoyòu)　N：grapefruit

26 柳橙 (liǔchéng)　　N：orange

27 小麥 (siǎomài) (xiǎomài)　　N：wheat

28 玉米 (yùmǐ)　　N：corn, maize

玉 (yù)　N：jade

臺灣最高的山叫「玉山」，因為遠遠地看，綠得像玉一樣漂亮。

米 (mǐ)　N：uncooked rice

用臺灣東部出產的米做飯特別好吃，因為那裡的空氣跟水都非常乾淨。

29 進口 (jìnkǒu)　　V/AT：to import/imported

(1) 這幾年臺灣從美國進口了很多蘋果、玉米。
(2) 從前在臺灣，進口車的價錢非常高，一般人都買不起。

出口 (chūkǒu)　V/AT：to export/exported

(1) 臺灣的水果，大部分從高雄 (Gāoxióng, Kaohsiung)、基隆 (Jīlóng, Keelung) 出口，賣到附近的國家去。
(2) 林小姐做的是出口生意，把臺灣做的衣服，賣到歐洲各國去。

30 天然資源 (tiānrán zīhyuán) (tiānrán zīyuán)

N：natural resource

天然 (tiānrán)　AT：natural

我覺得天然的風景比人工的美多了。

資源 (zīhyuán) (zīyuán)　N：resource

這個學校學生能用的資源很多，書、報、雜誌、電腦⋯都是。

31 礦產 (kuàngchǎn)　　N：minerals, mineral products

我國的礦產除了金、銀以外，還有鐵。

**32** 煤ㄇㄟˊ (méi)　　N：coal

　　煤ㄇㄟˊ礦ㄎㄨㄤˋ (méikuàng)　　N：coal mine

大部分的煤礦都在地底下，工作環境對健康很不好。

**33** 石ㄕˊ油ㄧㄡˊ (shíhyóu) (shíyóu)　　N：petroleum, oil

我們生活裡面，有很多東西都是石油做出來的，難怪石油又叫「黑金」。

石ㄕˊ頭ㄊㄡˊ (shíh·tóu) (shí·tóu)　　N：stone

小林的窗戶被人用石頭打破了。

油ㄧㄡˊ (yóu)　　N/SV：oil/to be oily

(1) 炸東西的油用過了，最好不要再用了。
(2) 小趙的頭髮油油的，好像好幾天沒洗了。

油ㄧㄡˊ膩ㄋㄧˋ (yóunì)　　SV：(said of food) to be greasy or oily

油炸的東西太油膩，吃太多，對身體不好。

汽ㄑㄧˋ油ㄧㄡˊ (qìyóu)　　N：gasoline, petrol

因為汽油越來越貴，坐公車的人就多起來了。

**34** 農ㄋㄨㄥˊ產ㄔㄢˇ品ㄆㄧㄣˇ (nóngchǎnpǐn)　　N：agricultural product

米、麥、青菜、水果什麼的，都是農產品。

產ㄔㄢˇ品ㄆㄧㄣˇ (chǎnpǐn)　　N：product, produce

我們公司的產品有：桌子、椅子、床、書架跟衣櫃。

**35** 新ㄒㄧㄣ鮮ㄒㄧㄢ (sīnsiān) (xīnxiān)　　SV：to be fresh

鄉下車少，空氣當然新鮮。

133

鮮ㄒㄧㄢ (xiān)　　SV：to be delicious, tasty; to be fresh

(1) 這個雞湯的味道很鮮，好喝極了。
(2) 李小姐買了些鮮花放在辦公室裡。

海ㄏㄞˇ鮮ㄒㄧㄢ (hǎisiān) (hǎixiān)　　N：sea food

在海鮮店吃得到各種不一樣的魚、蝦。

**36** 種ㄓㄨㄥˇ類ㄌㄟˋ (jhǒnglèi) (zhǒnglèi)　　N：type, variety, kind

這個市場，青菜的種類最多，青花菜、芥蘭菜都有。

類ㄌㄟˋ (lèi)　　M：kind, type, class, category

這一類的書都有很多畫，適合五、六歲的小孩看。

分ㄈㄣ類ㄌㄟˋ (fēn//lèi)　　VO：to classify

趙小姐的衣服多得不得了，她怕不好找，收衣服的時候都先分類，冬天的衣服一定不會跟夏天的掛在一起。

**37** 害ㄏㄞˋ (hài)　　V：to cause trouble to, to impair

我男朋友急著要我跟他一起出門，害我飯都來不及吃。

**38** 想ㄒㄧㄤˇ家ㄐㄧㄚ (siǎng//jiā) (xiǎng//jiā)　　VO/SV：to miss home/to be homesick

(1) 你離開家快一年了，一定常想家吧？
(2) 小英住校以後，非常想家，每天都打電話給媽媽。

## 注釋

1. "冬天差不多是十五度。再冷也不會到零下。" This is the weather of the valleys and the plains in Taiwan. In high mountains, the temperature may drop to below zero Celsius in winters. The people in Taiwan talk about temperature in Celsius, and that is why 台麗 still tells the temperature in Celsius.

2. "南部晴天的時候多，比北部暖和"　The Tropic of Cancer goes through 嘉義縣 (Jīayì Xiàn, Chia-yih County). Most of Taiwan is north of the Tropic of Cancer, in the subtropics. There is more sunshine in the south, and the temperature there is a little higher on average than in the north. The average temperature is above 20°C (68°F) for 8 to 9 months in the north, whereas it is above 20°C for 10 months in the south.

3. "春天秋天的氣溫變化很大"　The spring and autumn in Taiwan are both short, with frequent and wide changes in temperature. Sometimes the morning and evening temperatures differ by more than 10°C (50°F). Temperatures may also vary up to 10°C from one day to the next.

4. "一天吃一個蘋果，就不必看醫生了。"　is the familiar saying: "An apple a day keeps the doctor away."

5. "……有一條河，附近出產的米跟西瓜是臺灣最好吃的。"　This is a reference to 濁水溪 (Zhuóshuǐ Xī), the longest river (186 KM) in Taiwan, located on the western part of the island. The longest river on the east has a length of 84 KM. The main agricultural products in the 濁水溪 area are watermelon and rice.

## 文法練習

### 一　怎麼(一)回事　What is going on? What happened?

◎今天怎麼回事？
What is going on today?

用法說明：覺得情況不平常或奇特時，都可用這句話詢問事情發生的原因或經過。
Explanation: This is used to inquire further about a situation one feels is unusual or peculiar.

**練習**　根據所給情況用「怎麼回事」發問。

1. 下班時間還沒到，去找朋友，看見公司裡只有朋友一個人，別人都走了。
   You go to visit a friend during office hours, and you see that your friend is alone. Everyone else has left the office.
   →怎麼回事？別人都到哪裡去了？
   What happened? Where did everybody else go?

2. 看到同學的臉白得像紙一樣。
   _____

3. 看見妹妹的房間地上有很多髒東西。
   _____

4. 昨天才買的錶,今天就停了。
   _____

5. 室友這個星期都很晚回來,今天碰見他。
   _____

## 二 以為……,沒想到……

...... thought that ......, ...... didn't think that ......

◎ 我以為只是小感冒,沒想到咳了這麼久。
I thought that this was only a small cold, I had no idea that I would have a cough for this long.

用法說明:「以為」後面是不正確的想法,「沒想到」後面是「意料之外」的事實。
Explanation: Following 以為 is a mistaken thought idea (which one previously believed to be true), after 沒想到 is the unexpected or unpredictable truth.

▼ 練習    請用「以為……,沒想到……」改寫下面各句。

1. 我想王先生是學生,可是我弄錯了,他是老師。
   I thought Mr. Wang was a student, but I was mistaken: He's a teacher.
   → 我以為王先生是學生,沒想到他是老師。
   I thought that Mr. Wang was a student. I had no idea that he was a teacher.

2. 小高想做日本菜很容易,可是他錯了,麻煩得不得了。
   _____

3. 張小姐想這裡的冬天非常冷,可是她錯了,一點也不冷。
   _____

4. 大家都想他的病沒希望了,可是大家都錯了,他好了。
   _____

5. 我看李老師只有三十多歲，可是她告訴我她已經五十多歲了。

---

## 三　再……也……　No matter how ......

◎再冷也不會到零下。
No matter how cold it gets it won't go below zero.

用法說明：用於假設的情況，有「即使」或「無論怎麼」的意思。用「再」將情況推到最高程度，但即使在最高程度的情況下，「也」後面的結論仍然不變。「再」為副詞，用來修飾跟在後面的 SV、V，或 AV。

Explanation: This pattern is used in a hypothetical situation, and means "even if" or "no matter how......" The clause following 再 is an exaggerated and hypothetical expression of degree; the clause following 也 affirms that, even if this high degree were reached, the conclusion would not change. 再 is an adverb used to modify in combination with the SV, V, or AV that follows it.

### 練習

### （一）請用「再 SV 也……」回答下面各問題。
Please answer the questions below using "再 SV 也……".

1. 中文這麼難，你還要學嗎？
   With Chinese being so difficult, you still want to learn it?
   → 再難我也要學。
   　No matter how difficult it was, I'd still want to study it.

2. 有錢，就可以看不起別人嗎？

3. 照顧小孩很辛苦，你還願意生小孩嗎？

### （二）請用「再SV＋的＋N也……」完成下面各句對話。

1. 張：這次考試考了很多書裡沒有的東西。
   Chang: The test this time covered a lot of material which wasn't in the book.

李：是啊！這麼難，再用功的學生也考不好。
Lee: True! With a test this hard, no matter how hard-working a student was, he/she would still do poorly.

2. 張：沒想到這麼好的學校會有他這麼壞的學生！
李：不必奇怪，<u>再好的學校也　　　　　　</u>。

3. 張：這麼貴的衣服，誰買得起呢？
李：你放心！<u>再貴的衣服也　　　　　　</u>。

(三) 請用「再V也……」完成下面各句對話。

1. 張：我妹妹的男朋友離開她了，所以她一想起來就哭。
Chang: My little sister's boyfriend left her, so whenever she thinks of him she starts to cry.
李：再哭也沒有用了，最好不要再想他了。
Lee: No matter how much she cries it won't change matters. She should stop thinking about him.

2. 太太：我們去那家照像館照吧，他們照得比較好。
先生：不必了，你就是這個樣子，<u>再照也　　　　　　</u>。

3. 先生：我這件衣服弄髒了，你幫我洗一下。
太太：那麼髒！恐怕<u>再洗也　　　　　　</u>。

(四) 請用「再AV＋V也……」完成下面各句對話。

1. 張：這裡的風景真好，你畫一張吧！
Chang: The scenery here is really great. Why don't you do a painting?
李：不行！這麼美的風景，我再會畫也畫不好。
Lee: Impossible! With such a beautiful scene, no matter how talented I was, I still wouldn't be able to do it justice.

2. 張：老師要走了，有什麼話快說吧！
李：是啊！老師走了的話，<u>再想說也　　　　　　</u>。

3. 張：我聽說你很能吃，所以我做了這麼多菜。
李：太多了吧？我<u>再能吃也　　　　　　</u>。

## 四　一般來說／一般說來／一般而論
### Generally speaking ......

◎一般來說，南部晴天的時候多，比北部暖和。
Generally speaking, there are more clear days in the South, and the temperature is warmer than the North.

用法說明：「一般來說」強調「大部分的狀況都是這樣」。
Explanation: 一般來說 emphasizes that something is true in most instances and means "generally speaking".

▼ 練習　　請用「一般來說」回答下面各問題。

1. 西方小孩比東方小孩獨立嗎？
   Are Western children more independent than Eastern children?
   →一般來說，西方小孩比較獨立。
   Generally speaking, Western children are more independent than Eastern children.

2. 廣東菜辣不辣？
   _____

3. 這裡的秋天，氣溫變化很大嗎？
   _____

4. 補習班的學習環境怎麼樣？
   _____

5. 學校附近的房子，房租都很便宜吧？
   _____

139

## 五　並＋不／沒　not at all (indicates contradiction of the previous speaker's statement)

◎夏天又濕又熱，並不舒服。

It is both hot and humid in the summer, so (contrary to what you might think) it is really uncomfortable.

**用法說明**：「並」放在「不」或「沒」之前，加強否定的語氣，說明真實情況跟某種看法或一般看法不一樣。

Explanation: When 並 is placed in front of 不 or 沒, it strengthens the negative tone and indicates that the true situation differs from certain opinion or the general view.

### 練習

**(一) 請用「並＋不／沒」改寫下面各句。**

1. 大家都說這部電影很好看，可是我覺得不怎麼好看。
   Everybody says that this movie is very good, but I don't think it's particularly good.
   → 大家都說這部電影很好看，可是我覺得並不好看。
   　Everybody says that this movie is very good, but I think it's actually bad.
   or → 大家都說這部電影很好看，可是我並不覺得好看。
   　Everybody says that this movie is very good, but I, in fact, think it's bad.

2. 我以為林先生去過荷蘭，可是他說他沒去過。
   _____

3. 我室友學過三年中文，可是說得不太好。
   _____

4. 沙漠裡不是一點水也沒有。
   _____

5. 成績好的學生不一定都很用功。
   _____

第五課　氣候跟出產

## （二）請用「並＋不／沒」完成下面對話。

1. 張：你每天都來得這麼早，你住的地方很近吧？
   Chang: You come so early every morning. Your home must be really close to here.
   李：我住得並不近，不過我都很早出門。
   Lee: No, in fact I don't live very close at all, but I leave very early.

2. 張：張老師明天不能來，我以為她已經告訴你這件事情了。
   李：＿＿＿＿＿＿＿＿＿＿＿＿＿＿＿＿＿＿＿＿＿＿＿＿＿。

3. 張：小陳這麼聰明，成績一定很好。
   李：＿＿＿＿＿＿＿＿＿＿＿＿＿＿＿＿＿＿＿＿＿＿＿＿＿。

4. 張：老李幫了你一個大忙，你真應該謝謝他。
   李：＿＿＿＿＿＿＿＿＿＿＿＿＿＿＿＿＿＿＿＿＿＿＿＿＿。

5. 張：我這麼做是不是錯了？小王為什麼那麼生氣？
   李：＿＿＿＿＿＿＿＿＿＿＿＿＿＿＿＿＿＿＿＿＿＿＿＿＿。

## 六　V 起 O 來……　　When ...... starts V

◎尤其是颳起風來，真是冷得不得了。
Especially when the wind starts blowing, it is unbearable cold.

◎不知道下起雪來是什麼樣子。
I wonder what it's like when it snows.

用法說明：「V 起 O 來」放在句子前面的時候，用法跟第一課的一 (I) 一樣，只是多一個受詞，而這個受詞一定要放在「起來」的中間，不可以放在「起來」的後面。常常是說話者說明情況與剛剛提到的或預想的情況有什麼不同。

Explanation: When "V起O來" is founded at the beginning of the sentence, its usage is the same as in chapter 1, No. 1, Part 1. However when an object is given, the object must be placed between the 起 and the 來 of the 起來. The speaker often describes the situation of "V 起 O 來", which is somehow different from the situation just mentioned or expected.

# 實用視聽華語 3
Practical Audio-Visual Chinese

### ▼ 練習　　請完成下面各對話。

1. 張：小陳平常很多話都不敢說，為什麼喝了酒就不一樣了？
   Chang: Usually Little Chen is afraid to speak out. Why is he different after he drinks?
   李：他一喝起酒來就什麼都不怕了。
   Lee: As soon as he starts drinking, he's not afraid of anything.

2. 張：小王已經做了好幾個小時的事了，怎麼還不來吃飯？
   李：他做起事來_____。

3. 張：你妹妹說話聲音很低，沒想到唱歌聲音那麼高。
   李：是啊！她唱起歌來_____。

4. 張：我哥哥什麼都不喜歡，只有說到籃球的時候才有興趣。
   李：就是嘛！一說起籃球來，他_____。

5. 張：你第一次離開家，一定很想爸爸媽媽吧？
   李：是啊！每次想起他們來_____。

## 七　是 (A) SV

◎你們的蘋果是很好吃。
　Your apples are quite delicious (indeed).

用法說明：中文裡，「SV」的前面本來不需用「是」，但如果要表示強調或肯定對方的看法，就可加「是」。除了SV以外，也可以放在名詞、助動詞、副詞及表示心理狀態的動詞（如：喜歡、愛、討厭、知道、認識、了解等）前面。

Explanation: In Chinese, it is not necessary to place 是 in front of a SV, but 是 can be added for emphasis or for affirmation of the other party's statement or opinion. Besides a SV, a Noun, an Auxiliary Verb or an Adverb, you can also place after 是 a verb indicating state of mind (such as 喜歡, 愛, 討厭, 知道, 認識, 了解, etc.)

### ▼ 練習　　請用「是」完成下面各對話。

1. 張：我覺得這裡的氣溫變化非常大。
   Chang: I think that the temperature changes here are quite drastic.
   李：嗯，是非常大，有時候早晚氣溫會差十度。
   Lee: Uh huh, they are indeed. Sometimes it differs 10 degrees between morning and

第五課　氣候跟出產

night.

2. 張：這附近的房租很便宜，一個月大概兩三百塊。
   李：_____，所以我才在這裡租房子。

3. 弟弟：媽媽生病，你照顧她，好幾天沒睡覺了。今天我來吧。
   （應該／得／要）
   哥哥：_____。

4. 張：小王搬到哪裡去了？你一定知道，能不能告訴我？
   李：_____，不過地址我放在家裡，沒帶來。

5. 張：你跟老林是朋友，錢怎麼還算得這麼清楚？
   李：_____，可是我不能每次吃飯都讓他付錢啊！

## 八　像……什麼的　such as ...... and so on.

◎……，像葡萄柚、柳橙、香蕉、葡萄、李子什麼的。
……, such as grapefruit, oranges, bananas, grapes, plums, and so on.

用法說明：「像」是例如的意思，舉例說明時，因要舉出的東西太多，沒辦法一一列出，只要說出幾個，放在「像」的後面即可。

Explanation: 像 means "for example, such as." It is used to introduce a list when there are too many items for the speaker to list one by one and he/she just wants to mention a few sample items.

▼ 練習　　請用「像……什麼的」完成下面各句。

1. 我吃過很多中國菜，像宮保雞丁、青豆蝦仁、芥蘭牛肉什麼的。
   I've eaten lots of Chinese food: for example, Gongbao chicken, shrimp with peas, beef and broccoli, etc.

2. 我剛搬家，廚房裡的東西，像_____都還沒買。

3. 林小姐去過不少國家，像_____都去玩過。

4. 小王學過幾種語言，像_____，都說得不錯。

5. 你應該常做運動，像_____，對身體都很好。

## 九　害　cause (in a harmful way)

◎你害我更想家了。
You're causing me to miss home even more.

**用法說明**：這個「害」是「讓」或「使」的意思，語氣強烈一點，而且都是負面的。
Explanation: This 害 means "to make, to cause". The tone is fairly strong and is always negative.

**練習**　請用「害」改寫下面各句。

1. 你說這些話，會讓他睡不著覺的。
   If you tell him all this it's going to make him unable to fall asleep at night.
   → 你說這些話，會害他睡不著覺的。
   If you tell him all this it's going to make him unable to fall asleep at night. (implication is more negative: you will cause him to suffer).

2. 我給這個孩子穿得太少，所以孩子感冒了。
   _____

3. 天氣這麼壞，我們不能出去野餐了。
   _____

4. 物價太高，大家沒辦法生活了。
   _____

5. 老謝常常請我吃飯，所以我胖了不少。
   _____

## 課室活動　Classroom Activities

一、遊戲 (yóuxì, game)

1. This game is called 碰球. The teacher writes down on individual cards different types of agricultural produce, industrial produce and

minerals the class has learned. Each student is given one card and asked to remember the item written on it. The students then form a circle, each holding their card in front of him/her so that it is visible to the other students. One student starts the game by saying: 我的 X 碰 Y。e.g., 我的香蕉碰西瓜。The student representing 西瓜 must immediately respond by saying something such as: 我的西瓜碰鳳梨。

2. As a penalty, any student who fails to respond or who responds incorrectly must tell the class some of the produce/minerals of his/her country, e.g., 法國出產葡萄、李子……。

## 二、討論問題 (Discussion)

1. 請用圖片或實物介紹貴國的天然資源或農產品。
2. 請介紹一下貴國的氣候。

毛衣 (máoyī, sweater)

毛 (máo, hair)

## 短文　　簡介台灣（二）

台灣是個海島，一般來說，下雨的機會很大，可是因為夏天颳西南季風，這時就是西南部的雨季，到了冬天改颳東北季風，就是北部的雨季。這種冬雨，不但溼又冷，而且下的時間又長，所以台灣北部的氣候跟南部比起來，就差多了。另外每年四、五月是梅雨季節，差不多要下一個月的雨。梅雨下完了，天氣就熱起來了。

台灣溼熱的氣候，很適合農業的發展，所以農產品的種類非常多，除了米、茶以外，像甘蔗、甘藷、橘子、鳳梨、香蕉、花生什麼的，也都又多又好。

台灣的天然資源，除了北部以前出產過煤跟金子以外，現在已經沒什麼礦產了。又因為山多，森林也多，而且四邊都是海，所以漁業也非常重要。

## Vocabulary:

1. 季風 (jìfōng) (jìfēng): monsoon
2. 梅雨 (méiyǔ): (literally: plum rains) heavy spring rains
3. 甘蔗 (gānzhè): sugar cane
4. 甘藷 (gānshǔ): sweet potato, yam
5. 花生 (huāshēng): peanuts
6. 森林 (sēnlín): forest
7. 漁業 (yúyè): fishing industry

## 簡介台灣（二）

台灣是個海島，一般來說，下雨的機會很大，可是因為夏天颳西南季風[1]，這時就是西南部的雨季。到了冬天改颳東北季風，就是北部的雨季。這種冬雨，不但溼又冷，而且下的時間又長，所以台灣北部的氣候跟南部比起來，就差多了。另外，每年四、五月是梅雨[2]季節，差不多要下一個月的雨，梅雨下完了，天氣就熱起來了。

台灣溼熱的氣候，很適合農業的發展，所以農產品的種類非常多，除了米、茶以外，像甘蔗[3]、甘藷[4]、橘子、鳳梨、香蕉、花生[5]什麼的，也都又多又好。

台灣的天然資源，除了北部以前出產過煤跟金子以外，現在已經沒什麼礦產了。又因為山多、森林[6]也多，而且四邊都是海，所以漁業[7]也非常重要。

Day 1  P. 163-168
Day 2
         P. 169-173
Day 3  Review Key.
Day 4  ~~~~~~~~   Review
Day 5  test?

# 第六課　考不完的試

■ 在圖書館準備考試的學生（范慧貞提供）

（下課以後，高偉立走到前面找教授談話）

偉立：張老師，我剛剛看了考卷，有幾個地方不太明白。

教授：哦？什麼地方有問題？

偉立：我這題翻譯跟老師的差不多，為什麼要扣兩分呢？

教授：我看看。噢！「就」應該在主詞後面。文法錯了，當然要扣分。

偉立：還有這個呢？

教授：你把「再見」的「再」寫成「現在」的「在」了。下次小心一點兒。你考得不錯嘛！

偉立：我這次分數比上次低。題目不難，我都會，可是還寫錯，我太不小心了！所以我很生自己的氣。

教授：別生氣了！考試也算是一種練習，可以讓老師跟你自己了解你複習得夠不夠，學過的東西都記住了沒有。

偉立：還可以看出學生小心不小心。

教授：對了！還有問題嗎？

偉立：沒有了。謝謝，再見。

※　　※　　※　　※　　※　　※

（林建國踢開房門，把書往桌上一扔）

偉立：你怎麼啦？生什麼氣？

建國：今天心理學考得好爛[1]！昨天看的都沒考，真倒楣！

偉立：別的同學考得怎麼樣？

第六課　考不完的試

# Record of Study
## 修業證明書

國立臺灣師範大學　國語教學中心
National Taiwan Normal University
Mandarin Training Center
(Formerly Center for Chinese Language and Culture Studies)

| 學號: 050901777 | | | |
|---|---|---|---|
| 姓名 NAME : LIU, IRENE | | | 高念慈 IN CHINESE |
| 生日 Birth Date : 07/25/1972 | | 國籍 Nationality: 美 | |

| 註冊起訖日期 PERIOD OF ENROLLMENT | 個人班 INDIVIDUAL TUTORIAL | 合班 SMALL GROUP CLASS | 正式生 FULL TIME |
|---|---|---|---|
| Sep. 1, 2005-May. 31, 2006 | | X | X |
| Sep. 1, 2006-Feb. 28, 2007 | | X | X |

| 教材編號 UNIT CODE | 教材名稱 COURSE TITLE | 學習期間 PERIOD OF STUDY | 應上課時數 RHRS | 實際上課時數 AHRS | 成績 GRADE |
|---|---|---|---|---|---|
| A11041 | PRACTICAL AUDIO VISUAL CHINESE I | Sep. 1, 2005-Feb. 28, 2006 | 220 | 188 | 94.0 |
| A11053 | PRACTICAL AUDIO VISUAL CHINESE II | Mar. 1, 2006-Nov. 30, 2006 | 230 | 217 | 92.3 |
| X98870 | CHINESE PAINTING (I)- PLUM,ORCHID,BAMBOO,CHRYSANTHEMUM | Oct. 1, 2006-Nov. 30, 2006 | 14 | 12 | 82.5 |

| 應上課總時數 TOTAL NO. OF CLASS HOURS REGISTERED FOR | 464 |
|---|---|
| 實際上課總時數 TOTAL NO. OF CLASS HOURS ACTUALLY ATTENDED | 417 |

備　註 REMARKS:

## SUPPLEMENTARY INFORMATION

- *"Full Time"* indicates 10 or more hours of study per week.
- RHRS denotes "Registered Hours." AHRS denotes "Attendance Hours."
- MTC's grading system, the same as that used in all public schools and public schools and universities in Taiwan, is as follows:
  100-80=A　79-70=B　69-60=C　59-50=Pass Conditional (upon make-up exam)　49&Below=F
- Grades undisclosed upon request of the student.

Dec. 21, 2006
發出日期 Date of Issue

主任 周中天
Chung - tien Chou
Director

■學生修業證明書（范慧貞提供）

建國：不知道。不過，他們好像考得不錯。
偉立：先別難過，我們想想問題在哪裡。是不是你念書的方法不對？
建國：我高中也是這樣念的啊！
偉立：噢，我明白了。念大學跟念高中不一樣，一定得自動自發，才會有好成績。
建國：你的意思是……
偉立：平常要**多**看書，發現問題就去請教老師，也可以跟同學討論。
建國：對！一次小考考壞了沒關係，我現在就開始用功，期中考、期末考就不會有問題了。你得給我加油啊！
偉立：那當然，不過，下次生氣不要再踢門了。門並沒有錯啊！
建國：對不起，對不起。下次不敢了。

※　　※　　※　　※　　※　　※

(系辦公室)

偉立：胡老師，你好。**咦**，張老師不在？我的作業交給你，好不好？
助教：好啊，我正在改你們的作業呢[2]。
偉立：你今天臉色不太好，不舒服嗎[3]？
助教：大概是睡得不夠吧。明天要考法文，下星期一要交

報告,這幾天**不但**要看書,查資料,**還要**上課,改作業,差不多天天開夜車[4],累得不得了。

偉立:當助教真辛苦,還是只做學生比較好。

助教:是啊。我在臺灣念大學的時候,報告沒這麼多,也不必工作,輕鬆多了。

偉立:那你們的考試很多**嘍**?

助教:**也不算**多,你只要把書上或是老師說的背下來,考試及格[5]一定沒問題。

偉立:什麼都要背嗎?臺灣人好厲害啊!要是我,就死定了[6]。

助教:當然不是什麼都要背,其實背書也沒有你想的那麼難。你們老師不叫你們背書嗎?

偉立:很少。

助教:**所以啦**,要是你常常背,大概就不會覺得那麼難了。

偉立:我**寧可**寫報告,**也**不要背書。

助教:背書是很無聊,可是有些東西**非背不可**。學語言更需要背。

偉立:我們老師總是鼓勵我們要有自己的想法,寫報告比背書有意思多了。

助教(看看錶):我得去上課了,再見。

偉立:再見。

## 生詞及例句

**1** 考卷 (kǎo jyuàn) (kǎojuàn)　　N：exam paper, test booklet（M：份）

今天有二十個人來考試，請準備二十份考卷。

**2** 翻譯 (fānyì)

V/N：to translate, interpret/translator, interpreter, translation

(1) 這句中文用英文應該怎麼說，你會不會翻譯？
(2) 他跟外國人談生意的時候，常常帶著一個翻譯。
(3) 這本書的日文翻譯不太好，很多意思都弄錯了。

翻 (fān)

V：to translate; to turn (over, upside down, up, etc.) ; to rummage, to search

(1) 我們兩國生活習慣不一樣，有些句子翻譯的時候很難翻。
(2) 各位同學，今天我們念第六課，請翻到第八十五頁。
(3) 華人在船上吃魚的時候，吃完了一面，不可以把魚翻過來再吃，因為他們怕船也會翻過來。
(4) 小偷沒偷走什麼東西，可是把我的衣服翻亂了。
(5) 這本雜誌，我沒有時間慢慢地看，只隨便翻了一下。

**3** 扣分 (kòu//fēn)　　VO：to deduct points, take off credit

扣 (kòu)　　V：to deduct

老師說寫錯一個字要扣一分。

**4** 主詞 (jhǔcíh) (zhǔcí)　　N：subject (of a sentence)

詞 (cíh) (cí)　　N：word

名詞 (míngcíh) (míngcí)　　N：noun

動詞 (dòngcíh) (dòngcí)　　N：verb

「王小姐很喜歡貓」，這個句子裡，「王小姐」跟「貓」都是名詞；「喜歡」是動詞；「王小姐」也是這個句子的主詞。

### 歌詞 (gēcíh) (gēcí)　N：lyrics

這首歌的歌詞，又好懂又好唱，連小孩都會唱。

### 5 文法 (wénfǎ)　N：grammar

說日文的時候，動詞應該在名詞後面，要不然文法就錯了。

### 6 成 (chéng)

V/PV/RE：to become, to turn into, to complete/ to V as / [RE indicates success, completion, or accomplishment of an action]

(1) 老林跟小王才認識三個月，就成了好朋友了。
(2) 對不起，李先生，我把你看成張先生了。
(3) 我的錢不夠，我想我去不成了。

### 7 分數 (fēnshù)　N：score, grade (in an exam, course)

分 (fēn)　M：point(s), score(s) in (an exam, a sport, a contest)

小王這次考試的分數是全班最高的，九十六分。

### 8 低 (dī)　SV：to be low

一般來說，男人的聲音比較低。

### 9 題目 (tímù)　N：title, subject, topic

這篇文章的題目是「臺灣的出產」，介紹了很多農產品。

題 (tí)　M：for question or problem (in a test or an exercise)

考卷上一共有十個題目，第一題最容易。

## 10 算是 (suànshìh) (suànshì)  V：to be considered as

要是你的頭不疼了，你的病就算是好了。

## 11 了解／瞭解 (liǎojiě)

V/N：to know, to understand/knowledge, understanding

(1) 你跟小林剛認識，所以你不了解他。
(2) 你對我的了解還不夠，所以常常弄錯我的意思。

## 12 複習／溫習 (fùsí/wēnsí) (fùxí/wēnxí)  V：to review

學過的東西，得常複習，要不然很快就忘了。

## 13 記住 (jì//jhù) (jì//zhù)

RC：to remember, to fix in the mind, to commit to memory

小陳的電話號碼很難記，我總是記不住。

## 14 踢開 (tī//kāi)  RC：to kick away (literally or figuratively)

(1) 你為什麼把狗踢開？你這樣做是不對的。
(2) 老王覺得我對他沒有幫助了，就想把我踢開了。

### 踢 (tī)  V：to kick

馬生氣的時候才會踢人。

### 踢到 (tī//dào)  RC：to kick

小高沒踢到我，因為我跑得快。

## 15 心理學 (sīnlǐsyué) (xīnlǐxué)  N：psychology

### 心理 (sīnlǐ) (xīnlǐ)  N：thought and ideas; mentality

你做生意，要懂客人心理，兩塊九毛雖然只比三塊便宜一毛，但是願意買的人就多了。

## 第六課　考不完的試

**16 爛 (làn)**　SV：to be worn out ; to be rotten, decayed; (slang) rotten, terrible

(1) 這本書真爛，連書名都翻譯錯了。
(2) 這個蘋果放了一個星期，快爛了，不能吃了。

**17 倒楣 (dǎoméi)**

SV：to have bad luck or an unlucky break; to get into trouble

小林不但丟了書，還丟了錢，真倒楣！

**倒 (dǎo)**　V/RE：to fall over, [RE indicates toppling or falling over of the subject]

(1) 上次大地震，房子倒了二十幾間。
(2) 我不小心碰倒了桌上的茶杯，水都流出來了。

**18 高中 (gāojhōng) (gāozhōng)**

N：senior high school (10th, 11th and 12th grades)

小李十二歲就上高中了，比別人早了三年。

**19 自動自發 (zìhdòng zìhfā) (zìdòng zìfā)**

IE：self-motivated and spontaneous

這個孩子做什麼事都自動自發，從來不要我叫他。

**自動 (zìhdòng) (zìdòng)**

A/AT：to be automatic, voluntary/automatically, voluntarily

(1) 你不必用手開，只要站在前面，門就會自動打開。
(2) 李小姐的照像機是全自動的，誰都會用。

**被動 (bèidòng)**　SV：to be passive

老張很被動，什麼事都要別人說了，才去做。

**20 如果 (rúguǒ)**　A：if, in case, in the event of

如果你妹妹願意跟我約會，我一定會高興得睡不著覺。

## 實用視聽華語 3
Practical Audio-Visual Chinese 3

**21 討論 (tǎolùn)**　V：to discuss (formally)

上課時，李教授總是鼓勵我們把自己的意思說出來，跟大家一起討論。

**22 難過 (nán'guò)**　SV：to be sad, to be distressed

醫生說小王的病好不了了，我們都很難過。

**23 期末考 (címòkǎo) (qímòkǎo)**　N：final exam (at the end of the term)

期中考 (cíjhōngkǎo) (qízhōngkǎo)　N：mid-term exam

補考 (bǔkǎo)　N/V：make-up exam/to take a make-up exam

(1) 我弟弟的分數太低，一定得補考。
(2) 補考的成績還是不好的話，他就得再念一年了。

**24 加油 (jiā//yóu)**

VO：to make an extra effort, "Step on it !" ; to oil, lubricate, refuel; to cheer (an athlete)

加油站 (jiāyóujhàn) (jiāyóuzhàn)

N：gasoline (petrol) filling station

(1) 快沒油了，我們先去路口那個加油站加油吧！
(2) 加油吧！只要你用功，一定可以考好的。

**25 作業 (zuòyè)**　N：homework

老師留的作業太多，不但要寫字、寫句子，還要準備小考，恐怕三個鐘頭也做不完。

**26 臉色 (liǎnsè)**　N：complexion; facial expression

(1) 你的臉色很黃，是不是病了？
(2) 小張的臉色很難看，真的生氣了。

## 27 報告 (bàogào)  V/N：to report, to make known/a report (written or spoken)

(1) 我每天晚上看王小姐報告的電視新聞。
(2) 我今天晚上要寫報告,不能出去玩。

## 28 查 (chá)

V：to check, examine, inspect; to look into, investigate; to look up, consult

我不知道火車站的電話號碼是多少,請你幫我查查。

## 29 當 (dāng)  V：to work as, to serve as

我從小就想當醫生,可是我姐姐喜歡小孩,只想當個小學老師。

## 30 助教 (jhùjiào) (zhùjiào)  N：teaching assistant

張教授要我們把作業交給王助教改。

## 31 輕鬆 (cīngsōng) (qīngsōng)

SV/V：to be relaxed, easy, comfortable; to relax, wind down

(1) 作業都做完了,考試也考完了,我覺得真輕鬆。
(2) 考試考完了,我想去看電影,輕鬆輕鬆。

### 鬆 (sōng)  SV：to be relaxed, lenient, slack, loose

陳老師對學生太鬆了,所以學生都不用功。

## 32 背書 (bèi//shū)

VO：to recite a passage from memory; act of memorizing a passage

老師叫我們背書,我念了二十次才記住。

### 背 (bèi)

V/N：to memorize, to learn by heart, to recite from memory/ the back of the body, the back of an object

(1) 這幾個句子太難,我背了半天還記不住。
(2) 老林站了好久,背疼得不得了,躺在床上休息呢。

背ㄅㄟˋ下ㄒㄧㄚˋ來ㄌㄞˊ (bèi//siàlái) (bèi//xiàlái)

RC：to memorize, to commit to memory

我已經把你的電話號碼背下來了，0912835766，對吧？！

**33** 及ㄐㄧˊ格ㄍㄜˊ (jígé)　　V：to pass a test, pass an examination/to be qualified

這次考試比較難，所以五十分就算及格了。

**34** 厲ㄌㄧˋ害ㄏㄞˋ (lìhài)　　SV：to be fierce, formidable, sharp

(1) 你每次考試都一百分，真厲害！
(2) 王老師真厲害，誰沒交作業，就不許誰回家。我們都怕他。
(3) 小張好厲害，人前人後說的話不一樣。你要小心。

**35** 死ㄙˇ定ㄉㄧㄥˋ了ㄌㄜ˙ (sǐhdìng·le) (sǐdìng·le)　　IE：(slang) will surely die

我媽叫我十點回家，現在十二點了，我死定了！

死ㄙˇ (sǐh) (sǐ)　　V/SV/RE：to die/to be dead

(1) 小李很小的時候，父母就死了。
(2) 這條河的水都變綠了，難怪河裡有好多死魚。
(3) 如果在沙漠裡旅行，沒有水喝，恐怕就會渴死。

**36** 其ㄑㄧˊ實ㄕˊ (císhíh) (qíshí)　　A：actually, in fact, as a matter of fact

老王說他會做飯，其實他只會烤麵包。

**37** 寧ㄋㄧㄥˊ可ㄎㄜˇ / 寧ㄋㄧㄥˊ願ㄩㄢˋ (níngkě/níngyuàn)

AV：would rather, had better, would sooner

我寧可餓死，也不要吃我哥哥做的菜，太難吃了。

**38** 無ㄨˊ聊ㄌㄧㄠˊ (wúliáo)

SV：to be bored ; to be boring and uninteresting; to be a nuisance; to be nonsensical

(1) 我一個人在家很無聊，所以想約朋友去跳舞。
(2) 我昨天在車上碰到一個很無聊的人，他總是想找我說話。

## 第六課　考不完的試

**39 非⋯不可 (fēi...bùkě)**　PT：must, have to, is indispensable, will inevitably

不考試就不能畢業，所以你非考不可。

**40 想法 (siǎngfǎ) (xiǎngfǎ)**　N：way of thinking, point of view

小林的想法很奇怪，一般人很難了解他。

**看法 (kànfǎ)**　N：point of view, opinion, way of looking at things

我覺得小王一定申請不到獎學金，你的看法怎麼樣？

**做法 (zuòfǎ)**　N：way of doing things

老李家吃的魚只有紅燒跟糖醋，沒有別的做法。

**說法 (shuōfǎ)**　N：way of speaking, an orally expressed view

恐龍 (kǒnglóng, a dinosaur) 是怎麼死的？說法有好幾種。

**教法 (jiāofǎ)**　N：teaching method, way of teaching

小學老師跟大學教授的教法不太一樣吧？

### 歎詞跟語助詞　Interjections and Particles

1. **哦 (ó)**　I：[indicates doubt ; "really?!"]

   張：我昨天給你打過電話。
   李：哦？沒有人告訴我啊！

2. **咦 (yí)**　I：[indicates surprise]

   咦？他怎麼有我的電話號碼？

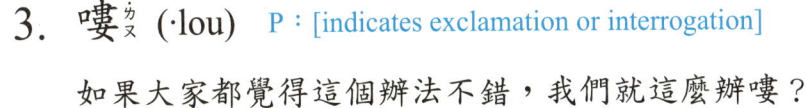

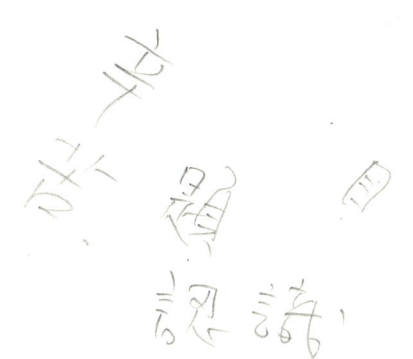

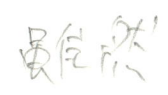

3. **嘍 (·lou)**　P：[indicates exclamation or interrogation]

   如果大家都覺得這個辦法不錯，我們就這麼辦嘍？

## 注釋

1. 爛 is a slang term used in Taiwan, popularized by some television programs in the early "80s. 爛 literally means "decayed or rotten", but in this case it is used to describe something which is lousy or extremely bad. Originally it was used in this manner mostly by young people, but it has since become widely used and does not sound as extreme as it did several years ago.

2. "我正在改你們的作業呢！" means: "I'm right in the middle of correcting your assignments."

3. "你今天臉色不好，不舒服嗎？" means: "You don't look well today. Are you not feeling well?" This is an expression of concern. Some other ways to say this are. "你還好吧？(Are you all right?)"and"你怎麼了？ (What's the matter with you? or What's wrong with you?)"However, the latter is considered somewhat straightforward and impolite and should not be used when speaking with an elder.

4. 開夜車 is a slang term used by students meaning: "to stay up late at night in order to complete an assignment or study for an exam", "to burn the midnight oil".

5. 考試及格 means "to pass an exam". One usually has to get a grade of at least 60 points in order to pass an exam in Taiwan.

6. 死定了 is a slang term used by young people. It literally means "one will certainly die." It is used to describe the dire importance of a particular situation. It is similar to saying: "That will be the death of me (if something happens)." Another Chinese pattern to convey the same meaning is "……完了".

## 文法練習

### 一　N1V成N2　N1 turned into N2 (via V)

◎你把「再見」的「再」寫成「現在」的「在」了。
　You wrote the 再 from 再見 like the 在 from 現在。

用法說明：這個「成」是 PV，是「成為」的意思，N1 經由 V 這個動作成為 N2。因為也有「處置」的作用，所以常跟「把」一起用。動詞如果是看、聽、說、寫、念，就有「弄錯了」的意思。

Explanation: 成 is used here as a post verb. It means the same thing as 成為 (to turn into, become)". Thus, this pattern can be translated as "N1 becomes N2 via the action of V", 把 is often used together with this pattern because the sentence shows manipulation of an object. If the main verb is 看, 聽, 說, 寫, and 念 then this pattern usually indicates that the change or manipulation was faulty or resulted in a mistake.

### 練習

**(一) 請根據提示，用「V 成」完成下面各句。**

1. 這間書房，我打算改成客房，因為常有客人來住。（客房、改）
   I plans to convert this study into a guest room because guests often stay over.

2. 這篇文章是用法文寫的，我看不懂，你幫我 ___翻英文___，好不好？（英文、翻）

3. 我覺得她頭髮的樣子很好看，我也想 ___剪她那個樣___。（她那個樣子、剪）

4. 我們有六個人，這個蛋糕當然得 ___分六塊___。（六塊、分）

5. 這個地方原來只有兩萬人，現在已經 ___發展一個大城市___ 了。（一個大城市、發展）

**(二) 請根據提示，用「V 成」跟「把」完成下面各句。**

1. 你聽錯了，你把十四聽成四十了。（十四、四十、聽）

2. 小林的中文真不好，又 ___念不好___。（綠、路、念）

3. 李小姐站得太遠，所以我 ___看不到___。（她、張小姐、看）

4. 我同學 ___說我哥哥是做麵包的時候___，真好笑！
   （我哥哥是做麵包的、我哥哥是麵包做的、說）

5. 我弄不清楚這兩個字怎麼用，常常 ___寫的的關___（得、的、寫）

## 二　算是　to be considered as
　　不算　does not count as,

◎ 考試也算是一種練習…
Exams could be regarded as practices...

◎ 也不算多。
(Here, 也 indicates a contradiction of the previous speaker's statement)
But that isn't much.

用法說明：「算是」的意思「可以說是」，語氣較不肯定，後面可以是名詞或修飾語，如果是SV，最好加「的」，表示一個狀態或情況。「不算」是「算是」的否定，語氣較不肯定。

Explanation: 算是 means "one could say that it is ..." and carries a slight tone of uncertainty. 算是 can be followed by a noun or a modifier. If 算是 is followed by an SV, it is best to add a 的，which acts as a nominalizer. 不算 is the opposite of 算是, and its tone is not so certain.

### 練習　用「算是」完成句子。

1. 李先生在德國住了二十年，可以算是德國人了。
   Mr. Li has lived in Germany for twenty years, so could be considered a German now.

2. 你的頭不疼了，病就算是 _好了_ 。

3. 我家離學校六公里，算是 _很遠_ 。

4. 我們念的書都很難，這本算是 _很～無聊_ 。

5. 張小姐念中學的時候有一百七十公分，在女同學當中算是 _很高_ 。

### 練習　請把下面各句改成「不算」的句子。

1. 在這個學校申請獎學金算是容易的。
   It's quite easy to apply for a scholarship at this school.
   → 在這個學校申請獎學金不算難。
   　It's not difficult to apply for a scholarship at this school.

第六課　考不完的試

2. 那個學生的成績在班上算是高的。
   那個學生的成績在班上<u>不算是高的</u>。

3. 教書的工作算是辛苦的。
   教書的工作<u>不算是辛苦的</u>。

4. 這個冰箱的價錢跟你的比起來，算是便宜的。
   這個冰箱的價錢跟你的比起來，<u>不算是便宜的</u>。

5. 你們這兒的火車一小時跑一百五十公里，算是快的。
   你們這兒的火車一小時跑一百五十公里，<u>不算是快的</u>。

## 三　V住

(indicates the resulting stabilization, or fixation of an action)

◎…學過的東西都記住了沒有？
Do you (solidly) remember everything that you have studied?

**用法說明**：這個「住」是 RE，表示「穩固」。RC 的 Actual Type 跟 Potential Type 都可用。

Explanation: This 住 is a RE (resultative verb ending), and it indicates the stabilization or fixation of a verb's action. The RC can be used in either Actual Type form or Potential Type form.

▼ 練習　請根據所給「V住」填入合適的 RC。

1. 記住：
   (1) 我的電話號碼很好記，你一定記得住。
       My phone number is easy to memorize: You'll definitely remember it.
   (2) 這本書，我才念了一次，當然<u>不一定記住</u>。
   (3) 這些句子，我背了半天，可是一個字都<u>記不住</u>。

2. 坐住：
   (1) 三個月大的孩子，怎麼<u>會坐住</u>？
   (2) 我弟弟很愛玩，在家裡一分鐘也<u>坐不住</u>。

165

3. 站住：
   (1) 沒關係，我不累，不必坐，我還 __站得住__ 。
   (2) 高太太 __站不住__ ，得找個椅子坐下來了。
   (3) 我一叫小張，他就 __站住了__ 。

4. 拿住：
   (1) 這麼大的杯子，小孩一定 __拿得住__ 。
   (2) 那個瓶子，我 __拿不住__ ，就打破了。

5. 停住：
   (1) 小林的車開得太快，__沒停住__ ，所以出事了。
   (2) 飛機剛起飛，怎麼 __會停住__ ？

## 四　多 V (O)　V more

◎平常要多看書。

(You) need to read more in general.

用法說明：「多」在此做副詞用，修飾後面的動詞，強調程度應該加強。客套話可重疊「多」。如欲說明程度，可在V之後加上「一點」、「一些」或「Nu-M」。此時「多」就不可重疊。

Explanation: 多 is used here as an adverb which describes the verb that follows, indicating increased frequency or degree. To soften the tone of 多 and make it more polite, it can be repeated. To indicate only a small or specific increase in frequency, place 一點, 一些, or "Nu M" after the verb without repeating 多.

▼ 練習　請把「多」插入下面各句適當位置。

1. 這件事很清楚，不必我說。
   This matter is very clear; I don't need to explain it.
   → 這件事很清楚，不必我多說。
   This matter is very clear; I don't need to explain further.

2. 運動對身體健康有很大的幫助。

3. 再吃一點嘛！我做的菜不好吃嗎？

4. 一袋蘋果不夠，你應該再買一些。
_____

5. 你不必今天就回去，在這裡住幾天吧！
_____

6. 以後要麻煩你照顧我的孩子了。（「多」可重疊）
_____

7. 我什麼都不懂，要跟你學習。（「多」可重疊）
_____

## 五　不但……，還……　　Not only......, but also ......

◎ 這幾天不但要看書、查資料，還要上課、改作業……
Lately, I not only have had to study and do research, but I also have had to go to class, correct homework…

用法說明：這個句型跟第四課的「不但……，也……」差不多，但是用「還」時，程度比用「也」更進一步。

Explanation: This sentence pattern is very similar to the "不但…，也…" pattern found in Chapter 4; however, the use of 還 instead of 也 implies a slightly stronger tone.

▼ 練習　　請用「不但……，還……」完成下面句子。

1. 陳先生不但有三輛汽車，還有一架小飛機。
   Not only does Mr. Chen have three cars, but he also has a small airplane.

2. 張先生不但念過大學，還_____。

3. 王小姐不但去過歐洲，還_____。

4. 這個地方不但有公路，還_____。

5. 老李真倒楣，不但被偷過，還_____。

167

## 六　所以啦　so, you see I was right about this…

◎偉立：很少。（老師很少叫我們背書）
　助教：所以啦，要是你常常背，大概就不會覺得那麼難了。
　Weili: Rarely. (My teacher rarely tells us to memorize a passage.)
　T.A.: So, (as what I said before) if you often memorize passages, you probably won't feel it is so difficult.

用法說明：在對話中，說話者用「所以啦」表示從剛才對方說的話就知道自己先前的看法是對的。
Explanation: In conversation, the speaker uses 所以啦 to express that we know what I said previously was right from what the other party said.

**練習**　請用「所以啦」完成下面對話。

1. 媽媽：要常常複習功課，成績才會好。
   Mom: Only regular review can bring you good grades.
   孩子：上次考試，我沒時間準備，考得好爛。
   Child: I didn't have time to prepare for my last exam. I got really bad grades.
   媽媽：所以啦，學過的東西一定得複習，才記得住。
   Mom: So, as I have said before, you must review and then you will remember what you have learned.

2. 姐姐：這幾天天氣變化大，出門一定要帶著外套。
   妹妹：我好多同學都感冒了。
   姐姐：_所以啦，要多加小心_。

3. 太太：做紅燒魚得放點糖才好吃。
   先生：哦，是嗎？我剛才沒放。難怪這麼難吃。
   太太：_所以啦，以後要放_。

4. 張：你晚出門還比我早到。你叫我走七號公路，可是我以為九號公路比較近。
   李：_所以啦，這就是你不聽_。

5. 張：你住校以後，是不是比以前獨立了？
   李：是啊，我爸媽都這樣說。
   張：_所以啦，那不就是好事_。

## 七　寧可VP1，也VP2（寧願……，也……）
### would rather VP1 than VP2

◎我寧可寫報告，也不要背書。
I would rather write a report than memorize a passage.

**用法說明**：VP1 本來是不喜歡做的事，但因不願改變 VP2 的情況，VP1 變得可以接受了。

Explanation: In this pattern VP1 is something the subject doesn't really want to do, but rather something he is willing to accept, in order to avoid a change in the situation given by VP2. This pattern implies that although VP1 is not completely ideal, in comparison with VP2 it is the more acceptable alternative.

**練習**　請用「寧可……，也……」完成下面對話。

1. 張：你怎麼在家裡洗衣服，沒跟他去看電影？
   Chang: Why did you stay home washing clothes instead of going to the movies with him?
   李：那個人很沒趣，我寧可在家洗衣服，也不要跟他去看電影。
   Li: That guy is very uninteresting; I'd rather stay at home and wash clothes than go to the movies with him.

2. 張：錢那麼少，你為什麼不換工作？
   李：這個工作可以學到很多東西，所以我 _____才不才奐_____ 。

3. 張：學校的大鍋菜吃膩了，我們到郵局旁邊那家飯館去吃吧！
   李：那家飯館的菜太難吃，我 ____寧可吃也不要____ 。

4. 張：快睡吧，天快亮了。
   李：這本書太好看了，我寧可不 ____睡____ 。

5. 張：你跟王小姐借一件衣服去參加舞會吧！
   李：我不喜歡她，我寧可沒有 ____一件衣服____ 。

## 八　非……不可　have to, definitely must, is indispensable (for a particular action)

◎ ……可是有些東西非背不可。
…… but there are some things you must memorize.

用法說明：「非……不可」的意思是「不……不行」。
Explanation: This pattern indicates that you must definitely carry out a specific action due to either necessity or strong desire.

### 練習　請用「非……不可」完成下面對話。

1. 張：怎麼樣才會有好成績？
   Chang: What must one do to get good grades?
   李：要有好成績，非用功不可。
   Li: If you want to have good grades, you must work very diligently.

2. 張：這裡的冬天需不需要裝暖氣？
   李：冬天的溫度都在零下，_非有沒有暖氣_。

3. 張：哎喲！怎麼辦？我把哥哥的照像機弄壞了。
   李：如果他知道了，_非打我_。

4. 張：急什麼？再坐一會兒嘛！
   李：不行，還有半個小時火車就要開了，我 _非走不可_。

5. 張：你怎麼又要找房子？
   李：我的房東要賣房子，所以我 _非走不可_。

## 九　歎詞跟語助詞的用法
The use of Interjections & Modal Particles

第六課　考不完的試

## （一）哦　Oh, (really)?

◎哦，什麼地方有問題？
Oh (really)? Where is the problem?

**用法說明**：放在句首，語調高揚，對聽到的情況表示疑惑、驚訝。
Explanation: When 哦 is placed at the beginning of a sentence and spoken with a questioning tone, it indicates doubt or surprise about what one has just heard.

**練習**　請用「哦」完成下面對話。

1. 張：王教授這個週末要請我們全班吃飯。
   Chang: Professor Wang wants to treat us to a meal this weekend.
   李：哦，真的嗎？他為什麼要請我們吃飯？
   Li: Oh, really? Why does he want to treat us to a meal?

2. 張：助教說期末考不考法文了。
   李：哦，_那就好不是好拳拳_。

3. 張：林小姐病了好幾個星期了。
   李：哦，_病快點好_。

4. 張：上次考試，我的學生有一半不及格。
   李：哦，_那麻口不是就好拳拳_。

5. 張：我哥哥大學畢業半年了，可是還不想找工作。
   李：哦，_罗找口立_。

## （二）咦　Yi? (What?) (indicates surprise)

◎咦，張老師不在？
Huh? Teacher Zhang isn't here?

**用法說明**：放在句首，語調高揚，對眼前的狀況表示驚訝或疑問。近似自言自語。
Explanation: 咦 is placed at the beginning of a sentence and is spoken with a questioning tone, indicating doubt or surprise about what one has just seen, as if the speaker is talking to himself.

## 練習

**(一) 根據所給情況，用「咦」表示驚訝或疑問。**

1. 開燈，可是燈不亮？
   You turned on the switch, but the light doesn't shine.
   → 咦，燈壞了？
   Huh? Is the light broken?

2. 早上起來，看見廚房地上都是水。
   → 咦，為什麼有水_____？

3. 吃晚飯的時候回家，發現沒有人在家。
   → 咦，不是會嗎_____？

4. 室友出門了，可是你看見他的鑰匙還放在桌上，沒帶走。
   → 咦，不好吧_____？

5. 聽說陳助教去了日本，可是今天在路上遠遠地看見他。
   → 咦，不會吧_____？

**(二) 請在「欸」、「哦」、「咦」三詞當中，選擇合適的，填進空格裡。**

1. ___咦___，電視怎麼沒聲音了？
2. （看錶）___欸___，他不是說好了三點一定到嗎？
3. ___哦___，聽你的意思，好像不願意幫忙。
4. ___咦___，我記得你不吃辣的，怎麼點了宮保雞丁？
5. ___咦___，誰把我的桌子搬走了？
6. ___哦___，你已經知道他出國的事了？

172

第六課　考不完的試

## （三）嘍 (indicates exclamation or interrogation)

◎那你們的考試很多嘍？
　So you have a lot of tests?

用法說明：「嘍」是「了」跟「ou」的合音。「了」在此強調達到某一程度。放在句尾，語調高平，徵詢對方以求確定。

Explanation: 嘍 is the combined sound of 了 and "ou". The 了 here emphasizes that a certain level is reached. 嘍 is placed at the end of a statement and pronounced with a high flat tone to ask the other party to confirm the statement.

**練習**　請用「嘍」完成下面對話。

1. 張：我們要去歐洲旅行三個月。
   Chang: We want to travel in Europe for three months.
   李：那你們帶的行李一定不少嘍？
   Li: Then I guess you'll have to bring a lot of luggage, huh?

2. 張：這學期，我只選了兩門課。
   李：那 _選這個嘍_ ？

3. 張：我一天見不到我女朋友就沒辦法念書。
   李：那 _不好嘍_ ？

4. 張：這次考試，全班都考得很好。
   李：_嘍 好好嘍_ ？

5. 張：上週末我一個人在家，電視也壞了，真不知道做什麼才好。
   李：_出去玩好嘍_ ？

| 課室活動 | Classroom Activities |

## 一、角色扮演 (Role Playing)

1. Two students: One acts as a strict teacher, the other as a student who

has not finished his/her homework. The student offers excuses to avoid being punished. Some useful supplementary words include: 嚴 (yán; to be strict), 罰 (fá; to punish), 原諒 (yuánliàng; to forgive), 原因 (yuányīn; reason), 懶 (lǎn; to be lazy), 藉口 (jièkǒu; excuse).

2. Two students: One acts as a parent, the other as a young teenage daughter who has been sitting in front of the TV set for two hours. The parent knows that the daughter has not prepared for her exam tomorrow. The two should improvise a conversation suitable for this situation. Some useful supplementary words include: 數學 (shùsyué) (shùxué; mathematics), 歷史 (lìshǐh) (lìshǐ; history), 化學 (huàsyué) (huàxué; chemistry), 公式 (gōngshìh) (gōngshì; formula), 節目 (jiémù; program), 催 (cuēi) (cuī; to urge; hurry along), 管 (guǎn; to discipline; to be concerned about; to be in charge of; to manage).

## 二、討論問題 (Discussion)

1. 你覺得哪種老師好？常考試的，還是不常考試的？說說你的看法。
2. 你念高中或大學時，最怕考哪一門功課？為什麼？最低分數多少？
3. 貴國老師常叫學生背書嗎？背書有什麼好方法？

下星期一考心理學。　　下星期二考法文。　　下星期三考地理。　　我快變成「烤鴨」了！

## 第六課　考不完的試

**短文**　　　　　　　老師的話

各位同學：

如果沒有問題了，就把考卷收起來吧！從這次的考試，我發現你們大部分的人都有寫字的問題。寫漢字只有多練習、多寫。老師也是這樣學的。我知道你們不喜歡背書，可是學語言非背不可，要不然你怎麼記得住字的寫法、念法，還有文法。學語言一定要多聽、多說、多練習，敢開口、不怕錯，才學得好。

我想你們會選中文課，一定對中文有一點興趣，有興趣就應該自動自發、隨時發現問題，並且找機會練習。如果只有上課的時候學習，那是不夠的。更不可以考試前一天才開夜車。學語言，聽、說、讀、寫都一樣，不可能一天就學會，一定得慢慢來，不能急。

大家加油吧！好，現在我們念下一課，請翻到第八十五頁。

175

## Vocabulary:

1. 各 (gè) : each
2. 讀 (dú) : to read

### 老師的話

各¹位同學：

如果沒有問題了，就把考卷收起來吧！從這次的考試，我發現你們大部分的人都有寫字的問題。寫漢字只有多練習、多寫。老師也是這樣學的。我知道你們不喜歡背書，可是學語言非背不可，要不然你怎麼記得住字的寫法、念法，還有文法？學語言一定要多聽、多說、多練習，敢開口、不怕錯，才學得好。

我想你們會選中文課，一定對中文有一點興趣，有興趣就應該自動自發、隨時發現問題，並且找機會練習。如果只有上課的時候學習，那是不夠的。更不可以考試前一天才開夜車。學語言，聽、說、讀²、寫都一樣，不可能一天就學會，一定得慢慢來，不能急。

大家加油吧！好，現在我們念下一課，請翻到第八十五頁。

# 第七課 念大學容易嗎

■ 大學指考 臺北市立成功高中考場（聯合報記者陳再興攝）

（活動中心，李平端著咖啡找位子）

李平：嗨，你也在這裡啊？看什麼書？
建國：心理學。我上次考得好爛，下星期再考不好，就慘了。
李平：難怪你這麼用功。下星期還早嘛！
建國：可是我心裡壓力好大啊！
李平：才一個小考就讓你有這麼大的壓力，要是你還在臺灣，恐怕早就變成神經病了。
建國：太誇張了吧？我記得我小時候，考試也不怎麼多啊！
李平：那是因為你只念到小學三年級，沒考過高中、大學[1]。

（偉立走過來）

偉立：嗨！你們好，在談什麼？
李平：剛剛他說考試有壓力，我告訴他臺灣的學生要念高中、大學都得通過考試。因為人人都想念大學[2]，有的人要上有名的大學，有的人要念熱門的科系，所以很早就開始準備，差不多每天都有複習考。下了課還要去補習。這才是壓力。
建國：天哪！那他們一定不敢出去玩了，恐怕連睡覺的時間都不夠。
李平：這樣已經不錯了。六〇年代還要考初中呢！那時候義務教育只有六年[3]。一九六八年以後才改成九年。
偉立：那你們大學怎麼考呢？
李平：以前有聯考。就是每年七月所有的大學聯合起來，在

同一天舉行考試。每年有十萬多人參加，只錄取三萬多人[4]，競爭非常激烈。二〇〇二年開始，進大學的路比較多了。除了參加大學指考以外……

偉立：大學指考？

李平：就是以前的大學聯考。高中成績好的學生，還可以先參加學科能力測驗，然後學校看測驗的成績，再決定把哪個學生推薦到哪個學校去。要不然學生也可以用這個成績，自己申請理想的大學。

偉立：只看學科能力測驗的成績嗎？

■大學指考 考生跟陪考家長（聯合報記者潘俊宏攝）

李平：當然不是，還要參加大學的面試，他們才會決定錄取誰。

偉立：那現在臺灣學生考大學的壓力小多了吧？

李平：那得看要念什麼大學或科系了。有的學生覺得壓力比以前更大。

建國：**幸虧**我們家移民了，**要不然**我一定念不了大學。

李平：有的父母怕孩子受不了這種壓力，就想辦法把孩子送到外國去念書。像我舅舅，就把我表弟送來了。

建國：他多大了？現在住在哪裡？

李平：住在我姑姑家，念八年級。他在臺灣的時候，不喜歡背書，有好幾科不及格。我舅舅擔心他考不上好大學

■大學指考考完後（聯合報記者游文寶攝）

，他自己也願意到外國看看，所以就來了。
偉立：現在情形怎麼樣？
李平：他來了半年了。雖然喜歡老師的教法，但是上課的時候不敢問問題，下了課功課常做得不對，也不知道怎麼寫報告，所以成績並不理想。
建國：我剛來的時候也一樣。他**會**慢慢適應**的**。
李平：我也這麼希望。我覺得他的問題是父母不在這裡，心裡很孤單。雖然有我姑姑照顧，但總還是不夠。因為有的事情你只會跟父母說，不好意思告訴別人。
偉立：嗯，這真是麻煩。
李平：還好我們政府早就注意到這些小留學生的問題[5]，大家

■成功嶺大專學生受訓（范慧貞提供）

也發現把孩子送出來念書，並不是最好的辦法。
建國：沒念大學的人，工作好找嗎？
李平：高中畢業找工作並不容易。所以有的就進專科學校或技術學院學習一種技術，有的補習一年再考，可是男孩子**滿**了十八歲就得先去當兵[6]了。
建國：這些人**只好**等當完兵再念大學嘍？
李平：是啊！
偉立：那麼多人都要念大學，人人都念得起嗎？
李平：以前臺灣的大學，**不管**公立的、私立的，學費**都**沒有你們這裡這麼高[7]，那時候政府的想法是如果學費太高，有錢人才念得起大學，那很不公平。可是現在政府給大學的補助少了，學費就越來越貴了。
偉立：臺灣學生出國留學的人多不多？
李平：跟九〇年代比起來少多了。現在有的人覺得出國留學太辛苦，寧願留在國內念研究所。
建國：噢，對了！你的論文寫完了嗎？以後有什麼計畫？
李平：**寫得差不多了**。拿到學位以後，我**不是**留在這裡做研究，**就是**回臺灣工作。
建國：他們一定很歡迎你這位李博士回國服務。

## 生詞及例句

**1 活動中心 (huódòng jhōngsīn) (huódòng zhōngxīn)**

N：activity center

**活動 (huódòng)** V/N：to move about, to exercise / activity

(1) 人老了，應該常活動，總是坐著並不好。
(2) 我常常參加別系的活動，所以認識的人比較多。

**中心 (jhōngsīn) (zhōngxīn)** N：center, heart, central point

這個語言中心只教學生德文跟法文。

**2 端 (duān)** V：to hold something level with both hands; to carry

想要在餐廳當服務生，就得先學端盤子。

**3 位子 (wèi·zih) (wèi·zi)** N：seat, place, position

這輛車還沒客滿，還有幾個位子。

**4 慘 (cǎn)** SV：to be tragic, pitiful, miserable

(1)如果你姐姐發現你把她的照像機弄壞了，你就慘了。
(2)這個地方因為地震死了很多人，真慘！

**5 壓力 (yālì)** N：pressure, stress

老趙的工作太多，壓力很大。

**壓 (yā)** V：to press, to push down, to weigh down

風太大，請你拿本書把這些紙壓著。

**6 神經病 (shénjīngbìng)**

N：insanity, mental illness (usually used in anger or jest as an exaggeration, rather than to describe actual insanity)

你神經病啊？怎麼把醋加進咖啡裡？

神經 (shénjīng)　N：nerve

剪頭髮不會疼，就是因為頭髮沒有神經。

神 (shén)　N：god

老趙什麼神都信 (to believe)，所以從來不敢做壞事。

7 誇張 (kuājhāng) (kuāzhāng)　SV：to be exaggerated, to be overstated

王大文說他家的房子住得下一百個人，真是太誇張了。

8 通過 (tōngguò)　V：to pass, pass through

聽說這次心理學期末考很容易，大家都通過了。

9 熱門 (rèmén)

SV：to be in great demand, to be very popular (area of study, learning, subject, field)

這幾年學電腦很熱門，連很小的孩子都去學了。

冷門 (lěngmén)　SV：opposite of 熱門

10 天哪 (tiān·na)　IE：Goodness !, Good heavens !, Gracious !

天哪！我怎麼這麼糊塗？忘了今天要期末考了。

哪 (·na)

P：(following words that end in "an", "en", serves the same function as"啊")

(1) 這些青菜是那個農人剛剛送給我的，好新鮮哪！
(2) 不要怕，有問題就問哪！

11 年代 (niándài)　N：era, generation, a decade of a century

我奶奶 (grandmother) 那個年代還沒有手機。

代(dài)　M：generation

上一代的人總是不了解這一代年輕人的想法。

## 12 初中 (chūjhōng) (chūzhōng)

N：junior high school (7th, 8th and 9th grades)

我念初中一年級的時候，就住校了，所以比較獨立。

## 13 義務教育 (yìwù jiàoyù)　N：compulsory education

我們小學、初中都是義務教育，非念不可。

義務 (yìwù)　N：duty, obligation, responsibility

雖然我是你妹妹，可是我沒有義務給你介紹女朋友吧？！你自己去找啊！

教育 (jiàoyù)　N：education

臺灣的教育辦得很好，到處都有學校。

教育部 (jiàoyùbù)　N：the Ministry of Education

教育界 (jiàoyùjiè)　N：educational circles, educational world

## 14 聯合 (liánhé)　V：to combine, to unite, to ally

我們學校打算聯合另外兩所高中一起考試。

聯合國 (Liánhé Guó)　N：United Nations

聯考 (liánkǎo)

N：a standardized entrance exam for school (high school, college, etc.)

今年參加高中聯考的學生比去年多了三千人。

## 15 同一天 (tóngyìtiān)　Dem-Nu-M：the same day

沒想到我的生日跟王教授的同一天，都是三月十一號。

同ㄊㄨㄥˊ (tóng)　　CV/DEM：together, with ; same

(1) 我每天同姐姐一起去上課。
(2) 我跟小陳在同一棟大樓上課，所以我常常碰到他。

不ㄅㄨˋ同ㄊㄨㄥˊ（不ㄅㄨˋ一ㄧˊ樣ㄧㄤˋ）(bùtóng) (bùyíyàng)

SV/N：different from, distinct from/difference

(1) 我跟室友的習慣不同，他早睡早起，我晚睡晚起。
(2)「大」跟「太」這兩個字有什麼不同？

同ㄊㄨㄥˊ樣ㄧㄤˋ (tóngyàng)　　AT：the same, similar

我們對教育有同樣的看法，都覺得學習環境對學生很重要。

## 16 舉ㄐㄩˇ行ㄒㄧㄥˊ (jyǔsíng) (jǔxíng)

V：to hold (a meeting, ceremony, etc.), to convene, take place

舉ㄐㄩˇ辦ㄅㄢˋ (jyǔbàn) (jǔbàn)　　V：to hold (an activity)

我們系要舉辦一個歡迎新生的茶會，可是在哪裡舉行，還沒決定。

舉ㄐㄩˇ (jyǔ) (jǔ)　　V：to hold up, raise, lift

警察叫小偷把手舉起來。

舉ㄐㄩˇ手ㄕㄡˇ (jyǔ//shǒu) (jǔ//shǒu)

VO：to raise one's hand (to vote or to speak-up)

有問題的人請舉手。

舉ㄐㄩˇ重ㄓㄨㄥˋ (jyǔjhòng) (jǔzhòng)　　N：weight lifting

老謝練過舉重，舉起一百公斤的東西，一點也不困難。

## 17 錄ㄌㄨˋ取ㄑㄩˇ (lùcyǔ) (lùqǔ)

V：to admit, to accept (applicants after an examination or application process)

想進我們公司做事的人很多，一百個人來考，我們只錄取了三個人。

錄用 (lùyòng)　V：to employ; to take somebody on the staff

小王他們公司這幾年的發展不太好，已經三年沒有錄用新人了。

18 競爭 (jìngjhēng) (jìngzhēng)　V/N：to compete/competition

只有一個工作機會，可是競爭的人有幾百個。

19 激烈 (jīliè)

SV：(of action and argument) to be intense, sharp, fierce, acute, violent

警察跟小偷打得太激烈了，有人被打死了。

20 學科能力測驗（學測）
(Syuékē Nénglì Cèyàn) (Xuékē Nénglì Cèyàn)

N：Scholastic Aptitude Test

學科 (syuékē) (xuékē)　N：branch of learning, discipline, subject

「學科」指的是國文、英文、地理……什麼的，唱歌、畫畫都不算。

能力 (nénglì)　N：ability, capability, aptitude

謝小姐做事的能力，誰都比不上，又好又快。

測驗 (cèyàn)　N/V：test/to test

(1) 我們期末考，除了口試、筆試，還有聽力測驗。
(2) 口試是測驗學生聽跟說的能力。

21 理想 (lǐsiǎng) (lǐxiǎng)　SV/N：to be ideal/ideal

(1) 我很久沒練習寫字了，成績一定不理想。
(2) 我的理想是大學畢業以後，進大公司做事。

22 面試 (miànshìh) (miànshì)　V/N：to interview/interview

(1) 上次面試的時候，我太緊張，老闆的問題我都沒聽清楚，所以他

們沒錄取我。
(2) 想要進這所學校當老師，得先通過筆試，才能參加面試。

面談 (miàntán)　V/N：to interview/personal interview

那家公司的老闆跟我面談以後，才決定買我們公司的產品。

23 幸虧 (sìngkuēi) (xìngkuī)　A：fortunately, luckily

幸虧沒下雨，要不然就不能去野餐了。

24 舅舅 (jioù·jiou) (jiù·jiu)　N：uncle (mother's brother)

舅媽 (jioùmā) (jiùmā)　N：aunt (wife of mother's brother)

25 表弟 (biǎodì)

N：younger male cousin (on mother's side or paternal aunt's side)

表哥 (biǎogē)　N：older male cousin (on mother's side or paternal aunt's side)

表姐 (biǎojiě)

N：older female cousin (on mother's side or paternal aunt's side)

表妹 (biǎomèi)

N：younger female cousin (on mother's side or paternal aunt's side)

26 考上（考取）(kǎo//·shàng)(kǎo//cyǔ)(kǎo//qǔ)

RC：to pass an entrance examination (for school, a job, a license, etc.)

恭喜你考上了最好的大學。

27 情形 (cíng·síng) (qíng·xíng)　N：situation, condition, circumstances

小張的爸爸還沒有找到工作，媽媽又病了，所以最近他們家的情形很不好。

28 孤單 (gūdān)　SV：to be alone, to be lonely

我現在碰到了困難，沒有人能幫我，我覺得很孤單。

### 29 不好意思 (bùhǎoyì·sih) (bùhǎoyì·si)

IE：to find it embarrassing, to be ill at ease; to feel shy or bashful, ashamed

我已經二十歲了，不好意思再跟父母要錢了。

### 30 注意 (jhùyì) (zhùyì)

V：to pay attention to, to take notice of

各位請注意，飛機要起飛了。

### 31 專科學校 (jhuānkē syuésiào) (zhuānkē xuéxiào)

N：a technical college, vocational school

臺灣的專科學校有兩年的，也有五年的。

#### 科系 (kēsì) (kēxì)

N：department (in a college or university)

這個大學有很多科系，像中文系、心理系，都很有名。

#### 科 (kē)

M：a branch of academic or vocational study; a division or subdivision of an administrative unit or section

感冒應該看哪一科的醫生？

### 32 技術學院 (jìshù syuéyuàn) (jìshù xuéyuàn)

N：Institute of Technology

五年制 (zhì, system) 專科學校畢業的學生，可以念兩年的技術學院。

#### 技術 (jìshù)

N：skill, technique; technology

小王開車的技術不錯，你可以放心坐他的車。

### 33 當兵 (dāng//bīng)

VO：to join the army, to serve in the military

在臺灣，當兵是男孩子的義務。

### 34 不管/不論/無論…都… (bùguǎn/búlùn/wúlùn…dōu…)

PT：no matter (what, how, whether, etc.), regardless of

不管大人、小孩,坐公車都得買票。

**管** (guǎn)

V：to be in charge of, to run, be responsible for; to mind, attend to, bother about, to be concerned about

(1) 你別管他,讓孩子自己決定吧!
(2) 老林已經坐下了,地上好髒,他也不管。

**管不了** (guǎn·bùliǎo)　　RC：cannot manage, handle, supervise

十個孩子,我一個人管不了。

**管不著** (guǎn·bùjháo) (guǎn·bùzháo)

RC：no authority to manage, handle, or interfere

這是我家的事,你管不著。

**35 私立** (sīhlì) (sīlì)　　AT：privately run

**公立** (gōnglì)　　AT：established and maintained by the government

公立大學都是政府辦的,一般來說,學費比私立的便宜很多。

**國立** (guólì)　　AT：nationally run

**市立** (shìhlì) (shìlì)　　AT：municipally run

**36 公平** (gōngpíng)　　SV：to be fair, just, impartial, equitable

為什麼爸爸給哥哥的錢比較多?我覺得不公平。

**37 國內** (guónèi)　　N：inside the country, domestic

**國外** (guówài)　　N：outside the country, overseas, abroad

國內風景好的地方,高先生都去過了,下次他打算到國外去看看。

**38 論文** (lùnwén)　　N：thesis, dissertation, treatise（M：篇）

190

我的畢業論文很長,一共有七百多頁。

### 39 學位ㄒㄩㄝˊㄨㄟˋ (syuéwèi) (xuéwèi)　N：academic degree

大學畢業就有學士學位，如果沒有學位很難跟別人競爭。

### 40 博士ㄅㄛˊㄕˋ (bóshìh) (bóshì)　N：PhD degree, doctorate

老張大學畢業以後，念了七年的研究所，才拿到博士學位。

## 專有名詞　Proper Names

大學指考（大學指定科目考試）
(Dàsyué jhǐhdìng kēmù kǎoshìh) (Dàxué zhǐdìng kēmù kǎoshì)
N: College Entrance Examination

## 注釋

1. **"沒考過高中、大學"** In 2001 Taiwan discontinued the use of the Joint Examination for high school. The reason was that many people felt that it was unfair and unobjective for the fate of the students to be decided by a single exam, after having studied diligently in junior high school for three years. Therefore the Ministry of Education of the R.O.C., after having researched the problem thoroughly, decided to adopt a multi-faceted admission policy, Students may be admitted by several different methods, e.g.「推薦甄選」、「申請入學」and「登記分發」. The admission criteria includes grades, leadership, performing skills etc., in addition to the scores of the Basic Aptitude Test（基本學力測驗）taken twice during the last semester of junior high school. In the year 2002 the use of the Joint Examination for university was also discontinued.

2. **人人都想念大學** means "Everyone wants to go to college." As stated in Note 4 of Lesson 1, study is of primary importance in Taiwan. The purpose of study in high school is to get into a college and obtain a degree, thereby assuring one of a good job and future career.

3. **義務教育** means "compulsory education", In 1922, the Chinese government decided to adopt an educational system similar to the American system. However, only the six years of elementary school was made compulsory at that time and everyone had to pass an exam to go to a junior high school. In 1968, compulsory education was extended to nine years, thereby including junior high school.

4. 錄取三萬多人 refers to the rate of students who pass the Joint Examination of Universities and are admitted to a college. This figure used to be around 30% of all examinees, but has been gradually increasing. In 1991, 41% of those who took this exam were admitted to college. The rate of students who pass the 大學指考 and admitted to a college was 81.4% in 2005. It was 81.3% in 2006.

5. 小留學生的問題 Some parents do not want their children to receive their education in Taiwan because of the difficulty in getting into high school and college. Therefore they take their children to be educated in other countries, often to the States. Boys formerly could not go abroad after age 16 due to regulations concerning the compulsory military service. According to these old regulations, young children were not allowed to have their own passports either. So some of the parents simply left their children with relatives or friends in the States while they went back to Taiwan to work or care after other members of the family. These children left in the U.S. lacked proper identification papers and often had no immediate family. They encountered many problems and sometimes went astray. The number of these 小留學生 in the States has been estimated to be approximately 50 thousand. In 1988, the Taiwanese government changed the law so that children now can have their own passports. Boys under 18 are now also allowed to study abroad first, then come back to serve in the army.

6. 當兵 Military service in Taiwan is compulsory for all healthy males. The average service is two years, which must be served between the ages of 18-45. Students can request a draft deferment while they are in an accredited college or graduate program.

7. 學費都沒有你們這裡這麼高. For the 1991-92 school year the average tuition at public universities in Taiwan was NT$ 12,837 per semester. The average tuition at private universities was NT$ 38,456 per semester. For the 2006-2007 school year the tuition at public universities are from NT$ 20,200 to 39,560 per semester. The tuition at private universities are from NT$70,460 to 41,250. It varies from school to school.

第七課　念大學容易嗎

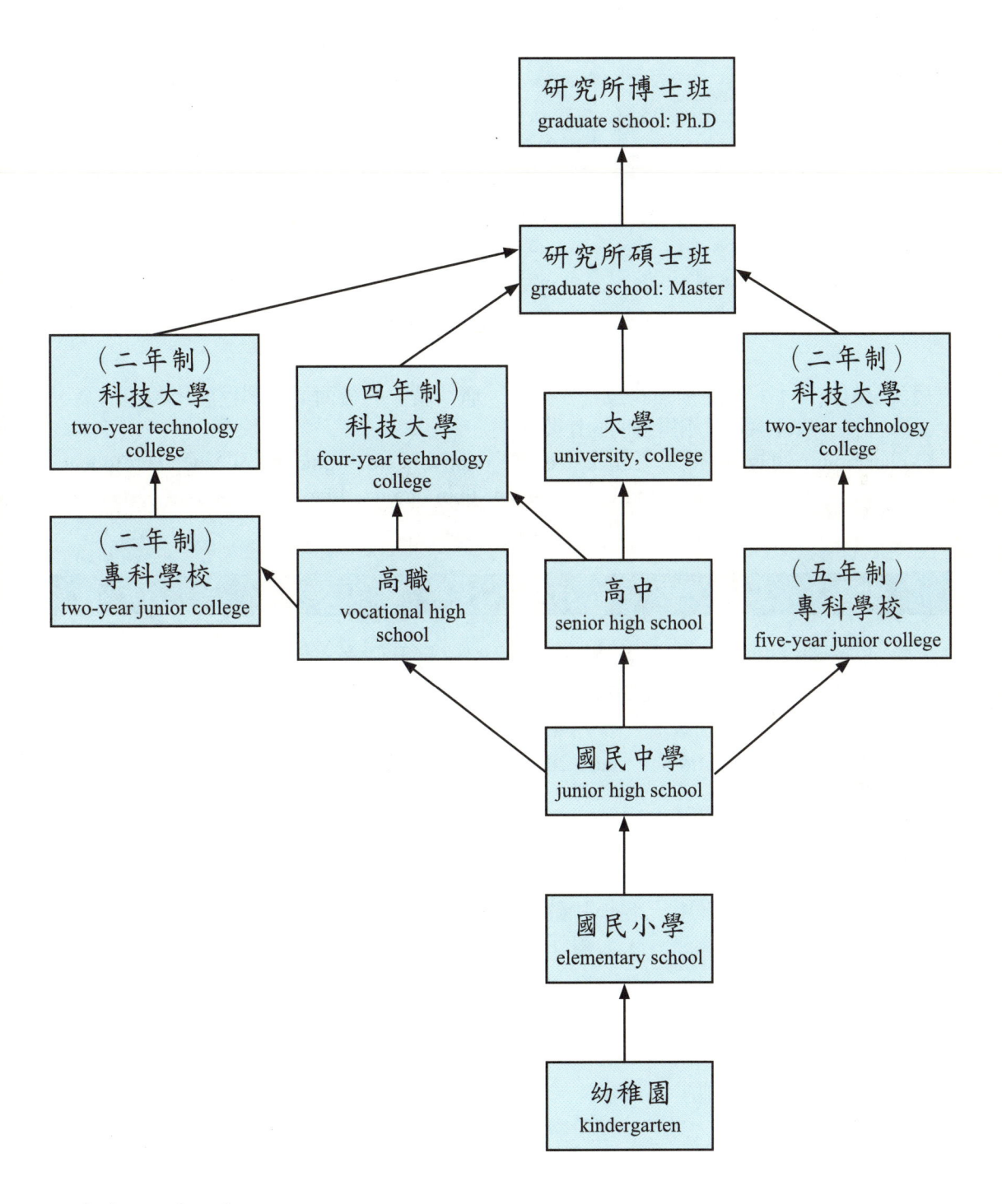

```
                    研究所博士班
                    graduate school: Ph.D
                           ↑
                    研究所碩士班
                    graduate school: Master
        ↗         ↑         ↑         ↖
(二年制)      (四年制)              (二年制)
科技大學      科技大學      大學      科技大學
two-year      four-year    university,  two-year
technology    technology    college    technology
college       college                   college
   ↑             ↑      ↑      ↑          ↑
(二年制)         高職    高中         (五年制)
專科學校       vocational senior        專科學校
two-year       high      high          five-year
junior college school   school       junior college
                   ↑      ↑              ↑
                   國民中學
                   junior high school
                         ↑
                    國民小學
                    elementary school
                         ↑
                      幼稚園
                    kindergarten
```

■ 臺灣的教育制度

## 文法練習

> 一　才 (V) NU M (N)，就……
> only V NU M (N) and ......
>
> ◎才一個小考就讓你有這麼大的壓力。
> Only one small test and you're so stressed-out.

用法說明：「才」在這裡強調數量「少」，而「就」的後面則強調程度比期望的高。前後兩句做相對鮮明的比照。

Explanation: In this usage, 才 emphasizes the relatively small quantity of N which produces a result（preceded by 就）grater than one would expect. The two parts of the sentence express a clear contrast.

### ▼ 練習　請用「才 (V) NU M (N)，就……」完成下面對話。

1. 張：昨天晚上她做了二十道菜，可是我們只有五個客人。
   Chang: Last night she made 20 dishes, but we only had 5 guests.
   李：才五個客人，就做了二十道菜！怎麼吃得完？
   Li: Only five guests and she made 20 dishes?! How could you eat it all?

2. 張：我吃飽了，不吃了。
   李：你才＿＿＿＿＿＿＿，你平常吃兩碗的啊？

3. 張：這兩個句子我是用三個小時翻完的。
   李：才＿＿＿＿＿＿＿，太慢了吧！

4. 張：今天是我第一次上中文課，我學了三十個中國字。
   李：才＿＿＿＿＿＿＿不錯嘛！

5. 張：我買了一個鳳梨，四塊半。
   李：才＿＿＿＿＿＿＿，好貴啊

## 二 才 (used to refute or top the previous speaker's statement)

◎這才是壓力。

Now, this is what you call pressure.

**用法說明**：這個「才」是用來反駁別人的意見。

Explanation: In this usage, 才 indicates that the speaker is refuting or topping the previous speaker's statement.

### 練習　請用「才」完成下面對話。

1. 張：今天的地震好大啊！
   Chang: The earthquake today was really big!
   李：今天的不算什麼，上次的才大呢！
   Li: Today's was nothing, but last time's, that was really big!

2. 張：請隨便坐！對不起，我的房間很亂。
   李：哪裡，__我才來一下__。

3. 張：我記得你很喜歡背書，不喜歡寫報告。
   李：我才 __沒有__ ，你弄錯了。

4. 張：不要叫我請客，我沒錢。
   李：__你才說什麼__ ，大家都知道你有很多房子。

5. 張：你這麼晚回家，不怕你爸爸生氣嗎？
   李：我才 __沒有，我爸爸比我晚__ ，他自己也很晚回家。

## 三　幸虧 / 幸好 / 還好 / 好在……，要不然……
### Fortunately ......., otherwise ......

◎ 幸虧我們家移民了，要不然我一定念不了大學。
Fortunately, our family immigrated; otherwise, I definitely wouldn't be able to go to college.

用法說明：表示慶幸，「幸虧」的後面是已成的事實，如果這個事實沒發生的話，「要不然」後面的情形就會發生。

Explanation: This pattern indicates that the speaker is happy that the fact stated after 幸虧 has occurred or is true. If this were not the case, the undesirable situation following 要不然 would have occurred.

### 練習　請用「幸虧……，要不然……」改寫下面句子。

1. 要是他坐了那班飛機，他也死了。
   If he had been on that flight, he would have died too.
   → 幸虧他沒坐那班飛機，要不然也死了。
   Fortunately, he didn't take that flight; otherwise, he would have died too.

2. 要是你上次考試不及格，今天就得補考了。

3. 要是昨天下雨，我們搬家就有問題了。

4. 要是丟了的那個東西很值錢，我媽一定很著急。

5. 我喝了這麼多汽水，要是附近沒有洗手間，就麻煩了。

第七課　念大學容易嗎

## 四　會……的　will, should

◎他會慢慢適應的。
He will be able to slowly adjust.

**用法說明：**「會」在這裡表示「將來很可能」。「的」表示肯定，語氣較婉轉。
Explanation: Here, 會 indicates that the future situation indicated is likely, and 的 indicates that it is definite, so the tone, while definite, is relatively mild and tactful.

**練習**　請用「會……的」完成下面對話。

1. 張：你哥哥明天一定來嗎？
   Chang: Is you older brother definitely coming tomorrow?
   李：你放心，他一定會來的。
   Li: Don't worry, he should definitely come.

2. 張：這件事情不告訴爸爸，行不行？
   李：不行，如果你不告訴他，他會 ~~生氣~~ 。

3. 張：我妹妹的男朋友離開她了，她不吃也不喝，怎麼辦？
   李：別擔心，她會 ~~好的~~ 。

4. 張：你出國以後，大概就不容易再見到你了。
   李：沒關係，我會 ~~再見你~~ 。

5. 張：怎麼辦？我的病恐怕好不了了。
   李：你想得太多了，只要你聽醫生的話，不會 ~~有好的~~ 。

## 五

### (I) 滿 NU-M-(N)　to reach or fully attain NU M (N)

◎……，可是男孩子滿了十八歲就得先去當兵了。
……, but when boys reach 18 years of age, they first have to serve in the army.

197

實用視聽華語 3
Practical Audio-Visual Chinese

用法說明：「滿 NU-M-(N)」表示已達到某種「實足」的程度。

Explanation: This pattern expresses a state of having reached or fully attained a specified quantity.

▼ 練習　　請用「滿 NU-M-(N)」完成下面對話。

1. 張：你今年二十歲了吧？
   Chang: You're 20 years old this year, aren't you?
   李：我的生日是下個月三號，還差一個多星期才滿二十歲。
   Li: My birthday is the 3rd of next month, so I still have a little over a week until I'm twenty.

2. 張：你說這家商店送香水 (perfume)，他們怎麼沒送我？
   李：買東西滿 _五十元_ ，才送一瓶香水。

3. 張：選這門課的人才三個，學校還讓王教授教嗎？
   李：如果不滿 _三個人_ ，恐怕就有問題。

4. 張：你怎麼有這麼多的時間去旅行？不必上班嗎？
   李：我到公司已經滿了 _十天_ ，可以有兩個星期的假。

5. 張：我常坐你們公司的飛機，我買票可以便宜一點吧？
   李：對不起！還沒滿 _十二次_ ，沒辦法便宜。

## (II) V 滿　something is filled by the action

用法說明：「滿」在此為結果動詞語尾，Actual Type 跟 Potential Type 都可以。

Explanation: This 滿 is a RE (resultative verb ending). The RC can be used in either Actual Type form of Potential Type form.

▼ 練習　　請填上合適的「V 滿」結果動詞形式。

1. 先把這個箱子裝滿，再裝另外一個。
   First, fill this suitcase then the other one.

2. 那家旅館還 _沒滿人_ ，還有空房間。

3. 對林教授的課有興趣的人不多，教室總是 _坐不滿_ 。

4. 老師要我們寫五頁的報告，我查的資料才這麼一點，怎麼 ___滿了___？
5. 他房間的牆上 ___寫滿了___ 他自己的畫。

## 六 只好
### to have no alternative but to ......, can only, cannot but

◎這些人只好等當完兵再考大學嘍？
Then these people have to first do military service before taking he exam for college?

用法說明：「只好」表示「只能這麼做」，所以「只好」的後面是此刻唯一能行的辦法。語氣有稍許無奈。

Explanation: 只好 indicates that something is the only alternative. This alternative always follows 只好. The tone implies that this final alternative is not necessarily ideal either.

**練習** 請用「只好」完成下面句子。

1. 我買不到機票，只好坐火車。
   I couldn't get an airplane ticket, so I had no choice but take the train.
2. 明天的期末考，我還沒準備好，只好 ___準備___。
3. 我們不出產小麥，只好 ___吃麥___。
4. 小李的成績太爛了，只好 ___準備___。
5. 我不願意離開家，可是鄉下沒有什麼工作機會，我只好 ___出產小麥___。

## 七　不管／不論／無論……都……

regardless of whether ....... (all), no matter whether ....... (all)

◎以前臺灣的大學，不管公立的私立的，學費都沒有你們這裡這麼高。

Universities in Taiwan, (regardless of) whether they are public or private, all have lower tuition than those in America.

用法說明：「不管」的後面可加疑問詞 (QW)、選擇式 (A/not A) 或兩個相對的詞，表示不同的情況。雖然有不同的情況，「都」後面的事實都不受影響。

Explanation: You can place a Question Word, a Choice Type structure (A/not A), or two opposites after 不管 to indicate possible situations. This pattern indicates that even if this situation (or situations) occurs, it will not influence the fact expressed after 都.

### 練習　請用「不管……都……」完成下面對話。

1. 張：如果明天下雨，你還去不去？
   Chang: If it rains tomorrow, will you still go?
   李：不管天氣怎麼樣，我都要去。
   Li：I'll be going no matter what the weather is like.
   　　不管天氣好不好，我都要去。
   　　I'll be going whether it rains or not.
   　　不管天氣好壞，我都要去。
   　　I'll be going whether the weather is good or bad.

2. 張：我看你別去了，那個地方太遠了。
   李：不管＿＿＿＿＿＿＿＿＿＿＿＿＿＿＿＿＿。

3. 張：你喜歡吃法國菜，還是義大利菜？
   李：不論＿＿＿＿＿＿＿＿＿＿＿＿＿＿＿＿＿。

4. 張：我想請你來我家玩，你下星期，哪天有空？
   李：不論＿＿＿＿＿＿＿＿＿＿＿＿＿＿＿＿＿。

5. 張：參觀這個博物館，每個人都得買票嗎？
   李：無論 _去都要買_ 。

## 八　V得差不多了　almost finished (via V)

◎寫得差不多了。
I'm almost finished writing it.

用法說明：「V 得差不多了」表示某件事情在進行中，而且快要達到預期中的目標。
Explanation: This pattern indicates that some action is in progress and that the desired goal will soon be reached or attained.

**練習**　請用「V 得差不多了」回答下面問題。

1. 明天的考試，你準備好了沒有？
   Have you finished preparing for tomorrow's test?
   → 準備得差不多了。
   I'm pretty much done.

2. 王先生要買你們公司的電腦，這件事談得怎麼樣了？
   _談得差不多了_

3. 野餐要吃的東西都買了嗎？
   _都買了得差不多了_

4. 你衣服洗好了沒有？我們該走了！
   _都洗的得差不多了_

5. 客人都來了嗎？可以開始了吧？
   _來了得差不多了_

## 九　不是……，就是……

If not A......, then must be B......

◎我不是留在這裡做研究，就是回臺灣工作。
I either stay here to do research work or go back to Taiwan to work.

201

實用視聽華語 3
Practical Audio-Visual Chinese

用法說明：「不是」後面的情況跟「就是」後面的情況，兩者當中一定有一種成立。
Explanation: This pattern indicates that of the two situations mentioned after 不是 and 就是, one of them is certain to occur or is certain to be true.

### 練習　請根據提示用「不是……就是……」回答下面問題。

1. 老張到哪裡去了？（辦公室、女朋友家）
   Where did old Chang go?
   → 他不是在辦公室，就是在女朋友家。
   　He's either at the office or at his girlfriend's house.

2. 你在這家餐廳吃飯都吃什麼？（宮保雞丁、青豆蝦仁）
   _____

3. 這裡冬天的天氣怎麼樣？（颱風、下雨）
   _____

4. 你這兩天在忙什麼？（查資料、寫報告）
   _____

5. 這是誰的書？（哥哥的、姐姐的）
   _____

## 課室活動　Classroom Activities

### 一、角色扮演 (Role Playing)

1. Three students. One student acts as a teacher, the second acts as a student who got the highest score on a recent test, and the third as a classmate who accuses the other student of having cheated on his test. The actors should try to express the lively discussion one might expect in such a situation. Some useful supplementary words include: 作弊 (zuò//bì; to cheat on an exam, in a contest, or in gambling), 懶 (lǎn; to be lazy), 偷看 (tōukàn; to peek), 答案 (dá'àn; answer), 侮辱

(wǔrù; to insult; humiliate), 忌妒 or 嫉妒 (jìdù or jídù; to be jealous of).

2. Two students: One acts as a parent who is visiting the U.S. from Taiwan. The other acts as his/her friend who has been living in the States for a long time. The parent wants his/her child to study in the States and is asking about the education system. The parent should ask questions such as: 怎麼選學校？怎麼申請？大概的教育制度 (zhìdù; system) 怎麼樣？ Some useful supplementary words include: 以上 (yǐshàng; more than; over; above), 學區 (xuéqū; school district), 設備 (shèbèi; facilities; equipment).

## 二、討論問題 (Discussion)

1. 在你們國家，學位越高越容易找工作嗎？為什麼？
2. 在貴國，學生念書的壓力大不大？最嚴重的情形怎麼樣？
3. 貴國的教育制度 (zhìdù; system) 跟臺灣有什麼不同？你覺得你們的制度有什麼問題？有沒有辦法改變？
4. 你覺得女孩子也應該當兵嗎？為什麼？

## 短文　　　　　　　　大學生在想什麼

　　九〇年代後期，台灣社會開始有了一些新名詞，像「新新人類」、「草莓族」什麼的。這些新詞的意思是年輕一代有自己的想法，跟他們的父母、老師不太一樣。

　　「新新人類」為什麼新呢？因為他們的做法、想法都跟以前的人不同。比方說，不管別人覺得客氣不客氣，「新新人類」都會把自己的想法說出來。而且他們覺得「只要我喜歡，有什麼不可以」，所以想做什麼，就做什麼。

　　「草莓族」說的是在大學或研究所念了很多書，可是吃不了苦的年輕人。聽說他們找工作要「錢多、事少、離家近」；上班的時候希望「位高、權重、責任輕」。這樣的想法讓他們的父母、老師怎麼想都很難了解。不過也有想法比較新的老闆覺得「草莓族」怕苦，就會想辦法很快地把事情做完，比較有效率。

　　從前人覺得每個人都應該好好地工作，可是現在有些年輕人覺得為什麼非那麼辛苦地工作不可？！只要能得到自己想要的東西，用什麼方法都沒有關係。每個人都可以有自己的想法，哪一種想法才對社會有幫助呢？

## Vocabulary:

1. 新新人類 (sīnsīnrénlèi) (xīnxīnrénlèi): Generation X
2. 草莓族 (cǎoméizú): this class of people are like strawberries, good-looking but cannot endure any pressure/stress
3. 位高、權重、責任輕 (wèigāo、cyuánjhòng、zérèn cīng) (wèigāo、quánzhòng、zérèn qīng): high status, lots of power and few responsibilities
4. 效率 (siàolyǜ)(xiàolǜ): efficiency

## 大學生在想什麼

　　九〇年代後期，台灣社會開始有了一些新名詞，像「新新人類₁」、「草莓族₂」什麼的。這些新詞的意思是年輕一代有自己的想法，跟他們的父母、老師不太一樣。

　　「新新人類」為什麼新呢？因為他們的做法、想法都跟以前的人不同。比方說，不管別人覺得客氣不客氣，「新新人類」都會把自己的想法說出來。而且他們覺得「只要我喜歡，有什麼不可以」，所以想做什麼，就做什麼。

　　「草莓族」說的是在大學或研究所念了很多書，可是吃不了苦的年輕人。聽說他們找工作要「錢多、事少、離家近」；上班的時候希望「位高、權重、責任輕₃」。這樣的想法讓他們的父母、老師怎麼想都很難了解。不過，也有想法比較新的老闆覺得「草莓族」怕苦，就會想辦法很快地把事情做完，比較有效率₄。

　　從前人覺得每個人都應該好好地工作，可是現在有些年輕人覺得為什麼非那麼辛苦地工作不可？！只要能得到自己想要的東西，用什麼方法都沒有關係。每個人都可以有自己的想法，哪一種想法才對社會有幫助呢？

# 第八課 你也打工嗎

■ 在便利商店打工的高中生（劉秀芝提供）

（學校湖邊）

偉立：天晴了，真好。（拿出口香糖）要不要？

美真：好啊。（拿了一片）前幾天一直下雨，又濕又冷。

台麗：今天**不冷不熱**，風也不大，這種天氣很舒服，出來野餐最好了。

建國（拿出可樂）：來，一個人一罐，我請客，別客氣。

美真：你今天**可**真大方[1]！

偉立：那是因為他昨天剛拿到第一次打工賺的錢。

台麗：哦？！那是該好好兒地慶祝**一下**。

美真：才請我們喝一罐可樂，太小氣了吧？該請吃大餐**才**對。

建國：你忍心把我辛苦賺來的錢一次就吃**光**啊？

偉立：他是很辛苦，每次都很晚才回來，累得一躺下就睡著了。早上不但聽不見鬧鐘的聲音，我叫他也叫不醒。

美真：你**到底**打什麼工啊？**怎麼這麼**累？

建國：我在一家小酒館[2]做服務生，越晚客人越多。

台麗：你為什麼不找個輕鬆一點的工作？

建國：我什麼經驗都沒有，而且酒館的小費也多，我想存點錢去旅行。這裡還有麵包、蘋果，誰要吃，自己來。

美真：（拿起一個麵包）你一個星期去幾次？

建國：星期三、星期六，晚上八點到十二點。有時候還要替別人代班。

台麗：（拿了一個蘋果）老闆怎麼樣？

建國：（又開了一罐可樂）大家都說他是小氣鬼。每個鐘頭只

給我們兩塊錢。有一次我不小心打破了一個杯子，他不但扣我錢，還罵我笨手笨腳。

偉立：那是常有的事情，老闆總是這樣的。我第一次在餐廳打工的時候送錯了菜，老闆把我罵了一頓，就叫我走路[3]了。

美真：你現在在哪裡打工？

偉立：我每星期在圖書館打六個小時的工。

美真：做些什麼？

偉立：有人來借書、還書的時候，我登記一下。

台麗：那很輕鬆嘛！

偉立：也不一定，得看什麼時候。要是沒人來的話，我可以看點書，這是最大的好處。

建國：下一次我也要去申請在圖書館工讀，有錢賺，可以看書，還可以欣賞漂亮的女生[4]。

偉立：你們兩個呢？也打工嗎？

美真：我上個週末才去替一個臺灣人看孩子[5]。我從來沒有帶小孩的經驗，孩子一哭，我就手忙腳亂，不知道怎麼辦才好了。

台麗：我剛來，想先適應一下環境，而且我這學期有獎學金，所以沒有打工。不過，在臺灣我一直當家教[6]。

偉立：（拿起一個蘋果）你教什麼？

台麗：我到一些中學生家去教他們英文。有些父母很客氣，每次去都有點心吃；有些學生不用功，教起來很累，

這個錢也不好賺。

美眞：現在臺灣學生打工的情形很普遍，送報啊，做店員啊，到公司做小妹[7]啊，到速食店去當服務生啊，還有人去擺地攤，做什麼的都有。

偉立：真的嗎？我以爲華人父母都只要孩子念書，不讓他們打工。

美眞：那是從前，臺灣社會改變了。現在很多人覺得打工是一種很好的經驗，不但可以學到課本裡沒有的東西，還可以賺零用錢。

建國：哎喲！我不能忍了，喝太多了，我得去上廁所[8]了。

■在工廠打工的高中生（劉秀芝提供）

第八課　你也打工嗎

## 生詞及例句

**1 湖 (hú)**　N：lake

臺灣最大的湖叫日月潭 (Rìyuè Tán, Sun Moon Lake)，有山有水，風景真美。

**2 口香糖 (kǒusiāngtáng) (kǒuxiāngtáng)**

N：chewing gum （M：片／包）

**3 一直 (yìjhíh) (yìzhí)**　A：always, all along, continually

我室友回國以後一直沒給我寫信，不知道他現在怎麼樣了？

**4 可樂 (kělè)**　N：cola (the beverage) （M：罐／瓶）

我喜歡喝汽水，不喜歡喝可樂，因為可樂喝起來味道像藥一樣。

**5 請客 (cǐng//kè)(qǐng//kè)**

VO：to host, to invite, to treat someone (to dinner, etc.)

小林說他要請客，不知道他要請我吃飯，還是看電影。

**6 大方 (dàfāng)**　SV：to be generous; natural and poised

(1) 你男朋友真大方，送你這麼貴的禮物。
(2) 你表妹又漂亮又大方，難怪這麼多人喜歡她。

**7 賺 (jhuàn) (zhuàn)**　V：to earn; to make a profit

我表姐念大學的學費都是自己打工賺來的。

**8 小氣 (siǎocì) (xiǎoqì)**　SV：stingy, mean

那個服務生幫你拿了兩件行李，你只給一塊錢，太小氣了吧？

211

小氣鬼 (siǎociguěi) (xiǎoqìguǐ)　N：cheapskate, tightwad, miser

王先生從來不請客，大家都說他是小氣鬼。

鬼 (guěi) (guǐ)　N：ghost; spirit; demon; devil

雖然我妹妹聽了鬼故事以後，都怕得不敢自己一個人上洗手間，但是她還是愛聽。

酒鬼 (jiǒuguěi) (jiǔguǐ)　N：heavy drinker, drunkard

老王是個酒鬼，一喝多了就打孩子。

9 忍心 (rěnsīn) (rěnxīn)

V：to be hardhearted enough to, to have the heart to, to bear to

小張沒考上大學，可是他正在生病，你忍心告訴他這個壞消息嗎？

忍 (rěn)　V：to put up with, tolerate, bear, endure

我忍了很久，最後還是跟小張說了。

忍住 (rěn//jhù) (rěn//zhù)

RC：to control oneself, to keep oneself from doing something

方先生聽說他母親死了，忍不住哭了起來。

10 光 (guāng)　RE：used up, exhausted

剛開學，要買的東西太多，我帶來的錢很快就用光了。

11 鬧鐘 (nàojhōng) (nàozhōng)　N：alarm clock

昨天晚上我忘了定鬧鐘，今天就起晚了。

鬧 (nào)　V：to create a disturbance, to agitate, to trouble, to disturb

(1) 孩子一生病，就鬧得全家都睡不好。
(2) 小美的男朋友跟別的女孩約會。她氣得去男朋友家鬧，把東西都打壞了。我跟她說：「這樣不好，還是跟男朋友談談吧。」
(3) 這個房子聽說鬧鬼 (be haunted)，所以沒人敢住。

## 12 叫醒 (jiào//sǐng) (jiào//xǐng)　RC：to wake someone up

已經七點半了，弟弟還在睡，你為什麼還不叫醒他？

### 醒 (sǐng) (xǐng)　V：to be awake

媽媽一叫我，我就醒了，可是還躺在床上不想起來。

## 13 到底 (dàodǐ)

A：in the end, at last, finally; to completion, to the end, in the final analysis (used in an interrogative sentence to indicate an attempt to get to the bottom of the matter)

你昨天說要去，今天又說不要去，你到底要不要去？

## 14 經驗 (jīngyàn)　N：experience

這種工作，我沒做過，一點經驗也沒有，可是我一定會好好地學。

### 有經驗 (yǒu jīngyàn)　SV：to be experienced

我們需要一位有經驗的醫生，你剛畢業，不行。

### 對…有經驗
[duèi…(X)… yǒu jīngyàn] [duì…(X)…yǒu jīngyàn]

PT：has experience in... (X)

我表姐是小學老師，對教小孩子很有經驗。

## 15 小費 (siǎofèi) (xiǎofèi)　N：a tip, pourboire

要是餐廳的服務很好，我就多給一點小費。

實用視聽華語 **3**
Practical Audio-Visual Chinese

**16 存錢 (cún//cián) (cún//qián)**　VO：to deposit money, to save up

(1) 我哥哥說他要存錢買一個照像機。
(2) 我爸爸給我的錢,我還用不著,先存在銀行裡吧!

**存 (cún)**　V：to deposit, to keep

我打工賺的錢還沒用,都存起來了。

**17 代班 (dài//bān)**　VO：to fill in for someone's shift at work

張大年病了,不能去打工,今天晚上我得代他的班。

**代課 (dài//kè)**　VO：to substitute teach

林教授明天不能來,誰願意代他那門心理學的課呢?

**18 老闆 (lǎobǎn)**　N：the boss, the owner of a shop or business

**19 罵 (mà)**　V：to scold（M：頓）

王美英今天被老師罵了,因為又忘了做功課。

**20 笨手笨腳 (bèn shǒu bèn jiǎo)**　IE：to be clumsy

我真是笨手笨腳,這個月已經打破了七個盤子了。

**笨 (bèn)**　SV：to be stupid

**腳 (jiǎo)**　N：foot

腳太大或太小都不容易買到鞋。

**21 頓 (dùn)**　M：(used for meals, scoldings)

我生日那天,朋友們請我吃了一頓大餐。

**22 叫/請…走路 (jiào/cǐng …zǒulù) (jiào/qǐng… zǒulù)**

PT：to fire someone, to dismiss someone from a job

第八課　你也打工嗎

小陳三天沒來上班了，是不是老闆請他走路了？

**23 還 (huán)**　V：to repay, give back, return

俗話 (súhuà, a common saying) 說：「有借有還，再借不難」，你上次借的錢還沒還，我怎麼可能再借你？

**24 登記 (dēngjì)**　V：to register, to enter one's name, to sign up

住旅館的時候要先在櫃台 (counter) 登記名字、身份證 (shēnfènzhèng, ID card) 號碼。

**25 一下 (yísià) (yíxià)**　Nu-M：a little, a while

(1) 你要不要進來坐一下？
(2) 你頭髮的樣子改變一下，也許會好看一點。

**下 (sià) (xià)**　M：(for downward actions of the hand)

人的心，平常一分鐘跳多少下？

**26 好處 (hǎochù)**　N：advantage, benefit

在臺灣學中文的好處是可以天天練習。

**壞處 (huàichù)**　N：disadvantage, harm

你知道喝酒的壞處很多，你怎麼還喝那麼多？

**27 工讀 (gōngdú)**

V：work-study, work arranged for students by the school

念大學的時候，我在圖書館工讀了兩年。

**工讀生 (gōngdúshēng)**　N：students who do work-study

在速食店、加油站服務的人，很多都是工讀生。

215

讀 (dú)　V：to read; to go to/attend school or college

(1) 「還」這個字可以讀「hái」，也可以讀「huán」，對不對？
(2) 小王考上了兩個研究所，還沒決定要讀哪一個。

讀書 (dú//shū)　VO：to study, to read

(1) 我表哥現在還在大學讀書，還沒畢業。
(2) 我下了課以後，還要再讀兩個小時的書才休息。

### 28 女生 (nyǔshēng) (nǚshēng)　N：school age girl, female student

男生 (nánshēng)　N：school age boy, male student

臺灣的學生宿舍，男生、女生是分開的。

### 29 週末 (jhōumò) (zhōumò)　N：weekend

有人覺得禮拜五晚上，週末就開始了。

### 30 看 (kān)　V：to look after, to take care of, to watch for

錢先生跟他太太要去旅行，請我去替他們看房子。

看家 (kān//jiā)　VO：to mind the house

留這隻狗看家，我很放心，牠 (tā, it) 叫得很大聲，小偷一定不敢來。

### 31 帶 (dài)　V：to take care of (a child), to bring up the young

我沒想到把孩子帶大這麼不容易，不但要照顧他吃、穿，還要教育他。

### 32 手忙腳亂 (shǒu máng jiǎo luàn)

IE：to be in a great flurry, to be in a frantic rush

那幾個男生在廚房裡手忙腳亂地給我們做飯。

## 亂 (luàn)

SV/A/RE：to be messy, disordered, confused/disorderly, groundlessly/disordered, untidy, rumpled

(1) 小弟，你的房間真亂：桌上、地上、床上都有書。你怎麼知道我借你的那本書在哪裡？
(2) 你說我拿了你的書，我沒有！你沒看見我拿，你怎麼可以亂說？
(3) 我桌上的資料是要交給老師的，你別弄亂了。

### 33 家教 (jiājiào)　N：a private tutor

李文德的成績不好，所以他媽媽給他請了個家教，到家裡來給他補習。

### 34 普遍 (pǔbiàn)　SV：to be widespread, common, universal

學生在考試以前開夜車是很普遍的情形。

## 普通 (pǔtōng)　SV：to be common, mediocre, ordinary

我們只是普通朋友，沒有特別的關係。

### 35 店員 (diànyuán)　N：shop assistant, sales person (in a shop)

你一直在那家鞋店當店員嗎？

### 36 擺地攤 (bǎi//dìtān)

VO：to display goods for sale on a mat out on the street

在臺北擺地攤的都賣些什麼東西？

## 擺 (bǎi)　V：to display, spread out, place

如果把那個書架擺在書桌右邊，用起來比較方便。

## 地攤 (dìtān)　N：a mat on which to display goods for sale outdoors

地攤上的東西雖然便宜，可是不一定好。

37 社會 (shèhuèi) (shèhuì)　N：society

社會學 (shèhuèisyué) (shèhuìxué)　N：sociology

我在大學念社會學系，研究人跟人的關係。

38 改變 (gǎibiàn)　V/N：to change, alter, transform

醫生告訴王太太她有小孩了以後，她開始注意到自己的身體有了變化：慢慢地變「胖」了。另外，她還變得比以前愛吃酸的東西，也比以前容易生氣。她決定有些生活習慣也得改變：她不能再像以前那樣亂跑亂跳，也不能喝酒什麼的。想到自己就要從太太變成媽媽了，要適應這樣的改變，需要一點時間。

39 課本 (kèběn)　N：textbook

你們心理學的課，用什麼課本？

課文 (kèwén)　N：text in a school book

這本會話 (conversation) 書，每一課都分三部分：生字、句型 (jùxíng, sentence pattern) 跟課文。

40 零用錢 (língyòngcián) (língyòngqián)

N：pocket money, money for incidental expenses, allowance

每個月除了房錢，飯錢，我還需要二十塊零用錢看電影、喝飲料。

41 上廁所 (shàng//cèsuǒ)　VO：to go to the toilet, to use the restroom

我不敢喝太多水，就是怕要上廁所，太麻煩！

廁所 (cèsuǒ)　N：toilet, lavatory

這是男廁所，你不要走錯了。

## 注釋

1. "你今天可真大方！" means: "You are really generous today!". "太小氣了吧？！" means: "Aren't you stingy!". This kind of joking can be used among good friends, however, in other situations it is considered to be very rude.

2. 小酒館 refers to a "pub". These are getting more popular in Taiwan. Many people just call them by their English name—pub.

3. 叫……走路 means "to tell (somebody) to leave". In other words, to fire someone. The slang expression 炒魷魚 (chǎo//yóuyú) was derived from Cantonese and has the same meaning, and it is used as follows: 他被老闆炒魷魚了 (He was fired by the boss.), 老闆想炒我魷魚 (The boss wants to fire me.) This expression literally means "to stir-fry squids". It came to represent getting fired because squid curls up when it is fried, and there is an expression for leaving a job 捲鋪蓋 (juǎn//pūgài, to roll up one's bedding). Thus the curling, rolled up fried squid evokes the idea of firing someone from a job. The formal expression for being fired is 解雇 (jiěgù), e.g. 他被老闆解雇了 and 老闆想解雇我.

4. 男生／女生 is short for 男學生／女學生. In Taiwan, these are general terms referring to any young person or anyone who looks young, since most young people are students. Sometimes the young people are called 男孩／女孩, because Chinese consider unmarried young people to still be children (孩子). Most Taiwanese are not used to referring to a person as 男人／女人, because these terms imply a certain air of disapproval. The terms 那個男的／女的 would be used instead.

5. 看孩子, i.e. baby sitting, is not popular in Taiwan. Most Taiwanese parents do not feel comfortable hiring an acquaintance or a stranger to care for their children. They either leave the children with their parents, take the children out with them, or choose not to go out.

6. 家教 is short for 家庭教師. It refers to a private tutor or teacher. People hire 家庭教師 to help their child with his/her studies, especially if the child's scholastic record indicates that he/she may not be able to pass the 聯考. 家教 usually go to the child's house once or twice a week for two or three hours each time.

7. 在公司做小妹 means "to work at a company as an office helper". 小妹 literally means "little sister". In Taiwan, some companies hire girls who attend school in the evening as daytime office helpers. Office helpers perform simple tasks such as delivering documents, answering phone calls, receiving visitors, etc. Boys who do this job are called 小弟, however, they are far less common.

8. 上廁所 means "to go to the toilet". It is more polite to say 去／用洗手間, meaning "to use the washroom". Many students use the slang expression 上一號. Another more subtle expression is 去方便一下.

實用視聽華語 3
Practical Audio-Visual Chinese

## 文法練習

### 一　不SV1不SV2
### neither SV1 nor SV2 (somewhere in between)

◎今天不冷不熱……
　Today is neither hot nor cold ……

**用法說明**：兩個 SV 都是單音節，意思相對。「不SV1不SV2」表示介於兩者之間的程度。

Explanation: This pattern is used with two single-syllable stative verbs with opposite meanings. "不 SV1 不 SV2" indicates that the actual situation is somewhere between the two stated extremes.

**練習**　請用「不 SV1 不 SV2」改寫下面各句。

1. 這條褲子不太長也不太短，你穿正合適。
   This pair of pants is neither too long nor too short; it fits you perfectly.
   → 這條褲子不長不短，你穿正合適。
   　This pair of pants is just right in length; it fits you perfectly.

2. 我準備的菜不太多也不太少，剛夠四個人吃。
   _____

3. 十五、六歲的小孩，不算大也不算小，問題比較多。
   _____

4. 那個桌子不太高也不太矮，正合我的需要。
   _____

5. 這件衣服穿了幾年，不新了，可是也不舊，丟了可惜，留著也不想穿，真麻煩。
   _____

220

第八課　你也打工嗎

## 二　可 (used to emphasize the tone of the speaker)

◎你今天可真大方！
You really are generous today!

用法說明：多用於口語，放在副詞、動詞、助動詞、SV……等前面，表示強調語氣。可以表示a. 不以為然，b. 強調程度，一般有感嘆的意味。句末常有語氣助詞，如啊、呢、了、啦等。SV之前可以有真、太等副詞。c. 必須如此，有勸導或期盼的語氣。d. 事情好不容易完了。

Explanation: This is used more often in informal speech. It is placed in front of an Adverb, a V, a SV, etc, to express a stronger tone. It is used to indicate a. disagreement with the previous speaker, b. to emphasize degree, usually indicating a tone of exclamation. Modal particles like 啊、呢、了、啦 are often used at the end of the sentence, however, if 可 is used with a SV, the adverbs 真 or 太 are often placed before the SV. c. the thing must be done in this way, with a tone of advice or expectation, or d. to show that that matter is very difficult to resolve.

### 練習

（一）請把「可」放在句中合適的地方。

例：我等了那麼久，你來了。
I've waited so long. you've arrived.
→ 我等了那麼久，你可來了。
I've waited so long; you're finally here.

a. 1. 我不像你這麼有錢，想買什麼就買什麼。

2. 老張不是小孩子，你以為他會聽你的嗎？

3. 誰說王大年什麼都不懂，他知道的事情多呢！

b. 1. 李小姐真愛看電影，她每天都要看一場。

2. 這太奇怪了，我昨天放在這裡的東西怎麼不見了？

221

3. 移民是一件大事啊！要好好地計畫，不能隨便。
_____

c. 1. 這個藥每四個鐘頭吃一次，你別忘了。
_____

2. 這次的考試很重要，考不好就不能畢業，我們得好好地準備。
_____

3. 李愛美不能不來，小王今天請客都是為了她。
_____

d. 1. 這一個月的衣服，我洗完了。
_____

2. 這麼多的課，我都上完了。星期天要好好地休息休息了。
_____

3. 你回來了！這麼晚了，電話也打不通，害我急得吃不下飯。
_____

(二) 請根據提示，用「可」或「那可」完成下面對話。

例：張：怎麼辦？我寫好的報告丟了。（麻煩）
　　Chang: What should I do? I've lost the report that I finished.
　　李：那可麻煩了。
　　Li: What a pain!

a. 1. 張：小王那麼笨手笨腳的，一定不會跳舞。（會跳）
　　　李：你錯了，他可_____

2. 張：在加油站打工，小費一定很多。（不一定）
　　李：那可_____，得看哪一區。

b. 1. 張：你在超級市場打工，一個小時七塊錢，小王呢？（多）
　　　李：他賺的可_____。

2. 張：這個週末我哥哥姐姐的孩子都要到我家來。（熱鬧）
　　李：那可_____。

3. 張：我打破盤子的事，老闆知道了嗎？（不得了）
　　李：怎麼能告訴他？！要是他知道了，那可_____。

4. 張：我有車，可以幫你搬家。（太好了）
   李：那可＿＿＿＿＿＿。

5. 張：我這學期的學費都被偷走了！（怎麼辦）
   李：那可＿＿＿＿＿＿。

c. 1. 孩子：我從今天開始用功，期末考一定要每科都及格。
         （說了就要做到）
      媽媽：＿＿＿＿＿＿。

   2. 張：最近天氣變化很大，感冒的人很多。（要小心）
      李：＿＿＿＿＿＿。

   3. 張：我們要坐九點的火車，你來晚了，就不等你了。
         （得準時）
      李：＿＿＿＿＿＿。

d. 1. 張：老陳的博士論文寫了四年，昨天交出去了。（寫完）
      李：他＿＿＿＿＿＿。

   2. 孩子：唉喲！已經十一點了。怎麼沒有人叫我起床？
      媽媽：＿唉喲＿！我已經叫了你八百次了！

   3. 教授：王大明，學校剛剛決定下學期給你獎學金。（放心）
      學生：這次申請獎學金的人這麼多，我一直擔心申請不到，＿＿＿＿＿＿。

（三）請老師先念一次下面的故事，學生聽完以後，老師再分句或分段再念一次，叫學生用「可」說出自己的看法。「可」的四種用法，每種都應該用到。

李文德大學畢業一年多，一直找不到工作。有一天在路上碰到一個以前的同學。這個同學在補習班教英文，他願意去跟老闆說，讓李文德也到他們的補習班工作。李文德就這樣教起書來了。他很高興不必再跟父母要錢，可以自己賺錢生活了。因為他的教法不錯，很受學生歡迎，課越來越多。每天工作十幾個小時，除了吃飯、睡覺以外，連生病都不休息。錢雖然越賺越多，可是身體越來越壞，後來就病倒了。看醫生，把賺來的錢都用光了還不夠。李文德現在才明白，健康比什麼都重要，以後不敢再這樣：只知道賺錢，不管身體了。

## 三　V一下　V one time, V once, V a bit

◎那是該好好地慶祝一下。
In that case, we should do some proper celebrating.

◎有人來借書、還書的時候，我登記一下。
When people come to borrow and return books, I check them in and out.

◎想先適應一下環境，……
(I) would like to be accustomed here, ....

用法說明：「下」是動量詞 (Mv)。「一下」是「一會兒」的意思。「V一下」表示一次短促的動作。「V一下」使語氣比較婉轉，感覺不那麼嚴肅。

Explanation: 下 serves as a measure word for verbs. 一下 means 一會兒 (for a moment, for a very brief time). V 一下 indicates one short action. However, V 一下, should not always be taken literally. It often serves to simply lighten the tone of a statement or request to make it more polite.

▼ 練習　請用「V 一下」改寫下面句子。

1. 你新買的公寓，我們可不可以參觀參觀？
   Can we take a tour of your new apartment?
   →你新買的公寓，我們可不可以參觀一下？
   　Can we take a quick tour of your new apartment?

2. 這裡風景不錯，我們下車欣賞欣賞吧！
   _____

3. 考完了，我們開個舞會輕鬆輕鬆。
   _____

4. 這兩件衣服，我比較了以後，覺得還是綠的好。
   _____

5. 來、來、來，我給你們介紹。
   _____

## 四 才 (indicator of prerequisite)

◎該請我們吃大餐才對。
It's only fitting that you should treat us to eat a big meal.

◎孩子一哭，我就手忙腳亂，不知道怎麼辦才好了。
As soon as a child cries, I get in a fluster; I don't know what to do (to properly resolve the situation).

**用法說明**：這個「才」跟第三課一樣，也是強調「條件」，但「才」後面常是「好」、「對」、「行」、「可以」等字。

Explanation: Here, 才 is used in the same way as in Chapter 3, indicating the conditions required to achieve a desired state or outcome. However, in this use of 才, the words 好, 對, 行, or 可以 are often placed after it.

### 練習　請用「才對」、「才好」改寫下面句子。

1. 這篇報告很難寫，我不知道應該怎麼開始。
   This report is very difficult to write; I don't know how to start.
   →這篇報告很難寫，我不知道怎麼開始才好。
   This report is very difficult to write; I don't know how to start (in order to get good results).

2. 老林幫了我很多忙，我不知道應該怎麼謝謝他。
   _____

3. 學生考壞了，罵沒有用，應該多鼓勵。
   _____

4. 跟人約會，一定要準時到。
   _____

5. 跟人借錢，當然要還。
   _____

## 五　V光　V up (use up, exhaust), V till it is used up

◎你忍心把我辛苦賺來的錢一次就吃光啊？
You would have the heart to take my hard-earned money and swallow it up in one shot?

用法說明：「光」在此是 RE，是「完」、「盡」、「一點不剩」的意思，使用時均為 Actual Type。可跟「把」一起用。

Explanation: Here, 光 serves as a RE, meaning that some thing is finished, used up, exhausted, or done to the greatest extent possible. It is used in the Actual Type form, and can be used together with 把.

### ▼ 練習

(一) 請用「把」跟「V 光」改寫下面句子。

1. 冰箱裡的啤酒，老闆都喝完了。
   The boss drank all of the beer in the refrigerator.
   →老闆把冰箱裡的啤酒都喝光了。
   　　The boss drank up all of the beer in the refrigerator.

2. 我給弟弟的錢，他都用完了。
   _____

3. 我們助教值錢的東西，小偷都偷走了。
   _____

4. 天氣太熱，這個孩子就把身上的衣服全脫了。
   _____

5. 老師說的話，我全都忘了。
   _____

(二) 請根據提示，用「V 光」完成下面對話。

1. 張：這部電影真難看。（走）
   Chang: This movie is really bad.
   李：難怪看到一半，人都走光了。
   Li: No wonder everybody walked out halfway through the movie.

2. 張：你怎麼不願意跟王大年約會？（死）
   李：他太小氣，全世界的男孩子都_____，我也不要跟他出去。

3. 張：我做的炸雞味道怎麼樣？（搶）
   李：好極了。你看，一拿出來就_____。

4. 張：我要去圖書館借心理學。（借）
   李：別去了，最近大家都要交報告，這一類的書都_____。

5. 張：這家花店的花真好看！（賣）
   李：是啊！好快就_____。

## 六 到底 after all, in the final analysis

◎你到底打什麼工啊？
So what work do you actually do?

用法說明：用於疑問句，表示追究事情的真相，是「究竟」的意思。「到底」可在主語前，也可在主語後。主語是疑問詞時，應在「到底」後面，「到底」句尾不可有「嗎」，但可用「呢」或「嘛」。

Explanation: 到底 is used in questions to indicate an attempt to find out the truth or get to the bottom of a matter. 到底 can be placed either before or after the subject, unless the subject is a QW, in which case 到底 must always come first. If 到底 is used, do not place 嗎 at the end of the sentence. Instead, use the particle 呢 or 嘛.

### 練習

（一）請用「到底」完成下面各句。

1. 你昨天說要去中國大陸，今天說要去歐洲，到底要去哪裡啊？
   Yesterday you said you wanted to go to mainland China, and today you said you want to go to Europe. Where do you really want to go?

2. 老丁說他女朋友很漂亮，可是我們都沒見過，到底_____？

3. 老王說這個字對，小林說那個字對，到底_____？

實用視聽華語 3

4. 張小姐不喜歡運動，也不喜歡看電影、看書，她到底_____？

5. 我幫你，你不高興，我不幫你，你也不高興，你到底_____？

## （二）改錯 Correct the errors.

1. 你到底去不去嗎？

2. 誰到底有這個門的鑰匙？

---

### 七　怎麼這麼……

Why so...? (used in a question or a rhetorical question)

◎怎麼這麼累？
Why are you so tired?

用法說明：「怎麼」的意思是「為什麼」。「怎麼這麼……」可表示疑問或感歎。如果表示感歎，可以不必回答。「這麼」的後面通常加SV，但少數動詞或助動詞(AV)亦可使用。

Explanation: 怎麼 means "why" or "how". "怎麼這麼……", can be used to express a question or make an exclamation through a rhetorical question, depending on the speaker's tone. The word or phrase following "怎麼這麼……" is usually a SV, but certain verbs and auxiliary verbs can be used also.

▼練習　請根據所給情況，用「怎麼這麼……」表示疑問或感歎。

1. 今天的氣溫有三十三度。
   The temperature of today is 33 degrees.
   →怎麼這麼熱？！
   How did it get so hot?!

2. 弟弟這次小考只考了二十五分。
   _____

3. 室友說昨天吃了一天水餃，今天還想吃。
   _____

4. 哥哥說他女朋友叫他做什麼他都願意，要他死也可以。

5. 看見朋友什麼舞都會跳，而且跳得非常好。

## 八、TW才　just or only TW (indicating not long ago)

◎ 我上個週末才去替一個臺灣人看孩子。
Just last weekend I went to baby-sit for a Taiwanese person.

用法說明：「才」放在時間詞(TW)或表示時間的短語後面。強調說話者覺得事情發生在「不久以前」，即使十年、八年前的事亦可。

Explanation: In this usage 才 is placed after a TW or a phrase indicating time. It emphasizes the speaker's feeling that something occurred relatively recently, even if it was eight or ten years ago.

**練習**　請把「才」放在句中合適的地方。

1. 我昨天吃過北京烤鴨，今天不想再吃了。
   I ate Peking Duck yesterday; I don't want to have it again today.
   → 我昨天才吃過北京烤鴨，今天不想再吃了。
   　I just ate Peking Duck yesterday; I don't want to have it again today.

2. 老師上個月告訴你這件事，你怎麼就忘了？

3. 這篇論文是一年以前寫成的，資料還算很新。

4. 王先生十年前畢業，所以還不到四十歲。

5. 你出門以前上過廁所，怎麼現在又要上了？

## 九　……啊，……啊，……啊，……
### (used in lists for pauses)

◎現在臺灣學生打工的情形很普遍，送報啊，做店員啊，到公司做小妹啊，……

In Taiwan today the occurrence of students doing part-time work is very common; they deliver papers…work in stores…work as errand girls in companies……

**用法說明**：在列舉人、地、事、物時，「啊」在每一項後面，表示停頓的語氣。

Explanation: Here, when listing people, places, events, objects, times, etc., 啊 is placed after each item to indicate a pause, often as the speaker thinks of the next item on the list.

### ▼ 練習　　請把「啊」放在句中合適的地方。

1. 媽媽剛剛上街買了一大袋東西，雞蛋、麵包、水果，什麼都有。
   Mom just went out and bought a big bag of things: eggs, bread, fruit, etc.
   →媽媽剛剛上街買了一大袋東西，雞蛋啊、麵包啊、水果啊，什麼都有。
   Mom just went out and bought a big bag of things: eggs, bread, fruit, etc.

2. 這裡的春天風景很好，山、水、花，都特別美。
   _____

3. 昨天野餐去的人很多，張先生、李小姐，都去了。
   _____

4. 弟弟真像爸爸，不管眼睛、鼻子、頭髮的顏色，都像得不得了。
   _____

5. 李教授去過的地方可多了，像紐約、倫敦(Lúndūn, London)、巴黎(Bālí, Paris)，這些大城市他當然都去過。
   _____

| 課室活動 | Classroom Activities |
|---|---|

## 一、角色扮演 (Role playing)

1. Two students: One acts as a manager of a McDonald's fast food restaurant. The other is a student who wants to get a part-time job （打工）there. The manager has advertised for someone to help in the restaurant, so the student has come for an interview. The two should try to develop a spirited discussion of the job requirements, job benefits, and the student's qualifications as an employee so the manager can reach a decision.
可能用到的詞：工錢 (wages), 薪水 (xīnshuǐ; salary), 個性 (gèsing) (gèxìng; personality), 職務 (jhíhwù) (zhíwù; official duties), 職位 (jhíhwèi) (zhíwèi; position in a job).

2. 四個學生，四個人在同一家公司工作：Person A has an MBA and is serious and hard-working. He/she was hired only two weeks ago. Person B, an average employee who also tends to be a bit emotional, has been working here for ten years. Person C, an easy-going guy who studies part-time at college in the evening, has been working here for four years. Person D is the director of the office. A has to finish an assignment today but is unable to concentrate because B and C are chattering and laughing loudly. A asks them to quiet down and tells them to take work a little more seriously. This causes an argument to break out amongst the three. A few minutes

later the director walks in. How does he handle this, and how do the other three respond? Each student should appropriately act out his/her role.

可能用到的詞：企管碩士 (cìguǎn shuòshìh) (qìguǎn shuòshì; Master of Business Administration), 神氣 (shéncì) (shénqì; putting on airs; to be cocky; overweening), 認真 (rènjhēn) (rènzhēn; to be serious, conscientious), 吵架 (chǎo//jià; to quarrel, wangle), 教訓 (jiàosyùn) (jiàoxùn; to lecture somebody for wrongdoing), 主任 (jhǔrèn) (zhǔrèn; director of an office or department).

## 二、討論問題 (Discussion)

1. 高中時打工，你覺得早不早？
2. 學生打工，你聽說過可能碰到什麼不好的事？
3. 如果你需要錢，可是打工以後就沒時間念書了，你怎麼辦？

我念高中的時候就半工半讀了。

我念大學的時候也半工半讀。

我現在上班了，還是半工半讀。

半天工作、半天讀報。

## 第八課　你也打工嗎

| 請依序填入個人基本資料 | ※此頁全為必填欄位 |||
|---|---|---|---|
| ※ 身份證字號 | □□□□□□□□□ 身份證字號 □　護照號碼 □ |||
| ※ 自訂密碼 | □□□□□□ | ※密碼確認 | □□□□□□ |
| ※ 姓　　名 ||||
| ※ 國　　籍 || ※ 血型 | O□　A□　B□　AB□ |
| ※ 性　　別 | 男□　女□ |||
| ※ 出生日期 | □□年 □□月 □□日 |||
| ※ 婚姻狀況 | 單身□　已婚□ |||
| ※ 服役狀況 | 免役□　未役□　待役□　役畢□　屆退伍□<br>退伍日期 □□年 □□月 □□日 |||
| ※ 行動電話 | □□□□□□□□□ | ※聯絡電話 ||
| ※ 電子郵件 ||||
| ※ 聯絡時間 | □□年 □□月 □□日 上午□ 下午□ 晚上□ |||
| ※ 聯絡地址 ||||
| ※ 教育程度 | 博士□　碩士□　學士□　高中□　國中以下□<br>畢業□　肄業□　在學□ |||
| ※ 就讀時間 | □□年 □□月 至 □□年 □□月 |||
| ※ 最高學歷 | 學校名稱 | 科系名稱 | 科系類別 |
| ※ 希望從事工作 ||||
| ※ 希望工作地點 ||||

■ 網路上的履歷表（范慧貞提供）

## 短文　　　　　怎麼填履歷表[1]

十月三十日 星期五 晴

今天到系辦公室交作業，看到助教正在上網填表，她告訴我那是中文履歷表，原來她計畫畢業後回台灣工作。她說，在台灣找工作，除了請別人介紹、自己看報上的廣告，或是大公司去學校找人以外，還可以上人力銀行[2]的網站[3]。不管用什麼方法，都應該填好履歷表寄去，等接到通知再去面談。

我想看看中文的履歷表到底怎麼填，就站在旁邊看。沒想到表上很多字都不認識，助教就翻譯給我聽。原來「國籍[4]」是問你是哪國人。「電子郵件[5]」是問email地址。「聯絡[6]時間」是問什麼時候打電話給你最合適。「教育程度[7]」是問你高中畢業、大學畢業，還是有博士學位。「服役狀況[8]」是問當兵[9]的情形。

助教把這些個人[10]的基本資料都填好了以後，也下載了一張給我，她說我可以自己填一填，也許明年去台灣找工作的時候，就用得著了。

## Vocabulary:

1. 履歷表 (lyǔlìbiǎo) (lǚlìbiǎo) : curriculum vitae
2. 廣告 (guǎnggào): advertisement
3. 人力銀行 (rénlì yínháng): human resource agency
4. 國籍 (guójí): nationality
5. 電子郵件 (diànzǐ yóujiàn): e-mail
6. 聯絡 (liánluò): to get in touch with, to make contact with
7. 程度 (chéngdù): level
8. 服役 (fúyì): to be on active duty; to serve in the army
9. 狀況 (jhuàngkuàng) (zhuàngkuàng): condition
10. 個人 (gèrén): to be personal
11. 基本 (jīběn): to be basic, fundamental

## 怎麼填履歷表[1]

十月三十日　星期五　晴

今天到系辦公室交作業，看到助教正在上網填表，她告訴我那是中文履歷表，原來她計畫畢業後回台灣工作。她說，在台灣找工作，除了請別人介紹、自己看報上的廣告[2]，或是大公司去學校找人以外，還可以上人力銀行[3]的網站。不管用什麼方法，都應該填好履歷表寄去，等接到通知再去面談。

我想看看中文的履歷表到底怎麼填，就站在旁邊看。沒想到表上很多字都不認識，助教就翻譯給我聽。原來「國籍[4]」是問你是哪國人。「電子郵件[5]」是問email地址。「聯絡[6]時間」是問什麼時候打電話給你最合適。「教育程度[7]」是問你高中畢業、大學畢業，還是有博士學位。「服役[8]狀況[9]」是問當兵的情形。

助教把這些個人[10]的基本[11]資料都填好了以後，也下載了一張給我，她說我自己可以填一填，也許明年去台灣找工作的時候，就用得著了。

# 第九課 誰最漂亮

■中華民國小姐選美（行政院新聞局　葉銘源攝）

（林建國的表姐站在宿舍門口）

表姐：怎麼回事？你們怎麼現在才來？我等得急**死了**[1]。

建國：對不起，來晚了。來參加你們學校園遊會的人太多，路上**都**塞車了。

美眞：就是啊！路上都是車，半天**都**動不了。

表姐：哦？真沒想到，我們這裡從來不塞車的。這幾位是……？

建國：噢！我**來**介紹一下，這是我表姐丁小青，他是高偉立，（用手指著說）謝美真，李平。

表姐：大家好！

李平、美眞、偉立：你好！

建國：你們宿舍好難找啊！

表姐：是嗎？怎麼會呢[2]？

建國：你們校園很大。每一棟大樓都離得很遠，而且名字都看不清楚。所以我們就迷路了。

表姐：**早知道**我**就**去車站接你們了。

李平：沒關係。這樣我們正好有機會欣賞一下你們美麗的校園。

偉立：我們先走一走，運動運動，等一下可以多吃一點兒。

建國：你們學校環境真好，還是私立學校有錢。

李平：這些房子不但漂亮，而且每一棟都有自己的特色。

美眞：你們這裡，秋天的樹好美，什麼顏色都有。

表姐：春天的花更美呢！走吧！我們到湖邊去。現在恐怕人

已經很多了。

※　　※　　※　　※　　※　　※

（四人下車）

李平：你們餓嗎？

美眞：餓**倒是**不餓，**可是**可以吃一點東西。

偉立：**既然**不怎麼餓，我們**就**去吃pizza³吧！

李平、美眞、建國：好啊！

※　　※　　※　　※　　※　　※

（四人邊吃邊說）

偉立：今天的園遊會真熱鬧！

美眞：是啊！林建國，你表姐好漂亮！那雙眼睛好像會說話。我好羨慕她那頭又黑又亮的長頭髮。

李平：嗯，你表姐很大方。

建國：很多人都覺得她不但大方，個性也很溫和。追她的人多得不得了。

偉立：我丟飛鏢的時候，旁邊收錢的那個女孩子，你們注意到沒有？

建國：對，對，對，那個女生身材真是好**得沒話說**⁴，尤其是那雙長腿。笑起來也很迷人。難怪那個攤位前面擠了

那麼多人。

美真：你們男生就注意女生的身材。

李平：她笑起來很甜，可惜近看皮膚不夠細。

偉立：你來這裡幾年了，你覺得這裡的女孩跟台灣女孩比起來怎麼樣？

李平：我們都覺得眼睛大，鼻子高，嘴巴小，皮膚細白，才好看[5]。一般說來，西方女孩比較高大，沒有亞洲女孩秀氣。但是西方女孩的活潑、大方，亞洲女孩就**比不上**了。

美真：你去買冰淇淋的時候，我們在熱狗攤位看見一個很帥的男生，像電影明星王德華那麼英俊。

建國：英俊**是**英俊，**可是**我不喜歡他那種態度，自以為比別人有魅力。

偉立：對！我最討厭這種人。我覺得我雖然醜，可是我頭腦好，又溫柔，怎麼沒有人發現呢？大家都只看外表。

建國：**誰叫**你總是不修邊幅？其實你一點也不醜。如果你把鬍子刮乾淨，打扮一下，還可以算帥哥[6]呢！

第九課　誰最漂亮

■園遊會（吳俊銘攝）

實用視聽華語 3
Practical Audio-Visual Chinese

## 生詞及例句

1. 園遊會 (yuányóuhuèi) (yuányóuhuì)　　N：an outdoor fair

2. 塞車 (sāi//chē)　　VO：to be jammed with traffic

   我今天下班的時候，路上塞車，塞了二十分鐘，車子都動不了。

3. 校園 (siàoyuán) (xiàoyuán)　　N：campus, school yard

   放假了，校園裡一個人也沒有。

4. 棟 (dòng)　　M：(used for buildings)

   這棟十二層(céng, floor, story)的公寓，一共住了二十四家人。

5. 迷路 (mí//lù)　　VO：to lose one's way / bearings, to get lost

   李新給我的地址不對，所以我迷路了。

6. 正好 (jhènghǎo) (zhènghǎo)　　A：happen to, chance to, as it happens..

   我去找老謝的時候，他正好要出門。

7. 美麗 (měilì)　　SV：to be beautiful

   這條路開好了以後，大家都可以欣賞到台灣東部美麗的風景了。

8. 特色 (tèsè)　　N：special or distinctive characteristic

   校園大，學生少，是我們學校的一個特色。

9. 樹 (shù)　　N：tree（M：棵 kē）

242

## 第九課　誰最漂亮

### 10 倒是 (dàoshìh) (dào·shì)　A：yet, nevertheless, contrary to expectations

張：走了半天了，你累不累？
李：我累倒是不累，可是很渴。

### 11 既然 (jìrán)　A：since, now that

張：怎麼辦？小趙說如果不吃西餐，他就不去了。
李：既然他非吃西餐不可，我們就聽他的吧。

### 12 羨慕 (siànmù) (xiànmù)　V/SV：to admire, to envy/to be envious

(1) 小高的工作又輕鬆又能賺很多錢，我們都很羨慕他。
(2) 你女朋友真漂亮，大家都羨慕得不得了。

### 13 個性 (gèsìng) (gèxìng)　N：individual character, personality

王大年想做什麼就做什麼，從來不管別人，我最受不了這種個性的人。

### 14 溫和 (wūnhé) (wēnhé)　SV：to be temperate, mild, moderate

小王個性溫和，跟人說話總是客客氣氣的。從來不會為了一點小事，弄得大家心裡不舒服。

### 溫柔 (wūnróu) (wēnróu)　SV：to be gentle and soft

我哥那雙眼睛看人的時候很溫柔，讓人很快就覺得輕鬆了。

### 15 追 (jhuēi) (zhuī)　V：to pursue, chase after

李愛美又聰明又溫柔，如果你想追她，就約她去看電影吧！

### 16 丟飛鏢 (diōu//fēibiāo) (diū//fēibiāo)　VO：to throw darts

李文德才丟了三支飛鏢，就有兩支打中(dǎjhòng) (dǎzhòng, to hit the target)了紅心(bull's-eye)，好厲害啊！

243

丟ㄉㄧㄡ (diōu) (diū)　　V：to throw, cast, fling

王大明把脫下來的髒衣服丟進洗衣機 (washing machine) 裡。

飛ㄈㄟ鏢ㄅㄧㄠ (fēibiāo)　　N：a dart（M：支 zhī）

17 身ㄕㄣ材ㄘㄞˊ (shēncái)　　N：figure, build, physique

陳小姐每天慢跑、游泳，難怪身材這麼好。

18 腿ㄊㄨㄟˇ (tuěi) (tuǐ)　　N：leg（M：條）

一般來說，長得高的人腿都比較長。

19 迷ㄇㄧˊ人ㄖㄣˊ (mírén)　　SV：to be charming, enchanting, spellbinding

張助教的聲音很迷人，讓人忍不住想跟他多聊聊。

迷ㄇㄧˊ (mí)　　V/N：to be fascinated, spellbound or charmed by, to be infatuated with /a (sports, etc.) fan, enthusiast

(1) 我表哥很迷籃球，沒事就去打。
(2) 王英英是一個電影迷，只要有好電影，她一定去看。

20 攤ㄊㄢ位ㄨㄟˋ (tānwèi)　　N：a stall, a booth

在這個市場裡，樓上的攤位都是賣水果的。

攤ㄊㄢ子˙ (tān·zih) (tān·zi)　　N：a stand, a street stall

這兩天學校舉行運動會，老王就在學校門口擺了個攤子賣飲料。

21 擠ㄐㄧˇ (jǐ)　　V/SV：to squeeze, to press, to force in/crowded, crammed, packed

(1) 車上的人太多，我擠不上去。
(2) 市場裡人很多，擠得不得了。

244

## 第九課　誰最漂亮

**22** 皮膚 (pífū)　　N：skin, epidermis

你的皮膚真好，又紅又白，像蘋果一樣。

皮包 (píbāo)　　N：handbag, briefcase

這個皮包的樣子和顏色比較適合年輕人用。

**23** 細 (sì) (xì)　　SV：to be fine, delicate

我的頭髮又細又少，怎麼弄都不好看。

**24** 嘴巴 (zuěi·bā) (zuǐ·bā)　　N：mouth（M：張）

小李嘴巴很甜，你得小心他說的不是真的。

**25** 秀氣 (siòu·ci) (xiù·qi)　　SV：to be delicate, refined, graceful

你弟弟寫的字像女孩兒寫的一樣，好秀氣！

**26** 活潑 (huópō)　　SV：to be lively, vivacious, vigorous

王大文上課討論的時候，話很多，很活潑。

**27** 冰淇淋 (bīng·cílín) (bīng·qílín)　　N：ice cream

冰淇淋的口味很多，我特別喜歡吃香草 (vanilla) 的。

**28** 熱狗 (règǒu)　　N：hot dog（M：根）

**29** 電影明星（影星）

(diànyǐng míngsīng) (yǐngsīng) (diànyǐng míngxīng) (yǐngxīng)

N：movie star

明星 (míngsīng) (míngxīng)　　N：a (movie, t.v., music, etc.) star

李新打球，打得那麼好，全國的人都認識他，是最受歡迎的籃球明星。

歌星 (gēsīng) (gēxīng)　　N：singer

歌手 (gēshǒu)　　N：singer

小林本來只是個歌手，現在他的歌到處都聽得到，已經變成大歌星了。

**30 英俊 (yīngjyùn) (yīngjùn)**　　SV：good-looking, handsome, dashing

你欣賞的那個電影明星就是臉好看，很英俊，可惜身材不怎麼樣。

**31 態度 (tàidù)**　　N：attitude

昨天那家餐廳的服務生，態度很不客氣，我們都很生氣。

**32 魅力 (mèilì)**　　N：glamour, enchantment, attractiveness

王德華長得很好看，又會說話，很有魅力，不管男的、女的都很迷他。

**33 討厭 (tǎoyàn)**

V/SV：to dislike, to loathe, to hate/disgusting, repugnant, disagreeable, annoying

(1) 我最討厭又溼又冷的天氣。
(2) 老李又嘮叨了，真討厭。

**34 醜 (chǒu)**　　SV：to be ugly

我小時候不好看，哥哥姐姐都叫我「醜小鴨」。

**35 頭腦 (tóunǎo)**　　N：brain

王小姐的頭腦非常清楚，公司裡那麼多錢都是她在管，一毛錢都沒錯過。

腦子 (nǎo·zih) (nǎo·zi)　　N：brain

老趙常頭疼，看了醫生以後，才發現腦子裡長了個東西。

## 36 外表 (wàibiǎo)　N：appearance

有些人覺得外表好看，機會就多，所以去美容。其實個性跟能力更重要。

## 37 不修邊幅 (bù siōu biānfú) (bù xiū biānfú)

IE：untidy/untidy in dress

我舅舅穿得很隨便，總是不修邊幅。

## 38 鬍子 (hú·zih) (hú·zi)　N：mustache, beard, whiskers

我女兒說我留鬍子看起來好像老了十歲。

## 39 刮 (guā)　V：to shave

臺灣的理髮廳，除了給客人剪頭髮，也給客人刮鬍子。

## 40 打扮 (dǎbàn)　V：to get dressed up, to put on make-up

明天是我男朋友的生日，我一定要打扮得漂亮一點。

## 41 帥哥 (shuàigē)　N：handsome young man

是不是只有帥哥、美女才能當明星？

帥 (shuài)　SV：to be handsome, elegant in appearance

王先生雖然不年輕了，可是很會打扮，所以還是很帥。

▼ 專有名詞　**Proper Name**

1. 王德華 (Wáng Déhuá)　　Wang, De-Hua

## 注釋

1. **我等得急死了** means "I've waited so long that I died of anxiety." This is an exaggeration of course. This expression is used mostly by women.

2. **怎麼會呢？** means "How could this be?" It is short for 怎麼會這樣呢？ It indicates that a situation is contrary to a person's expectations.

3. **Pizza.** The full translation is 義大利脆餅 (Yìdàlì cuìbǐng), which means "crispy Italian pastry". Many people just say "pizza", written 披薩 (pīsà).

4. **好得沒話說** is used in positive situations. For negative situations other expressions are used, such as 不是普通的 SV (e.g. 笨) (extraordinarily stupid) or SV (e.g. 笨) 得離譜 (lípǔ) (stupid even beyond the rule book). These phrases, however, would be considered impolite by anyone other than very close friends.

5. This reflects the Taiwanese standard of beauty. Taiwanese do not consider dark skin to be beautiful. Most Taiwanese women like to keep their skin light, so they often carry parasols under the sun.

6. **帥哥** came into popular use just a few years ago. It means "handsome young man". 帥 means "dashing," or "smart-looking". A 帥哥 not only has a good looking face but also has a good build and stylish clothes.

## 文法練習

### 一　SV 死了　SV to death, extremely SV

◎我等得急死了。

I got extremely anxious waiting.

用法說明：「SV 死了」跟「SV 極了」、「SV 得不得了」意思差不多，但程度更強。是一種誇張的語氣。大部分表示不好的意思。

Explanation: "SV 死了" means almost the same thing as "SV 極了", "V 得不得了", but the tone is even stronger. It expresses exaggeration and usually has negative connotations.

第九課 誰最漂亮

▼ **練習** 根據所給提示用「SV 死了」完成下面對話。

1. 張：那家飯館的菜怎麼樣？（難吃）
   Chang: How's the food at that restaurant?
   李：難吃死了！我從來沒吃過那麼難吃的菜。
   Li: Awful! I've never eaten anything so disgusting.

2. 張：你房東對你這麼壞，你為什麼不搬家？（麻煩）
   李：搬家___麻煩死了___，我寧願看他的臉色。

3. 張：明天期中考，你今天應該早一點睡。（緊張）
   李：我___緊張死了___怎麼睡得著呢？

4. 張：申請獎學金的人那麼多，小王能申請到真不容易。（高興）
   李：是啊！他___高興死了___！他說要請客。

5. 張：老林的女朋友不但漂亮，身材好，還很溫柔。（羨慕）
   李：就是嘛！大家都___羨慕死了___。

> 二 都 even
>
> ◎來參加你們學校園遊會的人太多，路上都塞車了。
> So many people came to your school fair that even the road was jammed with traffic.

用法說明：「都」表示情況「甚至達到這種程度」，放在要強調的事情之前，說話時應輕讀。

Explanation: 都 shows that conditions have reached such an extreme level that even a certain situation has occurred. 都 is placed in front of that situation and should be spoken lightly with no emphasis.

▼ **練習**

（一）請把「都」放在句中合適的地方。

1. 今天是媽的生日，我才買蛋糕的。你怎麼忘了？
   I bought a cake because today is Mom's birthday. How could you forget?
   → 今天是媽的生日，我才買蛋糕的。你怎麼都忘了？

249

I bought a cake because today is Mom's birthday. How could you forget?

2. 我才打破一個杯子，老闆就罵了半個小時，我被氣哭了。
   _____

3. 老陳真小氣！病得那麼重，還不願意看醫生。
   _____

4. 林小姐越來越漂亮了，兩年沒見，我差一點不認識了。
   _____

5. 我男朋友一直說我胖，說得我不敢再吃了。
   _____

(二) 請老師先念一次下面的故事，學生聽完以後，老師再分句或分段再念一次，叫學生用「都」說出自己的看法。

小林這個人小氣得不得了，不但從來沒有買過禮物送給別人，自己也從來不買新衣服。衣服破了，也不丟，還拿來穿。有時候還因為想少用一點錢，就不吃早飯，連晚飯也不管飽不飽，只吃一碗速食麵就算了。冬天洗澡(xǐzǎo, to take a bath)，能不用熱水，就不用熱水，所以常常感冒，可是他怕用錢，也不去看醫生。總是喝喝水，睡睡覺，讓它自己好。這樣的生活害他瘦得好像風一大，就會被颳跑。雖然還很年輕，頭髮已經白了一半。小林的媽媽本來覺得他不亂用錢很好，可是看他這個樣子，也受不了了。

## 三　來 V　let (S) V

◎我來介紹一下，…
　Let me introduce you ...

用法說明：這個「來」表示要做某件事，並不真正向說話者移動，由「來」前面的主語進行「來」後面的「要做的事」。有緩和語氣的作用。

Explanation: When used this way, 來 does not express the action "come". Instead, it shows that the subject before 來 is about to perform the action indicated in the verb following 來. It serves to give the statement a casual, friendly tone.

第九課　誰最漂亮

### ▼ 練習　請用「來 V」完成下面對話。

1. 媽媽：我累了，今天我可不要洗碗了。
   Mom: I'm tired. I really don't want to wash dishes today.
   大女兒：我來洗吧！
   Eldest Daughter: I'll wash them!

2. 張：我們去南部旅行，車票，我買，旅館，誰訂？
   李：旅館，我來 訂吧 。

3. 張：這個桌子太重，我一個人搬不動。
   李：我來 搬吧 。

4. 張：我們去哪兒吃飯，決定了沒有？
   李：你常在外面吃，還是你來 我家吃 吧！

5. 張：這條山路我沒走過，不敢開車去。
   李：小王正好在這兒，他走過好幾次，讓他來 開 吧！

### 四　早知道（…）（我/我們）就…了。

If (I) had known beforehand that ... then ...

◎早知道我就去車站接你們了。
If I had known beforehand, I would have gone to meet you at the train station.

用法說明：「早知道」的後面是已成的事實，但並不是說話者所期望的，語言環境清楚時，這個已成的事實可省略。「就」的後面是說話者遺憾（或後悔）應做而未做的事。

Explanation: The words following 早知道 show a fact or situation that exists, but that the speaker had not expected to occur. When the context is clear, then the fact or situation can be omitted. Following 就 is something that the speaker should have and would have done if he had known about the situation beforehand. This pattern expresses the speaker's regret.

251

**實用視聽華語 3**

▼ 練習　　請根據所給情況,用「早知道(…)(我/我們)就…了。」表示遺憾。

1. 本來要選張教授的課,後來沒選,現在聽說他的課非常有趣。
   Originally, I wanted to take Professor Chang's class, but I didn't. Now I hear that his class is really interesting.
   → 早知道我就選了。
   　If I had known, then I would have taken it.

2. 從前不知道有這個獎學金,現在才聽說這個獎學金,而且申請的人都申請到了。
   *早知道我就申請*

3. 留在家裡做功課,沒跟朋友去看電影。後來聽朋友說電影非常好看。
   *早知道我就去看電影了*

4. 地理系畢業以後,一直找不到合適的工作。
   *早知道我就⋯⋯*

5. 幫妹妹搬家,可是她不但不謝謝我,還說我把她的東西弄丟了。
   *早知道我不幫*

---

五　…倒是…,可是(不過/就是)…

**Well, it is ... however ...**

◎ 餓倒是不餓,可是可以吃一點東西。
　I'm not really hungry, but I could eat a little something.

用法說明:「倒是」前面是重覆對方的問題或說法,「倒是」後面才是真正的回答。說「倒是」的目的是說話者可利用這個時候考慮如何回答,亦可使語氣較婉轉。「倒是」後面肯定、否定都可以。「是」可省略,但大部分的人省略「倒」。

Explanation: Preceding 倒是 is the opening response to the other party's question or comment, but following 倒是 is the speaker's real answer. 倒是 allows the speaker some time while deciding upon an answer and also serves to soften the tone of the reply. The words following 倒是 can be either positive or negative. Either 倒 or 是 can be omitted, but usually it is 倒 which is omitted.

第九課　誰最漂亮

### 練習　請用「…倒是…，可是（不過／就是）…」回答下面問題。

1. 這個花瓶好漂亮，你買吧！
   This flower vase is beautiful; you should buy it!
   → 漂亮是漂亮，可是價錢太貴，我買不起。
   　 It may be beautiful, but it's too expensive: I can't afford it.

2. 你為什麼不跟他們一起去，你不喜歡游泳嗎？
   _____

3. 你想不想看電影？
   _____

4. 你為什麼不坐公車去？車票不貴啊！
   _____

5. 你會說法文啊？我以為你沒學過。（請用否定句回答）
   _____

## 六　既然…，就…　Since ..., then ...

◎既然不怎麼餓，我們就去吃 pizza 吧！
Since you're not that hungry, then let's go eat pizza!

用法說明：「既然」的後面是已發生或認定會發生的事實，「就」的後面是說話者因為這個事實而表示的意見。
Explanation: Following 既然 is an existing fact or something that is considered to happen, and following 就 is a position that the speaker takes using this fact as a basis.

### 練習　請用「既然…，就…」完成下面對話。

1. 張：小王沒什麼經驗，做這件事恐怕有問題。
   Chang: Little Wang has no experience, I'm afraid that he'll have trouble doing this.
   李：既然他沒什麼經驗，就另外找人做吧！
   Li: Since he doesn't have any experience, then let's look for somebody else to do it!

2. 張：週末出去玩的人多，我怕塞車。
   李：你既然_____。

253

3. 張：王美美又大方又活潑，我好欣賞她！
   李：既然 _____。

4. 張：我想吃冰淇淋，可是這個攤位的已經賣完了。
   李：既然 _____。

5. 張：這個公寓房租太貴，我恐怕租不起。
   李：既然 _____。

## 七　SV 得沒話說　indescribably, beyond words

◎那個女生身材真是好得沒話說。
That girl's figure is absolutely amazing.

用法說明：強調程度很高，高到沒有合適的話可以形容。大部分用在好的情況，若用在不好的情況，似乎說話者並不在乎。

Explanation: This pattern emphasizes that the level of something is so high that no words can properly describe it. Usually it is used in positive situations, but sometimes it is used to describe negative situations and gives the impression that the speaker really does not care.

### 練習　請用「SV 得沒話說」完成下面對話。

1. 張：小王的成績好棒，每一科都是 A。
   Chang: Little Wang's grades are excellent; he has an A in every class.
   李：是啊！他的成績真是棒得沒話說。
   Li: That's right! His grades are really amazing.

2. 服務生A：我沒看過這麼大方的人，我每次幫他開門，他都給我二十塊。
   服務生B：這個人真是 _____。

3. 張：你的房子真便宜！房租跟水電費加起來才一百塊錢。
   李：是啊！這房子真的 _____。

4. 張：李愛美真漂亮，學校裡每個男生都很迷她。
   李：她是 _____。

5. 張：那個人的衣服髒得好像幾年沒換了。
   李：那是 _____。

第九課　誰最漂亮

## 八　比不上　cannot compare to, cannot compete with, is no competition for

◎…但是西方女孩的活潑、大方，亞洲女孩就比不上了。
...but Chinese girls can't compare to American girls in terms of vivaciousness and natural poise.

用法說明：「上」表示達到一定的水準。這個 RC 僅使用 Potential Type。
Explanation: 上 indicates that the subject has reached a certain level (of quality, accuracy, standard, etc.) This RC is used in Potential Type form (not Actual Type).

### 練習　請用「比不上」完成下面對話。

1. 張：你跟小王，誰的打工經驗多？
   Chang: Between you and Li'l Wang, who has more work experience?
   李：他的經驗比較多，我比不上他。
   Li: He has more experience than I. I am no competition for him.

2. 張：東方小孩獨立，還是西方小孩獨立？
   李：西方小孩獨立多了，_____比不上我_____。

3. 張：你覺得哪一國的葡萄酒好喝？
   李：法國葡萄酒世界有名，_____比不上美國的_____

4. 張：這家旅館雖然便宜，可是服務不好。
   李：小旅館的服務當然_____好，比不上我的_____

5. 張：林教授的課每一次教室裡都坐得滿滿的。
   李：是啊，他的魅力_____好，可是比不上我的_____。

255

實用視聽華語 3

> 九 誰叫…？
> 
> Who told (asked) you to...? (rhetorical question)
> 
> ◎誰叫你總是不修邊幅？
> Who asked you to always be so sloppily dressed?

用法說明：不是問句。「誰叫」的後面是說明某件事情發生的原因，而此原因是有道理的，不該埋怨的。

Explanation: Sentences like these are rhetorical questions. Following 誰叫 is an explanation that some bad situation is due to the other party's own shortcoming. It implies that the other party has no right to complain.

▼ 練習　請用「誰叫」完成下面對話。

1. 張：你們為什麼不等我，先走了？
   Chang: Why did you leave and not wait for me?
   李：誰叫你不準時？我們再等你，就來不及了。
   Li: Who told you to be late? We would be late if we had waited for you.

2. 張：平常小林的成績不錯，沒想到這次考得這麼爛！
   李：誰叫他 _____？

3. 張：真倒楣，老闆又扣我錢了！
   李：誰叫你 _____？

4. 張：我自己付錢吧！不好意思讓你哥哥請客。
   李：有什麼不好意思，誰叫他 _____？

5. 張：你男朋友對你這麼不好，你為什麼不離開他？
   李：沒辦法，誰叫我 _____？

第九課　誰最漂亮

| 課室活動 | Classroom Activities |

一

1. 遊戲：猜 (cāi; to guess) 猜我是誰？（你知道我是誰嗎？）

    Before class, the teacher prepares cards with people's names on them, one per student. The names should be of people well known to the class such as celebrities, classmates, professors etc. Each student is given a card and is asked to describe the person on his/her card to the class. They can even liven it up by using body language and mannerisms typical of the person. Their description may begin with statements such as：我是男的。我很高，我有六呎高。我的頭髮… The rest of the class is to guess the identity of this person. The game can be made more exciting by dividing the class into two teams which compete against each other.

    Some useful supplementary words include: 禿（頭）(tūtóu; bald), 肚子 (dù·zīh) (dù·zi; belly; abdomen), 金頭髮藍眼睛的 (blonde-haired and blue-eyed), 戴眼鏡 (dài yǎnjìng; wear glasses), 胸部 (syōngbù) (xiōngbù; chest, bosom), 安靜 (ānjìng; quiet), 屁股 (pì·gǔ; buttocks, rear end).

2. Read the following narrative of this chapter and discuss or debate with the class the pros and cons of beauty contests. Some useful supplementary words include: 贊成 (zànchéng, agree, approve), 反對 (con, against), 內在美 (nèizàiměi, inner beauty), 三圍 (sānwéi, measure of figure).

257

## 二、討論問題 (Discussion)

1. 你選學校，會先看看校園怎麼樣嗎？為什麼？
2. 內在美 (nèizàiměi, inner beauty)、外在美 (wàizàiměi, outer beauty)，哪個重要？你的看法怎麼樣？
3. 怎麼樣可以讓自己更有魅力？

這些衣服，我下午來拿。

老闆，我來拿衣服。

已經洗好了，小姐。早上送衣服來的是你媽吧？！

## 短文　　報上的短評[1]

今天是「世界小姐」選美[2]報名[3]的最後一天,已有三十二位小姐填好報名表。這次參加的小姐,年齡[4]都比以前小了很多,大部分高中都還沒有畢業。他們雖然看起來活潑、大方,可是都打扮得太老,並不適合她們的年紀。很多人擔心像她們這麼年輕,生活經驗跟常識[5]都不夠,如果選她們來代表[6]現代[7]的美女,合適嗎?而且以前選出來的世界小姐也鬧過不少新聞:不是生過孩子,就是照過裸照[8],要不然就是跟別人的先生有不正常[9]的關係。這也是為什麼每年都有人在討論這個活動還要不要再辦的原因[10]。

到底什麼才是『美』?我們又為什麼要選美?我覺得政府有義務教育年輕人:不要以為有漂亮的臉,迷人的身材就是美。腦子裡面有沒有東西才是更值得注意的。

## Vocabulary:

1. 短評 (duǎnpíng): short critique
2. 選美 (syuǎnměi) (xuǎnměi): beauty contest
3. 報名 (bào//míng): to enroll
4. 年齡 (niánlíng): age
5. 常識 (chángshih) (chángshì): common sense
6. 代表 (dàibiǎo): to represent
7. 現代 (siàndài) (xiàndài): modern
8. 裸照 (luǒjhào) (luǒzhào): nude photos
9. 正常 (jhèngcháng) (zhèngcháng): normal
10. 原因 (yuányīn): reason

# 第十課 你選誰

■投票（行政院新聞局 黃仲新攝）

(活動中心)

偉立：那邊有位子，我們坐那兒吧！（兩人過去坐下）

錢太太：我的英文不好，每次語言交換你都很辛苦，真抱歉！

偉立：沒什麼！只要對你有幫助，我就很高興了。

錢太太：你真好，謝謝你！剛剛外面那些人在說什麼？我就聽懂了幾句話，好像是選舉參議員的事，對嗎？

偉立：對了，我們十一月初舉行國會議員選舉，所以最近有很多政見發表會，也有人到處幫他們的黨拉票[1]。

錢太太：除了選參議員，還要選眾議員嗎？

偉立：對，國會議員包括參議員和眾議員。

錢太太：多久選一次？

偉立：眾議員**每**兩年選一次；參議員任期六年，每兩年輪流改選三**分之**一。

錢太太：那你們什麼時候選州長、市長呢？

偉立：州長、市長有的兩年選一次，有的四年選一次。

錢太太：你是民主黨，還是社會黨？

偉立：我是民主黨。

錢太太：你幫民主黨拉票了嗎？你一定希望他們贏吧！

偉立：那還用說[2]？我大哥這次就幫州長候選人助選。

錢太太：那一定很忙嘍？

偉立：是啊，每天**為了**競選經費跑來跑去，不是安排政見發表會、布置場地，就是發傳單。忙得吃飯都沒時間。

錢太太：你大哥怎麼那麼熱心？

偉立：他念研究所的時候，在國會工讀，認識了一些國會議
　　　員，學了很多，很有興趣往政治這**方面**發展。

錢太太：**這麼說**，也許有一天你會是總統的弟弟呢！

偉立：（笑）到總統府的路可不好走啊！你們怎麼選總統？

錢太太：我們以前是**由**國會代表人民**來**選舉，從一九九六年
　　　　開始，才直接由人民來選舉[3]。

偉立：也是四年選一次嗎？

錢太太：是，我們也是四年選一次。

偉立：那你們的國會議員怎麼選的呢？

錢太太：我們的國會議員就是立法委員。怎麼選的，我以後

■計票（行政院新聞局　葉銘源攝）

263

再告訴你吧。（看錶）
偉立：好吧！時間不早了，我們該學英文了。

※　　※　　※　　※　　※　　※

（公車站）
助教：嗨！高偉立，等車啊[4]？
偉立：是啊，我剛投完票，想回宿舍吃飯。你買東西啊[4]？
助教：嗯，買了些雞蛋、鮮奶[5]跟洗衣粉。我**正要**去學校，要不要我送你[6]？我當你的司機。我的車就停在前面。

■政見發表會（行政院新聞局　劉光哲攝）

偉立：好啊，謝謝。（兩人過去上了車）

助教：投票的人多不多？

偉立：不少，我等了好久才輪到。

助教：你投過幾次票了？

偉立：兩年前的大選，我還**不到**十八歲，沒有選舉權，所以這次是第一次。

助教：你的票投給誰了？

偉立：我當然支持民主黨的候選人，我覺得他們競選時答應選民的事情，比較容易做到。不像有些候選人只是文宣做得好，政見聽起來不錯，可是好好地想想，就會發現其實都做不到。

助教：**你看**，你支持的人有希望當選嗎？

偉立：誰敢說？這一次競爭很激烈。你呢？你投過幾次票？

助教：兩次。我們是滿了二十歲，在一個地方住滿六個月，才可以投票。

偉立：哦，原來是這樣。宿舍到了，我要下車了，謝啦，再見。

## 生詞及例句

**1 抱歉 (bàociàn) (bàoqiàn)**　IE/SV：sorry/to be sorry, to regret

(1) 抱歉！路上塞車，所以來晚了。
(2) 不能幫小陳的忙，我覺得對他很抱歉。

**抱 (bào)**　V：to hug, to embrace, to hold or carry in one's arms

孩子哭了，媽媽把他抱起來，他就不哭了。

**道歉 (dàociàn) (dào//qiàn)**　VO：to apologize

這件事情是我錯了，我跟你道歉。

**2 選舉 (syuǎnjyǔ) (xuǎnjǔ)**　N：election

找什麼人做這件事，選舉是最公平的辦法。

**改選 (gǎisyuǎn) (gǎixuǎn)**　V：to re-elect

這些人已經做了很多年了，應該改選了。

**助選 (jhùsyuǎn) (zhùxuǎn)**　V：to help elect, to assist a campaign effort

王先生有很多幫別人助選的經驗。

**大選 (dàsyuǎn) (dàxuǎn)**　N：general election

臺灣四年舉行一次總統(zǒngtǒng, president)大選。

**3 參議員 (cānyìyuán)**　N：senator

**4 月初 (yuèchū)**　TW：the beginning of the month

下個月初，二號到六號我們要舉行這學期的期中考。

**年初 (niánchū)**　TW：the beginning of the year

第十課　你選誰

月底 (yuèdǐ)　　TW：the end of the month

我媽給我的零用錢太少，不到月底就用完了。

年底 (niándǐ)　　TW：the end of the year

我在銀行工作，每年年底都特別忙。

**5** 國會議員 (guóhuèi yìyuán) (guóhuì yìyuán)

N：member of parliament

國會 (guóhuèi) (guóhuì)　　N：parliament, congress

議員 (yìyuán)　　N：member of a legislative assembly

議員的工作就是幫選民看著政府，好好地做事，而且不可以亂用錢。

市議員 (shìhyìyuán) (shìyìyuán)

N：member of a municipal assembly

議會 (yìhuèi) (yìhuì)　　N：council, assembly, parliament

**6** 政見發表會 (jhèngjiàn fābiǎohuèi) (zhèngjiàn fābiǎohuì)

N：political convention

政見 (jhèngjiàn) (zhèngjiàn)　　N：political views

參加選舉的人都應該在政見發表會上說清楚自己的政見，選民才知道選誰比較好。

發表會 (fābiǎohuèi) (fābiǎohuì)

N：convention or exhibition of new ideas or products

這個歌星的新歌發表會，總是有非常多的歌迷來參加。

發表 (fābiǎo)　　V：to make public, make known, express an idea

李助教的研究報告是在上個月的國家地理雜誌上發表的。

**7** 黨（政黨）(dǎng) (jhèngdǎng) (zhèngdǎng)

267

實用視聽華語 3

N：political party

8 拉票 (lā//piào)　VO：to solicit votes

最近老趙到處拉票，請大家選他們黨的參議員候選人。

拉 (lā)　V：to pull, to tug

這個門太重，我拉不動，打不開。

9 眾議員 (jhòngyìyuán) (zhòngyìyuán)

N：member of the House of Representatives (U.S.); Member of Parliament (M.P.) (U. K.)

10 包括 (bāokuò)　V：to include, consist of, comprise of

套餐包括菜、飯、湯，還有飲料。

11 和（和）(hàn, hé)　CONJ：and

因為王小姐有漂亮的臉和迷人的身材，追她的人多得不得了。

12 任期 (rèncí) (rènqí)　N：term of office, tenure of office

任 (rèn)　M：(for the terms of an office)

參議員的六年任期快滿了，你要選誰做下一任的參議員？

13 輪流 (lúnliú)　V/A：to take turns/by turns, in turn

(1) 這個星期的衣服你洗，下個星期我來洗，大家輪流。
(2) 我舅媽生病，我舅舅跟我表弟輪流去醫院照顧她。

14 X分之Y (X fēnjhīh Y) (X fēn zhī Y)　IE：the fraction Y of X

(1) 全世界人口有五分之一是中國人。
(2) 中國人口是世界人口的五分之一。

15 州長 (jhōujhǎng) (zhōuzhǎng)　N：governor (of a state)

第十課　你選誰

州ㄓㄡ (jhōu) (zhōu)　N/M：state (section of nation)

美國一共有五十個州，你住在哪一州？

市ㄕˋ長ㄓㄤˇ (shìhjhǎng) (shìzhǎng)　N：mayor (of a city)

市議會開會的時候，議員們如果不了解市政府的作法，市長有義務對他們說清楚。

校ㄒㄧㄠˋ長ㄓㄤˇ (siàojhǎng) (xiàozhǎng)

N：principal / head of a school, head-master

班ㄅㄢ長ㄓㄤˇ (bānjhǎng) (bānzhǎng)　N：class leader

在中學當過班長，對申請大學有幫助，可以加分。

**16** 贏ㄧㄥˊ (yíng)　V：to win

我們來比比誰跑得快，贏的人請客，好不好？

**17** 候ㄏㄡˋ選ㄒㄩㄢˇ人ㄖㄣˊ (hòusyuǎnrén) (hòuxuǎnrén)　N：candidate (for office)

這一次出來競選的候選人都很年輕。

**18** 為ㄨㄟˋ了ㄌㄜ˙ (wèi·le)　CV：so as to, in order to, for the purpose of

為了讓我媽高興，她生日的時候，我唱了首歌給她聽。

為ㄨㄟˋ (wèi)　CV：on someone's behalf, for someone's sake

今天是你的生日，這些菜都是為你做的。

**19** 競ㄐㄧㄥˋ選ㄒㄩㄢˇ (jìngsyuǎn) (jìngxuǎn)

V：to enter an election, to run for office, to campaign for office, to enter a beauty contest

王愛美姐姐很漂亮，大家都說她可以競選臺灣小姐。

**20** 經ㄐㄧㄥ費ㄈㄟˋ (jīngfèi)　N：operating funds of an organization（M：筆）

系裡的經費不夠，只能買兩部電腦。

## 21 安排 (ānpái)　V：to arrange matters, to plan

我姐姐安排了一個很好的機會，介紹我跟陳小姐見面。

### 排 (pái)　V/M：to line up, arrange in order/M. for rows, lines

(1) 買票的時候，那個人排在我們後面，所以看電影的時候，他就坐在我們旁邊。
(2) 你把教室裡的桌子排好，就可以回去了。
(3) 我看電影的時候，都喜歡坐在最後一排。

## 22 布置（佈置）(bùjhìh) (bùzhì)

V/N：to arrange, set-up/arrangement

(1) 我姑姑剛搬家，房子還沒布置好，看起來很亂。
(2) 百貨公司的櫥窗 (chúchuāng, show window) 一年四季的布置都不同，一看就知道現在是哪個季節了。

## 23 場地 (chǎngdì)　N：place, site

這個新歌發表會的場地很大，坐得下一萬人。

### 場 (chǎng)　M：(used for an event or happening)

這場雨下了兩個鐘頭。

## 24 發傳單 (fā//chuándān)　VO：to issue a handbill/leaflet

那些媽媽們在路口發傳單，是為了讓大家注意孩子的教育問題。

### 發 (fā)　V：to distribute (leaflets), to issue (a handbill)

考卷發完了，誰沒拿到的，請舉手。

### 傳 (chuán)　V：to pass, pass on

我說「停」的時候，這個球傳到誰手裡，誰就得唱歌。

### 傳單 (chuándān)　N：handbill, leaflet

競選傳單上一定有候選人的姓名、相片、政黨和政見。

### 25 熱心 (rèsīn) (rèxīn)

SV/A：to be warmhearted, enthusiastic/zealously, enthusiastically

不管是誰的事,張助教都很熱心地幫忙。

### 26 政治 (jhèngjhìh) (zhèngzhì)   N：politics

我對政治完全沒有興趣,我不想競選議員。

### 27 方面 (fāngmiàn)   N：aspect, position, side, party

學中文,聽、說、讀、寫,你覺得哪一方面最困難?

### 28 總統 (zǒngtǒng)   N：president (of a republic)

不管什麼事,國會如果沒有通過,恐怕總統也不能做。

總統府 (zǒngtǒng fǔ)

N：the residence and office of a president, presidential palace

### 29 由 (yóu)   CV：by, up to (someone)

考試時間一般都由老師決定。

### 30 代表 (dàibiǎo)   V/N：to represent, to stand for/representative, delegate

(1) 我們代表中文系,歡迎你們來參觀。
(2) 這幾位都是今年選出來的學生代表。

### 31 直接 (jhíhjiē) (zhíjiē)   A：directly

間接 (jiànjiē)   A：indirectly

這件事,你應該直接問他,不要問別人。間接聽到的消息,不一定是對的。

32 立法委員 (lìfǎ wěiyuán)　N：legislator

　　立法 (lì//fǎ)　VO：to legislate

　　委員 (wěiyuán)　N：committee member

　　委員會 (wěiyuánhuèi) (wěiyuánhuì)　N：a commission

　　王先生當立法委員的時候，參加的是教育委員會，跟別的委員一起立了一個新法，讓鄉下孩子念書有更多補助。

　　立法院 (Lìfǎ Yuàn)　N：Legislative Yuan

33 投票 (tóu//piào)　VO：to vote, to cast a ballot

　　(1) 舊社會的女人不能選舉，立法以後女人才能投票。
　　(2) 去年的總統選舉，你的票投給誰了？

34 鮮奶 (siānnǎi) (xiānnǎi)　N：fresh milk（M：瓶／盒）

　　有的臺灣人冬天不習慣喝冰的鮮奶，總要熱一熱再喝。

　　牛奶 (nióunǎi) (niúnǎi)　N：(cow's) milk

　　吃母奶長大的孩子比吃牛奶的健康。

35 洗衣粉 (sǐyīfěn) (xǐyīfěn)

　　N：laundry detergent (powder)（M：包／盒／袋）

　　奶粉 (nǎifěn)　N：powdered milk（M：罐／包）

　　我姐姐的孩子只喝這種奶粉沖泡 (chōngpào, to brew) 的牛奶，喝別的會不舒服。

36 司機 (sīhjī) (sījī)　N：a driver, a chauffeur

37 選舉權 (syuǎnjyǔcyuán) (xuǎnjǔquán)　N：the right to vote

　　等我有了選舉權，我一定要選像你這樣不愛錢，又願意替大家服務的人。

第十課　你選誰

權 (cyuán) (quán)　　N：a right; power, authority

(1) 我們沒有權管別人的私生活。
(2) 我們老闆怕太太，所以公司裡，權最大的是老闆太太。

人權 (réncyuán) (rénquán)　　N：human rights

想說什麼就可以說什麼，是最重要的人權。

特權 (tècyuán) (tèquán)　　N：a privilege, a peculiar

老張有什麼特權？為什麼我們都得站著，他可以坐著？

38 支持 (jhīhchíh) (zhīchí)　　V/N：to support, to back/support, backing

張：你給鄉下孩子比較多的補助，這個做法很對，我完全支持。
李：謝謝你對我的支持。

39 答應 (dāying)　　V：to promise, to agree ; to answer, to reply, to respond

(1) 這件事，我真的做不到，所以沒辦法答應你。
(2) 媽媽叫你，你為什麼不答應？

40 選民 (syuǎnmín) (xuǎnmín)　　N：voter, elector

這個地方的選民，好像對這次的選舉都不太關心。

41 文宣 (wúnsyuān) (wénxuān)　　N：propaganda; advertisement

競選的時候，文宣很重要，除了傳單，還有電視、報紙的廣告和網路新聞。

42 你看 (nǐ kàn)　　IE：in your opinion

老錢今天沒來，你看，他會不會生病了？

43 當選 (dāngsyuǎn) (dāngxuǎn)　　V：to be elected

這次競選的人太多，十個人裡面，只有一個人會當選。

## 專有名詞 Proper Names

1. 民主黨 (Mínjhǔ Dǎng) (Mínzhǔ Dǎng)　　Democratic Party
2. 社會黨 (Shèhuèi Dǎng) (Shèhuì Dǎng)　　Socialist Party

## 注釋

1. 拉票 means "to solicit votes," but not necessarily on a formal basis. 助選 means to solicit votes formally.

2. "那還用說嗎？" means "Does one even need to mention it?", "Of course," "Certainly." It is casual and should not be used in speaking to elders or superiors.

3. According to the revised Constitution of the Republic of China, the president is elected every four years by the citizens, not by the 國民大會 as prior to 1996. This revision was made in July, 1994. 國民大會 is the National Assembly. Members of the National Assembly are known as 國民大會代表. They were elected by the people every six years. They were authorized to vote for the President and Vice President, and revise the Constitution. The number of seats in the National Assembly varied with the population.

Formerly included in Parliament were the following three groups: 立法院, 監察院, and 國民大會. The members of 立法院, members of the 監察院 (Jiānchá Yuàn, Control Yuan), and 國民大會代表 who came to Taiwan with Chiang Kai-shek were allowed to retain their seats until December 1991. Their continued presence represented the legitimate rule of the government of the Republic of China over all of China.

Members of the 監察院, or Control Yuan, are known as 監察委員. They were elected by provincial assemblymen and city councilors every six years. Their responsibilities include impeachment and censoring of officials. The first members of the Control Yuan were elected in 1948. A constitutional change enacted in 1992 removed the 監察委員 from Parliament, and they shall be nominated and, with the consent of the Legislators, appointed by the President now.

立法院 is the Legislative Yuan, the body of the national government which proposes and debates bills and passes laws. The legislators are known as 立法委員. They are elected by the people every three years. The number of seats varies with the population. The first legislators were elected in 1948.

4. "等車啊？" and "你買東西啊？" are greetings. See Note 4 of Lesson 1.

5. 鮮奶 means "fresh milk." Many Taiwanese people are not used to drinking cold milk. They often buy powdered milk and make warm milk themselves. If you mention 牛奶, the first

idea that comes to most Taiwanese is warm milk made from powder. Many people do not drink fresh milk because they have an allergy to it which causes gastric disorders.

6. "要不要我送你？" means "Do you want me to give you a lift?" (Literally: "Do you want me to send you there?") Another way to say this is "要不要搭個便車？" 搭便車 (dā//biànchē) means to get a lift from someone or to hitchhike, e.g. 我要搭別人的便車去紐約。

## 文法練習

### 一　每 Nu + M₁ (N) + V+ 一 + M₂
V once/have one every Nu -M

◎ 眾議員每兩年選一次。
Members of the House of Representatives are elected once every two years.

**用法說明**：說明某個動作發生的規律。
Explanation: This pattern explains the rate of occurrence for some action.

▼ 練習　請用「每 Nu+M₁(N)+V+ 一 +M₂」改寫下面各句。

1. 我們念完六課就考一次。
   After we finish going over 6 chapters then we have a test.
   → 我們每六課考一次。
   　We have a test once every six chapters.

2. 這個機場，五分鐘就有一架飛機起飛。
   _____

3. 這個園遊會有很多攤位，十公尺就有一個。
   _____

4. 在這個國家，兩個人就有一輛汽車。
   _____

5. 奧林匹克運動會 (Àolínpīkè Yùndònghuì, Olympic Games) 四年就舉行一次。
   _____

## 二　X 分之 Y　(fraction) Y/X

◎參議員任期六年，每兩年輪流改選三分之一。
One third of the senators run for election every two years. Their term is six years.

**用法說明**：表示把某個整體分成 X 分，取其中 Y 分。
Explanation: This pattern refers to Y parts out of a total of X parts. （"X 分之 Y" in simple fraction form = Y/X）

▼ **練習**　請用「X 分之 Y」改寫下面句子。

1. 這個學校，五個學生當中只有一個是女的。
   Only one out of every five students in this school is female.
   → 這個學校的學生只有五分之一是女的。
   　Only 1/5th of this school's students are female.

2. 我星期天買了六個蘋果，才兩天，就壞了兩個。
   _____

3. 小張做生意的錢有一半是他爸爸給的。
   _____

4. 我弟弟念高中，上學期的期末考一共考了八科，有兩科不及格。
   _____

5. 你成績這麼好，申請獎學金一定沒問題。(100%)
   _____

## 三

### (I) 為了　for the purpose of, so as to, in order to

◎每天為了競選經費跑來跑去。
He runs around every day seeking out campaign funds.

**用法說明**：「為了」後面是目的或目的物，再後面是要達成此目的的做法或手段。如果先說做法或手段，後面應該說「是為了」。

Explanation: Following 為了 is a purpose or a desired object. After this, the method through which the goal is to be attained is given. When the positions of the method and goal are inverted, then 為了 is changed to 是為了 and placed between them.

▼ 練習　請根據提示，用「為了」及「是為了…」回答下面問題。

1. 小高為什麼每個週末都去圖書館？（查資料）
   Why does Little Gao go to the library every weekend?
   →小高為了查資料，所以每個週末都去圖書館。
   　In order to look up information, Little Gao goes to the library every weekend.
   →小高每個週末都去圖書館，是為了查資料。
   　The reason Little Gao goes to the library every weekend is to look up information.

2. 林建國為什麼到酒館打工？（多賺小費）
   _____

3. 你哥哥怎麼每天開夜車？（通過博士班的考試）
   _____

4. 那個參議員怎麼這麼早就開始跟選民拉票？（競選總統）
   _____

5. 小李為什麼一個人到那麼遠的地方去工作？（理想）
   _____

6. 你搬了好幾次家了，到底是為什麼？（孩子）
   _____

## (II) 為 ＋ N/PN ＋ V

for, in order to benefit (a person, group, organization, etc.)

**用法說明**：「為」的前面有主語，後面是名詞或代名詞 (PN)，再後面是動詞，表示做某事是特別給該名詞或代名詞做的。

Explanation: Here 為 is preceded by the subject and followed by a noun (or pronoun) and verb. It indicates that the action is performed by the subject particularly for the benefit of the noun (or pronoun) mentioned. The difference between 爲 and 爲了 is that following 爲了 is a reason or goal, whereas, following 爲 is the recipient of the benefits of an action.

### 練習　請把「爲 N / PN」放在句中合適的地方。

1. 今天是你的生日，所以我做了一個蛋糕。
   Today is your birthday, so I made a birthday cake.
   → 今天是你的生日，所以我爲你做了一個蛋糕。
   　Today is your birthday, so I made a birthday cake for you.

2. 王先生競選的時候，答應做的事都沒做到。
   _____

3. 做父母的總想在家裡布置一個舒服的生活環境。
   _____

4. 你每天忙到這麼晚才回家，老闆應該對你好一點才對。
   _____

5. 張校長辛苦了很多年，我們學校才有這麼好的成績。
   _____

## 四　方面　aspect, direction, field, area

◎ …很有興趣往政治這方面發展。
　… very interested in going into the field of politics.

用法說明：「方面」有「範圍」、「範疇」的意思。前面可用名詞、數字，或「這」、「那」、「哪」、「每」、「各」、「別的」…等。

Explanation: 方面 means field, scope or category, but in translation this often remains unspoken. One can place a noun, a numeral, or a demonstrative 這, 那, 哪, 每, 各, or 別的 … in front of 方面.

### 練習　請把「方面」放在句中合適的地方。

1. 老趙剛到美國的時候，吃的、住的都不習慣。

第十課　你選誰

When Old Zhao first arrived in America, he was neither accustomed to the food nor the lifestyle.
→ 老趙剛到美國的時候，吃的、住的方面都不習慣。
　When Old Zhao first arrived in America, he was uncomfortable both from the standpoint of food and lifestyle.

2. 小張念研究所是為了研究社會的問題。
　_____

3. 王大明只會念書，追女朋友，完全沒有經驗。（可以加「這」）
　_____

4. 法國話，我只會說，文法我一點都不懂。
　_____

5. 如果你競選市議員，只要發表政見就行了，別的都由我們來替你安排。
　_____

6. 你學中文，聽、說、讀、寫哪個有困難？
　_____

7. 李先生當立法委員的時候，特別注意教育、政治、外交 (foreign affairs) 這三個問題。
　_____

## 五　這麼說

### If you put it that way, then ...... /If so , then ......

◎這麼說，也許有一天你會是總統的弟弟呢！
If it's as you say it is, then maybe someday you'll be the younger brother of the president!

**用法說明**：「這麼說」意思是「如果按照你說的」，後面是說話者根據對方說的話所做的推測。如果並不確定自己所做的推測，可在句尾加「嘍」。

Explanation: 這麼說 means "If things are as you say , then ..." After 這麼說 the speaker states his or her conclusion or prediction based on what the other party has said. If the speaker is not so confident about his conclusion 嘍 can be added at the end of the sentence.

### 練習　請用「這麼說」完成下面對話。

1. 張：如果你真的找不到人幫忙，就打電話給我吧！
   Chang: If you really can't find anybody to help, then give me a call!
   李：這麼說，你答應了。
   Li: If you put it that way, then I guess you've agreed to do it.

2. 張：冰淇淋、蛋糕，我都愛吃。
   李：這麼說，＿＿＿＿＿＿＿＿＿＿＿＿＿＿＿。

3. 張：我先生念大學的時候，我才念小學。
   李：這麼說，＿＿＿＿＿＿＿＿＿＿＿＿＿＿＿。

4. 張：小林從來沒生過病，連感冒都很少。
   李：這麼說，＿＿＿＿＿＿＿＿＿＿＿＿＿＿＿。

5. 張：謝教授教書，已經教了二十年了。
   李：這麼說，＿＿＿＿＿＿＿＿＿＿＿＿＿＿＿。

## 六　由 N／PN 來 V(O)　up to N to V

◎我們以前是由國會代表人民來選舉。
Previously, (the president) was elected by representatives from the Parliament representing the people.

用法說明：「由」的後面是施行動作者，「來」的後面是要做的事（請參看第九課文法練習三）。這個句型表示做這件事的責任或權利歸施行動作者。賓語放在句首或句尾都可以。語言環境清楚時可省略。

Explanation: After 由 is the performer of the action, and after 來 is the necessary action. (Please refer to sentence pattern 3 in Chapter 9) This pattern shows that this person has the responsibility or right to perform the given action. The object can be placed either at the beginning or the end of the sentence. When the context is clear, 由 can be omitted.

### 練習　請用「由 N／PN 來 V (O)」完成下面句子。

1. 我媽說我只要把書念好就行了，學費的事由她來想辦法。

My mother said all I have to do is concentrate on doing well in school. She will be responsible for dealing with the tuition.

2. 氣候，我已經介紹完了，這裡到底出產什麼，由＿＿＿＿＿＿。

3. 張教授只教文法，說話練習由＿＿＿＿＿＿。

4. 我們家的小事，我可以決定，可是大事就由＿＿＿＿＿＿。

5. 明天的舞會，我布置場地，飲料由＿＿＿＿＿＿。

6. 不管誰想跟市長見面，都得先由＿＿＿＿＿＿。

## 七　正要　just about to, on the verge of

◎我正要去學校。
I'm just about to go to school.

**用法說明**：強調「剛準備做」某件事，雖然還沒做，可是幾乎已經開始做了。也可以說「正想」或「正打算」。
Explanation: This emphasizes that one is just about to do something, and although you have not done it yet, you have, for all practical purposes, started. You could also say 正想 (just thinking about) or 正打算 (just planning to).

### 練習　請用「正要」改寫下面句子。

1. 我剛拿起刮鬍刀，準備刮鬍子，你就打電話來了。
   I had just picked up the razor when you called.
   → 我正要刮鬍子，你就打電話來了。
   I was just about to shave when you called.

2. 老張來找我室友的時候，他剛準備出門。
   ＿＿＿＿＿＿＿＿＿＿＿＿＿＿＿＿

3. 我剛準備問老師這個問題，沒想到老師先問我了。
   ＿＿＿＿＿＿＿＿＿＿＿＿＿＿＿＿

4. 老李說他真倒楣！他剛準備回家，就下起大雨來了。
   ＿＿＿＿＿＿＿＿＿＿＿＿＿＿＿＿

5. 我媽剛準備上車，就聽到我爸在叫她。
   _____

## 八 不到 not yet, under, less than

◎我還不到十八歲，沒有選舉權。
I still hadn't reached 18 yet; I didn't have the right to vote.

用法說明：「不到」的後面加「數字」，表示尚未達到那個程度，但相差不多。
Explanation: When 不到 is placed before a number it indicates that one has not yet arrived at that point. However, it also implies that it is not very far off.

### 練習 請用「不到」完成下面句子。

1. 這麼多衣服，媽媽不到半個小時就洗完了，好快啊！
   Mom washes all these clothes in less than half an hour, that's fast!

2. 這個電影大人才能看，你不到_____，不可以看。

3. 我搬到這兒才五個月，還不到_____，所以認識的人不多。

4. 這個冰箱好便宜，只要九十多塊，還不到_____。

5. 小王他們學校很小，每班學生才十幾個，還不到_____。

## 九 你/我看 in your/my opinion

◎你看，你支持的人有希望當選嗎？
In your opinion, does the candidate you support have a chance of winning the election?

用法說明：「看」在此處是「想」或「認為」的意思，「我看」的後面是說話者的看法或建議，「你看」的後面都是問句，詢問對方的看法。
Explanation: Here, 看 means think or believe. Following 我看 is the speaker's own thought or opinion, and following 你看 is a solicitation for another's opinion.

### 練習　請用「我看」回答下面問題。

1. 你看，明天會不會下雨？
   What do you think, will it rain tomorrow?
   → 我看，一定不會。一般來說，這個時候很少下雨。
   In my opinion, it definitely won't rain. Generally speaking, it seldom rains during this period.

2. 你看，我什麼時候去看張老師比較好？
   _____

3. 你看，小張跟小王，誰可能申請到獎學金？
   _____

4. 王先生的政見發表會，你看，在哪兒舉行才合適？
   _____

5. 小陳期末考又三科不及格，你看，老師會不會讓他補考？
   _____

## 課室活動　Classroom Activities

一

1. 角色扮演 (Rolc Playing)

    Two students: One student acts as a curious Chinese 小留學生, the other as his/her tutor. The 小留學生 saw someone distributing leaflets concerning the upcoming presidential campaign. So he/she has come to the tutor with such questions as: 你們國家怎麼選總統？是不是直接選舉？要不要選代表？為什麼要選代表？什麼人可以做候選人？什麼人可以投票？沒有參加政黨的人也可以競選嗎？

可能用到的詞：家世背景 (family background), 聲望 (popularity, prestige, reputation), 學歷 (syuélì) (xuélì; record of formal schooling), 資格 (qualifications), 承諾 (chéngnuò; promise to undertake, undertake to do something), 條件 (conditions, requirements)

2. 遊戲

This game can be played by paired students or by a larger group. First, have the students memorize the following names: 額頭 (étóu, forehead), 下巴 (siàbā)(xiàbā, chin), 耳朵 (ěr·duo, ear), 眼睛, 鼻子, 嘴巴. Then have the students make fists with both hands and touch their noses（鼻子）. The leader, usually the teacher on the first round, then says: 鼻子, 鼻子, 鼻子—耳朵 (or another facial part from the list above). The third time that 鼻子 is repeated, it should be spoken more slowly, tipping off the other players that he is about to change. Everyone must move both his/her fists at the same time the new part is called out (in this case, 耳朵). All players, including the leader, must quickly move both fists from the 鼻子 to 耳朵. Anyone who touches any part of the face part other than 耳朵 loses, including the leader himself. The loser then must take over as leader. But before he does so, he must share with the class, in Mandarin, his views on what issues should be emphasized in a presidential campaign.

3. 辦一個競選班長的政見發表會。

## 二、討論問題 (Discussion)

1. 總統、市長、國會議員……這些人有什麼特權？你覺得這樣對嗎？說說你的看法。
2. 如果你有投票權，你會把票投給什麼樣的候選人？哪一類的候選人，你會告訴別人不要選他？

你看，這是我上次的傳單，這次競選我恐怕沒希望了！

因為我答應選民的事一件也沒做到。

哇！好極了，這些傳單，這次還可以再用。

## 短文　　　　幫同學助選

各位同學：

大家好！你們都知道李大偉這次要競選學生聯合會代表，就像傳單上說的，大偉是個關心校園問題，了解同學需要，而且又熱心服務的人。各位一定還記得，上次放假的時候，小偷到學生宿舍來偷東西，大偉為了追小偷，不管外面下著大雨，也不怕小偷手裡拿著刀子，追了十幾分鐘，才把同學的東西追回來。從這件事情，我們也發現校園安全已經成了問題。只要大偉當選了代表，一定會跟學校一起來想辦法，讓大家可以放心地在校園裡活動。除了安全問題，大偉也會請學校多準備經費買書、買電腦、辦活動；另外像補助學費、安排工讀機會、學校餐廳價錢什麼的，也都是他特別注意的問題。如果您願意給他一個為您服務的機會，就請您別忘了下禮拜一把票投給最理想的學聯會代表候選人＝3號李大偉！3號李大偉！謝謝您的支持。

## Vocabulary:

1. 各 (gè): each
2. 學生聯合會（學聯會）(syuéshēng liánhéhuèi) (xuéshēng liánhéhuì): students association
3. 安全 (āncuán) (ānquán): security/safety
4. 三號: No. 3. In Taiwan each election candidate carries a special personal number through the election campaign. This is so that the voters can identify and remember them more easily. These numbers are all decided by drawing lots. Most of the candidates hope to be "number one."

## 幫同學助選

各位₁同學：

　　大家好！你們都知道李大偉這次要競選學生聯合會₂代表，就像傳單上說的，大偉是個關心校園問題，了解同學需要，而且又熱心服務的人。各位一定還記得，上次放假的時候，小偷到學生宿舍來偷東西，大偉為了追小偷，不管外面下著大雨，也不怕小偷手裡拿著刀子，追了十幾分鐘，才把同學的東西追回來。從這件事情，我們也發現校園安全₃已經成了問題。只要大偉當選了代表，一定會跟學校一起來想辦法，讓大家可以放心地在校園裡活動。除了安全問題，大偉也會請學校多準備經費買書、買電腦、辦活動；另外像補助學費、安排工讀機會、學校餐廳價錢什麼的，也都是他特別注意的問題。如果您願意給他一個為您服務的機會，就請您別忘了下禮拜一把票投給最理想的學聯會代表候選人：3號₄李大偉！3號李大偉！謝謝您的支持。

# 第十一課 臺灣故事

■ 中華民國國慶日的活動：舞龍（新聞局提供）

（演講廳）

偉立：你覺得他的演講怎麼樣？你同意他的看法嗎？

李平：這位教授講的是中國大陸的民主運動，我們臺灣的情形不太一樣。

偉立：有什麼不同？

李平：大陸實行的是共產主義。

偉立：那你們到底實行什麼主義呢？

李平：**這就要從**孫中山先生**說起了**。孫中山，你聽說過嗎？

偉立：是 Dr. Sun Yat-Sen 嗎？

李平：對了！他在一九一一年革命成功，推翻了腐敗的清朝政府，建立了中華民國。想要建設一個三民主義[1]的新中國，沒想到不久就發生了內戰[2]。然後又是世界大戰。

偉立：第二次世界大戰的時候，中國不是跟日本打仗嗎？

李平：嗯！一共打了八年[3]。就**因為**長時間打仗**的關係**，社會一直沒辦法安定，人民的生活很苦，毛澤東領導的共產黨就在這個時候發展起來了。

偉立：後來呢？

李平：戰爭結束以後，日本把臺灣還給中華民國。國民政府[4]的力量這時候已經弱了很多，**再加上**共產黨的勢力越來越大，控制了大陸大部分的地方。因為情形越來越嚴重，蔣介石就決定把政府遷到臺灣去。

偉立：這是哪一年的事？

李平：一九四九年，這是歷史上很重要的一年。**從**這個時候**起**，中華民國在臺灣，實行三民主義；中華人民共和國在大陸，實行共產主義。因為**各有各的**制度，就有了不同的發展。

偉立：有什麼不同？

李平：我們政府一直希望臺灣將來能**像**歐美國家**一樣**進步、民主，所以在教育、社會、政治、經濟各方面都做了很多建設。中國大陸怎麼實行共產主義，我不清楚，不過，東歐的共產國家後來都放棄了共產主義，這不是就證明共產主義並不適合人類社會嗎？你說對不對？

■ 雙十節慶祝大會（新聞局提供）

偉立：對啊！我認為民主化才是最好的辦法。

※　　※　　※　　※　　※　　※

（高偉立敲門）

錢太太：嗨！高偉立。歡迎，歡迎。來，這雙拖鞋給你穿[5]。

偉立：噢！謝謝。錢先生呢？還沒下班嗎？

錢太太：快了。他公司最近比較忙。同同[6]，高哥哥[7]來了！

大同（過來）：高哥哥，你好。

偉立：嗨！大同，生日快樂，這個送給你。

■ 中華民國國慶日的活動：舞獅（新聞局提供）

大同：謝謝。

偉立：你不打開看看嗎？（大同看了看媽媽）

錢太太：沒關係，打開看看吧[8]！

大同：哇！印第安人！謝謝高哥哥。

偉立：沒什麼，小東西[9]。大同真有禮貌。

錢太太：哪裡，應該的。他最喜歡看漫畫書了，謝謝你的禮物。

大同：高哥哥，我看過好多印第安人的電影，現在他們都到哪裡去了？

偉立：歐洲人移民過來以後，印第安人就**一天比一天**少了。你們的歷史課教到哪兒了？

大同：剛剛念到獨立戰爭，殖民地的代表們決定要建立一個獨立的國家，跟統治國的軍隊打了一仗以後，宣布獨立。

錢太太：不錯嘛！**多少**學了**一點**[10]。

偉立：是啊！好棒啊！你的同學都**像**你**這樣**記得這麼清楚嗎？噢，還有一個「南北戰爭」，我們歷史上只有這一次內戰，你們以後一定也會學到。

大同：媽，我餓了。可以吃飯了嗎？

錢太太：等一下，你**先**吃點蘋果，**等**爸爸回來，我們**再**吃飯。

## 生詞及例句

**1** 演講廳 (yǎnjiǎngtīng)　N：auditorium, lecture hall

演講 (yǎnjiǎng)／講演 (jiǎngyǎn)　（M：場／次）

V/N：to deliver a speech, give a lecture /lecture, speech

講 (jiǎng)　V：to speak, explain

政治系昨天請總統來演講，他講的是「政黨跟政府的關係」。

講價 (jiǎng//jià)　VO：to bargain, to haggle over prices

我跟擺地攤的講了半天的價，他只願意便宜一塊錢。

**2** 同意 (tóngyì)　V/N：to agree, give consent/agreement, consent

(1) 李小姐的男朋友不是好人，我不同意把房子租給他。
(2) 沒有我姐姐的同意，你不可以進她的房間。

**3** 民主運動 (mínjhǔ yùndòng) (mínzhǔ yùndòng)

N：democratic movement

民主 (mínjhǔ) (mínzhǔ)　N/SV：democracy/to be democratic

這個國家非常不民主，連搬家都得政府同意才行。

運動 (yùndòng)　N：movement, campaign, drive (political, social, etc.)

參加這次學生運動的大部分是男學生。

**4** 實行 (shíhsing) (shíxíng)

V：to carry out, to implement, to put into practice

如果經費不夠，這個計畫實行起來就有困難。

294

## 5 共產主義 (gòngchǎnjhǔyì) (gòngchǎnzhǔyì)

N：communism

主義 (jhǔyì) (zhǔyì)　　N：doctrine, "-ism"

哪個國家是最早實行民主主義的國家？

共產黨 (gòngchǎndǎng)（共黨 (gòngdǎng)）　　N：communist party

## 6 革命 (gémìng)　　V/N：to revolt, to overhaul/a revolution（M：次/場）

(1) 這個國家的政府不民主，人民才起來革命的。
(2) 法國大革命的時候，死了多少人？

改革 (gǎigé)　　N/V：a reform/to reform

(1) 臺灣學生要念大學，不像以前那樣一定要通過考試了，這是教育改革的一部分。
(2) 我們這裡的選舉文化有問題，只要有錢就可以買票、做票，當選國會議員。很多大學教授都認為非改革不可了。

## 7 成功 (chénggōng)　　N/V/SV：success/to succeed/to be successful

(1) 成功是每一個人都希望的。有的人要有名，有的人要有錢；可是如果不好好地做，很難成功。
(2) 老張生意做得很大，賺了很多錢，非常成功。

## 8 推翻 (tuēifān) (tuīfān)　　V：to overthrow, overturn, topple

牛頓 (Newton) 這個說法，到現在還沒有人能推翻。

推 (tuēi) (tuī)　　V：to push, to shove

那個門我推了半天都推不開，後來才發現應該往外拉。

## 9 腐敗 (fǔbài)　　SV：rotten, decayed ; corrupt

這個政府裡的人只關心怎麼讓自己賺更多的錢，真腐敗。

腐ㄈㄨˇ爛ㄌㄢˋ (fǔlàn)　V：to rot, to decay, to decompose, to putrefy

上次買的青菜，放在冰箱裡，忘了吃，都腐爛了。

10　建ㄐㄧㄢˋ立ㄌㄧˋ (jiànlì)　V：to establish, to set up, to found

亞洲最早建立的民主國家是哪一國？

11　建ㄐㄧㄢˋ設ㄕㄜˋ (jiànshè)　V/N：to build, to construct/construction

(1) 王市長答應選民一定要把這個城市建設好。
(2) 這個地方的交通建設，完全沒有計畫，才會到處塞車。

12　內ㄋㄟˋ戰ㄓㄢˋ (nèijhàn) (nèizhàn)　N：civil war（M：場／次）

13　打ㄉㄚˇ仗ㄓㄤˋ (dǎ//zhàng)　VO：to go to war, to engage in combat, to battle

這個世界上有哪個國家從來沒跟別的國家打過仗？

14　安ㄢ定ㄉㄧㄥˋ (āndìng)　N/SV：stability / to be stable, to be settled

(1) 老張決定不再換工作，或搬家了，因為孩子念書需要安定。
(2) 在一個安定的社會裡，大部分人民都有工作，吃得飽，穿得暖，很少人會去偷、去搶。

15　人ㄖㄣˊ民ㄇㄧㄣˊ (rénmín)　N：the people, citizen

這個國家的人民都支持他們的政府嗎？

國ㄍㄨㄛˊ民ㄇㄧㄣˊ (guómín)　N：the people

只要是中華民國的國民就可以接受九年的義務教育。

公ㄍㄨㄥ民ㄇㄧㄣˊ (gōngmín)　N：citizen

老趙剛移民美國，還沒有拿到公民權，不能投票。

市ㄕˋ民ㄇㄧㄣˊ (shìhmín) (shìmín)　N：residents of a city

在臺北市住滿六個月的市民才能選市長。

## 16 領導 (lǐngdǎo)　　N/V：leadership, guidance / to lead, guide

(1) 有了總統的領導，我們一定會打贏這場仗。
(2) 這次的民主運動是誰領導的？

## 17 戰爭 (jhànjhēng) (zhànzhēng)　　N：war, combat（M：場／次）

(1) 全世界最重要的兩次戰爭，就是第一次跟第二次世界大戰。
(2) 男人跟女人的戰爭，誰都贏不了。

## 18 結束 (jiéshù)　　V：to end, finish, conclude

期末考一考完，學期就結束了。

## 19 力量 (lìliàng)　　N：strength, power

我一個人的力量不夠，得大家聯合起來一起做才行。

## 力氣 (lìcì) (lìqì)　　N：energy, power

老陳在山上迷了路，餓了三天。我們發現他的時候，他連走路的力氣都沒有了。

## 20 弱 (ruò)　　SV：feeble, weak, frail

李教授的病剛好，所以身體還很弱。

## 21 勢力 (shìhlì) (shìlì)　　N：force, power, influence

用這種電腦的人越來越多，所以這家公司在市場上的勢力也越來越大。

## 22 控制 (kòngjhìh) (kòngzhì)

N/V：control, command/to control, manipulate, dominate

(1) 在不民主的國家，人民的生活都受到政府的控制。
(2) 演講的時候，得控制好時間。

23 嚴重 (yánjhòng) (yánzhòng)　　SV：serious, grave, critical

小錢這次感冒很嚴重，病了一個月才好。

嚴 (yán) / 嚴格 (yángé)　　SV：to be strict, severe

丁老師很嚴，一個字寫錯了，就要扣兩分。

24 遷 (ciān) (qiān)　　V：to move to another place

辦公室太小了，我們老闆想遷到附近的新大樓去。

25 歷史 (lìshǐh) (lìshǐ)　　N：history

這棟老房子已經有三百年的歷史了，很多地方都壞了。

26 各 (gè)　　DEM：various, each, every

(1) 這兩個菜都是豬肉做的，可是各有各的味道。
(2) 各位同學，現在請你們把功課交給我。

27 制度 (jhìhdù) (zhìdù)　　N：system

這是一個新公司，制度都還沒有建立。

28 將來 (jiānglái)　　MA/N：in the future/the future

(1) 我現在替別人助選，將來自己要出來競選。
(2) 為了孩子的將來，孫太太覺得非搬家不可。

29 經濟 (jīngjì)　　N/SV：economy, financial status/to be economical, thrifty

(1) 一個國家如果政治安定，經濟才能發展。
(2) 坐飛機不像坐火車需要那麼多時間，比較經濟。

30 放棄 (fàngcì) (fàngqì)　　V：to abandon, give up, renounce

我看沒有希望申請到獎學金了，我們放棄吧！

## 第十一課　臺灣故事

**31 證明 (jhèngmíng) (zhèngmíng)**

N/V：proof, evidence/to prove, to confirm

(1) 你一直說你是對的，請證明給我看。
(2) 小李生病，不能去上課，他應該拿一張醫生證明給老師看。

**證明書 (jhèngmíngshū) (zhèngmíngshū)**

N：a certificate (of a person's qualifications, abilities, etc.)（M：張）

進我們公司以前，一定要交一張健康證明書。

**證書 (jhèngshū) (zhèngshū)**　N：a certificate（M：張）

我大學沒念完，沒拿到畢業證書，現在找工作有困難。

**32 人類 (rénlèi)**　N：humankind, the human race

**人類學 (rénlèisyué) (rénlèixué)**　N：anthropology

人類學研究一切跟人類有關係的事情，越來越熱門了。

**33 認為 (rènwéi)**　V：to believe that, consider that

這個候選人在政治方面沒有什麼經驗，我認為他不會當選。

**34 民主化 (mínjhǔhuà) (mínzhǔhuà)**

N/V：democratization/to democratize

(1) 臺灣的民主化很快，現在連總統做了什麼不對的事，人民都可以講話了。
(2) 你們國家想要民主化，一定要改變制度。

**西化 (sīhuà) (xīhuà)**　N/V：westernization/to westernize

現在很多臺灣人喜歡吃漢堡(hànbǎo, hamburg)、熱狗，喝咖啡、可樂，吃東西的習慣已經西化了。

**制度化 (jhìhdùhuà) (zhìdùhuà)**　N/V：systematization/to systematize

我們公司已經完全制度化了，什麼人做什麼事，拿多少錢，都是一定的。

### 電腦化 (diànnǎohuà)　N/V：computerization / to computerize

(1) 辦公室電腦化可以讓老闆少用一些人，大家做事也快一點。
(2) 我們學校已經電腦化了，所以學生要上網選課。

### 自動化 (zìhdònghuà) (zìdònghuà)　N/V：automation/to automate

### 暖化 (nuǎnhuà)　N/V：warming/to make warm

因為汽車、冷氣用得太多，全世界的天氣越來越熱，氣候暖化的情形很嚴重。

## 35 拖鞋 (tuōsié) (tuōxié)　N：slippers, thongs（M：雙）

### 拖 (tuō)　V：to pull, drag, haul; to drag on, delay; to mop

(1) 箱子太重了，我拿不動，只好拖回家。
(2) 這篇報告上星期就該交了，你怎麼拖到今天才交？
(3) 地上有水，請你拖一拖。

## 36 禮貌 (lǐmào)　N：courtesy, manners, social etiquette

別人說話的時候，你應該注意聽，這是禮貌。

### 有禮貌 (yǒu lǐmào)

SV：to be courteous, to have good manners, to be polite

客人還在喝咖啡，你就一直看錶，真沒禮貌。

## 37 漫畫書 (mànhuàshū)　N：comic book

### 漫畫 (mànhuà)　N：caricature, cartoon

王愛美她們每天搶報紙，就是為了看漫畫。

## 第十一課 臺灣故事

**38 殖民地 (jhíhmíndì) (zhímíndì)** N：colony

印度 (Yìndù, India) 以前是英國的殖民地，大部分的人都會說英文。

**39 統治 (tǒngjhìh) (tǒngzhì)** V/N：to govern, to rule/governance; dominion

(1) 日本統治了臺灣五十年，直到一九四五年才把臺灣還給中華民國。
(2) 一九九七年英國結束了對香港的統治，這是歷史上的一件大事。

**40 軍隊 (jyūnduèi) (jūnduì)** N：army, troops, armed forces（M：支）

第二次世界大戰的時候，好幾個國家的軍隊聯合起來打仗。

**軍人 (jyūnrén) (jūnrén)** N：soldier, serviceperson

如果軍人為國家打仗，打死了，政府有義務照顧他們的家人。

**陸軍 (lùjyūn) (lùjūn)** N：ground forces, land forces, army
**海軍 (hǎijyūn) (hǎijūn)** N：naval forces, navy
**空軍 (kōngjyūn) (kōngjūn)** N：air force

總統是三軍統帥 (a commander-in-chief)，所以不管是陸軍、海軍或空軍都要聽他的。

**41 宣布 (syuānbù) (xuānbù)** V：to declare, proclaim, announce

大家請注意，我現在要宣布一個好消息。

**布 (bù)** N：cloth（M：塊／尺）

你這麼高，只買兩尺布做衣服，怎麼夠呢？

**42 多少 (duōshǎo)** A：how many, how much; more or less, somewhat

小高說了半天，你一塊錢都不借也不好意思，多少借給他一點吧！

## 專有名詞  Proper Names

1. 孫中山 (Sūn Jhōngshān) (Sūn Zhōngshān)
   Sun Yat-sen (1866 - 1925)
2. 清朝 (Cīng Cháo) (Qīng Cháo)　Ch'ing Dynasty (1644 - 1911)
3. 中華民國 (Jhōnghuá Mínguó) (Zhōnghuá Mínguó)
   Republic of China (1912 - present)  (government in Taiwan since 1949)
4. 三民主義 (Sānmín Jhǔyì) (Sānmín Zhǔyì)
   Three Principles of the People
5. 第二次世界大戰
   (Dièrcìh Shìhjiè Dàjhàn) (Dì'èrcì Shìjiè Dàzhàn)
   World War II
6. 毛澤東 (Máo Zédōng)　Mao Tse-tung (1893 - 1976)
7. 蔣介石 (Jiǎng Jièshíh) (Jiǎng Jièshí)　Chiang Kai-shek (1887 - 1975)
8. 國民政府 (Guómín Jhèngfǔ) (Guómín Zhèngfǔ)
   National Government
9. 中華人民共和國
   (Jhōnghuá Rénmín Gònghéguó) (Zhōnghuá Rénmín Gònghéguó)
   The People's Republic of China (1949 - present) (government in Mainland China)
10. 東歐 (Dōng Ōu)　East Europe
11. 印地安人 (Yìndì'ān rén)　American Indians
12. 南北戰爭 (Nánběi Jhànjhēng) (Nánběi Zhànzhēng)
    the American Civil War (1861- 1865)

## 注釋

1. 三民主義 the Three Principles of the People. Dr. Sun Yat-sen (1866-1925) authored this three-part theory in 1898 as an ideal for shaping the Chinese nation and as a means to promote the political and economic status of Chinese people. The three parts consist of 民

族主義 (racial rights), 民權主義 (political rights), and 民生主義 (rights for life and the pursuit of happiness). 民族主義 establishes equal rights to all races in the Chinese nation, and declares that Chinese citizens have rights equal to other citizens of the world. 民權主義 asserts that everyone has an equal right to participate in politics and the running of government. According to 民生主義 everyone should have equal access to daily necessities of life, including education, food, housing, clothing, transportation and recreation.

2. 內戰 means "civil war." The Republic of China, established in 1912, was the first republic in Asia. Democracy was a new concept to the Chinese and therefore faced some opposition at the beginning. In 1915 袁世凱 (Yuán ShìhKǎi) (Yuán Shìkǎi) claimed that he was the emperor and tried to restore imperialism. 雲南, Yunnan Province declared itself independent. Military factions appeared in various places throughout the country, resulting in many local battles. In 1928 Chiang Kai-shek (1887-1975) and his troops succeeded in carrying out the Northern Expedition, clearing out all the warlords and once again unifying the country.

3. "一共打了八年" The Japanese invaded northeastern China in 1931. The war against Japan formally began in 1937, after they attacked 宛平 Wǎnpíng, a county close to 北平 Běipíng, the capital. The war ended eight years later in 1945 with the surrender of Japan. As part of the war settlement, Taiwan was returned to the Republic of China. It had been governed by Japan for fifty years as the result of a previous treaty signed during the Ch'ing Dynasty.

4. 國民政府 refers to The National Government of the Republic of China, before the Constitutional Central Government was formed in 1948. During that time 國民黨, the Kwomintang (KMT) or Nationalist Party, had full control of the government.

5. 這雙拖鞋給你穿 "Here, you can wear these slippers." Most people living in Taiwan have adapted this Japanese custom of leaving ones shoes at the doorway in order to keep the interior of the house clean.

6. "同同" The child's given name is 大同, but here the first syllable has been eliminated and the last syllable has been duplicated. Many parents like to address their children, especially young ones, in this manner as a term of endearment.

7. 高哥哥 "Brother Kao." In Chinese/Taiwanese society, children usually address older people of the same generation as 哥哥 or 姐姐, whether they are related or not. This expresses a feeling of closeness and familiarity.

8. "沒關係，打開看看吧！" means: "It's all right, go ahead and open it." As a custom, Chinese/Taiwanese people do not usually open gifts in front of the person who has presented the gift. This avoids giving the impression that the recipient is more concerned about the gift than about the giver or his goodwill.

9. "沒什麼，小東西。" means: "It's nothing, just a small token." Chinese/Taiwanese often say this when presenting a gift as a form of courtesy. Some people say 小意思 instead of 小東西.

10. **多少學了一點** means "so you have learned something." Statements such as this may imply two intentions. On one hand it might be 客氣話, a polite remark, resulting because 錢太太 does not want to make a big issue of her son's achievements before a guest. On the other hand it might be a joking statement which subtly contains some encouragement for her son.

## 文法練習

### 一

#### (I) 從……起    to start from ......

◎這就要從孫中山先生說起了。
In order to explain this, we need to begin by talking about Sun Yat-sen.

◎從這個時候起，中華民國在臺灣，實行三民主義……
Starting from this year, the Republic of China on Taiwan has been practicing the Three Principles of the People……

用法說明：「起」表示「開始」。「從」的後面常用時間詞，有時也可用表示地方的詞。

Explanation: 起 means "to start". This pattern means "to start from ......" 從 is often followed by a TW, or sometimes, a PW.

**練習**　　請用「從……起」改寫下面句子。

1. 我媽說我六歲以後就很少生病了。
   My mother says that after I turned six I hardly ever got sick.
   → 我媽說我從六歲起就很少生病了。
   My mother says that starting from the time I turned six years old I hardly ever got sick.

2. 小王找到了新工作，明天就不來這兒上班了。
   _____

3. 小張搬進來的那天，我們就成了好朋友。
   _____

4. 第十一課開始，李教授要改變教法。
___

5. 這條街上的商店，第七家開始，都是賣鞋的。
___

## (II) 這就要從……說起了
### to explain this one must begin by talking about ……

◎這就要從孫中山先生說起了。
In order to explain this, we need to begin by talking about Sun Yat-Sen.

用法說明：「這」表示「這件事」，「就要」是「就得」的意思。說話者要說明某件事，但這件事不是一兩句話可以說清楚的，現在打算從某一點開始談。因為「起」的意思是「開始」，所以前面還可以用其他動詞，如「找」、「做」、「寫」、「看」……等，表示開始做那件事。

Explanation: 這 refers to 這件事, 就要 means "then one must". The speaker wants to explain something cannot be clearly described in a brief statement, so he uses this pattern to introduce his explanation and indicate his starting point. Since 起 means "to start", other verbs, such as 找, 做, 寫, 看……, etc., can be placed in front of 起 to show what action one is starting.

▼ 練習　　請用「這就要從……說起了」回答下面問題，並再加以說明。

1. 張先生為什麼會競選州長？
   Why is Mr. Chang running for governor?
   → 這就要從他的政治理想說起了。他從小就對政治有興趣、關心社會問題。他一直在找機會證明自己政治方面的看法是對的
   To explain this one must begin by talking about his political ideals. Ever since he was young, he has been interested in politics and concerned about social issues. He has always been looking for a chance to prove that his political views are correct.

2. 你為什麼想學中文？
___

3. 我們學校離你家這麼遠,你為什麼要來這兒念大學呢?
   _____

4. 你跟你女朋友是怎麼好起來的?
   _____

5. 你怎麼會到××(地方)去打工的?
   _____

## 二　因為……的關係　Due to ...

◎就因為長時間打仗的關係,社會一直沒辦法安定,……
Due to the length of the war, society never had a chance to stabilize,…

用法說明:「因為」的後面大部分是名詞或簡單的短語。說話者不欲詳細說明原因,或覺得原因不必交代那麼清楚,就用「因為……的關係」表示。

Explanation: Usually, the word following 因為 is a noun or a simple clause, The speaker does not want to or does not think it is necessary to give an elaborate explanation for his/her statement; the connection between the first clause and the second clause is obvious and requires no further explanation.

▼ **練習**　請根據提示,用「因為……的關係」回答下面問題。

1. 你們為什麼不租大點兒的場地?(經費)
   Why don't you rent a larger site?
   →因為經費的關係,我們租不起大點兒的場地。
   　Due to funding, we cannot rent a larger site.

2. 你們怎麼準備了那麼多吃的東西?(颱風)
   _____

3. 趙老師今天怎麼只教了生詞?(時間)
   _____

4. 昨天這附近為什麼塞車?(學校開園遊會)
   _____

5. 小王怎麼這麼獨立?(從小住校)
   _____

## 三　再加上　furthermore; additionally

◎ 國民政府的力量這時候已經弱了很多，再加上共產黨的勢力越來越大，控制了大陸大部分的地方……

The power of the National Government was much weakened at this time. Furthermore, the Communist Party became increasingly powerful. Therefore, they controlled most of mainland China……

用法說明：「再加上」的前後都是造成後面事件的原因，可是「再加上」後面的原因比前面的更有決定性。

Explanation: The situations before and after 再加上 are all factors that contribute to the result that follows, but the factor stated after 再加上 is usually the final, determining factor which leads to the result.

### ▼ 練習　請用「再加上」完成下面句子。

1. 今天是週末，天氣又好，再加上期中考也考完了，所以出來玩的學生特別多。
It's the weekend, the weather is beautiful, and besides that, the mid-term exams are over; so there are especially many students outside today.

2. 這份工作很輕鬆，錢也多，再加上＿＿＿＿＿＿＿＿＿＿，所以我弟弟非常喜歡。

3. 那個地方颱風多，地震也多，再加上＿＿＿＿＿＿＿＿＿＿，不適合人住。

4. 我最近工作很忙，壓力很大，再加上＿＿＿＿＿＿＿＿＿＿，就病倒了。

5. 老張不但醜，而且不修邊幅，再加上＿＿＿＿＿＿＿＿＿＿，當然沒有女孩子會喜歡他。

## 四
### (I) 各有各的N　each has its own ……

◎ 各有各的制度。
Each has its own system.

用法說明：「各」表示「每一個」，指某個範圍內的每一個體，人、地、事、物都可以。
Explanation: 各 means 每一個 ("every single") person, place, thing, or event in a specific and understood setting.

### 練習　請用「各有各的 N」改寫下面各句。

1. 這些菜雖然都是牛肉做的，但是每一個都有不同的味道。
   Although all of these dishes are made with beef, every one of them has a distinct flavor.
   → 這些菜雖然都是牛肉做的，但是各有各的味道。
   　Although all of these dishes are made with beef, each one has its own distinct flavor.

2. 我想這幾家公司以後每一家都會有不同的發展。
   _____

3. 老李他們每個人的困難都不一樣，我真不知道怎麼幫助他們。
   _____

4. 孩子們現在都大了，都有他們自己的家了。
   _____

5. 畢業以後大家的計畫都不一樣，有的人還想念書，有的人只想找工作。
   _____


## (II) 各 V 各的　each V …… own ……

用法說明：表示所做的事雖然相同，但每個人是分別做的。
Explanation: Indicates that, although each action undertaken is identical, each person performs it individually.

### 練習　請用「各 V 各的」完成下面對話。

1. 張：你剛剛跟王小姐吃飯，是你請的客嗎？
   Chang: When you just ate with Miss Wang, was it you that treated?
   李：不，我們各付各的。
   Lee: No, we each paid our own bill.

2. 張：你跟你室友常一起出去玩嗎？
   李：我們興趣不同，所以都是 _____。

3. 張：你可以穿你姐姐的衣服吧？
   李：我們都是 _____，她的衣服樣子我都不喜歡。

4. 張：你已經吃過了？你不等你弟弟嗎？
   李：他不一定什麼時候下班，所以我們 _____。

5. 張：你跟你哥哥一起做生意嗎？
   李：他賣水果，我賣衣服，我們 _____。

## 五　像……一樣　like ....../similar to ......

◎我們政府一直希望臺灣將來能像歐美國家一樣進步、民主……
Our government always hoped that in the future Taiwan will be as developed and democratic as Western countries…..

用法說明：「像……一樣」表示兩個人、地、事物有類似之處，如果要說明類似之處，就加在「一樣」的後面。

Explanation: "像……一樣" indicates that two people, places or things have similar characteristics. To further explain how they are similar, a characteristic or condition can be placed after 一樣。

### 練習　請用「像……一樣」完成下面句子。

1. 我們學校各國學生都有，像聯合國一樣。
   Our school has students from all countries; it's just like the United Nations.

2. 這裡怎麼這麼亂，像_____一樣。

3. 我妹妹的皮膚像_____一樣，又白又細。

4. 老趙什麼都學不會，像_____一樣笨。

5. 張小姐打扮得好漂亮，像_____一樣。

## 六　一 M 比一 M

more and more/less and less/
......er and ......er (every) ......

◎……印地安人就一天比一天少了。
The Indian population is getting smaller and smaller every day.

**用法說明：表示程度逐漸加深。**
Explanation: This pattern indicates that the degree of something is gradually intensifying.

▼ **練習**　請用「一 M 比一 M」改寫下面句子。

1. 夏天到了，天氣就熱起來了。
   Summer has arrived, so the weather has started to get hotter and hotter.
   → 夏天到了，天氣就一天比一天熱了。
   Summer has arrived, so the weather has been getting hotter and hotter every day.

2. 這幾次的考試都很難，而且越來越難。
   _____

3. 我跟我妹妹都找到了工作，我媽覺得這幾年輕鬆多了。
   _____

4. 老師們都覺得這幾課書越到後面越難教。
   _____

5. 我這幾個朋友都很會說話，小王比小李會說話，小張比小王更會說話，小陳比他們都會說話。
   _____

## 七　多少 V 一點／一些／幾　M (more or less) V a little

◎多少學了一點。
You've learned a little something.

用法說明：「多少」是「或多或少」，「不管是多少，總……」的意思。多用作建議或對所提到的事故意表示不予重視的意思。

Explanation: 多少 means "more or less" or "no matter how much or how little, it's always ……." This pattern is mostly used to offer a suggestion or to downplay the thing mentioned in the conversation.

**練習** 請用「多少 V 一點／一些／幾 M」完成下面對話。

1. 張：老趙跟我借錢，我真不想借他。
   Chang: Old Zhao wants to borrow money from me. I really don't want to lend it to him.
   李：不借不好吧？多少借給他一點嘛！
   Li: I don't think it's a good idea not to lend Old Zhao anything. Give him a little something.

2. 張：你在美國住了兩年，英文說得不錯了吧？
   李：還說得不太好，不過多少＿＿＿＿＿＿。

3. 張：陳教授的課真無聊，我不想去上。
   李：你應該去上課，多少＿＿＿＿＿＿。

4. 張：我不舒服，不想吃東西。
   李：這些菜都是為你做的，多少＿＿＿＿＿＿。

5. 張：這個工作是你爸爸幫你找的嗎？
   李：是我自己找的，不過我爸爸多少＿＿＿＿＿＿。

## 八 像……這樣／那樣…… …… like …… (similar to)

◎你的同學都像你這樣記得這麼清楚嗎？
Do all of your classmates remember (things) as clearly as you?

用法說明：這個句型跟第五課的「像……什麼的」不同。「像」後面指出特定對象，「這樣」的後面是兩件事物相同的特點。

Explanation: This sentence pattern is not the same as the pattern "像……什麼的"(Chapter 5). Here, the word or phrase following 像 points out a specific object, and the word or phrase following 這樣 refers to a specific trait shared by that object and the subject.

**練習** 請用「像……這樣／那樣……」改寫下面句子。

1. 跟她一樣漂亮的女孩子多不多？
   Are there many girls as pretty as her?
   → 像她那樣漂亮的女孩子多不多？
   　Are there many pretty girls like her?

2. 我從來沒看過跟我弟弟房間一樣髒的地方。
   _____

3. 跟宮保雞丁一樣的菜，我都覺得太辣了。
   _____

4. 西瓜、香蕉這一類的水果，在臺灣到處都買得到。
   _____

5. 在餐廳當服務生好辛苦啊！
   _____

## 九　先……，等……，再……

### first ......, wait until ......, and then ......

◎你先吃點蘋果，等爸爸回來，我們再吃飯。
You have some apples first, wait until your father is back, and then we will have dinner.

**用法說明**：指出做三件事的順序。用於說話或動作當時及後來的情況。（請參看第三課文法練習五）
Explanation: This pattern shows the sequence of three actions, starting with the time a statement is made or an action is performed, and then moving into the situations that follow. (Please refer to sentence patterns 5 in Chapter 3.)

**練習** 請用「先……，等……，再……」回答下面問題。

1. 糖醋魚怎麼做？
   How do you make sweet and sour fish？
   → 你先把魚煎 (jiān, to fry with a little oil) 一下，等魚的兩面都黃了，再放糖跟

醋。
You fry the fish with a little oil first, wait until the fish is yellow on both sides, then add sugar and vinegar.

2. 你下了課，就直接回家嗎？
_____

3. 我想工讀，要怎麼申請？
_____

4. 你怎麼準備期末考？
_____

5. 這次的政見發表會，你要怎麼安排？
_____

| 課室活動 | Classroom Activities |
| --- | --- |

一

1. 角色扮演 (Role Playing)

The students select and play the role of one of the following political figures: 孫中山, 蔣介石, 毛澤東, 聯合國代表, or 現任中華民國總統. The teacher acts as a moderator for a televised discussion panel in which each of the five historical personalities participate. The moderator begins the discussion by asking them what they think about 臺灣的將來.

可能用到的詞：

改善 (gǎishàn; to improve), 資本主義 (zīběn zhǔyì; capitalism), 自由經濟 (free market economy), 思想 (sīxiǎng; thoughts), 和平 (hépíng; peace), 相處 (xiāngchǔ; to get along with one another).

2. 遊戲：搶椅子 (Musical Chairs)

Find out if the students know any songs in Mandarin. If they do not, teach them a simple one such as: 兩隻老虎，兩隻老虎，跑得快，跑得快。一隻沒有眼睛，一隻沒有尾巴 (wěi‧bā, tail)，真奇怪，真奇怪！Then have the students form a circle with their chairs. There should be one chair less than the total number of students. The game starts with the students circling around the chairs, singing the song they have just learned. When the teacher says 停, every student should quickly take a seat. The one who has no chair loses. He/She must describe in Chinese to the class some important event in their history, then he/she is removed from the game. Then one chair is removed and the game starts again. This is repeated until only one player is left.

## 二、討論問題 (Discussion)

1. 你認為我們會有第三次世界大戰嗎？如果會，你想原因 (reason) 是什麼？結果 (result) 會怎麼樣？
2. 你希望你們國家的領導人是什麼樣的人？他應該為人民做哪些事？
3. 請說一件貴國歷史上的大事。
4. 你對戰爭的看法怎麼樣？

## 短文　　爸爸的電子信₁

寄件者：爸爸
日期：2007_11_15 20:54
收件者：林建國
主旨：我從臺灣來了
附加檔案：picture 003.jpg(2.06MB) picture 002.jpg(2.32MB) picture 001.jpg(2.25MB)

建國：

　　最近功課忙吧？上個月我回臺灣，看了很多朋友，參觀了不少地方。

　　十月是臺灣最快樂的一個月，天氣好假日₂多，活動也多。第一個好日子就是雙十節₃，中華民國的國慶日₄。這是為了紀念₅一九一一年十月十日國父₆孫中山先生推翻清朝，革命成功。每年的這一天都有很多慶祝活動，像遊行₇、放煙火₈什麼的。跟這裡的獨立紀念日₉一樣熱鬧。像我這樣回國參加慶祝活動的華僑₁₀非常多。

　　十月二十五日是臺灣光復節₁₁，是二次大戰結束那年，日本政府把臺灣還給中華民國的日子。

　　這些年臺灣各方面的發展非常快，改變了很多。等明年一月我們全家回去的時候，你也會發現一切都跟你小時候不一樣了。好了，我們下次再談吧！

　　　　　　　　　　　　　　　　　　　　　　　　爸爸
　　　　　　　　　　　　　　　　　　　　　　　　11月15日

## Vocabulary:

1. 電子信 (diànzǐh sìn) (diànzǐ xìn): e-mail
2. 假日 (jiàrìh) (jiàrì): holiday
3. 雙十節 (Shuāngshíh Jié) (Shuāngshí Jié): Double Tenth, a holiday celebrating the formation of the Republic of China
4. 國慶日 (guócìng rìh) (guóqìng rì): date of a nation's formation
5. 紀念 (jì'niàn): to commemorate
6. 國父 (guófù): father of a nation
7. 遊行 (yóuxíng): parade
8. 放煙火 (fàng//yānhuǒ): to set off fireworks
9. 獨立紀念日 (Dúlì Jì niànrìh) (Dúlì Jì'niànrì): Independence Day
10. 華僑 (huáciao) (huáqiáo): Overseas Chinese
11. 臺灣光復節 (Táiwān Guāngfù Jié): Retrocession Day, day in which Taiwan was returned to the Republic of China

# 第十二課　看球賽

■棒球賽（行政院新聞局提供）

（體育館看台上）

建國：哇！剛才的球賽好精彩。我們七號打得真棒，他一個人就得了二十八分。

美真：對呀！他投籃投得好準，防守也不錯，**要不是**後來犯規太多，他還可以得更多分。

台麗：他投籃的動作很漂亮。人也帥，雖然頭有點禿，還是有好多女生都很迷他。

建國：是啊！給他加油的都是女生。他的魅力**還**真不小。

偉立：我覺得十五號也很好，每次搶到球都能得分。

美真：他那麼高，只要他站在籃下，誰都搶不到球。

建國：他跟隊友的默契也很好。他拿到球，**就是**沒機會投籃，**也**不會把球傳丟了，從來沒有出過錯！

台麗：上半場十三號打得不錯，不知道下半場教練為什麼不**讓**他打了？

偉立：可能因為他太愛出鋒頭，沒有團隊精神。你知道，比賽的時候，最重要的是合作。

建國：今天那個裁判不公平，好幾次對方犯規，他都假裝沒看見。幸虧我們有實力，要不然比數一定差得更多，不會只是九十八比九十三。

美真：所以好多人噓[1]他。

建國：真不知道他們從哪裡找來的爛裁判！我好幾次想進場把他拉出來。

偉立：我看見九號也**被**他氣得要打人了。

建國：九號，我認識。他常跟女朋友到我打工的酒館來玩。這個人很容易生氣，**動不動就**罵人。哎喲！**說到**打工，我得走了。今天有個同事生病，我得去代班。再見啦！

美真：談**得正**高興，你就要走了。

建國：那有什麼辦法，誰叫我答應他的呢？我非走不可了。去晚了，又要看老闆的臉色[2]。

台麗：那我們也走吧！

■籃球賽（行政院新聞局提供）

（在餐廳）

台麗：剛剛看大家這麼興奮，**讓**我想到以前在臺灣看棒球賽的情形。

偉立：在臺灣很多人看棒球賽嗎？

美真：我們最喜歡看的就是棒球賽跟籃球賽。

台麗：我聽我爸說我們的棒球隊第一次到美國比賽[3]，大家寧可不睡覺，也要看電視轉播[4]。打贏了，就放鞭炮慶祝[5]，大家都興奮得不得了。

美真：每次臺灣球員在外國比賽的時候，我老爸[6]都準備好多吃的、喝的，我們一邊看，一邊吃，真有意思。

偉立：我們家也一樣。尤其是我老爸，他不但一邊看，一邊吃，看到緊張的時候還又叫又罵。好像自己是教練一樣。

美真：我老哥[6]也總以為自己是教練。要是中華隊投手**一連**投了幾次四壞球，他就會對著電視大叫「換投手！」。

台麗：你老哥真有意思！

美真：還有一次，中華隊在最後一局打了一支再見全壘打，他興奮得跳起來，把桌上的杯子都打破了。

偉立：他跟我老爸一起看球賽一定很熱鬧。

美真：我老哥在南部念博士。有機會應該介紹他們認識認識。他還是很迷棒球。每次中華隊來比賽，他一定開幾

個小時的車去當啦啦隊,給他們加油。

台麗:如果中華隊打進決賽,聽說還有人特別自己花錢買機票,從臺灣飛到這裡看比賽。

偉立:像這樣的棒球迷,臺灣有不少吧?

台麗:是啊!臺灣棒球運動的發展越來越制度化了,現在有好幾支職業球隊[7],都是由大公司的老闆支持的。

偉立:我們職業球隊的球員大部分是從大學選出來的,很多校友捐錢給自己的大學發展校隊,打得好的球員就有機會參加職業球隊。

美真:欸,這麼說,要是書念不好,會打球也不錯[8]。

■臺北小巨蛋體育館(臺北市政府工務局新工處 馬景文攝)

## 實用視聽華語 3

### 生詞及例句

**1 球賽 (ciósài) (qiúsài)**　N：ballgame, match

你喜歡看哪一種球賽？籃球賽，網球賽，還是…？

**比賽 (bǐsài)**　N/V：compctition, match / to compete

(1) 你的毛筆字寫得這麼漂亮，要不要參加這次的書法比賽？
(2) 我們來比賽，看誰跑得快。

**決賽 (jyuésài) (juésài)**　N：(sports) finals

這次的游泳比賽，初賽有兩百多人參加，複賽(the semi-finals)還有一半的人，決賽就只有十個人在搶前三名了。

**2 體育館 (tǐyùguǎn)**　N：gym, gymnasium

我們校長覺得健康比讀書更重要，所以他決定先建體育館，等有了經費，再建圖書館。

**體育 (tǐyù)**　N：physical training, sports, physical education

我很愛運動，可惜我們一個星期只有兩個鐘頭的體育課。

**體育界 (tǐyùjiè)**　N：the sporting world

奧林匹克運動會 (Àolínpǐkè Yùndònghuì, Olympic Games) 是體育界的大事。

**3 看台（臺）(kàntái)**　N：grandstand

比賽還沒開始，看台上已經坐滿了人。

**月台（臺）(yuètái)**　N：railway platform

往南去的火車，都在第二月台上車。

**4 精彩 (jīngcǎi)**　SV：to be brilliant, excellent, splendid

第十二課　看球賽

李教授的課那麼精彩，你怎麼可能睡得著？

彩色 (cǎisè)　　AT：multicolored, colored

彩色電視的價錢比黑白的貴多了。

**5** 得分 (dé//fēn)

VO：to score points (in sports competitions, contests, tests, etc.)

這次考試，李新得了一百分。

得 (dé)　　V：to get, obtain, receive, gain

王大文才學游泳一個月，沒想到第一次參加比賽，就得了第五名。

得到 (dédào)　　RC：to get, obtain, receive, acquire

老謝去年打工，得到不少經驗。

**6** 投籃 (tóu//lán)　　VO：to shoot a basket (basketball)

老李投籃的時候，力氣不是太大，就是太小，投了三次都沒進。

籃 (lán)　　M：basket

我生病的時候，老孫來看我，送了一籃蘋果。

籃子 (lán·zih) (lán·zi)　　N：basket

你把要買的東西先放在籃子裡，等一下再提到門口去算帳。

**7** 準 (jhǔn) (zhǔn)　　SV：to be accurate

我的錶很準，一分都不差。

**8** 防守 (fángshǒu)　　N/V：defense / to defend, guard

(1) 小林他們球隊防守方面比較差，難怪贏不了。
(2) 這個地方很重要，所以有很多軍隊防守。

323

實用視聽華語 3

9 犯規 (fànguēi) (fànguī)　V：to commit a foul

打籃球的時候，如果帶球走，就犯規了。

犯 (fàn)

V：to violate a law, to have an attack of an old illness; to commit something wrong or bad

天氣不好，我媽腿疼的病又犯了。

10 動作 (dòngzuò)　N：movement, action

我室友又拉頭髮了，每次我看到這個動作，就知道她又緊張了。

11 禿 (tū)　SV：to be bald

王小姐吃的藥不對，頭髮忽然少了很多，頭上就禿了一塊。

禿頭 (tūtóu)　N："baldhead", bald-headed person

禿頭沒什麼特別，就像有些人高，有些人矮，有些人胖，有些人瘦一樣。

12 隊友 (duèiyǒu) (duìyǒu)　N：teammate

小高只管防守，所以拿到球一定傳給隊友，很少投籃。

隊 (duèi) (duì)　M：team, squad

參加這次比賽的，一共有五隊，法國隊打得最好。

校友 (siàoyǒu) (xiàoyǒu)　N：alumni, alumnus

每年有一千多人從這個學校畢業，所以他們的校友很多。

13 默契 (mòcì) (mòqì)　N：tacit agreement or understanding

我跟哥哥很有默契，我心裡想什麼，我敢說他都知道。

14 出錯 (chū//cuò)　VO：to make a mistake, to blunder, to err

324

小林打工的時候常出錯，不是送錯菜，就是打破盤子，所以老闆叫他走路了。

**15** 上半場 (shàngbànchǎng)　N：first half (of a game)

下半場 (siàbànchǎng) (xiàbànchǎng)　N：second half (of a game)

昨天那場籃球賽打得真爛，上半場結束人都走光了，下半場就沒人看了。

球場 (cióuchǎng) (qiúchǎng)　N：playing field, court, ball field

**16** 教練 (jiàoliàn)　N：coach, trainer

小王學開車的時候，只要做錯一個動作，就被教練罵得好慘。

**17** 出鋒頭 (chū//fōng·tóu) (chū//fēng·tóu)

VO：to show off, to seek the limelight

我弟弟穿這麼奇怪的衣服，就是為了出鋒頭，希望大家都注意他。

**18** 團隊精神 (tuánduèi jīngshén) (tuánduì jīngshén)

N：team spirit

你幫幫老李吧！我們都是同一家公司的人，應該有團隊精神。

精神 (jīngshén)　N：spirit, vigor, drive

我老哥最喜歡籃球，一說到籃球，精神就來了。

團體 (tuántǐ)　N/AT：group, organization/as a group

學校是個團體，你既然住校，過團體生活，就不可以只管自己方便，不管別人。

社團 (shètuán)　N：association; civic organization;

我們學校的社團很多，像吉他 (jitā, guitar) 社、登山 (dēngshān, mountain climbing) 社…什麼的。我只對演講有興趣，所以參加了演講社。

325

## 19 合作 (hézuò)　N/V/SV：cooperation/to cooperate/to be cooperative

(1) 請大家把書放回書架上再走，謝謝各位的合作！
(2) 學生要跟老師合作，才學得好。
(3) 這個病人非常合作，醫生叫他做什麼，他就做什麼，所以病好得很快。

## 20 裁判 (cáipàn)　N：a referee

不管什麼比賽，都有裁判，決定哪邊贏。

### 判 (pàn)　V：to judge, to decide

球賽剛開始的時候，八號在籃下的時間太長，所以裁判判他犯規。

## 21 對方 (duèifāng) (duìfāng)　N：opposing side, the other side

你們買房子的事，談得怎麼樣了？對方怎麼說？

## 22 假裝 (jiǎjhuāng) (jiǎzhuāng)

V：to pretend, make believe, simulate, feign

我問老陳什麼時候還我錢，他就假裝睡著了。

### 假 (jiǎ)　SV：to be false, fake, a sham, phony

我記得小林是禿頭，所以他的頭髮是假的吧！

## 23 實力 (shíhlì) (shílì)　N：strength (including resources and potentialities)

這次考試，沒時間準備，就看你的實力了。

## 24 比數 (bǐshù)　N：score (in a competition, contest, etc.)

### 比 (bǐ)

V：indicating the different scores won by two contestants or two contesting teams

這兩隊的實力差很多，所以昨天的比數也差很多，是十比一。

第十二課　看球賽

**25 噓 (syū) (xū)**　　V/ON：to hiss (off a court, field, or stage)/Hiss! Boo!

(1) 老錢的歌，唱得好爛，還沒唱完，大家就把他噓下來了。
(2) 噓！小聲一點，小心別人聽到！

**噓聲 (syūshēng) (xūshēng)**　　N：sound of hissing or booing

小趙上次演講，準備得不夠，得到的只有噓聲。

**26 動不動就 (dòng·bú dòng jiòu) (dòng·bú dòng jiù)**

PT：with little provocation, with out provocation, at the drop of a hat

老謝很討厭我，動不動就找我麻煩。

**27 同事 (tóngshìh) (tóngshì)**

N/V：colleague, co-worker / to work in the same place

小王是我的同事，我們在這家公司同事了三年了。

**28 看臉色 (kàn//liǎnsè)**

VO：to watch the facial expressions of others (literal meaning). Refers to paying attention to the mood of superiors and adjusting ones behavior accordingly

自己當老闆，就不必看別人的臉色了。

**29 興奮 (sīngfèn) (xīngfèn)**　　SV：to be excited

明天要去旅行，我妹妹今天晚上興奮得睡不著。

**30 棒球 (bàngcióu) (bàngqiú)**　　N：baseball

**球隊 (cióuduèi) (qiúduì)**　　N：ball team（M：支）

**校隊 (siàoduèi) (xiàoduì)**　　N：school team

小王棒球打得很好，參加校隊以後，常常代表學校跟別的球隊比賽。

**球員 (cióuyuán) (qiúyuán)**　　N：ball player

籃球比賽，每支球隊都要有五個球員上場。

### 31 轉播 (jhuǎnbò) (zhuǎnbò)

V：(of radio or TV broadcast) to relay, to broadcast from on site

這次的亞洲運動會，電視要不要轉播？

廣播 (guǎngbò)　N/V：a broadcast/to broadcast

(1) 我常一邊開車，一邊聽廣播，想要了解路上會不會塞車。
(2) 我找不到我的小孩了，能不能請服務的人幫我廣播一下？

播出 (bòchū)　V：to broadcast, transmit

電視上已經播出總統昨天的演講了。

播 (bò)　V：to broadcast

這首歌最近非常受歡迎，收音機 (radio) 常常播，有時候還一天播好幾次。

### 32 放鞭炮 (fàng//biānpào)　VO：to set off firecrackers

新年的時候，中國人一定放鞭炮。

放 (fàng)　V：to let go, set free, release; to place, put

(1) 十月十日是中華民國的生日，我們都會放煙火 (yānhuǒ, a firework) 慶祝。
(2) 孩子已經不小了，你可以放手了，不要再管那麼多。

鞭炮 (biānpào)　N：firecracker（M：串）

公司開門第一天，老闆買了一長串鞭炮來放。

### 33 投手 (tóushǒu)　N：pitcher

這個投手在這場比賽一共投了幾個球？

### 34 一連 (yìlián)　A：in succession, one after another

第十二課　看球賽

一連吃了幾天的漢堡，我真吃膩了。

**35** 壞球ㄑㄡˊ (huàicióu) (huàiqiú)

N："ball" (a pitch outside the "strike" zone in baseball)

好ㄏㄠˇ球ㄑㄡˊ (hǎocióu) (hǎoqiú)　N："strike" (in baseball)

老高投了兩好球、三壞球了，只有一次機會了。

**36** 局ㄐㄩˊ (jyú) (jú)

M：(for time periods in sports games：" set" in tennis, "inning" in baseball, etc.)

你昨天那場網球賽，前兩局都打得不錯。

出ㄔㄨ局ㄐㄩˊ (chūjyú) (chūjú)　V：to be "out" (in baseball)

對方投手的三個變化球，我都沒打到，我就被判出局了。

**37** 支ㄓ (jhīh) (zhī)　M：(used for stick-like things, also for army units, etc.)

這支球棒我已經用了好幾年了，該換了。

**38** 再ㄗㄞˋ見ㄐㄧㄢˋ全ㄑㄩㄢˊ壘ㄌㄟˇ打ㄉㄚˇ (zàijiàn cyuánlěidǎ) (zàijiàn quánlěidǎ)

N：game ending home run（M：支）

幸虧小林在最後一局打了一支再見全壘打，要不然比賽還不會結束。

全ㄑㄩㄢˊ壘ㄌㄟˇ打ㄉㄚˇ (cyuánlěidǎ) (quánlěidǎ)　N：home run（M：支）

安ㄢ打ㄉㄚˇ (āndǎ)　N：base hit, safe hit（M：支）

一ㄧ壘ㄌㄟˇ (yīlěi)　N：1st base

二ㄦˋ壘ㄌㄟˇ (èrlěi)　N：2nd base

小趙把球打出去以後，跑到二壘，對方才接到球，裁判說是二壘安打。

三ㄙㄢ壘ㄌㄟˇ (sānlěi)　N：3rd base

329

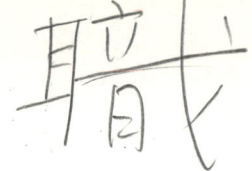

本壘 (běnlěi)　N：home base

打棒球的時候，只要有人跑回本壘就得分。

39 啦啦隊 (lāladuèi) (lāladui)　N：cheerleaders

你比賽的時候，我們去做啦啦隊，給你加油！

40 花錢 (huā//cián) (huā//qián)

VO/SV：to spend money/ to be uneconomical

(1) 老陳是個小氣鬼，連該花的錢也不願意花。
(2) 去歐洲旅行很花錢。

花時間 (huā//shíjiān)

VO/SV：to spend time, to take up time/to be time-consuming

41 職業 (jhíhyè) (zhíyè)　N/AT：occupation, profession /professional

(1) 這班學生的父母做什麼職業的都有，像醫生、老師、生意人什麼的。
(2) 老丁兩個哥哥都是職業軍人，隨時準備為國家打仗。

職員 (jhíhyuán) (zhíyuán)　N：clerk, employee

大家都以為張小姐是我們學校的老師，其實她是辦公室的職員，管學生選課的事。

42 捐錢 (jyuān//cián) (juān//qián)　VO：to contribute, donate money

我們想給那些沒有父母的孩子捐一點錢。

捐 (jyuān) (juān)　V：to contribute, to donate

孫太太決定移民以後，把家裡的書都捐給圖書館了。

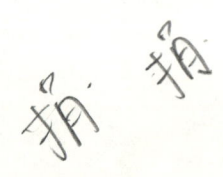

330

第十二課　看球賽

## 專有名詞　Proper Name

1. 中華隊 (Jhōnghuá Duèi) (Zhōnghuá Duì)
   Chinese team (from Taiwan)

## 注釋

1. 噓 means "to hiss or boo as an expression of hatred or disapproval." A slang term meaning the same thing is 開汽水, as in: 裁判不好，很多人開汽水。

2. 看老闆的臉色 means "to watch the boss's expression" and to act according to his/her mood. In this chapter 建國 means, "If I am late, I'll have to watch my boss's expression," or stated another way, "If I am late, I'll have to watch my boss express his displeasure."

3. 我們的棒球隊第一次到美國比賽　The first time that a baseball team from Taiwan competed in the United States was in 1969. The team traveled to Williamsport, Pennsylvania, to participate in the Little League Baseball World Series, and won the championship.

4. 大家寧可不睡覺，也要看電視轉播　Because of the difference in time zones, when the Taiwanese team began playing in the afternoon in the United States, it was midnight in Taiwan. Many people stayed up late to watch the televised games.

5. 放鞭炮慶祝 means to set off firecrackers in order to celebrate a special occasion. It is a Chinese custom to light firecrackers for almost any happy event, such as New Year's, store openings, weddings, etc.

6. 老爸、老媽、老哥、老姐　Here 老 does not mean "old." This form of address was formerly used only by young people, but now many people use these terms as an expression of endearment toward family members. These terms may be used both when addressing these people or when referring to them in conversation.

7. 職業球隊　The first four professional baseball teams in Taiwan were organized in November 1989.

8. 要是書念不好，會打球也不錯 means: "If one doesn't do well in his/her studies, then being good at sports isn't bad either." According to traditional Chinese values, study is of primary importance. However, when someone is not very successful in his/her studies, but excels in another activity, then family and friends strongly support that alternate career choice.

## 文法練習

### 一 要不是 if it were not for ......

◎要不是後來犯規太多，他還可以得更多分。
If he hadn't committed so many fouls later in the game, he could have gotten even more points.

用法說明：「要不是」的後面是已經發生的事實。如果這個事實沒發生，後半句的情況就成立。說話者有婉惜或慶幸的意思。

Explanation: Following 要不是 is something which has already occurred. If it were not for this event, the situation stated in the second half of the sentence would have become true. This can express that the speaker is either pleased or displeased with the result.

▼ 練習　請用「要不是」完成下面對話。

1. 張：你們怎麼來得這麼晚？
   Chang: Why did you come so late?
   李：小張起得太晚，要不是等他，我們早就到了。
   Lee: Little Chang got up too late. If we hadn't been waiting for him, we would have been here long ago.

2. 張：你不知道小王出國了嗎？
   李：沒人告訴我啊！要不是_____。

3. 張：你身體不錯嘛！一家都病倒了，你還好好的。
   李：是啊！要不是_____。

4. 張：恭喜你當選了，支持你的人真多啊！
   李：謝謝，要不是_____。

5. 張：難怪你願意給這個學生寫推薦信，他的成績真好。
   李：要不是_____。

## 二　還　unexpectedly

◎他的魅力還真不小。
His charm is unexpectedly big. (He is really charming.)

用法說明：表示出乎意料，含有「居然」的意思，可是語氣較弱，估計不可能的情況出現了。常有讚嘆的語氣。「還」字後面多用「眞」。
Explanation: This 還 indicates something quite unexpected has happened. It is similar to 居然, but its tone is softer. 還 is often followed by 眞, indicating a certain admiration.

**練習**　請把「還」放在句中合適的地方。

1. 小王平常不念書，期中考考那麼多科，他都及格了。
Usually Little Wang doesn't study. There were so many subjects tested in the mid-term exam, and he passed them all.
→ 小王平常不念書，期中考考那麼多科，他還都及格了。
Usually Little Wang doesn't study. There were so many subjects tested in the mid-term exam, and he still passed them all (unexpectedly).

2. 王先生說要請我吃飯，我以為只是客氣話，沒想到是真的。
_____

3. 大家都說這個獎學金很難申請，我只是試試看，後來真拿到了。
_____

4. 王大年都三十歲了，那麼愛看漫畫書，真像小孩子。
_____

5. 這家餐廳的菜好難吃，可是常常客滿。
_____

## 三　就是……，也……　even if ......, then ......

◎他拿到球，就是沒機會投籃，也不會把球傳丟了，從來沒出過錯！
When he gets the ball, even if he doesn't have a chance to make a basket, he won't lose the ball either; he never makes a mistake!

實用視聽華語 3

用法說明：「就是」的後面多半是一種假設情況，如果是事實，就有讓步的意味。「也」後面的結論或結果不因此而改變。

Explanation: Following 就是 is mostly a hypothetical situation which would normally adversely affect or contradict a given result. If it is a fact, it indicates a tone of yielding. However the statement following 也 indicates that the result or theory remains unchanged despite the hypothetical situation. This pattern is used to emphasize the certainty of a conclusion or opinion.

▼ 練習　　請用「就是……也……」完成下面對話。

1. 張：你為什麼不買這個東西？是不是沒錢？
   Chang: Why don't you buy this? Is it because you don't have money?
   李：這個東西好爛，我就是有錢，也不買。
   Lee: This thing is awful. Even if I had money, I wouldn't buy it.

2. 張：這個練習好難，你幫我做好不好？
   李：我也不會做啊！我就是_____。

3. 張：王小姐為什麼離開她男朋友了？
   李：別人的事我不太清楚。我就是_____。

4. 張：你明天要去上課嗎？
   李：明天期中考，就是_____。

5. 姐姐：你要多少錢才願意幫我帶孩子？
   妹妹：你的孩子這麼不聽話，就是_____。

6. 張：我昨天參加演講比賽，講得不好，很不好意思。
   李：這是你第一次參加比賽，就是_____。

7. 張：你跟你哥哥長得真像！大概只有你們自己家的人才不會弄錯吧？
   李：不對，就是_____。

四

(I) 讓　permit, allow, let/to make, to cause, to arouse

◎……不知道下半場教練為什麼不讓他打了？
　……I wonder why the coach didn't let him play in the second half?

第十二課　看球賽

用法說明：這個「讓」是「允許」、「聽任」的意思。
Explanation: This 讓 means to allow, permit, or let.

### 練習　　請用「讓」改寫下面句子。

1. 老謝的病很重，可是這件事不能告訴他，要不然他會難過。
   Old Xie's illness is very serious, but you must not tell him about it. Otherwise, he will feel depressed.
   → 老謝的病很重，可是這件事不能讓他知道，要不然他會難過。
      Old Xie's illness is very serious, but you must not let him know about it. Otherwise, he will feel depressed.

2. 媽媽說我不可以跟張小明交朋友，因為他太壞了。
   _____

3. 你不要替我做，我可以自己試試。
   _____

4. 你坐在這裡，我過不去，你站起來，我才可以過去。
   _____

5. 孩子大了，他的事情，他自己決定吧，你別管了。
   _____

## (II)

◎剛剛看大家這麼興奮，讓我想到以前在臺灣看棒球賽的情形。
Seeing everyone so excited just now made me remember watching baseball games in Taiwan.

用法說明：這個「讓」是「致使」、「引起」的意思。
Explanation: This 讓 means "to make, to cause, to give rise to, to arouse".

### 練習　　請把「讓」放在句中合適的地方。

1. 你假裝生病不去上課，爸爸很生氣。
   You pretended to be sick and didn't go to class; Dad is very angry.
   → 你假裝生病不去上課，讓爸爸很生氣。
      You pretended to be sick and didn't go to class; it has made Dad very angry.

335

2. 本來是我請趙老師吃飯，沒想到我帶的錢不夠，他替我付了帳，我真不好意思。
_____

3. 我是為了父母高興才念這個系的。
_____

4. 聽到這個歌，我想起從前的女朋友來了。
_____

5. 老丁跟他太太那麼有默契，我們羨慕死了。
_____

## 五　被 (passive voice)

◎我看見九號也被他氣得要打人了。
I also saw #9 become so angered by him that he wanted to hit someone.

用法說明：用於表示被動的句子。句型如下：動作接受者＋被＋動作施行者＋動詞＋補語。動作施行者如果清楚明顯時可省略。補語表示完成或結果。「被字句」多用於描述「說話者認為不如意的事」。「被字句」可用於告誡性的句子，但不可用於「要求」或「命令」的情況。表示否定的詞應在「被」之前。

Explanation: This pattern is used to show passive voice. The sentence pattern is as follows: object of verb＋被＋subject of verb＋Verb＋complement. If the identity of the subject is obvious, then it can be omitted. The complement shows the completion or result of an action. Most sentences using 被 describe a situation about which the speaker is displeased. This pattern can be used when one is warning or cautioning another, but cannot be used in requests or orders. The negative should be placed in front of 被.

### 練習

(一) 請把下面的句子改成被動句。

1. 風把我的帽子颳跑了。
   The wind blew my hat away.
   →我的帽子被風颳跑了。
   My hat was blown away by the wind.

2. 我同事打破了碗，老闆罵了他一頓。
　　_____

3. 我還想睡，可是我室友把我叫醒了。
　　_____

4. 孫中山先生把清朝政府推翻了。
　　_____

5. 張小明丟的球，把我妹妹的頭打破了。
　　_____

6. 那隻狗追得我弟弟到處跑。
　　_____

7. 雨水把這些資料都弄濕了。
　　_____

8. 小心，小李的球會打到你。（請用「別被……」）
　　_____

(二) 請改正下面各句，並說明原因。

1. 這本書是被張教授寫的。[sic.]
　→這本書是張教授寫的。因為這不是不如意的事。
　　This book was written by Professor Chang. [The first sentence is incorrect because this sentence does not describe a situation about which the speaker is displeased, so the use of 被 is inappropriate.]

2. 幸虧你的房租被小偷沒偷走。
　　_____

3. 這份報告，下星期四一定要被交給我
　　_____

## 六　動不動就 at the drop of a hat, with very little instigation

◎這個人很容易生氣，動不動就罵人。
　This guy gets angry very easily; he curses at people at the drop of a hat.

用法說明：「就」後面的情況極容易發生，頻率非常高。多用於負面事情。

Explanation: The situation following 就 occurs very easily and very frequently. This pattern is used to describe negative situations.

**練習** 請根據所給情況，用「動不動就」表示某一情況發生頻率很高。

1. 老趙身體真不健康，很容易感冒。
   Old Zhao is very unhealthy; he catches colds very easily.
   → 老趙身體真不健康，動不動就感冒。
   Old Zhao is very unhealthy; he catches colds at the drop of a hat.

2. 我們公司的老闆很容易生氣，常常給店員臉色看。

3. 我女朋友一有不高興的事就哭，真麻煩。

4. 張小明一碰到困難，就說「我死定了。」

5. 我房間的電視太老，常常壞，很容易就沒聲音了。

## 七 說到 speaking of, now that you mention...

◎說到打工，我得走了。
Speaking of working, I had better get going.

用法說明：「說到」的後面是剛才的話題，因為這個話題而想到別的事情，就引出後面的話。

Explanation: Following 說到 is a topic which was just mentioned. Mention of this topic reminded the speaker of something.

**練習** 請用「說到」完成下面對話。

1. 張：沒想到這兩個國家為了石油打起來了。
   Chang: I never expected that these two nations would start a war over petroleum.
   李：說到石油，我就想到我的車該加油了。

Lee: Speaking of petroleum, that reminds me that I should get some gas for my car.

2. 張：英國的殖民地很多都獨立了。
   李：說到殖民地，＿＿＿＿＿＿＿＿＿＿＿＿＿＿＿＿＿＿＿＿＿＿＿。

3. 張：老孫他們國家滿十八歲就有選舉權。
   李：說到選舉權，＿＿＿＿＿＿＿＿＿＿＿＿＿＿＿＿＿＿＿＿＿＿＿。

4. 張：昨天那場比賽，我們的校隊最有團隊精神。
   李：說到團隊精神，＿＿＿＿＿＿＿＿＿＿＿＿＿＿＿＿＿＿＿＿＿。

5. 張：我們教練的頭越來越禿了。
   李：說到教練，＿＿＿＿＿＿＿＿＿＿＿＿＿＿＿＿＿＿＿＿＿＿＿。

## 八　V 得正 SV　just in the midst of V SV

◎談得正高興，你就要走了。
Just when we are talking so merrily, you have to go.

用法說明：「V得正SV」表示一個動作正進行到某種程度，就有新的狀況發生。
Explanation: "V 得正 SV" indicates that an action has just progressed to a certain level or degree, when a new situation arises.

▼ 練習　請根據所給情況，用「V得正SV」描述下面的事情。

1. 你正在睡覺，睡得很舒服，媽媽把你叫醒了。
   You were in the midst of a comfortable sleep when Mother woke you up.
   → 我睡得正舒服，媽媽就把我叫醒了。
   I was just in the midst of sleeping very comfortably when Mom woke me up.

2. 大家正在看電視上的球賽，都很緊張，電視台就播廣告了。
   ＿＿＿＿＿＿＿＿＿＿＿＿＿＿＿＿＿＿＿＿＿＿＿＿＿＿＿＿＿＿＿＿＿＿

3. 同學們正在聽張教授講課，都很有興趣，可是下課的時間到了。
   ＿＿＿＿＿＿＿＿＿＿＿＿＿＿＿＿＿＿＿＿＿＿＿＿＿＿＿＿＿＿＿＿＿＿

4. 你一個人在家念書，覺得很無聊的時候，小王正好打電話來了。
   ＿＿＿＿＿＿＿＿＿＿＿＿＿＿＿＿＿＿＿＿＿＿＿＿＿＿＿＿＿＿＿＿＿＿

5. 你姐姐在房間裡哭，現在很難過，不希望別人去煩她。

## 九 一連 consecutively, successively, in a row...

◎要是中華隊投手一連投了幾次四壞球，……
If the Chinese Team's pitcher consecutively throws several sets of 4 balls,……

用法說明：表示同一情況或動作連續不斷的發生，後面是動詞，動詞後面應有表示次數或時間的數量詞。「一」可以省略。「一連」後面的短語如有否定詞「不」或「沒」，動詞應在數量詞和否定詞後面。

Explanation: This pattern shows that the same situation or action occurs repeatedly and without pause. A verb follows 一連, and after the verb should be a measure word that shows the number of times the action occurs or the time period of occurrence. 一 can be omitted. If the phrase after 一連 contains a negative, 不 or 沒, the verb should be placed after the measure word and the negative.

▼ 練習　　請把「一連」放在句中合適的地方。

1. 我寫了五封信給老錢，他都沒回。
   I wrote Old Qian five letters. He didn't write back at all.
   → 我一連寫了五封信給老錢，他都沒回。
   　I wrote Old Qian five letters in a row. He didn't write back at all.

2. 下了兩個星期的雨，今天晴了。

3. 上個月來了三個颱風，所以青菜都貴了。

4. 小陳打破了四個盤子，老闆就叫他走路了。

5. 我幾個晚上都沒睡好，所以看起來沒精神。

| 課室活動 | Classroom Activities |

## 一、組成短文 (Piecing together a narrative)

The teacher copies the following sentences on cards, one sentence per card, then gives the cards to the students in random order, one or two per person. After the students memorize their sentence(s) the cards are again collected, and the students take turns reciting their sentence(s). After all the sentences have been heard, the students figure out the order which best forms a good narrative.

還是坐著休息最舒服。

不管是籃球,還是足球 (zúqiú; soccer, football),

還有游泳,

都是為了一個球在球場裡跑來跑去,

可是一不小心就會喝水,

大概只有跳舞比較好了,

人人都說運動對身體、對精神都好,

他們不累嗎?

我也不懂為什麼有那麼多人喜歡看球賽。

在水裡游來游去當然不熱,

可以一邊聽好聽的歌,一邊跳;

可是我真不喜歡運動。

而且,誰贏誰輸 (shū; to lose in a game),有什麼關係呢?

情形不好,還可能會死呢!

想快就快,想慢就慢,多好啊!

可是,你想想,每次跑過、跳過以後,不都是又熱又渴嗎?!

The teacher may shorten or lengthen the contents of the narrative, depending on the number of students.

## 二、討論問題 (Discussion)

1. 每個人說說自己平常做什麼運動,為什麼喜歡這種運動?另外,再說說自己喜歡看什麼運動比賽,為什麼?

   可能用到的詞:有氧舞蹈 (yǒuyǎng wǔdào; aerobics), 拳擊 (cyuánjí) (quánjí; boxing), 騎自行車/騎腳踏車 (cí//zìhsíngchē / cí//jiǎotàchē) (qí//zìxíngchē/ qí//jiǎotàchē; bicycling), 散步 (sànbù; to take a walk, stroll), 打保齡球 (dǎ//bǎolíngcióu) (dǎ//bǎolíngqiú; to go bowling), 踢足球 (tī//zúcióu) (tī//zúqiú; to play soccer/football), 打撞球 (dǎ//jhuàngcióu) (dǎ//zhuàngqiú; to play billiards, pool), 排球 (volleyball), 桌球/乒乓球 (jhuōcióu / pīngpāngcióu) (pīngpāngqiú; Ping-Pong; table tennis), 曲棍球 (cyūgùncióu) (qūgùnqiú; hockey), 輸 (shū; to lose in a game).

2. 碰到不公平的裁判,你怎麼辦?
3. 球迷會做哪些特別的事?
4. 你認為當職業球員有什麼好處和壞處?

## 短文　　　系刊₁上的消息

※十一月十二日本校₂校慶₃，學校舉辦了很多慶祝活動，除了電影欣賞會、園遊會以外，還有運動會₄，非常熱鬧。

※本系₂三年級學生在這次園遊會有一個擲飛鏢的攤位，生意不錯，一共賺了九十六元₅，已捐給系裡做系刊的經費。

※本系四年級攤位賣的是中式點心，因為口味新鮮，特別受歡迎，攤位前一直擠得滿滿的，系主任都一連吃了十個水餃。

※本系在這次運動會的比賽成績是全校第六名₆，二年級高偉立同學參加一百公尺賽跑，得了第一名₆，成績是十二秒₇三，打破全校記錄₈，值得慶賀₉。

※本校跟紐約州立大學的籃球比賽，又激烈又精彩，結束時比數是九十七比一〇一，本校校隊因為默契好，犯規少，才贏了這比賽。

※十二月三日晚上七時，李國書教授在系辦公室樓上三〇八室演講，題目是：「中國的考試制度」。有興趣的同學請準時參加。

## Vocabulary:

1. 系刊 (sìkān)(xìkān): departmental publication
2. 本校 (běnsiào) (běnxiào): our school, this school
   本系 (běnsì) (běnxì): our department, this department
3. 校慶 (siàocìng) (xiàoqìng): holiday honoring the date of a school's formation．
4. 運動會 (yùndònghuèi) (yùndònghuì): athletic event
5. 元 (yuán): dollar (It means the same as "塊錢", but not so colloquial.)
6. 第六名 (dìliùmíng): sixth place
   第一名 (dìyīmíng): first place
7. 秒 (miǎo): second (unit of time)
8. 打破記錄 (dǎpò//jìlù): to break a record
9. 慶賀 (cìnghè) (qìnghè): to congratulate

# 第十三課 過節了

■端午節龍舟賽（行政院新聞局提供）

## 實用視聽華語 3

（陳台麗在房間裡）

台麗：喂，林建國嗎？我是陳台麗，麻煩你請高偉立聽電話[1]。

建國：好，你等一下。偉立，找你的，是陳台麗。

偉立：謝謝。（接過電話）喂，我是高偉立。

台麗：嗨，你好。我的電腦壞了，你的能不能借我用一下？

偉立：沒問題，你什麼時候來？

台麗：現在行嗎？

偉立：可以啊！你來吧！我三點才有課。

台麗：謝謝，我**這就**過去。

偉立：好，一會兒見。

※　※　※　※　※　※

（高偉立房間裡）

台麗：我後天要交一份報告，圖書館的電腦都有人在用，我只好來跟你借。

偉立：沒關係，**反正**我現在不用。

台麗：謝謝。（看到電腦旁的南瓜燈）哇！好可愛的南瓜。我萬聖節也做了個南瓜燈。

偉立：那一定很好玩。你的感恩節是怎麼過的？

台麗：除了感恩節那天去同學家吃火雞大餐以外，我都在家看書、寫報告。

偉立：真用功。那隻火雞味道怎麼樣？
台麗：不錯，可是太大了。同學媽媽烤了一隻十幾磅的大火雞，我們八九個人都沒吃完，我看，他們還要吃好幾天呢！另外還有南瓜派，我從來沒吃過，很香，很好吃。
偉立：南瓜派是我媽媽最拿手的點心，可惜我吃了過敏。既然你喜歡，以後有機會，我就帶一些給你嚐嚐。
台麗：謝謝。我看你們過感恩節好像跟聖誕節[2]差不多。
偉立：是差不多。感恩節是為了紀念我們祖先來到這裡以後，因為印第安人的幫助，才能在這塊土地上過著豐衣足食的生活。
台麗：聖誕節就完全是基督教[3]的節日了，對不對？
偉立：沒錯。你們在臺灣也過聖誕節嗎？
台麗：**只有**信教的人**才**過。有不少人**趁著**這個機會吃喝玩樂，商人更利用這個節日做廣告，推銷他們的東

■萬聖節快到了（劉秀芝提供）

西。好像跟宗教沒什麼關係了。

偉立：我們也覺得聖誕節一年比一年商業化了。其實聖誕節應該是全家人在一起，**歡歡喜喜**地吃飯、說笑、唱歌，享受溫暖的聖誕節氣氛。

■二〇〇七年臺北燈節主燈（范慧貞提供）

第十三課　過節了

台麗：欸，聽起來好像我們除夕吃年夜飯一樣。
偉立：那你怎麼過聖誕節？
台麗：我不信教，可是聖誕夜常去教堂做禮拜[4]，就是因為喜歡那裡的氣氛，可惜臺灣不下雪[5]，感覺就差很多。
偉立：聽說今年下雪的機會很多，你大概可以過一個銀色聖誕了。
台麗：我都等不及了。房東說今年的聖誕樹，要我跟美真幫忙裝飾。你等著看吧，那一定是全世界最漂亮的一棵。
偉立：好孩子！聖誕老人一定會送給你們一份特別的禮物！
台麗：討厭[6]！你**就是**愛開我的玩笑。小心聖誕老人今年不給你禮物了。
偉立：說到禮物，我正在頭疼不知道今年該買什麼給我老媽才好，她好像什麼都有了。
台麗：也許你可以直接問問她需要什麼。對了，我也該去買聖誕卡了，**再不**寄**就**太晚了。
偉立：聖誕節**什麼都**好，**就是**買禮物、寄聖誕卡太麻煩。
台麗：**我倒是**覺得對忙碌的現代人來說，寄聖誕卡是一個連絡感情的好辦法。
偉立（看錶）：別聊了，快打報告吧！
台麗：好，好，好，我一聊就忘了時間。謝謝你借我電腦。
偉立：別這麼客氣，我不急著用，你慢慢打[7]。

349

## 生詞及例句

**1 過節 (guò//jié)**    VO：to celebrate a festival or holiday

過年過節的時候，街上都很熱鬧。

**過 (guò)**    V：to pass (an occasion)

去年我的生日是一個人過的。

**春節 (Chūn jié)**    N：Chinese New Year/the lunar New Year

**母親節 (Mǔcīn jié) (Mǔqīn jié)**    N：Mother's Day

**父親節 (Fùcīn jié) (Fùqīn jié)**    N：Father's Day

**情人節 (Cíngrén jié) (Qíngrén jié)**    N：Valentine's Day

**2 反正 (fǎnjhèng) (fǎnzhèng)**    A：anyway, anyhow, in any case

(1) 你幾點來都可以，反正我都在家。
(2) 我不想參加這次考試，反正我也考不取。

**反 (fǎn)**    V/RE/AT：to turn over, turn inside out/to be reversed

(1) 我真受不了小陳，衣服穿髒了不洗，就反過來再穿。
(2) 那個孩子太小，分不清左右，又把鞋穿反了。
(3) 孩子念書，不要給他太多壓力，要不然會有反效果 (xiàoguǒ, effect; result)。

**3 可愛 (kě'ài)**    SV：to be lovable, likeable, adorable, cute

王老師的小女兒笑起來好甜，可愛極了。

**4 火雞 (huǒjī)**    N：turkey（M：隻）

**5 隻 (jhīh) (zhī)**    M：(used for one of a pair, also for boats, certain animals, etc.)

李先生的眼睛一隻大,一隻小。

**6** 磅 (bàng)　　M：pound

我比十年前胖了二十磅,差不多九公斤。

**7** 南瓜派 (nán'guāpài)　　N：pumpkin pie

　　南瓜 (nán'guā)　　N：pumpkin

　　派 (pài)　　N：pie

我女朋友最喜歡麥當勞的蘋果派。

　　南瓜燈 (nán'guādēng)　　N：jack-o'-lantern

新鮮南瓜並不適合做南瓜燈,還是拿來做派吧!

**8** 拿手 (náshǒu)　　SV：to be good at, adept at, expert

我老哥會打很多種球,也都打得不錯。籃球是他最拿手的運動。

**9** 過敏 (guòmǐn)　　V：to be allergic to something

我對海鮮過敏,不能吃魚蝦,一吃皮膚就會紅紅的,非常不舒服。

**10** 嚐 (cháng)　　V：to taste

你嚐嚐這個菜夠不夠鹹?

**11** 紀念 (jì'niàn)　　N/V：commemoration/to commemorate

(1) 這張畫既然是你小時候畫的,你就留起來做紀念吧!
(2) 王太太雖然死了很多年了,可是王先生一直忘不了她,就寫了一本書紀念她。

**12** 祖先 (zǔsiān) (zǔxiān)　　N：ancestors

聽說人類的祖先最早是從非洲來的。

祖父 (zǔfù)　　N：grandfather, father's father

祖母 (zǔmǔ)　　N：grandmother, father's mother

外祖父 (wàizǔfù)　　N：grandfather, mother's father

外祖母 (wàizǔmǔ)　　N：grandmother, mother's mother

13　土地 (tǔdì)　　N：land, soil, territory（M：塊／片）

王先生那塊土地建了大樓以後，比以前更值錢了。

14　豐衣足食 (fōng yī zú shíh) (fēng yī zú shí)

IE：to be well-clothed and well-fed

只要社會安定，我們就能過豐衣足食的生活。

15　基督教 (Jīdū jiào)　　N：Christianity (in Taiwan, refers to Protestantism)

天主教 (Tiānzhǔ jiào)　　N：Catholicism

佛教 (Fó jiào)　　N：Buddhism

回教 (Huí jiào)　　N：Islam

道教 (Dào jiào)　　N：Taoism

16　信教 (sìnjiào) (xìn//jiào)　　VO：to believe in a religion

相信 (siāngsìn) (xiāngxìn)　　V：to believe, to have faith in

(1) 不管信什麼教，每個人都只相信自己的神。
(2) 小王考試都考得很爛，我不相信他能得到獎學金。

17　趁著 (chèn·jhe) (chèn·zhe)

V：take advantage of an opportunity or situation, avail oneself of

我們趁著放假的時候，到海邊去玩了幾天。

趁 (chèn)　　V：take advantage of an opportunity or situation, avail oneself of

趁現在時間還早，我們先去喝杯咖啡，再回來坐車。

### 18 吃喝玩樂 (chīh hē wán lè) (chī hē wán lè)

IE：eat, drink and be merry; to idle away one's time in Epicurean, pleasure seeking pursuits

老陳除了吃喝玩樂，什麼事都不想做。

### 19 利用 (lìyòng)　V：to use, to take advantage of, to exploit

我覺得王愛美並不喜歡我，只是想跟我練習中文會話，她是在利用我。

### 20 做廣告 (zuò//guǎnggào)　VO：to advertise

生意人喜歡利用美女做廣告。

### 廣告 (guǎnggào)　N：advertisement

最近電視上有很多賣汽車的廣告。

### 廣 (guǎng)　SV：to be broad, extensive

老張的興趣很廣，慢跑、游泳、打球、看電影，什麼都喜歡。

### 21 推銷 (tuēisiāo) (tuīxiāo)　V：to promote sales

天氣不熱，冷氣機很難推銷。

### 推銷員 (tuēisiāoyuán) (tuīxiāoyuán)　N：salesperson

有人敲門，我開門一看，原來是賣洗衣粉的推銷員。

### 銷路 (siāolù) (xiāolù)　N：sales opportunity, market

因為廣告做得好，所以老陳他們公司的電腦銷路不錯，沒幾天就賣完了。

### 22 宗教 (zōngjiào)　N：religion

歷史上有沒有宗教戰爭？

### 23 商業化 (shāngyèhuà)

N/V/SV：commercialization/to commercialize/to be commercialized

商業 (shāngyè)　N：commerce, trade, business

我念大學的時候，選過幾門商業方面的課。

商人（生意人）(shāngrén) (shēngyìrén)

N：businessman, merchant, trader

商品 (shāngpǐn)　N：merchandise, goods, commodity

商人利用節日推銷商品，所以情人節越來越商業化了。

### 24 歡歡喜喜 (huān huān xǐ xǐ) (huānhuān-xǐxǐ)

SV：to be full of joy, extremely happy

考完試，放假了，大家都歡歡喜喜地出去玩了。

### 25 享受 (siǎngshòu) (xiǎngshòu)　V/N：to enjoy/enjoyment

(1) 這麼多好吃的東西，大家好好兒享受吧！
(2) 一天的事都忙完了，躺在床上欣賞音樂是我最大的享受。

### 26 溫暖 (wūnnuǎn) (wēnnuǎn)　SV/N：to be warm/warmth

(1) 老丁說不管怎麼樣，他都會幫助我，讓我覺得很溫暖。
(2) 這個社會上好人還是比壞人多，到處都有溫暖。

### 27 氣氛 (cì·fēn) (qì·fēn)　N：atmosphere, mood

媽媽今天都不說話，家裡氣氛怪怪的。

### 28 除夕 (chúsì) (chúxì)　N：the lunar New Year's Eve

### 29 年夜飯 (niányèfàn)　N：New Year's Eve dinner

除夕是一年的最後一天，華人的習慣是不管在多遠的地方上班上課，都要回家，跟家人一起吃年夜飯。

### 30 聖誕夜 (shèngdànyè)　　N：Christmas Eve

信基督教、天主教的人都相信耶穌 (Yēsū, Jesus) 是在聖誕夜出生的。

### 31 教堂 (jiàotáng)　　N：church, cathedral

### 32 做禮拜 (zuò//lǐbài)　　VO：to go to a church worship service

信教的人每個星期天都要去教堂做禮拜。

### 33 感覺 (gǎnjyué) (gǎnjué)

V/N：to feel, sense, perceive/feeling, sense, perception

(1) 你感覺到今天上課的氣氛跟平常有什麼不一樣嗎？
(2) 我對小陳那麼好，可是他一點感覺也沒有。

### 34 銀色 (yín sè)　　AT：silver

我祖父那頭銀色的短髮，真好看。

### 35 等不及 (děng·bùjí)　　RC：cannot bear to wait, unable to wait any longer

爸爸還沒回來，弟弟等不及，就自己先吃起來了。

### 36 裝飾 (jhuāngshìh) (zhuāngshì)　　V：to decorate, to adorn

我妹妹用花裝飾她的帽子。

### 37 棵 (kē)　　M：(used for trees, cabbage, grass, etc.)

這棵樹是去年才種 (zhòng, to plant) 的，現在已經長到兩公尺高了。

### 38 開玩笑 (kāi//wánsiào) (kāi//wánxiào)

VO：to crack a joke, to make fun of, to laugh at

實用視聽華語 3
Practical Audio-Visual Chinese

(1) 我常跟朋友開玩笑說：「我什麼教都不信，只信『睡覺』」。
(2) 這個玩笑開得太大了，難怪他那麼生氣。

### 39 聖誕卡 (shèngdànkǎ)　　N：Christmas card（M：張）

現在大家都用網路寄聖誕卡了，可愛的動畫 (animation)，讓收到的人看了更高興。

生日卡 (shēngrìhkǎ) (shēngrìkǎ)　　N：birthday card

母親卡 (mǔcīnkǎ) (mǔqīnkǎ)　　N：Mother's Day card

情人卡 (cíngrénkǎ) (qíngrénkǎ)　　N：Valentine's Day card

信用卡 (sìnyòngkǎ) (xìnyòngkǎ)　　N：credit card

我覺得帶太多錢不好，所以不管是買東西、吃飯，我都刷 (shuā, to swipe) 信用卡。

卡片 (kǎpiàn)　　N：card（M：張）

我同學把生詞寫在小卡片上，放在口袋裡，隨時拿出來複習。

### 40 忙碌 (mánglù)　　SV：to be busy, to be bustling about

住在城市裡的人，生活一定比較忙碌。

### 41 現代人 (siàndàirén) (xiàndàirén)　　N：modern man

現代化 (siàndàihuà) (xiàndàihuà)

N /V/ SV：modernization/to become modernized/to be modernized

(1) 交通建設的現代化是政府最關心的問題。
(2) 我住的地方離城市很遠，交通不方便，不容易現代化。
(3) 這棟大樓非常現代化，裡面的東西都是電腦控制的。

現代 (siàndài) (xiàndài)　　SV：to be modern, contemporary

陳教授雖然六十歲了，但是他的想法都很新、很現代。

第十三課　過節了

時代 (shíhdài) (shídài)　N：times, age, era, epoch

現在是電腦時代，不會用電腦，將來可能找不到工作。

42 連絡（聯絡）(liánluò)

V/N：to make contact with, to communicate with/contact

好久沒跟小王連絡了，你有他的消息嗎？

43 感情 (gǎncíng) (gǎnqíng)

N：emotion, sentiment, affection, feelings (between friends, relatives, etc.)

老李跟女朋友的感情一直很好，去哪裡兩個人都在一起。

### 歎詞　Interjections

1. 喂，喂 (wéi, wèi)　I: Hello; Hey!
   (1)（打電話的時候）
      李：喂，請問張老師在家嗎？
      張太太：在，請等一下。
   (2) 喂！那是你的東西嗎？

### 專有名詞　Proper Names

1. 萬聖節 (Wànshèng Jié)　Halloween
2. 感恩節 (Gǎn'ēn Jié)　Thanksgiving Day
3. 聖誕節 (Shèngdàn Jié)　Christmas

### 注釋

1. "麻煩你請高偉立聽電話。" This is how a Chinese would normally ask to speak with 高偉立 on the telephone. Though it means the same as asking: "May I please speak with 高偉立?", one should never use the expression: "我可以不可以跟高偉立說話？" "請問×××在不在？" is another way to ask for someone on the phone. If you are the one being asked for, you should answer by saying: "我就是", not "這就是他."

357

2. 聖誕節 means Christmas. 聖 means holy, sacred. 誕 means birth. So 聖誕節 means the day of the holy birth. If someone is not a Christian, he/she might call this holiday: 耶誕節. 耶 is short for 耶穌, Yēsū, the transliteration for "Jesus."

3. 基督教. 基督 means the Christ. 基督教 means Christianity. However, in Taiwan, when people mention 基督教, they frequently only think of Protestantism, while 天主教 refers to Catholicism.

4. 做禮拜 means to participate in a worship service at a Protestant church. The term for attending a Catholic mass is called: 望彌撒, wàng mísā.

5. 臺灣不下雪 Since Taiwan is in the subtropical and tropical zones, it has never snowed on most of the island. Occasionally there is snow in the high mountains.

6. "討厭！你就愛開我玩笑！" 討厭 here does not really express annoyance or disgust. When a close male friend teases a Chinese woman and she feels uncomfortable or doesn't know how to respond, she might say 討厭 even though she is not really upset. This feminine expression has evolved into a form of teasing or flirting.

7. "我不急著用，你慢慢打。" means "I am not in a hurry to use it, take your time (typing)." This is a polite remark, 客氣話. It is used to make someone feel comfortable about borrowing something and perhaps keeping it for some time.

## 文法練習

### 一　這就　right away, immediately

◎我這就過去。
I'll be right over.

用法說明：「這」表示「現在」，「就」表示「馬上」、「立刻」。「這就」的後面是動詞，表示馬上就做該動作。

Explanation: 這 means "now", whereas 就 means "immediately, right away". A verb placed right after 這就 indicates that the action will be performed immediately.

▼ 練習　請用「這就」完成下面對話。

1. 媽媽：建國，這個箱子我打不開，你來幫幫忙，好不好？
   Mother: Jianguo, I can't get this box opened. Will you come help me?

建國：好，我這就來。
Jianguo: OK, I'll be right over.

2. 張：明天烤肉的事，你還沒打電話告訴小王啊？
   李：_____。

3. 太太：你又忘了吃藥了！
   先生：_____。

4. 店員：對不起，我們要休息了。
   客人：_____。

5. 學生：助教說他一會兒就要走了，要我現在就到他那兒去拿資料。
   教授：那你_____。

## 二 反正 anyway......

◎沒關係，反正我現在不用。
　It doesn't matter; I won't use it now anyway.

**(I)**

用法說明：(A) 說話者認為做某件事或發生某種狀況，都沒什麼關係或沒有什麼大影響。(B) 說話者認為不必做對話中提到的某件事或做了那件事也沒什麼用。「反正」的後面是說話者的理由。

Explanation: (A) This is a kind of downplaying. The speaker thinks that the matter just mentioned is unimportant; it does not exert any influence on the matter at hand. (B) The speaker thinks that it is not necessary to do the thing mentioned in the conversation, or to do it is meaningless. Following 反正 is the reason(s) why it does not matter or why it is not necessary.

▼ 練習　請根據所給情況用「反正」描述下面的事情。

**(A)**

1. 桌上有一塊蛋糕，你怕胖不敢吃，可是又覺得已經發胖了，再吃一塊也沒關係。你說什麼？
   There's a piece of cake on the table. You are worried about gaining weight so you do not dare eat it. But on the other hand, you feel overweight already, so it would not

matter if you eat just one more piece. What do you say?
→ 我就再吃一塊吧,反正已經胖了。
　　I'll just eat one more piece; I'm already overweight anyway.

2. 你今天沒課,晚一點起來沒關係。你怎麼說?

3. 朋友問你:要不要一起去看電影?你覺得已經考完試了,去看場電影沒關係。你怎麼說?

4. 你媽覺得你的成績不夠理想,可是你認為每一科都及格,能畢業就行了,你怎麼說?

5. 你打工的時候常常睡覺,你同學問你:「不怕老闆叫你走路嗎?」你覺得這個工作太無聊,你早就不想做了,你怎麼說?

(B)
1. 你有一件漂亮衣服,你室友一直很欣賞,現在你胖了,穿不下了,你要送給室友。她高興得不得了,不停地謝你,你怎麼說?
You have a pretty dress; your roommate always admires it. You have gained weight and can no longer wear it. You want to give it to your roommate. She is very happy, and continues to thank you. What would you say?
→ 不必謝我,反正我也穿不下這件衣服了。
　　You don't have to thank me. I can no longer wear it anyway.

2. 你們的籃球校隊跟別的學校比賽,小王要去給他們加油。你認為你們的實力差太多,一定贏不了對方,不必去了。你怎麼說?

3. 老李學校開園遊會,他想請你妹妹去參觀,問你覺得怎麼樣。你知道你妹妹很討厭他,一定不會去,你怎麼說?

4. 你表妹一直在房間裡哭,因為男朋友離開她了。你覺得哭沒有用,男朋友也聽不到。你說什麼?

## 第十三課　過節了

### (II)

**用法說明：**跟「不管」連用，意思是因為不管怎麼樣，「反正」的後面的事實或想法都不會再改變。

Explanation: Used with 不管, meaning no matter what happens it will not change the fact or ideas following 反正.

**▼練習**　請根據所給情況用「不管……反正……」描述下面的事情。

1. 你有一件漂亮衣服，你一直很喜歡，可是現在你胖了，穿不下了，媽媽就把這件衣服送給別人了，你很不高興。這時候你會怎麼說？

   You had a pretty dress, you've always liked it. But you have gained weight and can no longer wear it. So your mother has given it away. You are very unhappy. What would you say in this case?

   → 不管我多喜歡這件衣服，反正媽媽已經送給別人了。

   　No matter how much I liked the dress, mother has given it away.

2. 你室友聽你說錢不夠用，他覺得你可以申請獎學金，叫你早一點申請，可是你覺得自己成績不好，多早申請都申請不到。你會怎麼說？

   _____

3. 你姐姐要你快一點，因為火車就要開了。可是你看看錶，覺得已經太晚了，走多快都來不及了，你會怎麼說？

   _____

4. 你的幾個朋友今天晚上都要去跳舞，你不要去。一個朋友跟你說跳舞很有意思；一個朋友說跳舞對身體好。你真的不想去，你會怎麼說？

   _____

5. 你很愛你女朋友，可是你爸媽不喜歡她，希望你離開她，可是你不要，你會說什麼？

   _____

## 三　只有⋯才⋯　only ...... ; only if ......

◎只有信教的人才過（聖誕節）。
Only people who believe in Christianity celebrate it (Christmas).

用法說明：「才」前面的短語是「才」後面的條件。本句型的「只有」強調唯一的條件，與第三課文法練習一的「才」有語氣上的差別。本句型語氣較強。

Explanation: The phrase before 才 is the necessary condition for the situation mentioned after 才. This 只有 emphasizes that this condition is the only one needed. The tone of this pattern is stronger than pattern 1 in Lesson 3.

### 練習　　請用「只有⋯才⋯」完成下面對話。

1. 張：我們公司想發展國外市場，你看，應該怎麼做？
   Chang: Our company wants to develop markets abroad. In your opinion, what should we do?
   李：我看，只有請對這方面有研究的人來領導，才可能開發 (open up) 國外市場。
   Lee: In my opinion, only by hiring people who have researched this field as leaders, can we open up and develop markets abroad.

2. 張：今天有點涼，你還要去游泳嗎？
   李：不去了，＿＿＿＿＿＿＿＿＿＿＿＿＿＿＿＿＿＿＿＿。

3. 張：百貨公司的東西好貴，我都買不起。
   李：那你去夜市吧，＿＿＿＿＿＿＿＿＿＿＿＿＿＿＿＿＿＿。

4. 爸爸：喂，喂，你不在家，孩子一直哭著找你，怎麼辦啊？
   媽媽：你把電視打開吧，＿＿＿＿＿＿＿＿＿＿＿＿＿＿＿＿。

5. 張：這件衣服亮亮的，晚上穿一定很好看。你要不要買？
   李：不要，如果＿＿＿＿＿＿＿＿，我大概沒有機會穿。

## 四　趁（著）　to take advantage of, to utilize

◎有不少人趁著這個機會吃喝玩樂……
A lot of people use this opportunity to eat, drink, and be merry.

用法說明：「趁著」是「利用」的意思，利用某條件或機會做一件事。「趁」的後面可加名詞、SV、動詞短語 (VP) 或短句。

Explanation: 趁著 means "to use", "to utilize", "to take advantage of" some requirement or opportunity to perform some action. Following 趁著 can be a noun, SV, verb phrase, or simple sentence.

### 練習　如果你看到下面情況，你會怎麼說，請用「趁（著）」。

1. 王太太一直想換個衣櫃，現在搬家了，就買了一個新的。
   Mrs. Wang has wanted to change her wardrobe for a long time. Now she has moved, and so she has bought a new one.
   → 王太太趁著搬家，換了一個新衣櫃。
   　Mrs. Wang is moving to a new house, so she's taken advantage of this opportunity to buy a new wardrobe.

2. 小王上班的時候不敢打電話給女朋友，老闆不在才敢打。
   ＿＿＿＿＿＿＿＿＿＿＿＿＿＿＿＿＿＿＿＿＿＿＿＿＿＿＿＿＿＿＿＿＿＿

3. 你看見同學不用功，你想告訴他：年輕的時候應該多學點東西。
   ＿＿＿＿＿＿＿＿＿＿＿＿＿＿＿＿＿＿＿＿＿＿＿＿＿＿＿＿＿＿＿＿＿＿

4. 朋友要去中國留學，你羨慕他有這個機會可以多了解中國人
   ＿＿＿＿＿＿＿＿＿＿＿＿＿＿＿＿＿＿＿＿＿＿＿＿＿＿＿＿＿＿＿＿＿＿

5. 媽媽不讓弟弟出去，可是弟弟看見媽媽沒注意他，就跑出去了。
   ＿＿＿＿＿＿＿＿＿＿＿＿＿＿＿＿＿＿＿＿＿＿＿＿＿＿＿＿＿＿＿＿＿＿

## 五　AABB（雙音節SV的重疊）
### Duplication of two-syllable SVs

◎全家人在一起，歡歡喜喜地吃飯、說笑、唱歌……
The whole family is together, joyfully eating, telling jokes, singing songs……

用法說明：雙音節的 SV 重疊時，一定是「AABB」的形式，跟雙音節動詞重疊時「ABAB」的形式不同。重疊的 SV 跟一般 SV 一樣，可以修飾名詞、動詞或做補語，但語氣較強，程度更深。在重疊的 SV 前面不可以再加副詞修飾。

Explanation: When you have the duplication of a two-syllable stative verb, it has to be in AABB format, unlike the ABAB format used for the duplication of two-syllable verbs. The functions of repeated stative verbs are the same as those of regular stative verbs- i.e., they can modify nouns or verbs, or serve as complements- but the mood is a bit stronger, the degree a bit more intense. Adverbs cannot be placed in front of a duplicated SV.

### ▼ 練習

(一) 請把下面各句中的形容詞改成重疊的形式。

A. 修飾名詞 modifying nouns
1. 沒想到這麼秀氣的女孩又會罵人又會打人。
   I never thought that such a refined girl would be capable of cursing at and hitting others.
   → 沒想到這麼秀秀氣氣的女孩又會罵人又會打人。
   I never thought that such an incredibly refined girl would be capable of cursing at and hitting others.

2. 趙小姐那種大方的態度，我們都很欣賞。
   _____

3. 乾淨的房間，誰都喜歡住。
   _____

B. 修飾動詞 modifying verbs
1. 老陳借到錢，就高興地回家了。
   After Old Chen succeeded in borrowing money, he happily returned home.

第十三課　過節了

→ 老陳借到錢，就高高興興地回家了。
　　After Old Chen succeeded in borrowing money, he joyfully returned home.

2. 我母親今年六十歲，我們打算給她熱鬧地慶祝一下。
　_____

3. 我辛苦地準備了半天，可是客人都沒來。
　_____

C. 做補語　as complements
1. 錢的事情，你一定要跟小謝算得很清楚。
   As far as money matters go, you should definitely keep things very clear with Little Xie.
   → 錢的事情，你一定要跟小謝算得清清楚楚的。
   　　As far as money matters go, you should definitely keep things extremely clear with Little Xie.

2. 李愛美每次跟男朋友約會，都打扮得很漂亮。
　_____

3. 媽媽總是把家裡弄得很舒服，所以我一放假就回家。
　_____

（二）請改正下面各句，並說明原因。

1. 錢大同的房間總是弄得乾淨乾淨的。
　_____

2. 昨天的「心理學」，小趙很輕輕鬆鬆地就考了一百分。
　_____

六　就是……　just...; merely...

◎你就是愛開我的玩笑。
　You just like to make fun of me.

用法說明：「就是」強調肯定某種性質或狀態，含「不認同」的意味。「就是」的後面加 SV、動詞或助動詞。

365

Explanation: 就是 emphasizes confirming a certain characteristic or state with a sense of disapproval. 就是 can be followed by a SV, a Verb, or a Aux. Verb.

**練習** 請用「就是」完成下面對話。

1. 張：真沒想到現在連校長都可以由我們教授來投票選舉了。
   Chang: I didn't expect that we professors can even vote for president of our university now.
   李：民主制度就是好，以前教授怎麼可能選校長？
   Lee: Democracy is good. How could professors vote for a university president before?

2. 張：小陳又去教同學寫作業了，他還真有時間！
   李：小陳＿＿＿＿＿＿＿＿＿＿＿＿，所以大家都喜歡他。

3. 張：小王打電話來說要晚一點到，叫我們再等他一下。
   李：又要等他！這個人＿＿＿＿＿＿＿＿＿＿＿＿，每次都害大家等半天。

4. 爸爸：我們還沒吃呢，兒子又把你做的南瓜派拿去請同學了。
   媽媽：這個孩子＿＿＿＿＿＿＿＿＿＿＿＿，覺得同學比我們重要。

5. 姐姐：你在哪裡剪的頭髮？看起來有一點老。
   妹妹：怎麼會呢？這個樣子＿＿＿＿＿＿＿＿＿＿＿＿，我同學都說好看。

## 七　再不 V(O)，就……

◎再不寄，就太晚了。
If you continue to put off mailing it, it will be too late.

用法說明：「再」是「還」的意思。「再不 V(O)，就……」表示如果「再」後面的情形繼續下去，就會發生「就」後面的結果。
Explanation: "再不 V(O)，就……" indicates that if the action following 再 continues as it is, the situation (usually negative) following 就 will result.

**練習** 請用「再不 V(O)，就……」完成下面句子。

1. 已經好幾個月沒有下雨了，如果再不下雨，就沒水用了。
   It hasn't rained in many months. If it continues to be dry, we won't have any water to use.

2. 你天天玩，不念書，如果你<u>再不　　　　　　</u>。

3. 你鬍子那麼長，<u>再不　　　　　　</u>。

4. 這場戰爭已經打了八年了，<u>再不　　　　　　</u>。

5. 我等小張的電話，等了半天了，他<u>再不　　　　　　</u>。

## 八　什麼都……，就是……

### everything is ......, except ......

◎聖誕節什麼都好，就是買禮物、寄聖誕卡太麻煩。
Everything about Christmas is wonderful, except buying presents and sending out Christmas cards which is too bothersome.

**用法說明：**「什麼都」表示所說的範圍內沒有例外，「就是」的後面是唯一的例外。「都」後面是肯定的，「就是」的後面則是否定的，反之亦然。

**Explanation:** 什麼都 indicates that, within the mentioned boundaries, there are no exceptions to the rule. Following 就是 is the sole exception to the rule. If the phrase following 都 is positive, then the phrase following 就是 is negative, and vice-versa.

▼ 練習　　請用「什麼都……，就是……」改寫下面句子。

1. 我弟弟除了玩以外，對哪件事都沒興趣。
   My little brother is not interested in anything other than having fun/fooling around.
   →我弟弟對什麼都沒興趣，就是喜歡玩。
   My little brother isn't interested in anything; he only likes to have fun.

2. 除了鴨子以外，我姑姑都吃。
   _____

3. 我媽罵我爸爸只會吃飯，別的事情都不會。
   _____

4. 李助教很愛看球賽，可是從來不看棒球賽。
   _____

5. 謝小姐男朋友矮了一點，別的都很好。
_____

## 九　倒是　but, on the contrary, however

◎我倒是覺得對忙碌的現代人來說，寄聖誕卡是一個連絡感情的好辦法。

On the contrary, I think that sending Christmas cards is a good way for busy modern-day people to keep in contact with friends.

用法說明：「倒是」的前後是相反的（不同的）情況或意見。語氣比「可是」舒緩，但「倒是」是副詞，「可是」是連接詞。「倒是」的「是」可以省略。

Explanation: The situations or opinions preceding and following 倒是 are different from each other. In this way it is similar to 可是, however, the tone is slightly more gentle. Also, 倒是 is an adverb whereas 可是 is a conjunction. The 是 in 倒是 can be omitted.

### ▼練習　請完成下面對話，用「倒是」表示不同的意見。

1. 張：那個穿藍外套的男孩真帥。
   Chang: That guy in blue jacket is really handsome.
   李：我倒是覺得他旁邊的那個更帥。
   Lee: But I think that the guy next to him is more handsome.

2. 張：這個房子冬天住好冷啊。
   李：夏天住倒是_____。

3. 張：小王對別人很小氣，從來沒請過客。
   李：他對自己倒是_____。

4. 張：老李這個人真奇怪，今天這麼冷，還穿短褲！
   李：就是嘛！天氣熱的時候，他倒是_____。

5. 張：她們兩個，矮的那個是姐姐。
   李：沒想到妹妹倒是_____。

| 課室活動 | Classroom Activities |

## 一、遊戲：你來猜猜 (cāi, to guess)

Before class the teacher copies some 生詞 the students have learned recently onto cards, one word per card. Then during class the teacher selects a card without revealing to the students what is written on it. The students try to figure out the word by asking questions such as：是吃的東西嗎？是紙做的嗎？是東西，還是人？是不是動物 (dòngwù; animal)？會不會動？能不能用？…… They may only ask "yes-no" or "choice type" questions, which the teacher answers. When the students think they have enough information, they guess what is written on the card. Anyone who guesses right wins a cookie or another reward provided by the teacher. Then the teacher goes to the next card, etc.

## 二、隨便談談 (Open discussion)

1. 請說說你最喜歡的節日是哪一天，為什麼？再說說你怎麼過萬聖節、感恩節、聖誕節，你都做些什麼？有什麼特別的活動嗎？可能用到的詞：

化裝 (disguise oneself), 化裝舞會 (costume party), 妖怪 (yāoguài; monster), 魔鬼 (móguěi) (móguǐ; devil), 巫婆 (wūpó; witch), 可怕的 (dreadful, terrible, fearsome, frightening), 遊行 (yóuxíng; parade), 刻 (kē; to carve), 打雪仗 (snowball fight), 堆雪人 (duēi//syuěrén) (duī//xuěrén; make a snowman), 禱告 (dǎogào; to pray), 上帝 (Shàngdì; God), 清教

徒 (cīngjiàotú) (qīngjiàotú; pilgrim), 基督徒 (jīdūtú, people who believe in Christianity), 天主教徒 (people who believe in Catholicism), 望彌撒 (wàng//mísā; to attend mass), 不給糖就搗蛋 (dǎodàn; this is a translation of the Western phrase "trick or treat", for which there is no traditional Chinese equivalent.)

2. 請介紹一個最能代表貴國文化的節日。
3. 貴國人過年、過節的時候，有什麼特別的吃的東西？
4. 大部分的節日都商業化了，你對這件事情的看法怎麼樣？

支票 (zhīpiào, check)
簽名 (qiēnmīng, to sign one'e name)

## 短文　　　　　華人的節日

農曆一月一日是新年,也叫春節,是華人最重要的節日,因為這是一年的開始,每個人不管在哪裏,除夕以前都要回家,全家一起吃年夜飯、放鞭炮、拿紅包。以前農業社會新年要到十五日過完元宵節才結束。現在時代不同了,一般公司只放四、五天假過年的氣氛跟以前比起來差多了。

元宵節也叫燈節,大家吃元宵,孩子們還提燈籠玩,因為明亮的燈籠會帶來好運。農曆五月五日端午節,是為了紀念兩千多年前的愛國詩人屈原。除了吃粽子,還有精彩的龍舟比賽。

八月十五的月亮又圓又亮,農人們的工作也做完了,全家人就一起賞月、吃月餅。慢慢就成了中秋節。可惜很多賞月時說的故事,都在阿姆斯壯上了月球以後被推翻了。

## Vocabulary:

1. 農曆 (nónglì): lunar calendar
2. 紅包 (hóngbāo): red envelope containing a gift of money
3. 元宵節 (Yuánxiāo jié): Lantern Festival, the fifteenth day of the first month of the lunar calendar
   元宵 (yuánxiāo): a dessert of glutinous rice flour balls with a center filled in broth
4. 提燈籠 (tí//dēnglóng): to carry a lantern
5. 好運 (hǎoyùn): good luck
6. 端午節 (Duānwǔ jié): Dragon Boat Festival, the fifth day of the fifth month of the lunar calendar
7. 詩人 (shīhrén) (shīrén): poet
8. 屈原 (Cyū Yuán) (Qū Yuán): (343 -290 B. C.) a famous poet of the Warring States period
9. 粽子 (zòng·zih) (zòng·zi): steamed food made of glutinous rice, meat, and other ingredients wrapped in bamboo leaves
10. 龍舟 (lóngjhōu) (lóngzhōu): dragon boat
11. 月亮 (yuèliàng): moon
    月球 (yuècióu) (yuèqiú): moon
12. 賞月 (shǎng//yuè): to enjoy a moonlit night
13. 月餅 (yuèbǐng) : mooncake
14. 中秋節 (Jhōngciōu Jié) (Zhōngqiū Jié): Mid-Autumn Festival
15. 阿姆斯壯 (Āmǔsīhjhuàng) (Āmǔsīzhuàng): Neil Armstrong, the first man on the moon

## 華人的節日

農曆[1]一月一日是新年，也叫春節，是華人最重要的節日，因為這是一年的開始，每個人不管在哪裏，除夕以前都要回家，全家一起吃年夜飯、放鞭炮、拿紅包[2]。以前農業社會，新年要到十五日過完元宵節[3]才結束。現在時代不同了，一般公司只放四、五天假，過年的氣氛跟以前比起來差多了。

元宵節也叫燈節，大家吃元宵[3]，孩子們還提燈籠[4]玩，因為明亮的燈籠會帶來好運[5]。農曆五月五日端午節[6]，是為了紀念兩千多年前的愛國詩人[7]屈原[8]，除了吃粽子[9]還有精彩的龍舟[10]比賽。

八月十五的月亮[11]又圓又亮，農人們的工作也做完了，全家人就一起賞月[12]、吃月餅[13]，慢慢就成了中秋節[14]。可惜很多賞月時說的故事，都在阿姆斯壯[15]上了月球[11]以後被推翻了。

# 第十四課　放假到哪裡去

■迪士尼樂園（盧德昭攝）

（高偉立、林建國房門口，門開著）

建國：嗨！你們怎麼來了？進來坐吧！

美真：我們去四樓跟一個同學借小說，**順便**上來看看你們在不在，有些事想跟你們請教一下。

偉立：什麼事？別客氣。

台麗：快放假了，我們打算去歐洲旅行，你們暑假才去過，哪些地方好玩？能不能給我們一點意見？

偉立：沒問題！歐洲**可**去的地方很多啊！我自己最喜歡法國巴黎，塞納河上每座橋都非常美麗，又各有特色。世界有名的羅浮宮、凡爾賽宮和巴黎鐵塔就更不用說了。

建國：我們在英國參觀了很多城堡，真希望我是個王子，跟自己喜歡的公主快快樂樂地生活在一起。

偉立：好羅曼蒂克[1]啊！又讓我想到了義大利的威尼斯。

建國：還有羅馬的大教堂，有好幾百年的歷史了，你們非去見識見識不可，保證值得！（對美真）你哥哥也一起去嗎？

美真：不行，他寒假要做實驗，不能一起去。真可惜！你們寒假有什麼計畫？

建國：（很著急地）等一下，我忘了告訴你們一個有意思的地方──蒙地卡羅。

台麗：噢，賭城，聽說過。

建國：你們可以去試試運氣，**說不定**這一次的旅費都能贏回來呢！

偉立：萬一輸光了呢？你這個賭鬼！

建國：**不賭就不賭**，去看表演[2]可以吧？那裡有些表演一定可以讓你大開眼界。

美真：你越說越興奮，我看，你就再跟我們去一次，當我們的導遊吧，小費不會少給的。

建國：這個錢，我恐怕賺不了，因為我爺爺今年八十歲，寒假我們全家要回臺灣給他過生日[3]，飛機票都已經訂好了。而且因為要在洛杉磯轉機，我們還打算**順便**去海洋世界和迪士尼樂園玩玩。想到他們的雲霄飛車、鬼屋和小小世界，我就等不及了。聽說在那裡玩三天三夜都不覺得過癮。

■臺灣陽明山國家公園：小油坑（范慧貞提供）

■臺灣東部的蘇花公路（范慧貞攝）

■臺灣中部的合歡山（劉秀芝提供）

美眞：你還真是長不大啊！不是玩，就是看動物表演。

建國：**難道**你不想去**嗎**？看動物表演也可以得到很多有關海洋動物的知識啊！

台麗：好啦[4]！知道你是動物專家。偉立，你呢？你要去哪裡？

偉立：我本來打算跟我二哥去尼加拉瀑布，可是現在我們決定去大峽谷跟黃石公園了。

台麗：我們臺灣有很多旅行團去這兩個地方，因為聽說去大峽谷得經過一片大沙漠，參加旅行團**一方面**省事，**一方面也**安全。

偉立：我覺得參加旅行團只能走馬看花，每次到了一個地方，不是忙著照相，就是排隊上廁所，還能有多少時間欣賞風景呢？！

台麗：你說得也對，難怪你們喜歡自助旅行。

美眞：大峽谷離黃石公園遠不遠？

偉立：遠倒是不算遠，雖然黃石公園冬天只有部分開放，但是我想去見識一下老忠實噴泉。回來就得打工了，我得存點兒錢，暑假才能去臺灣啊！這幾天我正在打聽訂機票、辦護照跟簽證這些事。

建國：嗨，你們的計畫聽起來都不錯，我也要趕快存錢，春假才能去佛羅里達州的海灘曬太陽，還可以去迪士尼世界玩。

美眞：**哎呀**！又是迪士尼！**算了**，**算了**，不跟你說了。

## 生詞及例句

**1 小說 (siǎoshuō) (xiǎoshuō)**　N：novel, short story（M：本／篇）

王：你喜歡看哪一類的小說？歷史的，還是戰爭的？
張：只要是短篇的就行，我沒時間看長篇的。

**2 順便 (shùnbiàn)**　A：incidentally; on the way, as one passes

你上樓的時候，順便把今天的報拿給爸爸，好嗎？

**3 意見 (yìjiàn)**　N：view, opinion, idea

這件事該怎麼辦？各位有什麼意見就說出來，別客氣。

**4 橋 (cíao) (qiáo)**　N：bridge（M：座 zuò）

以前要坐船才到得了那個小島，後來這座橋建好了，開車也能到了。

**5 塔 (tǎ)**　N：tower（M：座 zuò）

這棟公寓樓上的水塔很大，就是碰到停水，兩天也沒問題。

**6 城堡 (chéngbǎo)**　N：castle（M：座 zuò）

**7 王子 (wáng·zǐh) (wáng·zǐ)**　N：prince（M：位）

小李不但年輕、英俊、溫柔、大方，而且有很好的工作，是女孩子理想的「白馬王子」。

**8 公主 (gōngjhǔ) (gōngzhǔ)**　N：princess（M：位）

(1) 白雪公主跟七個小矮人的故事非常有名，沒有一個孩子沒聽過的。
(2) 歐洲的城堡，以前是王子、公主住的地方，現在只要有錢，一般人也可以把它買下來住了。

第十四課　放假到哪裡去

國王 (guówáng)　　N：king（M：位）

女王 (nyǔwáng) (nǚwáng)　　N：queen（M：位）

9 羅曼蒂克 (luómàndìkè)　　SV：to be romantic

王英英把房間裝飾得非常羅曼蒂克，到處都是粉紅色(pink)的，還有很多花。

10 見識 (jiànshih) (jiànshì)

N/V：general knowledge and experience, scope/to experience

(1) 小王常出國旅行，所以見識越來越廣。
(2) 陳助教說那個地方很特別，值得去見識一下。

11 保證 (bǎojhèng) (bǎozhèng)　　V：to guarantee, assure, ensure

我保證這些畫都是真的，有問題就來找我。

12 做實驗 (zuòshíhyàn) (zuò//shíyàn)

VO：to perform an experiment, to make a test

我們吃的藥都是先用動物(dòngwù, animal)做過實驗的，要不然市場上買不到。

實驗 (shíhyàn) (shíyàn)　　V/N：to experiment/experiment, test

實驗室 (shíhyànshih) (shíyànshì)　　N：laboratory

學外國話應該天天去語言實驗室聽錄音帶(lùyīndài, tape)。

13 賭城 (dǔchéng)

N：a gambling town (a city or town which has a large gambling industry, e.g. Las Vegas, Atlantic City)

賭場 (dǔchǎng)　　N：casino, gambling den

到賭城去玩的觀光客(tourist)，沒有一個不到賭場去賭一下的，都想看看自己能不能贏錢。

381

賭鬼 (dǔguěi) (dǔguǐ)　　N：an obsessive gambler

賭 (dǔ)　　V：to gamble, bet, wager

老謝一連賭了三天三夜了，真是個賭鬼！

打賭 (dǎ//dǔ)　　VO：to make a bet

我跟你打賭小林一定會贏，要是我說對了，你請我吃飯！

賭博 (dǔbó)　　N：gambling

老王會有今天都是賭博害了他，因為他在賭場把房子、車子跟銀行裡存的錢都輸光了。

14 運氣 (yùn·cì) (yùn·qì)　　N：fortune, luck

我的運氣真不錯，到了家才下雨。

幸運 (singyùn) (xìngyùn)　　SV：to be fortunate, lucky

我覺得我很幸運，到處都有人幫我的忙。

不幸 (búsìng) (búxìng)　　SV/A：to be unfortunate, to be sad/unfortunately

(1) 小王生下來，母親就死了，真不幸！
(2) 老王坐船去湖上看風景，不幸船翻了，他也死了。

15 說不定 (shuō·búdìng)　　MA/IE：perhaps, maybe

李：小錢怎麼一直沒消息？會不會出事了？
張：別著急，說不定他已經安全回到家了呢！

16 萬一 (wànyī)　　A：just in case, if by any chance

帶著你的信用卡吧，萬一錢用光了，也沒關係。

17 輸 (shū)　　V：to lose, to be defeated

昨天的球賽，我們打得不好，輸了十幾分。

### 18 表演 (biǎoyǎn)　　N/V：performance/to perform

(1) 我們這次的表演，有唱歌有跳舞，非常熱鬧。
(2) 李愛美的現代舞表演得很精彩，我一定要再看一次。

### 演 (yǎn)　　V：to perform, to act

那個電影明星太老了，演年輕人恐怕不合適。

### 上演 (shàngyǎn)

V：to open on the stage or screen, to premier (for movies and plays)

你剛剛說的那部電影是八月底上演的，已經演了快一個月了。

### 開演 (kāiyǎn)　　V：to start a performance or show

電影七點開演，我們六點四十五分在電影院 (a cinema) 門口見！

### 19 大開眼界 (dà kāi yǎnjiè)　　IE：to broaden one's horizons

第一次去迪士尼樂園，看到很多從來沒玩過的東西，我們都覺得大開眼界。

### 開眼界 (kāi//yǎnjiè)　　VO：to expand one's experience and horizon

錢小姐的鞋櫃裡有三百多雙鞋，什麼顏色的都有，真讓我開了眼界。

### 眼界 (yǎnjiè)　　N：field of view, range of vision

小王的眼界很高，找女朋友，不但要美麗大方，溫柔可愛，身材還要好，難怪一直找不到。

### 20 導遊 (dǎoyóu)　　N：tour guide

一個成功的導遊，除了帶著客人去玩，還要幫助客人了解那個地方的歷史、地理和文化。

### 21 爺爺 (yé·ye)

N：grandpa, grandfather(father's father); a respectful form of address for an old man

奶奶 (nǎi·nai)　　N：grandma, grandmother (father's mother)

22 轉機 (jhuǎn//jī) (zhuǎn//jī)　　VO：to make a connecting flight

從臺灣沒有飛機直飛中南美洲，得在美國轉機才到得了。

23 雲霄飛車 (yúnsiāo fēichē) (yúnxiāo fēichē)

N：roller coaster

醫生說有高血壓 (gāo xiěyā, high blood pressure) 的人，都不可以坐雲霄飛車。

雲 (yún)　　N：cloud（M：塊／片／朵 duǒ）

今天是個大晴天，藍天白雲，讓人看了都想跑出去玩。

24 海洋 (hǎiyáng)　　N：ocean, sea

地球 (the earth) 上四分之三的地方都是海洋。

25 過癮 (guò//yǐn)

SV/VO：to enjoy oneself to the full / to satisfy a craving

(1) 哇！今天吃得真過癮，好久沒吃這麼多海鮮了。
(2) 我從生病以後就沒喝過酒，今天想喝一小杯，過過癮。

26 動物 (dòngwù)　　N：animal（M：隻／頭／條）

陸地 (the land) 上最大的動物是大象 (dàxiàng, elephant)，海裡最大的動物是鯨魚 (jīngyú, whale)。

動物園 (dòngwùyuán)　　N：zoo（M：座）

海洋動物 (hǎiyáng dòngwù)　　N：marine life（M：條／隻／頭）

27 難道 (nándào)

A：(used to begin an emphatic, rhetorical question) Can it be possible that...?

(1) 你說你沒帶錢,難道連一塊錢都沒有嗎?
(2) 人人都知道張先生當選了國會議員,難道你還沒聽說嗎?

### 28 有關 (yǒuguān)　CV：to have something to do with, to be related to

有關參觀博物館的事,我們最好問問大家的意見。

### 跟…X…有關 (gēn ... X ... yǒuguān)

PT：has to do with ...X ; is related to...X

水果長得好不好跟天氣有關。

### 29 知識 (jhīhshìh) (zhīshì)　N：knowledge

只有課本上的知識是不夠的,經驗也很重要。

### 常識 (chángshìh) (chángshì)　N：common sense, basic knowledge

水當然往下流,這是常識嘛!

### 30 專家 (jhuānjiā) (zhuānjiā)　N：specialist, expert

王教授是心理方面的專家,因為他不但有博士學位,還有十多年的工作經驗。

### 書法家 (shūfǎjiā)　N：calligrapher

### 作家 (zuòjiā)　N：writer, author

陳先生是有名的作家,寫了很多本書。他也是書法家,毛筆字寫得非常漂亮。

### 專業 (jhuānyè) (zhuānyè)

AT/SV：major field of study, specialized trade/to be professional

(1) 陳小姐的專業知識不夠,做研究工作非常辛苦。
(2) 老李在大學念的就是電腦,所以這方面非常專業。

### 31 瀑布 (pùbù)　N：waterfall

要是很久不下雨，瀑布流下來的水也會變少。

**32** 旅行團 (lyǔsíngtuán) (lǚxíngtuán)　N：group tour, touring party

旅行社 (lyǔsingshè) (lǚxíngshè)　N：travel agency（M：家）

路口那家旅行社，只辦去歐洲的旅行團，只要有十六個客人，就出團。

團員 (tuányuán)　N：member of a group

我們這個旅行團有十六個團員，都是老人，動作比較慢，所以安排的活動都比較輕鬆，不需要走太遠。

**33** 省事 (shěng//shìh) (shěng//shì)

VO/SV：to save trouble, simplify matters/to be convenient

省錢 (shěng//cián) (shěng//qián)　VO/SV：to save money/economical

去飯館吃飯可以省不少事，可是不省錢。

省時間 (shěng//shíhjiān) (shěng//shíjiān)

VO/SV：to save time / to be time-saving

為了省時間，我們決定坐飛機去。

省油 (shěng//yóu)　VO/SV：to save gasoline/to be gas-saving

小車比大車省油。

省電 (shěng//diàn)　VO/SV：to save electricity/to be electricity-saving

每家冷氣機的廣告都說自己是最省電的。

省 (shěng)　N：province

聽說中國的四川 (Sichuān, Swechwan)省跟法國差不多一樣大。

**34** 安全 (āncyuán) (ānquán)　N/SV：safety/ to be safe, secure

(1) 為了安全，你最好不要把那麼多錢放在家裡。
(2) 在紐約，晚上一個人在路上走安全不安全？

### 安全帽 (āncyuánmào) (ānquánmào)

N：safety helmet（M：頂 dǐng）

這裡正在建大樓，不管誰進去，都得戴安全帽，要不然不安全。

### 安全帶 (āncyuándài) (ānquándài)　N：safety belt, seat belt（M：條）

飛機要起飛的時候，一定要坐在位子上，扣 (to buckle) 好安全帶，才安全。

## 35 走馬看花 (zǒu mǎ kàn huā)

IE：to gain a superficial understanding through cursory observation

那個博物館裡的東西太多，我們的時間不夠，只能走馬看花。

## 36 排隊 (pái//duèi) (pái//duì)　VO：to line up, to queue up

很多人在辦公室門口排隊拿申請表。

## 37 自助 (zìhjhù) (zìzhù)　AT：self-service

學生餐廳大部分都是自助餐，想吃什麼就拿什麼，然後去算帳。

## 38 開放 (kāifàng)　V/SV：to be open to public use/to be open-minded, liberal

(1) 這個圖書館假日也開放，你可以去那兒寫報告。
(2) 有些地方的人認為不穿衣服在沙灘上玩，沒什麼不好意思。他們這方面的看法比較開放。

## 39 打聽 (dǎtīng)

V：to make inquiries about; to ask around, to pry into; to enquire; to nose into; to inquire about/upon

小林對我們班一個女生非常有興趣，一直跟我打聽她的電話號碼。

## 40 護照 (hùjhào) (hùzhào)　N：passport（M：本）

不管誰要出國都得先辦一本護照，要不然就不能出去。

### 41 簽證 (ciān//jhèng) (qiānzhèng)　N：visa

如果你要去日本，一定要先拿到日本的簽證。

### 簽名 (ciān//míng) (qiān//míng)　VO/N：to sign ones name/signature

(1) 請你在這張表上簽個名，我就可以回公司報告，東西已經送到了。
(2) 你買的畫可能是假的，因為畫上的簽名一看就知道不是那個畫家的。

### 42 趕快 (gǎnkuài)　A：at once, quickly, immediately

你的病不輕，趕快去看醫生吧！

### 趕 (gǎn)　V/SV：to hurry, to rush; to catch up with/in a rush

(1) 這份資料我明天就需要用，請你幫我趕一趕。
(2) 這麼短的時間要看這麼多地方，太趕了吧！

### 趕上 (gǎn//·shàng)　RC：to catch up with ; to be in time for

現在已經三點了，我們趕不上三點半的飛機了。

### 43 春假 (chūnjià)　N：spring vacation

在臺灣，有些父母會利用學校放春假的時候，帶孩子出國旅行。

### 假日 (jiàrìh) (jiàrì)　N：holiday, day off

平常日子上班、上課，大家都很緊張，週末假日應該安排一些活動，讓自己輕鬆一下。

### 請假 (cǐng//jià) (qǐng//jià)　VO：to ask for leave

我感冒了，想請兩天假，在家休息。

### 病假 (bìngjià)　N：sick leave

第十四課　放假到哪裡去

事假 (shìhjià) (shìjià)
N：a leave of absence (to attend to private affairs), personal leave

我跟老闆請了兩個鐘頭的事假，去辦簽證。

**44** 曬太陽 (shài//tài·yáng)　VO：to bask in the sun

你看，很多老人坐在公園裡的椅子上曬太陽。

曬 (shài)　V：to dry in the sun , to bask

太陽 (tài·yáng)　N：the sun

今天太陽很大，把箱子裡的衣服拿出來曬曬吧！

月亮 (yuè·liàng)　N：moon

星星 (sīng·sīng) (xīng·xīng)　N：stars

迷路的時候，看天上的星星，也找得到路吧？

**45** 算了 (suàn·le)　IE：Forget it!

(1) 小錢不願意說就算了，我們問別人吧！
(2) 算了，別跟小孩子生氣了！

### ▼ 歎詞　Interjections

1. 哎呀 (āi·ya)　I: alas! [indicating surprise]

### ▼ 專有名詞　Proper Names

1. 巴黎 (Bālí)　Paris
2. 塞納河 (Sàinà Hé)　Seine River
3. 羅浮宮 (Luófú Gōng)　the Louvre
4. 凡爾賽宮 (Fán'ěrsài Gōng)　Versailles
5. 巴黎鐵塔 (Bālí Tiě Tǎ)　Eiffel Tower

389

6. 威尼斯 (Wēinísīh) (Wēinísī)　　Venice
7. 羅馬 (Luómǎ)　　Rome
8. 蒙地卡羅 (Méngdìkǎluó)　　Monte Carlo
9. 洛杉磯 (Luòshānjī)　　Los Angeles
10. 海洋世界 (Hǎiyáng Shìhjiè) (Hǎiyáng Shìjiè)　　Sea World
11. 迪士尼樂園 (Díshìhní Lèyuán) (Díshìní Lèyuán)　　Disneyland
12. 尼加拉瀑布 (Níjiālā Pùbù)　　Niagara Falls
13. 黃石公園 (Huángshíh Gōngyuán) (Huángshí Gōngyuán)　　Yellowstone National Park
14. 老忠實噴泉 (Lǎo Jhōngshíh Pēncyuán) (Lǎo Zhōngshí Pēnquán)　　Old Faithful Geyser
15. 佛羅里達州 (Fóluólǐdá Jhōu) (Fóluólǐdá Zhōu)　　Florida State
16. 迪士尼世界 (Díshìh ní Shìhjiè) (Díshìní Shìjiè)　　Disneyworld

## 注釋

1. 羅曼蒂克 is the transliteration of "romantic." The same word can also be translated as 浪漫 (làngmàn).

2. 表演 means "shows." People in Taiwan have begun to use the transliterated word 秀 (xiù) for "show" instead of 表演. You might hear someone ask: 那個歌星在哪裡作秀？ Another use of this word 秀 is in the expression 政治秀 which refers to a popularity-seeking action performed by a politician for the view of his electorate.

3. 給爺爺過生日 means "to celebrate grandfather's birthday." In Chinese society, people think every decade is a new stage of one's life, so every tenth birthday is particularly important and deserving of a celebration. Every tenth birthday over the age of 60 is especially important. This is the reason why the whole family of 林建國 is coming back to Taiwan to celebrate grandfather's birthday.

4. 好啦！ is a contraction of 好了啊. It is used to end talk on a particular subject. It is similar to saying: "Come on!", "Cut it out!", "No more!" etc.. In the text 美真 does not want to admit that she wants to go to Sea World, and so she does not wish to discuss it anymore.

## 文法練習

> 一　順便　conveniently, on the way without taking any extra trouble, at one's convenience
>
> ◎我們去四樓跟一個同學借小說，順便上來看看你們在不在，……
> We came to the fourth floor to borrow a novel from a classmate. Since we were here anyway, we came up to see if you were home.

用法說明：「順便」前面是本來要做的事，藉這個機會也可以方便地完成「順便」後面的事。

Explanation: Stated in front of 順便 is an initial action. Performance of this action creates a convenient opportunity to carry out a second action, described after 順便。

▼ 練習　下面的情形用「順便」怎麼說？

1. 你開車回家的時候碰到張教授，他就住在你家附近。
   While driving home you bump into Professor Chang, who happens to live near your house.
   → 張教授，我可以順便送你回家。
   　 Professor Chang! I could give you a lift home. It's on my way.

2. 室友要去郵局寄包裹，你請他幫你買幾張郵票。

3. 你到紐約看表演，正好有一個朋友住在紐約，你可以去看他。

4. 你看見弟弟要出門，你想叫他出去的時候把門關上。

5. 你的車沒油了，正好也髒了，你就把車開到加油站去加油，並且把車洗乾淨。

## 二　可 V（的）　worth V-ing

◎歐洲可去的地方很多啊！
There are a lot of places in Europe worth going to.

用法說明：這個「可」是「值得」的意思。「可 V（的）」可以放在名詞前，也可單獨使用，代表名詞。

Explanation: This 可 means "worth" or "worthwhile". "可V（的）" can be placed in front of a noun to describe it or the phrase can be used alone to take the place of a noun.

▼ 練習　　請用「可V（的）」完成下面句子。

1. 這件事，大家意見都不同，可討論的問題很多。
   Everybody's opinions differ on this issue. There are many points worthy of discussion.

2. 我的生活沒什麼變化，寫信的時候沒什麼可＿＿＿＿＿＿。

3. 那家飯館你去過，有什麼可＿＿＿＿＿＿，給我介紹一下。

4. 羅馬是個很老的城市，可＿＿＿＿＿＿地方很多。

5. 你從來不聽我的話，我跟你沒話可＿＿＿＿＿＿了。

## 三　說不定　perhaps/maybe

◎說不定這一次的旅費都能贏回來呢！
Who knows? Perhaps you'll win back all of the travel expenses this time!

用法說明：「說不定」的後面是短句。（如果主語清楚明顯可省略）。「說不定」、「也許」、「可能」、「大概」都表示臆測的語氣。但此四者中，越後面的詞情況發生的可能性越高。

Explanation: Following 說不定 is a clause. If the subject of the clause is clear then it can be omitted. The following four phrases indicate conjecture, listed in the order of increasing possibility: 說不定, 也許, 可能, 大概.

第十四課　放假到哪裡去

▼ 練習　　請把「說不定」放在句中合適的地方。

1. 我很多年沒回家了，會找不到回家的路了。
   I haven't been home in many years. I won't be able to find my way.
   → 我很多年沒回家了，說不定會找不到回家的路了。
   I haven't been home in many years. Maybe I won't be able to find my way.

2. 小王對政治很有興趣，將來會當參議員。
   _____

3. 你把你的困難告訴房東，房租可以少算一點。
   _____

4. 你去學校找找，王美美就在圖書館裡面看書。
   _____

5. 換換環境，小高的病會好得快一點。
   _____

### 四　不……就不……

◎不賭就不賭，去看表演可以吧？
Okay, then I won't gamble. Do you have any objection to my seeing the shows?

用法說明：「不」的後面可以是動詞、動詞短語 (VP) 或SV。這個句型表示勉強接受對方的說法，有妥協、無可奈何、委屈求全的語氣。後面的句子句尾常用「吧」。

Explanation: 不 can be followed by a verb, verb phrase, or SV. This sentence pattern shows that the speaker is forcing him/herself to accept what another has said. It expresses a tone of having no choice, compromising, or feeling wronged. 吧 is often placed at the end of the next sentence.

▼ 練習　　請用「不……就不……」完成下面對話。

1. 張：你怎麼對小陳說這種話？太沒禮貌了！
   Chang: How can you say something like that to Little Chen? That's so rude!

393

李：不說就不說，誰叫他這麼討厭？！
Lee: So I won't say it then! But who told him to be so disagreeable?!

2. 張：還有三天就期末考了，你還要去看電影！
   李：＿＿＿＿＿＿＿＿＿＿＿＿＿＿＿＿＿。

3. 媽媽：你不讓兒子去烤肉，他很不高興。
   爸爸：＿＿＿＿＿＿＿＿，他應該在家準備考試。

4. 張：小王覺得看孩子太辛苦，不願意做。
   李：＿＿＿＿＿＿＿＿，我們請別人吧！

5. 張：小陳說不能來參加你的生日舞會了。
   李：＿＿＿＿＿＿＿＿，反正人已經很多了。

## 五　難道……（嗎）？

### Is it possible that……? Could it be true that……?

◎難道你不想去嗎？
Is it possible that you don't want to go?

**用法說明**：「難道」的後面常用否定詞「不」或「沒」，表示懷疑或不相信的反問語氣。

Explanation: Following 難道 is a negative word like 不 or 沒, showing doubt or disbelief. The tone is that of a rebuttal or a rhetorical question.

▼ **練習**　請用「難道……（嗎）？」改寫下面句子。

1. 這件事全校都知道了，你怎麼沒聽說？
   Everybody in the whole school knows about this. How did you not hear about it?
   → 這件事全校都知道了，難道你沒聽說嗎？
   Everybody in the whole school knows about this. Is it possible that you didn't hear about it?

2. 你出去玩了一個月，真的還不過癮嗎？
   ＿＿＿＿＿＿＿＿＿＿＿＿＿＿＿＿＿＿＿＿＿＿＿＿＿＿＿

3. 這麼好的大學給你獎學金，你真的想放棄嗎？

394

4. 老丁打了這麼多年籃球，怎麼不知道這個動作是犯規的？

5. 小高罵得這麼難聽，你真的一點都不生氣？

## 六 一方面……，一方面也…… It is ..., and it is also ...

◎參加旅行團，一方面省事，一方面也安全。
When you travel with a tour group, it not only save a lot of effort, but it is also safe.

**用法說明**：說明做一件事的兩個原因，聽起來比較有條理。
Explanation: This explains two reasons in a particular situation. The pattern helps the speaker to present his ideas in an orderly fashion.

▼ 練習　　請用「一方面……，一方面也……」改寫下面句子。

1. 李小姐願意當助教，因為她可以選研究所的課，而且她對這個工作也有興趣。
Miss Lee wants to be a teaching assistant because she can take graduate courses. Furthermore, she also has interest in the work.
→ 李小姐願意當助教，一方面她可以選研究所的課，一方面她對這個工作也有興趣。
Miss Lee wants to be a teaching assistant, on the one hand, she is interested in the work, and on the other hand, she can also take graduate courses.

2. 我不參加那個旅行團，因為那些地方我都去過，而且我也沒時間。

3. 我老姐決定租這個公寓，因為房租便宜，交通也方便。

4. 那次革命沒成功，因為軍隊力量太弱，人民也希望安定。

5. 王英英能當電影明星，因為她身材好，而且也很會表演。

## 七　算了　forget it, never mind

◎算了，算了，不跟你說了。
Forget it; let's not talk about it anymore.

**用法說明**：表示這件事情就此作罷了。（表示說話者並不滿意。）可以獨立使用，後面也可以附加說明。或是放在句尾。

**Explanation**: 算了 is very similar to the phrases "forger it" and "never mind", meaning that no further effort or discussion is necessary, and often indicating dissatisfaction by the speaker. One can use 算了 by itself, add other speech afterwards, or attach 算了 to the end of a sentence.

### 練習　請用「算了」完成下面對話。

### （一）獨立使用，可附加說明

1. 張：老林對你這麼不客氣，你應該去罵他一頓。
   Chang: Old Lin is so rude to you. You ought to go tell him off.
   李：算了，跟這種人生氣不值得。
   Lee: Forget it. It's not worth getting mad at a person like that.

2. 張：對不起，雖然你說了兩次了，可是我還是沒聽懂，請你再說一次吧！
   李：＿＿＿＿＿＿＿＿＿＿＿＿＿＿＿。

3. 張：唉喲！我又忘了把你的書帶來了，我這就回家拿。
   李：＿＿＿＿＿＿＿＿＿＿＿＿＿＿＿。

4. 張：我昨天打電話的時候，跟你借的五毛錢，現在還你，謝謝！
   李：＿＿＿＿＿＿＿＿＿＿＿＿＿＿＿。

5. 張：我怎麼又輸了？我還要再賭一次，我不相信我的運氣真的這麼壞！
   李：＿＿＿＿＿＿＿＿＿＿＿＿＿＿＿。

### （二）放在句尾

1. 張：我請他好幾次，他都不願意來。
   Chang: I invited him many times, and he never wanted to come.
   李：既然這樣，我看算了吧！

Lee: If that's the case, I'd just say forget it!

2. 張：書店老闆說，這本漫畫書已經賣完了。
   李：那就 _____，我們買別的吧！

3. 張：我的頭很疼，全身都不舒服。
   李：要是你真的病了，就請假 _____。

4. 張：哎喲，怎麼辦？我把你的杯子打破了。
   李：_____，反正我的杯子多得很。

5. 太太：你姐姐跟我們借的錢，好幾年了都沒還，難道就算了嗎？
   先生：不 _____ 怎麼辦？誰叫她是我姐姐呢！

## 八　嘆詞「哎呀」的用法　The use of 哎呀 interjection

◎哎呀！又是迪士尼！
Oh no! Not Disney again!

用法說明：「哎呀」，語調低降、短促，放在句首。用法與第三課的「哎喲」差不多。表示驚訝、驚懼、驚喜、焦急、不耐煩時的呼聲。但不用於疼痛時的呻吟聲。一般來說，「哎呀」的程度比「哎喲」強，且負面的用法也比較多。

Explanation: The tone of 哎呀 starts low and descends. It's placed at the beginning of a sentence. The usage of 哎呀 is almost the same as 哎喲. It shows amazement, sudden fright, pleasant surprise, anxiety or impatience. It isn't used as a cry of despair or pain. Generally speaking, 哎呀 is stronger than 哎喲, and always used regarding a bad aspect.

▼ 練習　請根據下面情況用「哎呀」表示驚訝、驚懼、驚喜、焦急跟不耐煩。

1. 出門以後才想起來，煮 (zhǔ, to boil) 了一鍋湯，卻忘了關火。
   You suddenly remember that you had cooked a pot of soup, but forgotten to turn off the stove before you left the house.
   →哎呀，我忘了關火！
   Oh my God! I forgot to turn off the stove!!

2. 站在船邊欣賞風景，不小心鞋子掉進海裡去了。

3. 收到一份禮物，喜歡得不得了，可是覺得真不好意思讓對方花那麼多錢。

4. 聽朋友說他的病很嚴重，已經沒有藥可以醫了。

5. 想要好好地休息一下，哥哥的孩子卻在旁邊一直哭個不停。

## 課室活動 / Classroom Activities

一

1. The following assignment should be given to the students to prepare before class: The students are working for an organization which has invited some Taiwanese scholars to visit your country for two weeks. The students' assignment is to plan a program for those scholars, to show them places and things. During class, they are to compare their suggestions and work out the details on the program to be offered.

   Some useful supplementary words include: 太空中心 (space center), 紀念碑 (jì'niànbēi; monument), 國會山莊 (Guóhuèi Shānjhuāng) (Guóhuì Shānzhuāng; Capital Hill), 最高法院 (Supreme Court), 科學博物館 (science museum), 憲法 (xiànfǎ; constitution), 工廠 (gōngchǎng; factory), 購物中心 (gòuwù jhōngsīn) (gòuwù zhōngxīn; shopping center), 植物園 (Jhíhwùyuán) (Zhíwùyuán; botanical garden), 遊樂園 (yóulèyuán; amusement park), 地下鐵 (subway).

2. Role Playing

Two students. One student plays the role of an agent in a 旅行社 ( travel agency). The other is a customer. The customer is planning to take a trip to Europe for two weeks and asks for help from the agent about the travel route, airplane tickets, hotel rooms, special interest excursions, etc. The students should try to develop a lively conversation. Some useful supplementary words include: 航空公司 (hángkōng gōngsī; airlines), 雙人房 (double room), 單人房 (single room), 經濟艙 (jīngjìcāng; economy seating section in a plane or ship), 頭等艙 (tóuděngcāng; first class seating section in a plane or ship), 臥鋪 (wòpù; sleeping berth), 單程票 (dānchéngpiào; one way ticket), 來回票 (roundtrip ticket)

## 二、討論問題 (Discussion)

1. 每個人推薦一個最有特色、最值得去旅行的地方。要說清楚為什麼這個地方值得去。
2. 你喜歡去什麼樣的地方旅行？比較現代、舒服的地方？還是有很多歷史、文化可看的地方？
3. 說說坐雲霄飛車或參觀鬼屋的經驗。

## 短文

### 在台灣旅行

台灣的風景很美,可看的地方很多。台北郊區的陽明山國家公園,因為是火山區,有不少人來洗溫泉,花季時來賞花的人更多。再往南走有石門水庫、小人國、六福村野生動物園,都離台北不遠,是週末度假的好地方。中部的日月潭、溪頭、阿里山、合歡山都很有名。合歡山冬天可以滑雪,溪頭跟阿里山都是森林遊樂區,阿里山的日出、雲海、神木跟上山的老火車,都讓人難忘。

如果從台北順著海邊往東走,一邊是高山,一邊是大海,風景真是好得沒話說。到了花蓮,就可以從太魯閣上中部橫貫公路,一路青山綠水,空氣新鮮,無論你有什麼困難、壓力,都可以丟在一邊不管了。

墾丁在台灣的最南邊,不但有白色的海灘、乾淨的海水,還有熱帶森林,是最受歡迎的觀光度假地。

## Vocabulary:

1. 陽明山 (Yángmíng Shān): Yang Ming Mountain, a mountain in Taipei known for its beautiful scenery
2. 火山 (huǒshān): volcano
3. 溫泉 (wūncyuán) (wēnquán): natural hot-spring
4. 賞花 (shǎng//huā): to enjoy flowers in bloom
5. 石門水庫 (Shímén Shuǐkù): Shih-Men reservoir in 桃園 Táoyuán, south of Taipei
6. 小人國 (Siǎorénguó) (Xiǎorénguó): Miniatureland, a recreational area with miniature landscapes and architecture in 桃園 Táoyuán, south of Taipei
7. 六福村野生動物園 (Liùfúcūn Yěshēng Dòngwùyuán): Liufutsun Safari Park in 新竹 Xīnzhú, south of Taipei
8. 度假 (dù//jià): to spend a holiday
9. 日月潭 (Rìhyuè Tán) (Rìyuè Tán): Sun Moon Lake
10. 溪頭 (Sītóu) (Xītóu): a botanical park in central Taiwan
11. 阿里山 (Ālǐ Shān): Ali Mountain, a recreational park in southern Taiwan
12. 合歡山 (Héhuān Shān): Hehuan Mountain, a mountain in central Taiwan, location of the only ski area in Taiwan
13. 森林遊樂區 (sēnlín yóulèqū): natural forest resort
14. 日出 (rìhchū) (rìchū): sunrise
15. 雲海 (yúnhǎi): clouds resembling ocean waves which form around mountain peaks
16. 神木 (shénmù): extremely ancient tree
17. 順著 (shùn·zhe): to follow in the direction of

18. 花蓮 (Huālián): a port city in eastern Taiwan
19. 太魯閣 (Tàilǔgé): Taroko Gorge, a natural rock gorge in eastern Taiwan
20. 熱帶 (rèdài): tropical region
21. 觀光 (guānguāng) : to go sightseeing, to tour

## 在臺灣旅行

台灣的風景很美，可看的地方很多。台北郊區的陽明山[1]國家公園，因為是火山[2]區，有不少人來洗溫泉[3]，花季時來賞花[4]的人更多。再往南走，有石門水庫[5]、小人國[6]、六福村野生動物園[7]，都離台北不遠，是週末度假[8]的好地方。中部的日月潭[9]、溪頭[10]、阿里山[11]、合歡山[12]都很有名。合歡山冬天可以滑雪，溪頭跟阿里山都是森林遊樂區[13]，阿里山的日出[14]、雲海[15]、神木[16]跟山上的老火車，都讓人難忘。

如果從台北順著[17]海邊往東走，一邊是高山，一邊是大海，風景真是好得沒話說。到了花蓮[18]，就可以從太魯閣[19]上中部橫貫公路，一路青山綠水，空氣新鮮，無論你有什麼困難、壓力，都可以丟在一邊不管了。

墾丁在台灣的最南邊，不但有白色的海灘、乾淨的海水，還有熱帶[20]森林，是最受歡迎的觀光[21]度假地。

# INDEX I

# 詞類略語表

## GRAMMATICAL TERMS KEY TO ABBREVIATIONS

| | |
|---|---|
| A | Adverb |
| AT | Attributive |
| AV | Auxiliary Verb |
| CONJ | Conjunction |
| CV | Coverb |
| DC | Directional Compound |
| DEM | Demonstrative Pronoun |
| DV | Directional Verb |
| I | Interjection |
| IE | Idiomatic Expression |
| L | Localizer |
| M | Measure |
| MA | Movable Adverb |
| N | Noun |
| NP | Noun Phrase |
| O | Object |
| ON | Onomatopoeia |
| P | Particle |
| PRON | Pronoun |
| PT | Pattern |
| PV | Post Verb |
| PW | Place Word |
| QW | Question Word |
| RC | Resultative Compound |
| RE | Resultative Ending |
| S | Subject |
| SV | Stative Verb |
| V | Verb |
| VO | Verb Object Compound |
| VP | Verb Phrase |

403

# 文法練習索引

## A

| | | |
|---|---|---|
| ……a, ……a, ……a, …… | ……啊，……啊，……啊，…… | 8 |
| āi ·ya | 唉呀 | 14 |
| āiyāo | 哎喲 | 3 |

## B

| | | |
|---|---|---|
| bèi | 被 | 12 |
| bǐbúshàng | 比不上 | 9 |
| bìng bù /méi | 並不/沒 | 5 |
| búdàn ……, hái …… | 不但……，還…… | 6 |
| búdào | 不到 | 10 |
| bú dàn …, yě/érqiě (yě)/ bìngqiě(yě)… | 不但……，也／而且（也）／並且（也）…… | 4 |
| bùguǎn /búlùn /wúlùn …… dōu …… | 不管／不論／無論……都…… | 7 |
| bù ……jiùbù …… | 不……就不…… | 14 |
| (S) V bùliǎo jǐ Mī (N), (S) jiù …… | (S) V不了幾M(N)，(S)就…… | 1 |
| búshì ……, jiùshì …… | 不是……，就是…… | 7 |
| búsuàn | 不算 | 6 |
| bùzhī dào…… | 不知道…… | 3 |

## C

| | | |
|---|---|---|
| cái | 才 | 3,7,8 |
| TW cái | TW才 | 8 |
| cái (V) Nu M (N), jiù…… | 才(V) NuM(N)，就…… | 7 |
| N₁ V chéng N₂ | N₁ V成N₂ | 6 |
| chèn (.zhe) | 趁（著） | 13 |

| | | |
|---|---|---|
| chú·le……yǐwài/zhī wài, dōu…… | 除了……以外／之外，都…… | 4 |
| chú·le……yǐwài/zhī wài, hái…… | 除了……以外／之外，還…… | 4 |
| cóng……qǐ | 從……起 | 11 |

## D

| | | |
|---|---|---|
| dàodǐ | 到底 | 8 |
| dàoshì | 倒是 | 13 |
| ……dàoshì……, kěshì (búguò/jiùshì)…… | ……倒是……，可是（不過/就是）…… | 9 |
| V/SV ·de N/PN…… | V/SV得N/PN…… | 2 |
| N/NP V/SV ·de…… | N/NP V/SV得…… | 2 |
| V ·de chābùduō ·le | V得差不多了 | 7 |
| SV ·de méihuàshuō | SV得沒話說 | 9 |
| děng……zài…… | 等……再…… | 3 |
| V ·de zhèng SV | V得正SV | 12 |
| dōu | 都 | 9 |
| dòugbúdòng jiù | 動不動就 | 12 |
| duì NP láishuō…… | 對NP來說…… | 2 |
| S duì……yǒu xìngqù | S對……有興趣 | 1 |
| duō V(O) | 多V(O) | 6 |
| duōshǎo V yìdiǎn/yìxiē/jǐ M | 多少V一點／一些／幾M | 11 |

## E

| | | |
|---|---|---|
| ei, ei | 欸 | 2 |

## F

| | | |
|---|---|---|
| fèngmiàn | 方面 | 10 |
| fǎnzhèng | 反正 | 13 |
| fēi……bùkě | 非……不可 | 6 |

| | | |
|---|---|---|
| X fēn zhī V | X分之Y | 10 |

## G

| | | |
|---|---|---|
| gè V gè ·de | 各V各的 | 11 |
| N₁/NP₁ gēn N₂/NP₂ bǐqǐlái…… | N₁／NP₁跟N₂／NP₂比起來…… | 4 |
| gè yǒu gè de N | 各有各的N | 11 |
| V guāng | V光 | 8 |

## H

| | | |
|---|---|---|
| AABB | AABB（雙音節SV的重疊） | 13 |
| hái | 還 | 12 |
| hài | 害 | 5 |
| háishì…… | 還是…… | 1 |
| háishì……·baō | 還是……吧！ | 1 |
| hǎo SV ·de Nō! | 好SV的N！ | 4 |
| huì……·de | 會……的 | 7 |

## J

| | | |
|---|---|---|
| jiāqǐláǐ | 加起來 | 4 |
| Jìrán……, jiù…… | 既然……，就…… | 9 |
| ……QW……jiù……QW…… | ……QW……就……QW…… | 2 |
| QW+SV jìu V+QW & zě·me SV jìu.zě·me V | QW+SV就V+QW & 怎麼SV就怎麼V | 2 |
| jiùshì | 就是… | 13 |
| jiùshì·ma! | 就是嘛！ | 2 |
| jiùshì……, yě…… | 就是……，也…… | 12 |

## K

| | | |
|---|---|---|
| kànqǐlái……, jìushì…… | 看起來……，就是…… | 1 |
| kě | 可 | 8 |

406

| | | |
|---|---|---|
| kě V (·de) | 可V（的） | 14 |

## L

| | | |
|---|---|---|
| ·la | 啦 | 1 |
| lái | 來 | 1 |
| lái V | 來V | 9 |
| V lái V qù | V來V去 | 2 |
| lián……dōu/yě…… | 連……都／也 | 2 |
| ·lou | 嘍 | 6 |

## M

| | | |
|---|---|---|
| ·m | 嗯 | 1 |
| ·ma | 嘛 | 2, 3 |
| V mǎn | V滿 | 7 |
| mǎn Nu-M-(N) | 滿Nu-M-(N) | 7 |
| ……méi guān·xi……jiù hǎo·le | ……沒關係，……就好了 | 1 |
| (S) méi V jǐ M (N) (S) jiù…le | (S)沒V幾M(N)(S)就……了 | 1 |
| měi Nu+M₁(N)+V+yī +M₂ | 每Nu+M₁(N)+V+一+M₂ | 10 |
| méiyǒu yī M (N) bù/méi……de | 沒有一M(N)不／沒……的 | 4 |

## N

| | | |
|---|---|---|
| ·n | 嗯 | 4 |
| nándào……(·ma)? | 難道……（嗎）？ | 14 |
| níngkě VP₁, yě VP₂ | 寧可VP₁，也VP₂ | 6 |
| (níngyuàn……, yě……) | （寧願……，也……） | |
| nǐ/wǒ kàn | 你／我看 | 10 |

## O

| | | |
|---|---|---|
| ó | 哦 | 6 |

| òu | 噢 | 1 |

## Q

| V qǐlái…… | V起來…… | 1 |
| V/SV qǐlái | V/SV起來 | 4 |
| V qǐ O lái…… | V起O來…… | 5 |

## R

| ràng | 讓 | 12 |

## S

| shéijiào……? | 誰叫……? | 9 |
| shé·me dōu……, jiùshì…… | 什麼都……，就是…… | 13 |
| shì (A) SV | 是(A) SV | 5 |
| shùnbiàn | 順便 | 14 |
| shuōbúdìng | 說不定 | 14 |
| shuōdào | 說到 | 12 |
| SV sǐ·le | SV死了 | 9 |
| suàn·le | 算了 | 14 |
| suànshì | 算是 | 6 |
| suī rán……, kěshì…… | 雖然……，可是…… | 4 |
| suǒyǐ·la | 所以啦 | 6 |

## W

| ·wa | 哇 | 4 |
| wèi+N/PN+V | 為+N/PN+V | 10 |
| wèi·le | 為了 | 10 |

## X

INDEX I  文法練習索引

| | | |
|---|---|---|
| xiān……, děng……, zài…… | 先……，等……，再……。 | 11 |
| xiàng……shé·me·de | 像……什麼的 | 5 |
| xiàng……yíyàng | 像……一樣 | 11 |
| xiàng……zhèyàng/nàyàng…… | 像……這樣／那樣…… | 11 |
| xìngkuī/xìnghǎo/háihǎo/hǎozài……, yàobùrán…… | 幸虧／幸好／還好／好在……，要不然…… | 7 |

## Y

| | | |
|---|---|---|
| yàobúshì | 要不是 | 12 |
| yào/děikàn | 要／得看 | 3 |
| (yàoshì) ……dehuà | （要是）……的話 | 3 |
| yí | 咦 | 6 |
| yìbān lái shuō (yìbān ér lùn) | 一般來說（一般而論） | 5 |
| yìbiān……, yìbiān…… | 一邊……，一邊…… | 3 |
| yì M bǐ yì M | 一M比一M | 11 |
| yìfāngmiàn……, yìfāngmiànyě…… | 一方面……，一方面也…… | 14 |
| yìlián | 一連 | 12 |
| yīnwèi……·de guān·xi | 因為……的關係 | 11 |
| yǐwéi……, méixiǎngdào…… | 以為……，沒想到…… | 5 |
| V yíxià | V一下 | 8 |
| yóu N/PN lái V(O) | 由N/PN來V(O) | 10 |
| ……, yǒushíhòu hái…… | ……，有時候還…… | 3 |

## Z

| | | |
|---|---|---|
| zàibù V(O), jiù…… | 再不V(O)，就…… | 13 |
| zàijiāshàng | 再加上 | 11 |
| zài……yě…… | 再……也…… | 5 |
| zǎozhīdào (wǒ/wǒmén) jiù ….le | 早知道（……）（我／我們）就……了。 | 9 |

| | | |
|---|---|---|
| zěn·me (yì) huíshì | 怎麼（一）回事 | 5 |
| zěn·me zhè·me…… | 怎麼這麼…… | 8 |
| zhèjìu | 這就 | 13 |
| zhè jìu yào cóng……shuōqǐ·le | 這就要從……說起了 | 11 |
| zhèn·me shuō | 這麼說 | 10 |
| zhèngyào | 正要 | 10 |
| zhǐhǎo | 只好 | 7 |
| zhǐyào……,jìu…… | 只要……，就…… | 2 |
| zhǐyǒu …cái | 只有…才 | 13 |
| V zhù | V住 | 6 |
| zǒngshì | 總是 | 1 |

# 生詞索引 Vocabulary Index

| 通用拼音 | 漢語拼音 | 生詞 | 課數 |
|---|---|---|---|
| | **A** | | |
| | āiyā | 唉呀 | 14 |
| | āi·yāo | 哎喲　哎哟 | 3 |
| | āndǎ | 安打 | 12 |
| | āndìng | 安定 | 11 |
| | ānpái | 安排 | 10 |
| | ānquán | 安全 | 14 |
| āncyuándài | ānquándài | 安全帶　安全带 | 14 |
| āncyuánmào | ānquánmào | 安全帽 | 14 |
| | **B** | | |
| | bǎi | 擺　摆 | 8 |
| | bǎi//dìtān | 擺地攤　摆地摊 | 8 |
| | Bālí | 巴黎 | 14 |
| | Bālí tiětǎ | 巴黎鐵塔 | 14 |
| | bàng | 棒 | 1 |
| | bàng | 磅 | 13 |
| bangcióu | bàngqiú | 棒球 | 12 |
| bàngōngshìh | bàngōngshì | 辦公室　办公室 | 3 |
| bāngjhù | bāngzhù | 幫助　帮助 | 4 |
| | bànyè | 半夜 | 2 |
| bānjhǎng | bānzhǎng | 班長　班长 | 10 |
| | bào | 抱 | 10 |
| | bàogào | 報告　报告 | 6 |
| | bāoguǒ | 包裹 | 4 |
| | bāokuò | 包括 | 10 |

411

| 通用拼音 | 漢語拼音 | 生詞 | 課數 |
|---|---|---|---|
| bàociàn | bàoqiàn | 抱歉 | 10 |
| bǎojhèng | bǎozhèng | 保證　保证 | 14 |
|  | bàoyuàn | 抱怨 | 20 |
| Bāsī | Bāxī | 巴西 | 11 |
|  | Běijīng | 北京 | 2 |
|  | bèi | 背 | 6 |
|  | bèidòng | 被動　被动 | 6 |
|  | bèi//shū | 背書　背书 | 6 |
| bèisiàlái | bèi//xiàlái | 背下來　背下來 | 6 |
|  | bèn | 笨 | 8 |
|  | běnlěi | 本壘　本垒 | 12 |
|  | bèn shǒu bèn jiǎo | 笨手笨腳　笨手笨脚 | 8 |
|  | bǐ | 比 | 12 |
|  | biàn | 變　变 | 5 |
|  | biànhuà | 變化　变化 | 5 |
|  | biānpào | 鞭炮 | 12 |
|  | biǎo | 表 | 3 |
|  | biǎodì | 表弟 | 7 |
|  | biǎogē | 表哥 | 7 |
|  | biǎojiě | 表姐 | 7 |
|  | biǎomèi | 表妹 | 7 |
|  | biǎoyǎn | 表演 | 14 |
|  | bìng | 並　并 | 5 |
|  | bìngjià | 病假 | 14 |
| bìngciě | bìngqiě | 並且　并且 | 5 |
| bīngcílín | bīngqílín | 冰淇淋 | 9 |
|  | bǐsài | 比賽　比赛 | 12 |
|  | bǐshù | 比數　比数 | 12 |
|  | bò | 播 | 12 |

INDEX II　生詞索引

| 通用拼音 | 漢語拼音 | 生詞 | 課數 |
|---|---|---|---|
| | bòchū | 播出 | 12 |
| bóshìh | bóshì | 博士 | 7 |
| | bówùguǎn | 博物館　博物馆 | 4 |
| | bù | 布 | 11 |
| | búdàn | 不但 | 4 |
| | bùguǎn...dōu... | 不管…都… | 7 |
| | búguò | 不過　不过 | 2 |
| bùhǎoyìsih | bùhǎoyì·si | 不好意思 | 7 |
| | bǔkǎo | 補考　补考 | 6 |
| | bǔ//kè | 補課　补课 | 3 |
| | búlùn...dōu | 不論…都　不论…都 | 7 |
| | bùluògé | 部落格 | 3 |
| | bùtóng (bùyíyàng) | 不同（不一樣）不一样 | 7 |
| búsìng | búxìng | 不幸 | 14 |
| | bǔxí | 補習　补习 | 3 |
| | bǔxíbān | 補習班　补习班 | 3 |
| bù siōu biān fú | bù xiū biān fú | 不修邊幅　不修边幅 | 9 |
| bǔjhù | bǔzhù | 補助　补助 | 3 |
| bùjhìh | bùzhì | 布置　布置 | 10 |

## C

| | càidān | 菜單　菜单 | 2 |
|---|---|---|---|
| | càijià | 菜價　菜价 | 3 |
| | cáipàn | 裁判 | 12 |
| | cǎisè | 彩色 | 12 |
| | cǎn | 慘 | 7 |
| | cānguān | 參觀　参观 | 4 |
| | cāntīng | 餐廳　餐厅 | 2 |
| | cānyìyuán | 參議員　参议员 | 10 |

413

| 通用拼音 | 漢語拼音 | 生詞 | 課數 |
|---|---|---|---|
| | cèsuǒ | 廁所　厕所 | 8 |
| | cèyàn | 測驗　测验 | 7 |
| | chá | 查 | 6 |
| | chǎn | 產　产 | 5 |
| | cháng | 嚐　尝 | 13 |
| | chǎng | 場　场 | 10 |
| | chǎngdì | 場地　场地 | 10 |
| chángshìh | chángshì | 常識　常识 | 14 |
| | chǎnpǐn | 產品　产品 | 5 |
| | chèn | 趁 | 13 |
| | Chén, Táilì | 陳台麗　陈台丽 | 2 |
| | chéng | 成 | 6 |
| | chéngbǎo | 城堡 | 14 |
| | chénggōng | 成功 | 11 |
| | chéngjī | 成績　成绩 | 3 |
| | chéngjīdān | 成績單　成绩单 | 3 |
| chèn·jhe | chèn·zhe | 趁著　趁着 | 13 |
| chīh hē wán lè | chī hē wán lè | 吃喝玩樂　吃喝玩乐 | 13 |
| | chīkǔ | 吃苦 | 4 |
| | chǒu | 醜　丑 | 9 |
| | chú | 除 | 4 |
| | chuán | 傳　传 | 10 |
| | chuándān | 傳單　传单 | 10 |
| | chūchǎn | 出產　出产 | 5 |
| | chū//cuò | 出錯　出错 | 12 |
| | chúfǎ | 除法 | 4 |
| chūfōngtóu | chū//fēngtóu | 出鋒頭　出锋头 | 12 |
| chūjyú | chūjú | 出局 | 12 |
| | chūkǒu | 出口 | 5 |

414

INDEX II 生詞索引

| 通用拼音 | 漢語拼音 | 生詞 | 課數 |
|---|---|---|---|
|  | chūnjià | 春假 | 14 |
|  | chúle...yǐwài | 除了…以外 | 4 |
| chúsì | chúxì | 除夕 | 13 |
| chūjhōng | chūzhōng | 初中 | 7 |
|  | chūzū | 出租 | 3 |
| cíh | cí | 詞　词 | 6 |
|  | cóngláibù | 從來不　从来不 | 1 |
|  | cù | 醋 | 2 |
|  | cún | 存 | 8 |
| cúncián | cún//qián | 存錢　存钱 | 8 |

## D

| | dǎbàn | 打扮 | 9 |
| | dǎbùtōng | 打不通 | 3 |
| | dàcān | 大餐 | 2 |
| | dǎ//dǔ | 打賭　打赌 | 14 |
| | dàfāng | 大方 | 8 |
| | dàgēdà | 大哥大 | 2 |
| | dàguōcài | 大鍋菜　大锅菜 | 2 |
| | dàhòutiān | 大後天　大后天 | 13 |
| | dài | 帶　带 | 8 |
| | dài | 代 | 7 |
| | dài//bān | 代班 | 8 |
| | dàibiǎo | 代表 | 10 |
| | dài//kè | 代課　代课 | 8 |
| | dǎ//kāi | 打開　打开 | 1 |
| | dà kāi yǎnjiè | 大開眼界　大开眼界 | 14 |
| | Dàlù | 大陸　大陆 | 3 |
| | dāng | 當　当 | 6 |
| | dǎng | 黨　党 | 10 |

415

實用視聽華語 3
Practical Audio-Visual Chinese

| 通用拼音 | 漢語拼音 | 生詞 | 課數 |
|---|---|---|---|
|  | dāng//bīng | 當兵　当兵 | 7 |
|  | dāngxuǎn | 當選　当选 | 10 |
|  | dànhuā tāng | 蛋花湯　蛋花汤 | 2 |
| dànshìh | dànshì | 但是 | 4 |
|  | dǎtīng | 打聽　打听 | 14 |
| Dàsiágǔ | Dàxiágǔ | 大峽谷　大峡谷 | 4 |
| dàsyuǎn | dàxuǎn | 大選　大选 | 10 |
| Dàsyué jhǐh kǎo | Dàxué zhǐ kǎo | 大學指考　大学指考 | 7 |
| dān//sīn | dan//xīn | 擔心　担心 | 1 |
|  | dāyìng | 答應　答应 | 10 |
| dǎjhàng | dǎ//zhàng | 打仗 | 11 |
|  | dān·zi | 單子　单子 | 2 |
|  | dǎo | 島　岛 | 4 |
|  | dǎo | 倒 | 6 |
|  | dǎoméi | 倒楣 | 6 |
|  | dàochù | 到處　到处 | 5 |
|  | dàodǐ | 到底 | 8 |
|  | Dàojiào | 道教 | 13 |
| dào//ciàn | dào//qiàn | 道歉 | 10 |
| dàoshìh | dàoshì | 倒是 | 9 |
|  | dǎoyóu | 導遊　导游 | 14 |
|  | dé | 得 | 12 |
|  | dédào | 得到 | 12 |
|  | děngbùjí | 等不及 | 13 |
|  | dé//fēn | 得分 | 12 |
|  | dēngjì | 登記　登记 | 8 |
|  | dī | 低 | 6 |
|  | diànfèi | 電費　电费 | 3 |
|  | diànhuàfèi | 電話費　电话费 | 3 |

## INDEX II 生詞索引

| 通用拼音 | 漢語拼音 | 生詞 | 課數 |
|---|---|---|---|
| | diànnǎohuà | 電腦化　电脑化 | 11 |
| | diàntī | 電梯　电梯 | 1 |
| diànyǐng míngsīng | diànyǐng míngxīng | 電影明星　电影明星 | 9 |
| | diànyuán | 店員　店员 | 8 |
| Dìèrcìh Shìhjiè Dàjhàn | Dì'èrcì Shìjiè Dàzhàn | 第二次世界大戰　第二次世界大战 | 11 |
| | dìlǐ | 地理 | 1 |
| | dìng | 訂　订 | 3 |
| Dísìhní Lèyuán | Díshìní Lèyuán | 迪士尼樂園　迪士尼乐园 | 14 |
| Díshìhní Shìhjiè | Díshìní Shìjiè | 迪士尼世界 | 14 |
| | dìtān | 地攤　地摊 | 8 |
| | dìtú | 地圖　地图 | 1 |
| | diū | 丟 | 9 |
| dìjhèn | dìzhèn | 地震 | 4 |
| | dòng | 棟　栋 | 9 |
| | dòngbúdòngjiù | 動不動就　动不动就 | 12 |
| dòngcíh | dòngcí | 動詞　动词 | 6 |
| | dōngfāng | 東方　东方 | 1 |
| | Dōng Oū | 東歐　东欧 | 11 |
| | dòngwù | 動物　动物 | 14 |
| | dòngwùyuán | 動物園　动物园 | 14 |
| | dòngzuò | 動作　动作 | 12 |
| | dú | 讀　读 | 8 |
| | dǔ | 賭　赌 | 14 |
| | dù | 度 | 5 |
| | duān | 端 | 7 |
| | dǔbó | 賭博　赌博 | 14 |
| | dǔchǎng | 賭場　赌场 | 14 |
| | dǔchéng | 賭城　赌城 | 14 |

417

| 通用拼音 | 漢語拼音 | 生詞 | 課數 |
|---|---|---|---|
| | duìfāng | 對方　对方 | 12 |
| | dǔguǐ | 賭鬼　赌鬼 | 14 |
| | duì | 隊　队 | 12 |
| duèi …yǒujīngyàn | duì…yǒu jīngyàn | 對…有經驗<br>对…有经验 | 8 |
| duèi …yǒu//sìngcyù | duì…yǒu//xìngqù | 對…有興趣<br>对…有兴趣 | 1 |
| | dúlì | 獨立　独立 | 1 |
| | dú//shū | 讀書　读书 | 8 |
| duèiyǒu | duìyǒu | 隊友　队友 | 12 |
| | dùn | 頓　顿 | 8 |
| | duōshǎo | 多少 | 11 |

## E

| | éi,èi | 欸 | 2 |
|---|---|---|---|
| | ēn | 嗯 | 4 |
| érciě | érqiě | 而且 | 2 |
| | èrfángdōng | 二房東　二房东 | 3 |
| | èrlěi | 二壘　二垒 | 12 |

## F

| | fā | 發　发 | 10 |
|---|---|---|---|
| | fābiǎo | 發表　发表 | 10 |
| fābiǎohuèi | fābiǎohuì | 發表會　发表会 | 10 |
| | fā//chuándān | 發傳單　发传单 | 10 |
| | fān | 翻 | 6 |
| | fǎn | 反 | 13 |
| | fàn | 犯 | 12 |
| | Fán'ěrsài Gōng | 凡爾賽宮　凡尔赛宫 | 14 |
| | fàng | 放 | 12 |
| | fàng//biānpào | 放鞭炮 | 12 |

418

## INDEX II 生詞索引

| 通用拼音 | 漢語拼音 | 生詞 | 課數 |
|---|---|---|---|
| | fángdōng | 房東　房东 | 3 |
| | fángjià | 房價　房价 | 3 |
| | fángkè | 房客 | 3 |
| | fāngmiàn | 方面 | 10 |
| fàngcì | fàngqì | 放棄　放弃 | 11 |
| | fángshǒu | 防守 | 12 |
| fànguēi | fànguī | 犯規　犯规 | 12 |
| | fángzū | 房租 | 3 |
| | fānyì | 翻譯　翻译 | 6 |
| fǎnjhèng | fǎnzhèng | 反正 | 13 |
| | fāshāo | 發燒　发烧 | 5 |
| fājhǎn | fāzhǎn | 發展　发展 | 4 |
| | fēibiāo | 飛鏢　飞镖 | 9 |
| | fēi...bùkě | 非…不可 | 6 |
| | fēn | 分 | 6 |
| fònglí | fènglí | 鳳梨　凤梨 | 5 |
| fōng yī zú shíh | fēng yī zú shí | 豐衣足食　丰衣足食 | 13 |
| | fēnlèi | 分類　分类 | 5 |
| | fēnshù | 分數　分数 | 6 |
| | X fēnzhī Y | X分之Y | 10 |
| | fēnzū | 分租 | 3 |
| | Fójiào | 佛教 | 13 |
| FóluólǐdáJhōu | Fóluólǐdá Zhōu | 佛羅里達州<br>佛罗里达州 | 14 |
| | fù | 付 | 3 |
| | fǔbài | 腐敗　腐败 | 11 |
| | fǔlàn | 腐爛 | 11 |
| | fúwù | 服務　服务 | 2 |
| | fúwùshēng | 服務生　服务生 | 2 |
| | fúwùyuán | 服務員　服务员 | 2 |

419

## 實用視聽華語 3
### Practical Audio-Visual Chinese

| 通用拼音 | 漢語拼音 | 生詞 | 課數 |
|---|---|---|---|
| Fùcīnjié | Fùqīnjié | 父親節　父亲节 | 13 |
| fùsí | fùxí | 複習　复习 | 6 |

### G

| 通用拼音 | 漢語拼音 | 生詞 | 課數 |
|---|---|---|---|
|  | gǎibiàn | 改變　改变 | 8 |
|  | gǎigé | 改革 | 11 |
| gǎisyuǎn | gǎixuǎn | 改選　改选 | 10 |
|  | gǎn | 敢 | 2 |
|  | gǎn | 趕　赶 | 14 |
|  | gǎn'ēn jié | 感恩節　感恩节 | 13 |
| gǎnjyué | gǎnjué | 感覺　感觉 | 13 |
|  | gǎnkuài | 趕快　赶快 | 14 |
| gǎncíng | gǎnqíng | 感情 | 13 |
|  | gǎn//·shàng | 趕上　赶上 | 14 |
|  | gāosùgōnglù | 高速公路 | 4 |
|  | gāosùtiělù | 高速鐵路　高速铁路 | 4 |
|  | Gāo Wěilì | 高偉立　高伟立 | 1 |
|  | gāoyuán | 高原 | 4 |
| gāojhōng | gāozhōng | 高中 | 6 |
|  | gè | 各 | 11 |
| gēcíh | gēcí | 歌詞　歌词 | 6 |
|  | gémìng | 革命 | 11 |
|  | gēn...yǒuguān | 跟…有關　跟…有关 | 14 |
|  | gēshǒu | 歌手 | 9 |
| gēsīng | gēxīng | 歌星 | 9 |
| gèsìng | gèxing | 個性 | 9 |
|  | gōngbǎo jīdīng | 宮保雞丁　宮保鸡丁 | 2 |
| gòngchǎn jhǔyì | gòngchǎn zhǔyì | 共產主義　共产主义 | 11 |
|  | gōngdú | 工讀　工读 | 8 |
|  | gōngdúshēng | 工讀生　工读生 | 8 |

INDEX II　生詞索引

| 通用拼音 | 漢語拼音 | 生詞 | 課數 |
|---|---|---|---|
| | gōnglì | 公立 | 7 |
| | gōnglù | 公路 | 4 |
| | gōngmín | 公民 | 11 |
| | gōngpíng | 公平 | 7 |
| | gōngyù | 公寓 | 3 |
| gōngjhǔ | gōngzhǔ | 公主 | 14 |
| | guā | 刮 | 9 |
| guā//fōng | guā//fēng | 颱風　刮风 | 5 |
| | guàhào | 掛號　挂号 | 4 |
| | guāng | 光 | 8 |
| | guǎng | 廣　广 | 13 |
| | guǎngbō | 廣播　广播 | 12 |
| | Guǎngdōng | 廣東　广东 | 2 |
| | guǎnggào | 廣告　广告 | 13 |
| guān·sì | guān xì | 關係　关系 | 1 |
| guānsīn | guānxīn | 關心　关心 | 1 |
| | gūdān | 孤單　孤单 | 7 |
| | Gùgōng Bówùyuàn | 故宮博物院 | 4 |
| | gū·gu | 姑姑 | 2 |
| | guǐ | 鬼 | 8 |
| | gǔlì | 鼓勵　鼓励 | 1 |
| | guō | 鍋　锅 | 2 |
| | guò | 過　过 | 13 |
| guóhuèi | guóhuì | 國會　国会 | 10 |
| guóhuèi yìyuán | guóhuì yìyuán | 國會議員　国会议员 | 10 |
| Guójiā Dìlǐ Zájhìh | Guójiā Dìlǐ Zázhì | 國家地理雜誌　国家地理杂志 | 1 |
| | guójiā gōngyuán | 國家公園　国家公园 | 4 |
| | guò//jié | 過節　过节 | 13 |
| | guólì | 國立　国立 | 7 |

421

| 通用拼音 | 漢語拼音 | 生詞 | 課數 |
|---|---|---|---|
| | guómín | 國民　国民 | 11 |
| | guòmǐn | 過敏　过敏 | 13 |
| Guómín Jhèngfǔ | Guómín Zhèngfǔ | 國民政府　国民政府 | 11 |
| | guónèi | 國內　国内 | 7 |
| | guówài | 國外　国外 | 7 |
| | guówáng | 國王　国王 | 14 |
| | guòyǐn | 過癮　过瘾 | 14 |

## H

| | hài | 嗨 | 1 |
|---|---|---|---|
| | hài | 害 | 5 |
| hǎijyūn | hǎijūn | 海軍　海军 | 11 |
| | hǎitān | 海灘　海滩 | 4 |
| hǎisiān | hǎixiān | 海鮮　海鲜 | 5 |
| | hǎiyáng | 海洋 | 14 |
| | hǎiyáng dòngwù | 海洋動物　海洋动物 | 14 |
| Hǎiyáng Shìhjiè | Hǎiyáng Shìjiè | 海洋世界 | 14 |
| | hàn, hé | 和 | 10 |
| | hǎochù | 好處　好处 | 8 |
| hǎocióu | hǎoqiú | 好球 | 12 |
| | hé | 合 | 4 |
| | Hélán | 荷蘭　荷兰 | 4 |
| | héliú | 河流 | 4 |
| | héqǐ·lái | 合起來 | 3 |
| héshìh | héshì | 合適　合适 | 4 |
| | hézū | 合租 | 3 |
| | hézuò | 合作 | 12 |
| | hóngluó·bo | 紅蘿蔔　红萝卜 | 2 |
| | hóngshāo | 紅燒　红烧 | 2 |
| hóngshāo jhūròu | hóngshāo zhūròu | 紅燒豬肉　红烧猪肉 | 2 |

# INDEX II 生詞索引

| 通用拼音 | 漢語拼音 | 生詞 | 課數 |
|---|---|---|---|
| hòusyuǎnrén | hòuxuǎnrén | 候選人　候选人 | 10 |
| | hú | 湖 | 8 |
| | huá | 滑 | 5 |
| | huàichù | 壞處　坏处 | 8 |
| huàicióu | huàiqiú | 壞球　坏球 | 12 |
| | huán | 還　还 | 8 |
| Huángshíh Gōngyuán | Huángshí Gōngyuán | 黃石公園　黄石公园 | 14 |
| huānhuānsǐsǐ | huānhuānxīxǐ | 歡歡喜喜　欢欢喜喜 | 13 |
| | huánjìng | 環境　环境 | 3 |
| huācián | huā//qián | 花錢　花钱 | 12 |
| huāshíhjiān | huā//shíjiān | 花時間　花时间 | 12 |
| huèi | huì | 會　会 | 1 |
| | Huíjiào | 回教 | 13 |
| | húluó·bo | 胡蘿蔔　胡萝卜 | 2 |
| | huó | 活 | 3 |
| | huódòng | 活動　活动 | 7 |
| huódòngjhōngsīn | huódòng zhōngxīn | 活動中心　活动中心 | 7 |
| | huǒjī | 火雞　火鸡 | 13 |
| hùjhào | hùzhào | 護照　护照 | 14 |
| hú·zih | hú·zi | 鬍子　胡子 | 9 |

## J

| | jǐ | 擠　挤 | 9 |
| | jiǎ | 假 | 12 |
| | jiājiào | 家教 | 8 |
| | jiákè | 夾克 | 1 |
| | jiǎn | 剪 | 3 |
| | jiǎndāo | 剪刀 | 3 |
| | jiǎng | 講　讲 | 11 |

423

| 通用拼音 | 漢語拼音 | 生詞 | 課數 |
|---|---|---|---|
| | jiǎngjià | 講價　讲价 | 11 |
| Jiǎng Jièshíh | Jiǎng Jièshí | 蔣介石　蒋介石 | 11 |
| | jiānglái | 將來　将来 | 11 |
| jiǎngsyuéjīn | jiǎngxuéjīn | 獎學金　奖学金 | 3 |
| | jiǎngyǎn | 講演　讲演 | 11 |
| | jiànjiē | 間接　间接 | 10 |
| | jiànlì | 建立 | 11 |
| jiǎnsyùn | jiǎnxùn | 簡訊　简讯 | 3 |
| | jiànshè | 建設　建设 | 11 |
| jiànshìh | jiànshì | 見識　见识 | 14 |
| | jiǎn//tóu·fǎ | 剪頭髮　剪头发 | 3 |
| | jiǎo | 腳　脚 | 8 |
| | jiào//chē | 叫車　叫车 | 3 |
| | jiāofǎ | 教法 | 6 |
| | jiāogěi | 交給　交给 | 3 |
| | jiāohuàn | 交換　交换 | 3 |
| | jiàoliàn | 教練　教练 | 12 |
| | jiāo//péngyǒu | 交朋友 | 3 |
| jiàoshìh | jiàoshì | 教室 | 3 |
| | jiàoshòu | 教授 | 3 |
| | jiàotáng | 教堂 | 13 |
| | jiāotōng | 交通 | 3 |
| jiàosǐng | jiào//xǐng | 叫醒 | 8 |
| | jiàoyù | 教育 | 7 |
| | jiàoyùbù | 教育部 | 7 |
| | jiàoyùjiè | 教育界 | 7 |
| jiǎo·zih | jiǎo·zi | 餃子　饺子 | 2 |
| | jiào…zǒulù | 叫…走路 | 8 |
| jiàcián | jiàqián | 價錢　价钱 | 3 |

INDEX II 生詞索引

| 通用拼音 | 漢語拼音 | 生詞 | | 課數 |
|---|---|---|---|---|
| jiàrìh | jiàrì | 假日 | 假日 | 14 |
| | jiā//yóu | 加油 | | 6 |
| | jiāyóuzhàn | 加油站 | | 6 |
| jiǎjhuāng | jiǎzhuāng | 假裝 | 假装 | 12 |
| | jìchéngchē | 計程車 | 计程车 | 3 |
| | Jīdūjiào | 基督教 | | 13 |
| jièlán nióuròu | jièlán niúròu | 芥蘭牛肉 | 芥兰牛肉 | 2 |
| | jiéshù | 結束 | 结束 | 11 |
| | jígé | 及格 | | 6 |
| | jìhuà | 計畫 | 计画 | 3 |
| jīhuèi | jīhuì | 機會 | 机会 | 2 |
| | jīliè | 激烈 | | 7 |
| | jīngcǎi | 精彩 | | 12 |
| | jīngfèi | 經費 | 经费 | 10 |
| | jīngjì | 經濟 | 经济 | 11 |
| | jīngshén | 精神 | | 12 |
| jìngsyuǎn | jìngxuǎn | 競選 | 竞选 | 10 |
| | jīngyàn | 經驗 | 经验 | 8 |
| | jìngzhēng | 競爭 | 竞争 | 7 |
| | jìniàn | 紀念 | 纪念 | 13 |
| | jìnkǒu | 進口 | 进口 | 5 |
| jīn·zih | jīn·zi | 金子 | | 3 |
| | jìrán | 既然 | | 9 |
| | jìshù | 技術 | 技术 | 7 |
| Jìshùsyuéyuàn | Jìshù xuéyuàn | 技術學院 | 技术学院 | 7 |
| jiǒuguěi | jiǔguǐ | 酒鬼 | | 8 |
| jiòujiou | jiù·jiu | 舅舅 | | 7 |
| jiòumā | jiùmā | 舅媽 | 舅妈 | 7 |
| | jì//zhù | 記住 | 记住 | 6 |

425

| 通用拼音 | 漢語拼音 | 生詞 | 課數 |
|---|---|---|---|
| jyú | jú | 局 | 12 |
| jyǔ | jǔ | 舉 举 | 7 |
| jyuān | juān | 捐 捐 | 12 |
| jyuāncián | juān//qián | 捐錢 捐钱 | 12 |
| jyǔbàn | jǔbàn | 舉辦 举办 | 7 |
| jyuésài | juésài | 決賽 决赛 | 12 |
| jyūnduèi | jūnduì | 軍隊 军队 | 11 |
| jyūnrén | jūnrén | 軍人 军人 | 11 |
| jyǔshǒu | jǔ//shǒu | 舉手 举手 | 7 |
| jyǔsíng | jǔxíng | 舉行 举行 | 7 |
| jyǔjhòng | jǔzhòng | 舉重 举重 | 7 |

## K

| 通用拼音 | 漢語拼音 | 生詞 | 課數 |
|---|---|---|---|
| | kāifàng | 開放 开放 | 14 |
| | kāilù | 開路 开路 | 4 |
| kāi//wánsiào | kāi//wánxiào | 開玩笑 开玩笑 | 13 |
| | kāiyǎn | 開演 开演 | 14 |
| | kāi//yǎnjiè | 開眼界 开眼界 | 14 |
| | kān | 看 | 8 |
| | kànfǎ | 看法 | 6 |
| | kān//jiā | 看家 | 8 |
| | kàn//liǎnsè | 看臉色 看脸色 | 12 |
| | kàntái | 看台 | 12 |
| | kǎojuàn | 考卷 | 6 |
| kǎocyǔ | kǎo//qǔ | 考取 | 7 |
| | kǎo//shàng | 考上 | 7 |
| | kǎoyā | 烤鴨 烤鸭 | 2 |
| | kǎpiàn | 卡片 | 13 |
| | kē | 科 | 7 |
| | kē | 棵 | 13 |

INDEX II　生詞索引

| 通用拼音 | 漢語拼音 | 生詞 | | 課數 |
|---|---|---|---|---|
| | ké | 咳 | | 5 |
| | kěài | 可愛 | 可爱 | 13 |
| | kèběn | 課本 | | 8 |
| | kělè | 可樂 | 可乐 | 8 |
| | kèmǎn | 客滿 | 客满 | 2 |
| | Kěndīng | 墾丁 | 垦丁 | 4 |
| | kèrén | 客人 | | 2 |
| | késòu | 咳嗽 | | 5 |
| kèwún | kèwén | 課文 | | 8 |
| kēsì | kēxì | 科系 | | 7 |
| kōngjyūn | kōngjūn | 空軍 | 空军 | 11 |
| | Kǒng Miào | 孔廟 | 孔庙 | 1 |
| kòngjhìh | kòngzhì | 控制 | | 11 |
| | kǒu | 口 | | 4 |
| | kòu | 扣 | | 6 |
| | kòu//fēn | 扣分 | | 6 |
| | kǒuwèi | 口味 | | 2 |
| | kǒuxiāngtáng | 口香糖 | | 8 |
| | kǒuyīn | 口音 | | 1 |
| | kǔ | 苦 | | 4 |
| | kuàngchǎn | 礦產 | 矿产 | 5 |
| (kuājhāng) | kuāzhāng | 誇張 | 夸张 | 7 |
| | kùnnán | 困難 | 困难 | 3 |

## L

| | lā | 拉 | | 10 |
| | là | 辣 | | 2 |
| | ·la | 啦 | | 1 |
| | lái | 來 | 来 | 1 |
| | láibùjí | 來不及 | 来不及 | 3 |

427

實用視聽華語 3
Practical Audio-Visual Chinese

| 通用拼音 | 漢語拼音 | 生詞 | 課數 |
|---|---|---|---|
| lāláduèi | lāláduì | 啦啦隊　啦啦队 | 12 |
| | lán | 籃　篮 | 12 |
| | làn | 爛　烂 | 6 |
| lán·zih | lán·zi | 籃子　篮子 | 12 |
| | lā//piào | 拉票 | 10 |
| | lǎobǎn | 老闆　老板 | 8 |
| | láodāo | 嘮叨　唠叨 | 1 |
| Lǎojhōngshíh pēncyuán | Lǎozhōngshí pēnquán | 老忠實噴泉 老忠实喷泉 | 14 |
| | lèi | 類　类 | 5 |
| | lěngmén | 冷門　冷门 | 7 |
| lěngcì | lěngqì | 冷氣　冷气 | 5 |
| | lián …dōu … | 連…都 | 2 |
| | liánhé | 聯合　联合 | 7 |
| | Liánhé Guó | 聯合國　联合国 | 7 |
| | liánkǎo | 聯考　联考 | 7 |
| | liánluò | 連絡　连络 | 13 |
| | liánluò | 聯絡　联络 | 13 |
| | liǎnsè | 臉色　脸色 | 6 |
| | liǎojiě | 了解 | 6 |
| | liǎojiě | 瞭解　了解 | 6 |
| | lǐfǎtīng | 理髮廳　理发厅 | 3 |
| | lìfǎ | 立法 | 10 |
| | Lìfǎ Yuàn | 立法院 | 10 |
| | lìfǎ wěiyuán | 立法委員　立法委员 | 10 |
| | lìliàng | 力量 | 11 |
| | lǐmào | 禮貌　礼貌 | 11 |
| | lǐngdǎo | 領導　领导 | 11 |
| | lǐngdǎorén | 領導人 | 11 |

INDEX II 生詞索引

| 通用拼音 | 漢語拼音 | 生詞 | 課數 |
|---|---|---|---|
| | Lín Jiàn'guó | 林建國　林建国 | 1 |
| | lìngwài | 另外 | 4 |
| | língxià | 零下 | 5 |
| língyòng cián | língyòng qián | 零用錢　零用钱 | 8 |
| | lìhài | 厲害　厉害 | 6 |
| | Lǐ píng | 李平 | 4 |
| lìcì | lìqì | 力氣　力气 | 11 |
| lìshǐh | lìshǐ | 歷史　历史 | 11 |
| | liú | 流 | 4 |
| | liú | 留 | 2 |
| | liǔchéng | 柳橙 | 5 |
| lióucǐlái | liúqǐ·lái | 留起來　留起来 | 2 |
| lióusyué | liúxué | 留學　留学 | 2 |
| lióusyuéshēng | liúxuéshēng | 留學生　留学生 | 2 |
| lǐsiǎng | lǐxiǎng | 理想 | 7 |
| | lìyòng | 利用 | 13 |
| | ·lou | 嘍　喽 | 6 |
| | lóutī | 樓梯　楼梯 | 1 |
| | luàn | 亂　乱 | 8 |
| | lǚfèi | 旅費　旅费 | 3 |
| lùjyūn | lùjūn | 陸軍　陆军 | 11 |
| | lúnliú | 輪流　轮流 | 10 |
| lùnwún | lùnwén | 論文　论文 | 7 |
| | luó·bo | 蘿蔔　萝卜 | 2 |
| | Luófú Gōng | 羅浮宮　罗浮宫 | 14 |
| | Luómǎ | 羅馬　罗马 | 14 |
| | luómàndìkè | 羅曼蒂克　罗曼蒂克 | 14 |
| | Luòshānjī | 洛杉磯　洛杉矶 | 14 |
| lùcyǔ | lùqǔ | 錄取　录取 | 7 |

429

| 通用拼音 | 漢語拼音 | 生詞 | 課數 |
|---|---|---|---|
| lyǔsingshè | lǚxíngshè | 旅行社 | 14 |
|  | lǚxíngtuán | 旅行團　旅行团 | 14 |
|  | lùyòng | 錄用 | 7 |

## M

| | | | |
|---|---|---|---|
|  | ·m | 呣 | 1 |
|  | mà | 罵　骂 | 8 |
|  | ·ma | 嘛 | 2 |
|  | Màidāngláo | 麥當勞　麦当劳 | 2 |
|  | mǎlù | 馬路　马路 | 4 |
|  | mǎn | 滿　满 | 2 |
|  | mánglù | 忙碌 | 13 |
|  | mànhuà | 漫畫　漫画 | 11 |
|  | mànhuàshū | 漫畫書　漫画书 | 11 |
|  | Máo Zédōng | 毛澤東　毛泽东 | 11 |
|  | méi | 煤 | 5 |
| méiguān·sì | méiguān·xi | 沒關係　没关系 | 3 |
|  | méikuàng | 煤礦　煤矿 | 5 |
|  | měilì | 美麗　美丽 | 9 |
|  | mèilì | 魅力 | 9 |
|  | měiróng | 美容 | 3 |
|  | měiróngyuàn | 美容院 | 3 |
|  | Méngdìkǎluó | 蒙地卡羅　蒙地卡罗 | 14 |
|  | mí | 迷 | 9 |
|  | mǐ | 米 | 5 |
| miànshìh | miànshì | 面試　面试 | 7 |
|  | miàntán | 面談　面谈 | 7 |
|  | miào | 廟 | 1 |
|  | mílù | 迷路 | 9 |
|  | míng·bái | 明白 | 3 |

INDEX II　生詞索引

| 通用拼音 | 漢語拼音 | 生詞 | 課數 |
|---|---|---|---|
| | míngcí | 名詞　名词 | 6 |
| | míngdān | 名單　名单 | 2 |
| míngsīng | míngxīng | 明星 | 9 |
| mínjhǔ | mínzhǔ | 民主 | 11 |
| Mínjhǔ Dǎng | mínzhǔ Dǎng | 民主黨　民主党 | 10 |
| mínjhǔhuà | mínzhǔhuà | 民主化 | 11 |
| mínjhǔ yùndòng | mínzhǔ yùndòng | 民主運動　民主运动 | 11 |
| | mírén | 迷人 | 9 |
| mòcì | mòqì | 默契 | 12 |
| Mǔcīn jié | Mǔqīnjié | 母親節　母亲节 | 13 |
| mǔcīn kǎ | mǔqīn kǎ | 母親卡　母亲卡 | 13 |

## N

| | n | 嗯 | 4 |
|---|---|---|---|
| | na | 哪 | 7 |
| | nǎifěn | 奶粉 | 10 |
| | nǎinai | 奶奶 | 14 |
| Nánběi Zhànjhēng | Nánběi Zhànzhēng | 南北戰爭　南北战争 | 11 |
| | nándào | 難道　难道 | 14 |
| | nán'guā | 南瓜 | 13 |
| | nán'guā dēng | 南瓜燈　南瓜灯 | 13 |
| | nán'guài | 難怪　难怪 | 1 |
| | nán'guā pài | 南瓜派 | 13 |
| | nán'guò | 難過　难过 | 6 |
| | nánshēng | 男生 | 8 |
| | nào | 鬧　闹 | 8 |
| | nàozhōng | 鬧鐘　闹钟 | 8 |
| | náshǒu | 拿手 | 13 |
| | nèizhàn | 內戰　内战 | 11 |
| | nénglì | 能力 | 7 |

431

| 通用拼音 | 漢語拼音 | 生詞 | 課數 |
|---|---|---|---|
| | nì | 膩　膩 | 2 |
| | niánchū | 年初 | 10 |
| | niándài | 年代 | 7 |
| | niándǐ | 年底 | 10 |
| niáncīng | niánqīng | 年輕　年轻 | 4 |
| niáncīngrén | niánqīng rén | 年輕人　年轻人 | 4 |
| | niányèfàn | 年夜飯　年夜饭 | 13 |
| nǎo·zih | nǎo·zi | 腦子　脑子 | 9 |
| | Níjiālā Pùbù | 尼加拉瀑布 | 14 |
| | nǐkàn | 你看 | 10 |
| | níngkě | 寧可　宁可 | 6 |
| | níngyuàn | 寧願　宁愿 | 6 |
| nióunǎi | niúnǎi | 牛奶 | 10 |
| | nóngchǎnpǐn | 農產品　农产品 | 5 |
| | nóngmín | 農民　农民 | 4 |
| | nóngrén | 農人　农人 | 4 |
| | nóngyè | 農業　农业 | 4 |
| | nuǎnhuà | 暖化 | 11 |
| | nuǎn·huo | 暖和 | 5 |
| nuǎncì | nuǎnqì | 暖氣　暖气 | 5 |
| nyǔshēng | nǚshēng | 女生 | 8 |
| nyǔwáng | nǚwáng | 女王 | 14 |

## O

| | ó | 哦 | 6 |
|---|---|---|---|
| | òu | 噢　噢 | 1 |

## P

| | pái | 排 | 10 |
|---|---|---|---|
| | pài | 派 | 13 |

INDEX II  生詞索引

| 通用拼音 | 漢語拼音 | 生詞 | 課數 |
|---|---|---|---|
| pái//duèi | pái//duì | 排隊　排队 | 14 |
| | páigǔ | 排骨 | 2 |
| | pàn | 判 | 12 |
| | pèng | 碰 | 3 |
| | pèng//dào | 碰到 | 3 |
| | pèng//jiàn | 碰見　碰见 | 3 |
| | pèng//shàng | 碰上 | 3 |
| | piān | 篇 | 1 |
| | píbāo | 皮包 | 9 |
| | pífū | 皮膚　皮肤 | 9 |
| | píngdǐguō | 平底鍋　平底锅 | 2 |
| | píngyuán | 平原 | 4 |
| | pǔbiàn | 普遍 | 8 |
| | pùbù | 瀑布 | 14 |
| | pútáoyòu | 葡萄柚 | 5 |
| | pǔtōng | 普通 | 8 |

## Q

| ciān | qiān | 遷　迁 | 11 |
| ciānmíng | qiānmíng | 簽名　签名 | 14 |
| ciānjhèng | qiānzhèng | 簽證　签证 | 14 |
| ciāo | qiāo | 敲 | 3 |
| cíao | qiáo | 橋　桥 | 14 |
| cifēn | qìfēn | 氣氛　气氛 | 13 |
| cìhòu | qìhòu | 氣候　气候 | 5 |
| címòkǎo | qímòkǎo | 期末考 | 6 |
| cīng | qīng | 輕　轻 | 4 |
| cíng | qíng | 晴 | 5 |
| cǐng | qǐng | 請　请 | 3 |
| CīngCháo | Qīng Cháo | 清朝 | 11 |

433

| 通用拼音 | 漢語拼音 | 生詞 | 課數 |
|---|---|---|---|
| cīngdòu | qīngdòu | 青豆 | 2 |
| cīnghuācài | qīnghuācài | 青花菜 | 2 |
| cǐng//jià | qǐng//jià | 請假　请假 | 14 |
| cǐngjiào | qǐngjiào | 請教　请教 | 3 |
| cǐng//kè | qǐng//kè | 請客　请客 | 8 |
| Cíngrénjié | Qíngrénjié | 情人節　情人节 | 13 |
| cíngrénkǎ | qíngrén kǎ | 情人卡 | 13 |
| cīngsōng | qīngsōng | 輕鬆　轻松 | 6 |
| cíngtiān | qíngtiān | 晴天 | 5 |
| cíngsíng | qíng·xíng | 情形 | 7 |
| cǐng…zǔolù | qǐng…zǔolù | 請…走路　请…走路 | 8 |
| císhih | qíshí | 其實　其实 | 6 |
| cióuchǎng | qiúchǎng | 球場　球场 | 12 |
| cióuduèi | qiúduì | 球隊　球队 | 12 |
| cióusài | qiúsài | 球賽　球赛 | 12 |
| cióuyuán | qiúyuán | 球員　球员 | 12 |
| cìwūn | qìwēn | 氣溫　气温 | 5 |
| cìyóu | qìyóu | 汽油 | 5 |
| cíjhōngkǎo | qízhōngkǎo | 期中考 | 6 |
| cyuán | quán | 全 | 1 |
| cyuán | quán | 權　权 | 10 |
| cyuánguó | quán'guó | 全國　全国 | 1 |
| cyuánjiā | quánjiā | 全家 | 1 |
| cyuánlěidǎ | quánlěidǎ | 全壘打　全垒打 | 12 |
| cyuán shìhjiè | quán shìjiè | 全世界 | 1 |
| cyuánsiào | quánxiào | 全校 | 1 |

## R

| | règǒu | 熱狗　热狗 | 9 |
|---|---|---|---|
| | rèmén | 熱門　热门 | 7 |

INDEX II 生詞索引

| 通用拼音 | 漢語拼音 | 生詞 | 課數 |
|---|---|---|---|
| | rěn | 忍　忍 | 8 |
| | rèn | 任 | 10 |
| | rénkǒu | 人口 | 4 |
| | rénlèi | 人類　人类 | 11 |
| rénlèisyué | rénlèixué | 人類學　人类学 | 11 |
| | rénmín | 人民 | 11 |
| rèncí | rènqí | 任期 | 10 |
| réncyuán | rénquán | 人權　人权 | 10 |
| | rènwéi | 認為　认为 | 11 |
| rěnsīn | rěnxīn | 忍心　忍心 | 8 |
| rěnjhù | rěn//zhù | 忍住　忍住 | 8 |
| rèsīn | rèxīn | 熱心　热心 | 10 |
| | rónghuà | 融化 | 5 |
| | rúguǒ | 如果 | 6 |
| | ruò | 弱 | 11 |

## S

| | sāi//chē | 塞車　塞车 | 9 |
| | Sàinà Hé | 塞納河　塞纳河 | 14 |
| | sānlěi | 三壘　三垒 | 12 |
| SānMín Jhǔyì | SānMín Zhǔyì | 三民主義　三民主义 | 11 |
| | shā | 沙 | 4 |
| | shài | 曬 | 14 |
| | shài//tài·yáng | 曬太陽　晒太阳 | 14 |
| | shāmò | 沙漠 | 4 |
| | shāo | 燒 | 2 |
| | shàngbànchǎng | 上半場　上半场 | 12 |
| | shàng//cèsuǒ | 上廁所　上厕所 | 8 |
| | shāngpǐn | 商品 | 13 |
| | shāngrén | 商人 | 13 |

435

| 通用拼音 | 漢語拼音 | 生詞 | 課數 |
|---|---|---|---|
| | shāngyè | 商業　商业 | 13 |
| | shāngyèhuà | 商業化　商业化 | 13 |
| | shàng//wǎng | 上網　上网 | 3 |
| | shàngyǎn | 上演 | 14 |
| | shātān | 沙灘　沙滩 | 4 |
| shèhuèi | shèhuì | 社會　社会 | 8 |
| Shèhuèi Dǎng | Shèhuì Dǎng | 社會黨　社会党 | 10 |
| shèhuèicyué | shèhuìxué | 社會學　社会学 | 10 |
| | shètuán | 社團　社团 | 12 |
| | shén | 神 | 7 |
| | shēncái | 身材 | 9 |
| | shěng | 省 | 14 |
| | Shèngdànjié | 聖誕節　圣诞节 | 13 |
| | Shèngdàn kǎ | 聖誕卡　圣诞卡 | 13 |
| | shèngdànyè | 聖誕夜　圣诞夜 | 13 |
| | shěng//diàn | 省電　省电 | 14 |
| | shēnghuó | 生活 | 3 |
| | shēnghuófèi | 生活費　生活费 | 3 |
| shěng//cián | shěng//qián | 省錢　省钱 | 14 |
| shěng//shìh | shěng//shì | 省事 | 14 |
| shěng//shihjiān | shěng//shíjiān | 省時間　省时间 | 14 |
| | shěng//yóu | 省油 | 14 |
| | shénjīng | 神經　神经 | 7 |
| | shénjīngbìng | 神經病　神经病 | 7 |
| shēncǐng | shēnqǐng | 申請　申请 | 3 |
| shēngcǐng kiǎo | shēnqǐng biǎo | 申請表　申请表 | 3 |
| | shēngrì kǎ | 生日卡 | 13 |
| shīh | hī | 濕　湿 | 5 |

| 通用拼音 | 漢語拼音 | 生詞 | 課數 |
|---|---|---|---|
| shíhdài | shídài | 時代　时代 | 13 |
| shīhdù | shīdù | 濕度　湿度 | 5 |
| shìhhé | shìhé | 適合　适合 | 4 |
| shìhjià | shìjià | 事假 | 14 |
| shíhlì | shílì | 實力　实力 | 12 |
| shìhlì | shìlì | 勢力　势力 | 11 |
| shìhlì | shìlì | 市立 | 7 |
| shì mín | shìmín | 市民 | 11 |
| shīhrè | shīrè | 濕熱　湿热 | 5 |
| shíhtóu | shítóu | 石頭　石头 | 5 |
| shísíng | shíxíng | 實行　实行 | 11 |
| shíhyàn | shíyàn | 實驗　实验 | 14 |
| shíhyàn shìh | shíyàn shì | 實驗室　实验室 | 14 |
| shìhyìng | shìyìng | 適應　适应 | 5 |
| shìhyìyuán | shìyìyuán | 市議員　市议员 | 10 |
| shíhyóu | shíyóu | 石油 | 5 |
| shìhyǒu | shìyǒu | 室友 | 1 |
| shìhjhǎng | shìzhǎng | 市長　市长 | 10 |
|  | shōu | 收 | 4 |
|  | shòubùliǎo | 受不了 | 1 |
|  | shòucí | 受詞　受词 | 6 |
|  | shōudào | 收到 | 4 |
|  | shǒujī | 手機　手机 | 2 |
|  | shǒu máng jiǎo luàn | 手忙腳亂　手忙脚乱 | 8 |
|  | shōu//qǐ·lái | 收起來　收起来 | 4 |
|  | shū | 輸　输 | 14 |
|  | shù | 樹　树 | 9 |
|  | shuài | 帥　帅 | 9 |

437

| 通用拼音 | 漢語拼音 | 生詞 | 課數 |
|---|---|---|---|
| | shuàigē | 帥哥　帅哥 | 9 |
| | shūfǎ jiā | 書法家 | 14 |
| shuěifèi | shuǐfèi | 水費　水费 | 3 |
| shuěijiǎo | shuǐjiǎo | 水餃　水饺 | 2 |
| | shùnbiàn | 順便　顺便 | 14 |
| | shuōbúdìng | 說不定　说不定 | 14 |
| | shuōfǎ | 說法　说法 | 6 |
| shǔcíbān | shǔqíbān | 暑期班 | 3 |
| sǐh | sǐ | 死 | 6 |
| sǐhdìng·le | sǐdìng·le | 死定了 | 6 |
| sīhjī | sījī | 司機　司机 | 10 |
| | sīlì | 私立 | 7 |
| | sōng | 鬆　松 | 6 |
| | suǒyǒu·de | 所有的 | 3 |
| | suānlà tāng | 酸辣湯　酸辣汤 | 2 |
| | suàn·le | 算了 | 14 |
| suànshìh | suànshì | 算是 | 6 |
| suàn//jhàng | suàn//zhàng | 算帳（賬）算帐(账) | 2 |
| | suīrán | 雖然　虽然 | 4 |
| | Sūn Zhōngshān | 孫中山　孙中山 | 11 |
| sùshíh | sùshí | 速食 | 2 |
| sùshíhmiàn | sùshímiàn | 速食麵　速食面 | 2 |

# T

| | tǎ | 塔 | 14 |
|---|---|---|---|
| | tàidù | 態度　态度 | 9 |
| táifōng | táifēng | 颱風　台风 | 4 |
| Tàilǔ gé Xiágǔ | Tàilǔgé Xiágǔ | 太魯閣峽谷<br>太鲁阁峡谷 | 4 |

# INDEX II 生詞索引

| 通用拼音 | 漢語拼音 | 生詞 | 課數 |
|---|---|---|---|
|  | Táinán | 臺南 | 1 |
|  | Táiwān | 臺灣　台湾 | 1 |
|  | tàiyáng | 太陽　太阳 | 14 |
|  | tángcù | 糖醋 | 2 |
|  | tángcù páigǔ | 糖醋排骨 | 2 |
|  | tānwèi | 攤位　摊位 | 9 |
|  | tān·zi | 攤子　摊子 | 9 |
|  | tǎolùn | 討論　讨论 | 6 |
|  | tǎoyàn | 討厭　讨厌 | 9 |
|  | tàocān | 套餐 | 2 |
|  | tècān | 特餐 | 2 |
|  | tèquán | 特權 | 10 |
|  | tèsè | 特色 | 9 |
|  | tī | 踢 | 6 |
|  | tí | 題　题 | 6 |
|  | tián | 填 | 3 |
|  | tiándiǎn | 甜點　甜点 | 2 |
|  | tiān·na | 天哪 | 7 |
|  | tiānrán | 天然 | 5 |
| tiānrán zīhyuán | tiānrán zīyuán | 天然資源　天然资源 | 5 |
| Tiānjhǔjiào | Tiānzhǔjiào | 天主教 | 13 |
|  | tī//dào | 踢到 | 6 |
|  | tiě | 鐵　铁 | 4 |
|  | tiělù | 鐵路　铁路 | 4 |
|  | tī//kāi | 踢開　踢开 | 6 |
|  | tímù | 題目　题目 | 6 |
| tǐwūn | tǐwēn | 體溫　体温 | 5 |
|  | tǐyù | 體育　体育 | 12 |
|  | tǐyùguǎn | 體育館　体育馆 | 12 |

439

| 通用拼音 | 漢語拼音 | 生詞 | 課數 |
|---|---|---|---|
| | tǐyùjiè | 體育界 体育界 | 12 |
| tī·zih | tī·zi | 梯子 | 1 |
| | tōng | 通 | 3 |
| | tóng | 同 | 7 |
| | tōngguò | 通過 通过 | 7 |
| tóngshìh | tóngshì | 同事 | 12 |
| | tóngyàng | 同樣 同样 | 7 |
| | tóngyì | 同意 | 11 |
| | tóngyìtiān | 同一天 | 7 |
| tǒngjhìh | tǒngzhì | 統治 | 11 |
| tōngjhīhdān | tōngzhīdān | 通知單 通知单 | 2 |
| | tóu·fǎ | 頭髮 头发 | 3 |
| | tóu//lán | 投籃 投篮 | 12 |
| | tóunǎo | 頭腦 头脑 | 9 |
| | tóu//piào | 投票 | 10 |
| | tóushǒu | 投手 | 12 |
| | tū | 禿 | 12 |
| tuánduèi jīngshén | tuánduì jīngshén | 團隊精神 团队精神 | 12 |
| | tuántǐ | 團體 团体 | 12 |
| | tuányuán | 團員 团员 | 14 |
| | tǔdì | 土地 | 13 |
| tuēi | tuī | 推 | 11 |
| tuěi | tuǐ | 腿 | 9 |
| tuēifān | tuīfān | 推翻 | 11 |
| tuēijiàn | tuījiàn | 推薦 推荐 | 3 |
| tuēijiànsìn | tuījiànxìn | 推薦信 推荐信 | 3 |
| tuēisiāo | tuīxiāo | 推銷 推销 | 13 |
| tuēisiāoyuán | tuīxiāoyuán | 推銷員 推销员 | 13 |
| | tuō | 拖 | 11 |

440

INDEX II　生詞索引

| 通用拼音 | 漢語拼音 | 生詞 | 課數 |
|---|---|---|---|
| | tuōxié | 拖鞋 | 11 |
| | tūtóu | 禿頭　禿头 | 12 |

## W

| 通用拼音 | 漢語拼音 | 生詞 | 課數 |
|---|---|---|---|
| | ·wa | 哇 | 4 |
| | wàibiǎo | 外表 | 9 |
| | wàizǔfù | 外祖父 | 13 |
| | wàizǔmǔ | 外祖母 | 13 |
| | wǎnglù | 網路　网路 | 3 |
| | wǎngzhàn | 網站　网站 | 3 |
| | wǎngzhǐ | 網址　网址 | 3 |
| wǎngjhìh | wǎngzhì | 網誌　网志 | 3 |
| wángzǐh | wángzǐ | 王子 | 14 |
| wáncyuán | wánquán | 完全 | 1 |
| | Wànshèngjié | 萬聖節　万圣节 | 13 |
| | wànyī | 萬一　万一 | 14 |
| | wéi/wèi | 喂 | 13 |
| | wèi | 為　为 | 10 |
| | wèi·le | 為了　为了 | 10 |
| | Wēinísī | 威尼斯 | 14 |
| | wěiyuán | 委員　委员 | 10 |
| wěiyuánhuèi | wěiyuánhuì | 委員會　委员会 | 10 |
| wèi·zih | wèi·zi | 位子 | 7 |
| wūndù | wēndù | 溫度 | 5 |
| wúfǎ | wénfǎ | 文法 | 6 |
| wūnhé | wēnhé | 溫和 | 9 |
| wúnhuà | wénhuà | 文化 | 1 |
| wūnnuǎn | wēnnuǎn | 溫暖　温暖 | 13 |
| wūnróu | wēnróu | 溫柔　温柔 | 9 |
| wūnsí | wēnxí | 溫習　温习 | 6 |

441

| 通用拼音 | 漢語拼音 | 生詞 | 課數 |
|---|---|---|---|
| wúnsyuān | wénxuān | 文宣 | 10 |
| wúnjhāng | wénzhāng | 文章 | 1 |
|  | wùjià | 物價　物价 | 3 |
|  | wúliáo | 無聊　无聊 | 6 |
|  | wúlùn...dōu | 無論…都　无论…都 | 7 |

## X

| 通用拼音 | 漢語拼音 | 生詞 | 課數 |
|---|---|---|---|
| X fēn jhīh Y | X fēn zhī Y | X分之Y | 10 |
| sì | xì | 系 | 1 |
| sì | xì | 細　细 | 9 |
| siā | xiā | 蝦　虾 | 2 |
| sià | xià | 下 | 8 |
| siàbànchǎng | xiàbànchǎng | 下半場　下半场 | 12 |
| sīfāng | xīfāng | 西方 | 1 |
| siágǔ | xiágǔ | 峽谷　峡谷 | 4 |
| siān | xiān | 鮮　鲜 | 5 |
| siàndài | xiàndài | 現代　现代 | 13 |
| siàndàihuà | xiàndàihuà | 現代化　现代化 | 13 |
| siàndàirén | xiàndàirén | 現代人　现代人 | 13 |
| siǎngfǎ | xiǎngfǎ | 想法 | 6 |
| siāngfǎn | xiāngfǎn | 相反 | 4 |
| siǎngjiā | xiǎng//jiā | 想家 | 5 |
| siāngjiāo | xiāngjiāo | 香蕉 | 5 |
| siāngsìn | xiāngxìn | 相信 | 13 |
| siǎngshòu | xiǎngshòu | 享受 | 13 |
| siànmù | xiànmù | 羨慕　羡慕 | 9 |
| siānnǎi | xiānnǎi | 鮮奶　鲜奶 | 10 |
| siǎochīh | xiǎochī | 小吃 | 2 |
| siàoduèi | xiàoduì | 校隊　校队 | 12 |
| siǎofèi | xiǎofèi | 小費　小费 | 8 |

INDEX II  生詞索引

| 通用拼音 | 漢語拼音 | 生詞 | 課數 |
|---|---|---|---|
| siāolù | xiāolù | 銷路　销路 | 13 |
| siǎomài | xiǎomài | 小麥　小麦 | 5 |
| siǎocì | xiǎoqì | 小氣　小气 | 8 |
| siǎocì guěi | xiǎoqìguǐ | 小氣鬼　小气鬼 | 8 |
| siǎoshuō | xiǎoshuō | 小說　小说 | 14 |
| siàoyǒu | xiàoyǒu | 校友 | 12 |
| siàoyuán | xiàoyuán | 校園　校园 | 9 |
| siàojhǎng | xiàozhǎng | 校長　校长 | 10 |
| siārén | xiārén | 蝦仁　虾仁 | 2 |
| siàzài | xiàzài | 下載　下载 | 3 |
| síguàn | xíguàn | 習慣　习惯 | 2 |
| sīhuà | xīhuà | 西化 | 11 |
| sǐyīfěn | xǐyīfěn | 洗衣粉 | 10 |
| Siè,Měi jhēn | Xiè Měizhēn | 謝美真　谢美真 | 2 |
| sǐng | xǐng | 醒 | 8 |
| síngdòng diànhuà | xíngdòng diànhuà | 行動電話　行动电话 | 2 |
| sīngfèn | xīngfèn | 興奮　兴奋 | 12 |
| sìnghuèi | xìnghuì | 幸會　幸会 | 1 |
| sìngkuēi | xìngkuī | 幸虧　幸亏 | 7 |
| sínglǐ | xíng·lǐ | 行李 | 1 |
| sìngcyù | xìngqù | 興趣　兴趣 | 1 |
| sīngsīng | xīng·xīng | 星星 | 14 |
| sìngyùn | xìngyùn | 幸運　幸运 | 14 |
| sìnjiào | xìn//jiào | 信教 | 13 |
| sīnkǔ | xīnkǔ | 辛苦　辛苦 | 4 |
| sīnlǐ | xīnlǐ | 心理 | 6 |
| sīnlǐsyué | xīnlǐxué | 心理學　心理学 | 6 |
| sīnshǎng | xīnshǎng | 欣賞　欣赏 | 4 |
| sīnshēng | xīnshēng | 新生 | 1 |

443

實用視聽華語 3
Practical Audio-Visual Chinese

| 通用拼音 | 漢語拼音 | 生詞 | 課數 |
|---|---|---|---|
| sīnsiān | xīnxiān | 新鮮 新鲜 | 5 |
| sìnyòngkǎ | xìnyòngkǎ | 信用卡 | 13 |
| siòucì | xiùqì | 秀氣 秀气 | 9 |
| siōusí shìh | xiūxíshì | 休息室 | 3 |
| syū | xū | 噓 嘘 | 12 |
| syuǎn | xuǎn | 選 选 | 1 |
| syuānbù | xuānbù | 宣布 | 11 |
| syuǎnjyǔ | xuǎnjǔ | 選舉 选举 | 10 |
| syuǎnjyǔcyuán | xuǎnjǔquán | 選舉權 选举权 | 10 |
| syuǎnmín | xuǎnmín | 選民 选民 | 10 |
| syuéfèi | xuéfèi | 學費 学费 | 3 |
| syuéfēn | xuéfēn | 學分 学分 | 3 |
| syuékē | xuékē | 學科 学科 | 7 |
| Syuékē Nénglì Cèyàn | Xuékē Nénglì Cèyàn | 學科能力測驗 学科能力测验 | 7 |
| syuéwèi | xuéwèi | 學位 学位 | 7 |
| syuésí | xuéxí | 學習 学习 | 3 |
| syuěsié | xuěxié | 雪鞋 | 5 |
| syuěyī | xuěyī | 雪衣 | 5 |
| syūshēng | xūshēng | 噓聲 嘘声 | 12 |

## Y

| | yā | 壓 压 | 7 |
|---|---|---|---|
| | yālì | 壓力 压力 | 7 |
| | yán | 嚴 严 | 11 |
| | yǎn | 演 | 14 |
| | yángé | 嚴格 | 11 |
| | yǎnjiǎng | 演講 演讲 | 11 |
| | yǎnjiǎngtīng | 演講廳 演讲厅 | 11 |
| | yǎnjiè | 眼界 | 14 |

INDEX II  生詞索引

| 通用拼音 | 漢語拼音 | 生詞 | 課數 |
|---|---|---|---|
| yánjhòng | yánzhòng | 嚴重 严重 | 11 |
|  | yào·shi | 鑰匙 钥匙 | 1 |
|  | yā·zi | 鴨子 鸭子 | 2 |
| Yǎjhōu | Yǎ Zhōu | 亞洲 亚洲 | 4 |
|  | yé·ye | 爺爺 爷爷 | 14 |
|  | yí | 咦 | 6 |
|  | yìbān | 一般 | 5 |
|  | yìbān ér lùn | 一般而論 一般而论 | 5 |
|  | yìbān lái shuō | 一般來說 一般来说 | 5 |
|  | yìbān shuō lái | 一般說來 一般说来 | 5 |
| yìhuèi | yìhuì | 議會 议会 | 10 |
|  | yìjiàn | 意見 意见 | 14 |
|  | yìlián | 一連 一连 | 12 |
|  | yìlěi | 一壘 一垒 | 12 |
|  | yímín | 移民 | 1 |
|  | Yìndì'ān rén | 印第安人 | 11 |
|  | yíng | 贏 赢 | 10 |
|  | yīngjùn | 英俊 | 9 |
| yǐngsīng | yǐngxīng | 影星 | 9 |
|  | yínsè | 銀色 | 13 |
| yín·zih | yín·zi | 銀子 银子 | 2 |
|  | yǐwéi | 以為 以为 | 4 |
|  | yìwù | 義務 义务 | 7 |
|  | yìwù jiàoyù | 義務教育 义务教育 | 7 |
| yísià | yíxià | 一下 | 8 |
|  | yìyuán | 議員 议员 | 10 |
| yìjhíh | yìzhí | 一直 一直 | 8 |
|  | yóu | 油 | 5 |
|  | yóu | 由 | 10 |

445

| 通用拼音 | 漢語拼音 | 生詞 | 課數 |
|---|---|---|---|
| | yǒuguān | 有關　有关 | 14 |
| yǒujīngyàn | yǒu jīngyàn | 有經驗　有经验 | 8 |
| | yǒu lǐmào | 有禮貌　有礼貌 | 11 |
| | yóunì | 油膩　油腻 | 5 |
| yóucíshih | yóuqíshì | 尤其是 | 5 |
| yǒucyù | yǒuqù | 有趣 | 1 |
| yǒusìngcyù | yǒu xìngqù | 有興趣　有兴趣 | 1 |
| | yù | 玉 | 5 |
| | yuánlái | 原來　原来 | 4 |
| yuányóu huèi | yuányóuhuì | 園遊會　园游会 | 9 |
| | yuē | 約　约 | 3 |
| | yuèchū | 月初 | 10 |
| | yuèdǐ | 月底 | 10 |
| yuēhuèi | yuēhuì | 約會　约会 | 3 |
| | yuèliàng | 月亮 | 14 |
| | yuètái | 月台 | 12 |
| | yùmǐ | 玉米 | 5 |
| | yún | 雲　云 | 14 |
| | yùndòng | 運動　运动 | 11 |
| | yùnqì | 運氣　运气 | 14 |
| | yúnxiāo fēichē | 雲霄飛車　云霄飞车 | 14 |

## Z

| zàijiàn cyuánlěidǎ | zàijiàn quánlěidǎ | 再見全壘打<br>再见全垒打 | 12 |
|---|---|---|---|
| zájhìh | zázhì | 雜誌　杂志 | 1 |
| jhàngdān | zhàngdān | 帳單　帐单 | 2 |
| jhànjhēng | zhànzhēng | 戰爭　战争 | 11 |
| jhàogù | zhàogù | 照顧　照顾 | 1 |
| jhèngdǎng | zhèngdǎng | 政黨　政党 | 10 |

INDEX II 生詞索引

| 通用拼音 | 漢語拼音 | 生詞 | 課數 |
|---|---|---|---|
| jhèngfǔ | zhèngfǔ | 政府 | 4 |
| jhènghǎo | zhènghǎo | 正好 | 9 |
| jhèngjiàn | zhèngjiàn | 政見　政见 | 10 |
| jhèngjiàn fābiǎo huèi | zhèngjiàn fābiǎohuì | 政見發表會 政见发表会 | 10 |
| jhèngmíng | zhèngmíng | 證明　证明 | 11 |
| jhèngmíngshū | zhèngmíngshū | 證明書　证明书 | 11 |
| jhèngshū | zhèngshū | 證書　证书 | 11 |
| jhèngjhìh | zhèngzhì | 政治 | 10 |
| jhīh | zhī | 支 | 12 |
| jhīh | zhī | 隻　只 | 13 |
| jhíh | zhí | 值 | 4 |
| jhǐh | zhǐ | 指 | 4 |
| jhīhchíh | zhīchí | 支持 | 10 |
| jhíhdé | zhí·dé | 值得 | 4 |
| jhìhdù | zhìdù | 制度 | 11 |
| jhìhdùhuà | zhìdùhuà | 制度化 | 11 |
| jhǐhhǎo | zhǐhǎo | 只好 | 7 |
| jhíhjiē | zhíjiē | 直接　直接 | 10 |
| jhíhmíndì | zhímíndì | 殖民地　殖民地 | 11 |
| jhíhcián | zhí//qián | 值錢　值钱 | 4 |
| jhīhshìh | zhīshì | 知識　知识 | 14 |
| jhíhyè | zhíyè | 職業　职业 | 12 |
| jhíhyuán | zhíyuán | 職員　职员 | 12 |
| Zhōngbù héngguàn gōnglù | Zhōngbù Héngguàn Gōnglù | 中部橫貫公路 中部横贯公路 | 4 |
| Jhōngguó Dàlù | Zhōngguó Dàlù | 中國大陸　中国大陆 | 3 |
| Jhōnghuá | Zhōnghuá | 中華　中华 | 1 |
| JhōngHuáDuèi | Zhōnghuá Duì | 中華隊　中华队 | 12 |
| Jhōnghuá Mínguó | Zhōnghuá Mínguó | 中華民國　中华民国 | 11 |

447

| 通用拼音 | 漢語拼音 | 生詞 | 課數 |
|---|---|---|---|
| Jhōnghuá Rénmín Gònghéguó | Zhōnghuá Rénmín Gònghéguó | 中華人民共和國 中华人民共和国 | 11 |
| Jhōnghuá wúnhuà | Zhōnghuá wénhuà | 中華文化 中华文化 | 1 |
| jhǒnglèi | zhǒnglèi | 種類 种类 | 5 |
| jhōngsīn | zhōngxīn | 中心 | 7 |
| jhòngyìyuán | zhòngyìyuán | 眾議員 众议员 | 10 |
| jhōu | zhōu | 州 | 10 |
| jhōujhǎng | zhōuzhǎng | 州長 州长 | 10 |
| jhū | zhū | 豬 猪 | 2 |
| jhuàn | zhuàn | 賺 赚 | 8 |
| jhuǎnbò | zhuǎnbò | 轉播 转播 | 12 |
| jhuāng | zhuāng | 裝 装 | 5 |
| jhuǎnjī | zhuǎnjī | 轉機 转机 | 14 |
| jhuānjiā | zhuānjiā | 專家 专家 | 14 |
| jhuānkē syuésiào | zhuānkē xuéxiào | 專科學校 专科学校 | 7 |
| jhuānyè | zhuānyè | 專業 专业 | 14 |
| jhǔbō | zhǔbō | 主播 | 12 |
| jhuēi | zhuī | 追 | 9 |
| jhùjiào | zhùjiào | 助教 | 6 |
| jhǔn | zhǔn | 準 准 | 12 |
| jhǔnshíh | zhǔnshí | 準時 准时 | 5 |
| jhūròu | zhūròu | 豬肉 猪肉 | 2 |
| jhùsyuǎn | zhùxuǎn | 助選 助选 | 10 |
| jhǔyì | zhǔyì | 主義 主义 | 11 |
| jhǔcí | zhǔcí | 主詞 主词 | 11 |
| jhùyì | zhùyì | 注意 | 7 |
| zìhdòng | zìdòng | 自動 自动 | 6 |
| zìhdònghuà | zìdònghuà | 自動化 自动化 | 11 |
| zìhdòngzìhfā | zìdòng zìfā | 自動自發 自动自发 | 6 |

448

# INDEX II 生詞索引

| 通用拼音 | 漢語拼音 | 生詞 | 課數 |
|---|---|---|---|
| zīhyuán | zīliào | 資料 资料 | 3 |
| zīhyuán | zīyuán | 資源 资源 | 5 |
| zìhjhù | zìzhù | 自助 | 14 |
| | zōngjiào | 宗教 | 13 |
| | zǒngshì | 總是 总是 | 1 |
| | zǒngtǒng | 總統 总统 | 10 |
| | zǒngtǒngfǔ | 總統府 总统府 | 10 |
| | zǒu mǎ kàn huā | 走馬看花 走马看花 | 14 |
| | zū | 租 | 3 |
| | zū//chūqù | 租出去 | 3 |
| | zǔfù | 祖父 | 13 |
| | zuǐbā | 嘴巴 | 9 |
| | zǔmǔ | 祖母 | 13 |
| | zuòfǎ | 做法 | 6 |
| | zuò//guǎnggào | 做廣告 作广告 | 13 |
| | zuòjiā | 作家 | 14 |
| | zuò//lǐbài | 做禮拜 做礼拜 | 13 |
| | zuò//shíyàn | 做實驗 做实验 | 14 |
| | zuòyè | 作業 作业 | 6 |
| | zǔxiān | 祖先 | 13 |

449

國家圖書館出版品預行編目資料

新版實用視聽華語 / 國立臺灣師範大學主編. – 二版. – 臺北縣新店市：
正中, 2008. 2
　　冊；19×26公分　含索引

ISBN 978-957-09-1788-8（第1冊：平裝）
ISBN 978-957-09-1789-5（第1冊：平裝附光碟片）
ISBN 978-957-09-1790-1（第2冊：平裝）
ISBN 978-957-09-1791-8（第2冊：平裝附光碟片）
ISBN 978-957-09-1792-5（第3冊：平裝）
ISBN 978-957-09-1793-2（第3冊：平裝附光碟片）
ISBN 978-957-09-1794-9（第4冊：平裝）
ISBN 978-957-09-1795-6（第4冊：平裝附光碟片）
ISBN 978-957-09-1796-3（第5冊：平裝）
ISBN 978-957-09-1797-0（第5冊：平裝附光碟片）

1. 漢語　2. 讀本

802.86　　　　　　　　　　　　　　　　　　　　　96021892

## 新版《實用視聽華語》（三）

主　　　編　者◎國立臺灣師範大學
編　輯　委　員◎范慧貞・劉秀芝（咪咪）・蕭美美
召　　集　　人◎葉德明
著 作 財 產 權 人◎教育部
地　　　　　址◎(100)臺北市中正區中山南路5號
電　　　　　話◎(02)7736-7990
傳　　　　　眞◎(02)3343-7994
網　　　　　址◎http://www.edu.tw

發　　行　　人◎蔡繼興　　　　　　　香 港 分 公 司◎集成圖書有限公司－香港皇后大道中283號聯威
出　版　發　行◎正中書局股份有限公司　　　　　　　　商業中心8字樓C室
地　　　　　址◎(231)新北市新店區復興路43號4樓　　TEL：(852)23886172-3・FAX：(852)23886174
郵　政　劃　撥◎0009914-5　　　　　美 國 辦 事 處◎中華書局－135-29 Roosevelt Ave. Flushing, NY
網　　　　　址◎http://www.ccbc.com.tw　　　　　　11354 U.S.A.
　　　　　　　 E-mail：service@ccbc.com.tw　　　　TEL：(718)3533580・FAX：(718)3533489
門　　市　　部◎(231)新北市新店區復興路43號4樓　　日 本 總 經 銷◎光儒堂－東京都千代田區神田神保町一丁目
電　　　　　話◎(02)8667-6565　　　　　　　　　　　　　五六番地
傳　　　　　眞◎(02)2218-5172　　　　　　　　　　TEL：(03)32914344・FAX：(03)32914345

政府出版品展售處
教育部員工消費合作社　　　　　　　　　國立教育資料館
地　　　　　址◎(100)臺北市中正區中山南路5號　　地　　　　　址◎(106)臺北市大安區和平東路一段181號
電　　　　　話◎(02)23566054　　　　　　　　　電　　　　　話◎(02)23519090#125
五 南 文 化 廣 場　　　　　　　　　　　國家書店
地　　　　　址◎(400)臺中市中山路6號　　　　　地　　　　　址◎(104)臺北市松江路209號一樓
電　　　　　話◎(04)22260330#20、21　　　　　電　　　　　話◎(02)25180207

行政院新聞局局版臺業字第0199號(10575)　　　　分類號碼◎802.00.071
出版日期◎西元2008年2月二版一刷
　　　　　西元2012年10月二版六刷
ISBN 978-957-09-1793-2　　　　　　　　　　　GPN 1009700071
定價／**880**元（內含MP3）
著作人：范慧貞・劉秀芝（咪咪）・蕭美美　　　著作財產權人：教育部
◎本書保留所有權利
　如欲利用本書全部或部分內容者，須徵求著作財產權人同意或書面授權，請逕洽教育部。

版權所有・翻印必究　**Printed in Taiwan**

CHENG CHUNG BOOK CO., LTD.

CHENG CHUNG BOOK CO., LTD.

CHENG CHUNG
BOOK CO., LTD.

CHENG CHUNG
BOOK CO., LTD.